THE TWENTIETH CENTURY CONSTRUCTION OF "JUDAISM"

Essays on the Religion of Torah in the History of Religion

SOUTH FLORIDA STUDIES IN THE HISTORY OF JUDAISM

Edited by
Jacob Neusner
William Scott Green, James Strange
Darrell J. Fasching, Sara Mandell

Number 32
The Twentieth Century
Construction of "Judaism"

Essays on the Religion of Torah
in the History of Religion

by
Jacob Neusner

THE TWENTIETH CENTURY CONSTRUCTION OF "JUDAISM"

Essays on the Religion of Torah in the History of Religion

by

Jacob Neusner

Scholars Press
Atlanta, Georgia

THE TWENTIETH CENTURY CONSTRUCTION OF "JUDAISM"

Essays on the Religion of Torah
in the History of Religion

©1991
University of South Florida

Publication of this book was made possible by a grant from the Tisch Family Foundation, New York City. The University of South Florida acknowledges with thanks this important support for its scholarly projects.

Library of Congress Cataloging in Publication Data

Neusner, Jacob. 1932-
   The twentieth century construction of "Judaism" : essays on the religion of Torah in the history of religion / by Jacob Neusner.
   p.   cm. — (South Florida studies in the history of Judaism ; no. 32)
   Includes index.
   ISBN 1-55540-645-9 (acid-free paper)
   1. Judaism—Historiography. 2. Rabbinical liteature—History and criticism. I. Title. II. Series: South Florida studies in the history of Judaism ; 32.
BM160.N49 1991
296'.07—dc20   91-33564
                                                           CIP

Printed in the United States of America
on acid-free paper

Table of Contents

Preface

A portfolio of twenty-one recent papers addressing the audience beyond specialists likely to read my monographs, this book focuses upon Judaism within the history of religion and therefore addresses the academic field of the study of religion. The distinct subject, "religion," treated in abstract from a society's culture, its encompassing way of life, worldview, and a theory of itself as a distinct social entity, in the nineteenth century emerged as an object of academic inquiry. Before that time philosophy speculated about religious truth, but religion as a distinct aspect of analysis within the study of the social order had not reached definition. The systematic, critical, analytical study of "religion," aiming at generalizations about religion and not just descriptions of religions, defined within the academy – but mainly there – a principal focus of learning. Perhaps the reason was that, prior to the formation of a secularized component of the intellectual community, religiosity formed a given, too profoundly imbedded in consciousness to permit analysis on its own. Something so intimate within the consciousness and culture of a society could scarcely be abstracted and treated as a "thing" out there. But perhaps, too, interest in finding unity in diversity, in generalizing about religion out of the data of religions, had to await the moment at which, seeing other people up close, thoughtful European intellectuals recognized the task of finding a means of thinking about diversity. In the meeting with the protean and complex civilizations of Islam, India, and China, for example, Western scholars required a way of thinking about an "other" that lay totally beyond the available repertoire of metaphors and analogies by which, until then, the strange was transformed into something not wholly unlike the known and familiar.

Perhaps the first task in the study of religion – certainly the one that preoccupied scholarship within the academy – lay in forming of the diverse data of a given religious world a single, comprehensible entity, a whole, an -ism. India then was made to yield "Hinduism" and "Buddhism," the Muslim world, "Muhammedanism," in the analogy to

Christianity, the -ity of Christ; the complex and differentiated world of Israel, the holy people, "Judaism," and, by the way, the Christianities of the West, "Christianity." In the case of Judaism, in particular, Judaic theologians imparted to that "Judaism" a set of creedal definitions, for example, "Judaism is the religion of ethical monotheism," and, along these same lines, other constructs were so formulated as to sustain comparison and contrast with one another, upon the common and shared foundation of "religious belief," or even "religious belief and behavior." Within this intellectual effort, it goes without saying, the process of homogenization carried forward the theological work of distinguishing the normative from the schismatic, and the study of religions came to form a chapter within the theologies of religions. Lost in the confusion was the interest in generalization about religion, which had precipitated the intellectual initiative.

Now in none of the religions fabricated by the nineteenth century founders of the study of religion is -ism or -ity a native category. In Judaism, for example, the word for Judaism is not Judaism. It is "Torah." The word that stands for the entirety of the religious system names the symbol that captures the whole; or rather, it is the generative symbol that names the system, not the system that names the symbol. The system, if pressed to name itself, points (mutely) to the Torah, and "Judaism" – now requiring quotation marks – is the species of the -ism, the genus, religion, that takes shape within, and around, the Torah. But the realization that the category formations within which the study of religion was taking shape in fact generated theological thought, requiring the definition of religion through the theological statements treated as normative by religions, was a long time in coming.

The study of Judaism in the twentieth century forms one central arena in which the struggle properly to define a religion took place. The reason was, and remains, that Judaism is a religion that is familiar to the West and, because of Christianity's intimate theological and historical relationship to Judaism, important to the West as well. Yet Judaism was, and is, different from the principal religious formation of the West, the Christian one. The labor of comparison and contrast therefore proved both engaging but also accessible. Were Judaism altogether exotic, the West can have found enormous difficulty in making sense of the problem, as in general defining "the religion(s) of China" or "of Africa" or even "of India" faces extraordinary obstacles in the alien character of what is studied. Intersecting with Christianity throughout the history of Christianity, the West finds in its own paramount religious heritage usable metaphors and familiar similes, which serve to open the way for comparison and contrast. And not all of the metaphors proved misplaced, the similes distortions, by any means.

But a considerable labor of translation, from native to generally intelligible categories, would come to realization before (even) Judaism, a small and modest religion, with only a few bodies of believers, within a finite and accessible number of countries and cultures, would make its contribution to the definition of (a) religion, hence – through the comparison and contrasts of religions, – of religion in general. The initial labor of definition, carried on, as I said, by Judaic theologians, faced inward and addressed parochial problems, with little bearing on the study of the religion, Judaism, except as data in the contemporary aspect of the faith. But even there, as theologians proposed to define, they, too, confronted the extraordinary diversity of the data of Judaism(s), which, in the nature of things, theological study of Judaism would have to sift and sort out. So proposing that "Judaism" is the "religion of ethical monotheism," the theologians would invoke a category that is hardly native – not occurring in the canonical writings, not susceptible of translation, without considerable difficulty, from a Western language into the language of the canon. But what native category would serve, when the canon, then understood to encompass all religious writings produced by "Israel," that is, Jews, throughout recorded time – yielded nothing but confusion? The answer gained by theologians of Judaism before the end of the nineteenth century, and by history of religion by the end of the second decade of the nineteenth century, was to distinguish normative from sectarian or heretical Judaism. Judaism, conceived as a single, continuous "religious tradition," came to expression in diverse ways, but only some of these ways would be authoritative and so form a source for theological truth later on. The task of theology was then to distinguish the authoritative from the fraudulent within that single "Judaism." Within history of religion the hoary categories of orthodoxy and heresy came to expression in the category of "normative."

By the middle of the twentieth century, this received construct, "Judaism," with its fundamental qualification, "normative," had yielded an unwieldy and rickety construction indeed. For to hold together within a single category all of the data, distinguished then between the normative and the other, it was necessary at some point to appeal to a principle of verification and validations. Simply stated, how do I know what is normative and what is not? What data will instruct me on the norm? Appealing to the conception that pretty much everybody at all times was orthodox, and that the definition of "sectarian" or "not-normative" lay in counting who was the majority, who the minority, scholars of Judaism found themselves at an impasse. Archaeological data available for half a century before the mid-1950s, when the chronic frailty of the categories of learning came to crisis, simply denied that the norms set forth in the canonical writings characterized the routine and normal conduct of the people who were supposed to have lived up to those norms. The conception of a single, normative, linear, homogeneous, orthodox Judaism, corresponding in its main outlines through all time to what in the nineteenth and twentieth centuries came into being as Orthodox Judaism, proved to many to be implausible – and an obstacle to learning.

Beyond implausibility lay the task of the next half-century, which was to reconsider, through the case of Judaism, precisely what we mean by "a religion," viewed as an -ism or an -ity. I have devoted the first thirty years of my scholarly life, from 1960 onward, to that question, with special reference to the centuries, the first through the seventh, in which the canonical writings of the Judaism that has predominated from late antiquity to nearly our own day were taking shape and coming to closure. In these essays I summarize for a broader reading audience some of the results of my work in the recent past. In the prologue, I outline what I believe has been a revolution in the study of Judaism that began with the very preliminary and – we now know in retrospect – primitive and uncomprehending observations of the considerable figures of that time, Lieberman, Scholem, Smith, and, above them all, Erwin R. Goodenough. Part One presents free-standing essays that form the constructive part of my work. I present a theory of the formation of a particular Judaism, defined by its native category, in the context of any Judaism meaning, its particular Torah myth. Chapter Two sets forth a method that I have devised for the discovery of the formative history of Judaism within the canonical literature that defines our sources. Chapter Three then sets forth the first important step in the analytical work on the documents at hand. Chapter Six identifies what I conceive to be the principal integrative concept. Chapters Eight and Nine ask questions of classification of that particular Judaism. I borrow the classifications from the legacy of learning that I propose decently to inter, which has taken as certain that "Judaism is a biblical religion" and that "Judaism is a historical religion." I explain why both received certainties contradict the canonical evidence. In Chapter Ten I then show why these certainties turn out to be not so much wrong as monumentally irrelevant, this in my explanation of why "eternity" as commonly understood distorts the native category of "world to come."

Since all of the extant evidence on the Judaism of the Dual Torah is in literary form, I have had to devote much work to rereading the canonical writings. I have found myself required to translate everything not in English and to retranslate nearly everything that already had been translated. In Chapter Eleven I take up the definition of one important canonical document, the Tosefta. In Chapters Twelve and Thirteen I explain the work on which I am even now engaged.

Naturally my proposals on important problems have found a critical response, as in any healthy academic subject should take place. The character of the response, in the cases of E. P. Sanders and H. Maccoby, is addressed in Chapters Fourteen and Fifteen. Chapters Sixteen through Eighteen take up other recent books, which take different positions from those I have outlined.

Since the problem of defining a religion and defining religion forms the intellectual task that the study of religion must solve, I make my contribution to the theory of how the work is to be done. In Chapter Nineteen I take the case of Judaism as my example, offering a method in response to the problems of diversity within a single species of religion. In Chapter Twenty, finally, I direct attention toward a problem in the study and practice of religion that, in my view, faces all religions, therefore religion taken all in all and all together: religion, not merely religions. And that is where we started.

JACOB NEUSNER

Graduate Research Professor of Religious Studies
UNIVERSITY OF SOUTH FLORIDA
Tampa, St. Petersburg, Fort Myers, Sarasota, Lakeland

735 Fourteenth Avenue Northeast
St. Petersburg, Florida 33701 USA

METHODOLOGICAL PROLOGUE

1

The Twentieth Century Revolution: What Has Changed in Jewish Learning?

I began my college career as a freshman at Harvard in 1950 and from then to now have devoted my life to the study of Judaism. At a major turning in my career, forty years beyond the beginning of college, having concluded twenty-two years at Brown University and commenced a new career at University of South Florida, I ask myself the fundamental questions of a career such as mine has been: What do I think has changed, why have matters changed as they have, and what do I claim as my own role in the revolution of the second half of the twentieth century in the study of Judaism?

In 1950 everybody assumed that, in the first seven centuries C.E. (=A.D.) there was a single Judaism, corresponding to a single Christianity. That Judaism was a linear continuation of the Hebrew Scriptures ("Old Testament"), the original intent and meaning of which that Judaism carried forward. That same Judaism was normative, everywhere authoritative and accepted. Its canon was so uniform that any holy book, whenever edited, testified equally as any other book to the theological or normative position of that single, unitary Judaism. The allegations of the canonical documents about things people said or did were in general accurate, or had to be assumed to be accurate unless proved otherwise. True, a rational, skeptical attitude treated with caution obviously miraculous or otherwise "impossible" allegations, for example, about rabbis turning people into cows or dust into gold. But, in general, the canonical writings defined Judaism, and, as a matter of fact, Judaism dealt with historical facts. It was true, because its facts were true, and its representation of the meaning of Scripture accorded with the original intent and sense of the authors of Scripture as well. Today, not a single one of these principles of scholarship stands.

But for most of this century, New Testament scholarship in quest of the "Jewish background" or "the Jewish roots of Christianity" thought it could rely upon this literature of the one and only Judaism to tell them about that single, uniform Judaism to which earliest Christianity referred. If a sentence, taken out of context, in a seventh-century writing seemed to intersect, or even say the same thing, as a statement of Paul, then Paul could be assumed to have drawn upon "his Judaism," in making the statement that he did. And if people wanted to know the meaning of what Jesus said and could locate a pertinent statement in a fourth-century Babylonian rabbi's mouth, well, then, that tells us what "Rabbi Jesus" had in mind.

It is no surprise, therefore, that people commonly interpreted a passage of the New Testament by appeal to what that "single Judaism" taught. The holy books of that single Judaism, whenever and wherever they reached closure, told us what that one, unitary, harmonious Judaism had to say. So we could cite as evidence of opinions held in the first century writings edited in the sixth – a longer span of time than separates us from Columbus! Not only so, but everybody assumed that all Jews, except a few cranks or heretics, believed and practiced this single, unitary Judaism, which therefore was not only normal but normative. The Judaism of Jesus, in A.D. 30, was pretty much the same as the Judaism of Ezra, 450 B.C., and of Aqiba, in A.D. 130, and the Judaism of the Land of Israel (a.k.a. "Palestine") of the first century was the same as the Judaism of the Greek-speaking Jews of Alexandria at that same time or of the Aramaic-speaking Jews of Babylonia five hundred years later.

What then did we know and how did we know it? In 1950 we knew pretty much what people said, thought, and did. We knew it because the rabbinic sources reported what they said and did. If sources were not redacted or edited until much after the event, well, then, people had access to oral traditions, which they preserved word for word and handed on until they were written down wherever and whenever (and it did not matter). And since we knew lots of historical facts, we could write history in the way in which people assumed history should be written: the story of what happened, in order and sequence, beginning to end; the tale of what great men (rarely women) taught; the lessons to be learned from facts.

Scholarship then consisted of mainly the study of the meanings of words or phrases or sentences. If the reader knew the meaning of a sentence, then the reader knew what the person to whom that sentence was attributed really said and thought; and since everybody was assumed to hold the same views, or at least, talk about the same things, the reader could then write what "Judaism" taught about this or that. What happened if the reader had an unclear reading? The reader consulted manuscripts – written a thousand years later to be sure – and these would answer the reader's question and make the reader's history possible. So these three issues predominated: the study of the critical reading of a passage, the inquiry into the critical philology or the meaning of words, and the critical exegesis, or the meaning of sentences, all done against the background of the preparation of critical texts. To dismiss a person who disagreed with the reader view, the reader would call him or her (and there were very few women!) either uncritical or, better still, ignorant. Scholarly debate then was meant to discredit the other person, not to disprove a position contrary to one's own or even to help solve a problem held in common.

Today few scholars ignore or neglect the results of the century of work on text criticism, philology, and exegesis. We still need well-crafted versions of documents, formed out of the broad array of manuscript evidence, thoughtfully reworked. True, the century that closed in 1950 never witnessed the preparation of the required critical texts for most of the documents of the Judaic canon; but they were working on it. We of course need our dictionaries, and if the entire span of positivist study of Judaism failed to yield a decent Aramaic dictionary, even now one is coming. So the report card of the hundred years of positivist historicism shows many incompletes.

But in 1950, people took for granted, that same evaluation would contain unquestioned judgments in favor of excellence. For however partial the fulfillment of the great tasks – no definitive dictionaries, no critical texts for the most important writings – still, there were the achievements in critical history. After all, people contended, we no longer believe all those fables; now we bring to the documents' allegations a thoroughly critical spirit. In context, people were entirely right. For they looked back on the age prior to their own – just as we do – and where they remembered credulity, they now discerned honest independence of spirit, and a critical eye examined all claims. But the premises of the long period of historical critical scholarship corresponded, in their way, to the foundations of the age of faith: these documents yield history, meaning, an accurate picture of what pretty much everybody was thinking, saying, and doing. So when the reader has done the reader's work right, meaning, established a critical text, determined a critical definition of the meanings of words, phrases, sentences, examined the appropriate "parallels," meaning, other presentations of pretty much the same theme, then the reader could say what the text meant. And that statement took the form of history writing: what people said and did and thought then. That premise

explains the questions people asked: how they defined what they wished
to know. To put matters in a plain way: they wanted to know what they
thought they already knew – only better.

What called into question the fundamental positive-historical
suppositions about the character of the literary evidence was not the
discovery of other literary evidence, e.g., the Dead Sea Scrolls or the Nag
Hammadi library. The Dead Sea Scrolls presented us with the writings
of a Judaic religious community possibly identified with the Essenes; but
prior to the discovery of the library of the community, we had no
writings of that group. Nag Hammadi, in Egypt, yielded a vast library in
Coptic of Gnostic Christianity, of which, beforehand, we had scarcely a
hint. Literary evidence of one kind could readily be accommodated with
literary evidence of some other kind. Nobody in the decade after the
discoveries at the Dead Sea and in Nag Hammadi called into question
the accepted consensus concerning the character of the literary evidence
overall. That is to say, there really was one Judaism, the one about which
the rabbinic canon informs us; Qumran simply showed us a heretical
sect. What really shook the foundations was the accumulation of
evidence that there really was not a single Orthodox Judaism at all, only
diverse Judaisms. And that evidence derived from not writing but
material and concrete data: archaeology.

Specifically, most synagogues built from the third to the seventh
century, both in the Land of Israel and abroad, had decorated floors or
walls. Some symbols out of the religious life of Judaism or of Greco-
Roman piety occur nearly everywhere. These include the symbols for
the festival of Tabernacles. Other symbols, available, for example, from
the repertoire of items mentioned in Scripture, or from the Greco-Roman
world, never make an appearance at all. The symbols of Pentecost, for
instance, are rare indeed. A *shofar*, a *lulab* and *ethrog*, a *menorah*, all of
them Jewish in origin, but also such pagan symbols as a zodiac, with
symbols difficult to find in Judaic written sources – all of these form part
of the absolutely fixed symbolic vocabulary of the synagogues of late
antiquity. By contrast, symbols of other elements of the calendar year, at
least as important as those that we do find, turn out never to make an
appearance. And, obviously, a vast number of pagan symbols proved
useless to Judaic synagogue artists. It follows that the artists of the
synagogues spoke through a certain set of symbols and ignored other
available ones. That simple fact makes it highly likely that the symbols
they did use meant something to them, represented a set of choices,
delivered a message important to the people who worshiped in those
synagogues.

Because the second commandment forbids the making of graven
images of God, however, people have long taken for granted that

Judaism should not produce an artistic tradition. Or, if it does, it should
be essentially abstract and nonrepresentational, much like the rich
decorative tradition of Islam. But from the beginning of the twentieth
century, archaeologists began to uncover in the Middle East, North
Africa, the Balkans, and the Italian peninsula, synagogues of late
antiquity richly decorated in representational art. For a long time
historians of Judaism did not find it possible to accommodate the newly
discovered evidence of an ongoing artistic tradition. They did not
explain that art, they explained it away. One favorite explanation was
that "the people" produced the art, but "the rabbis," that is, the religious
authorities, did not approve it or at best merely tolerated it. That
explanation rested on two premises. First, because Talmudic literature –
the writings of the ancient rabbis over the first seven centuries of the
common era – made no provision for representational art,
representational art was subterranean and "unofficial." Second, rabbis
are supposed to have ruled everywhere, so the presence of iconic art had
to indicate the absence of rabbinic authority.

Aware of the existence of sources which did not quite fit into the
picture that emerged from Talmudic literature as it was understood in
those years or which did not serve the partly apologetic purposes of their
studies, scholars such as George Foot Moore, in his *Judaism: The Age of
the Tannaim* posited the existence of "normative Judaism," which is to be
described by reference to Talmudic literature and distinguished from
"heretical" or "sectarian" or simply "nonnormative" Judaism of "fringe
sects." Normative Judaism, exposited so systematically and with such
certainty in Moore's *Judaism*, found no place in its structure for art, with
its overtones of mysticism (except "normal mysticism"), let alone magic,
salvific or eschatological themes except within a rigidly reasonable and
mainly ethical framework; nor did Judaism as these scholars understood
it make use of the religious symbolism or ideas of the Hellenistic world,
in which it existed essentially apart and at variance. Today no informed
student of Judaism in late antiquity works within the framework of such
a synthesis, for this old way is no longer open. The testimony of
archaeology, especially of the art of the synagogues of antiquity, now
finds a full and ample hearing.

At stake was the conviction that the rabbinic canon was normative
and tells us how things were everywhere. Once the archaeological
evidence had made its impact, however, people came to recognize
diversity where they had assumed uniformity and harmony. Then the
conception of a single, normative Judaism, the same through five
hundred years, uniform wherever Jews lived, and broadly confessed by
almost all Jews almost everywhere, fell of its own weight. Scientific
studies on "Talmudic Judaism," which had begun about a century ago,

had rested on the presupposition that Talmudic literature might by itself yield a whole and accurate view of Judaism in the early centuries of the Common Era. Iconic evidence was simply ignored.

When the diversity of Jews in antiquity came to be recognized, then the other premises of the received tradition of learning lost the standing of self-evident truths. If there was no single, unitary, harmonious Judaism, then [1] the sources that portrayed that picture could no longer be taken at face value. If the sources stood only for their authors' opinions, not for broadly held norms, then [2] we could no longer assume that all sources everywhere, without regard to when they were redacted, attested to that same, single Judaism. And if people differentiated between a given document and the worldview and way of life of the Jews everywhere and through a half millennium or more, then [3] they had also to differentiate among the documents themselves. These three challenges to scholarship today outline not only what we now do not think we know. They also point toward what we think we know and how we think we know it; they account for the kinds of questions we now investigate. But it will take the rest of this book to spell out in detail the way in which the new learning reads the canonical writings and to account for the questions that today appear both urgent and also accessible to sustained scholarly research: what we think we know, how we think we know it.

Today no sophisticated student of Judaism in late antiquity works within the framework of the firmly established scholarly orthodoxy of 1950. The path to a conception of a single "normative Judaism" was closed by a number of scholars and by the infusion of new attitudes. First, Saul Lieberman who, drawing upon the early researches of S. Krauss and others, demonstrated how deeply embedded in late Hellenism were the methods and vocabulary of the Rabbis. But Lieberman went much further. He drew attention to the divisions within Jewry, thus implicitly admitting the existence of more than a single Judaism. What is important is Lieberman's willingness to take seriously the challenges of Hellenistic science, magic, and religion, not merely in the faith of "assimilated" Jews nor in the practices of the "ignorant masses" but in the bastions of the faith and their guardians.

True, Lieberman did not conclude that there was no single, unitary, harmonious normative Judaism, deriving in a linear path out of the Hebrew Scriptures or "Old Testament." He did not recognize that there were several Judaisms, each with its own points of special interest and concern, modes of selecting out of the Hebrew Scriptures passages of probative importance. He did not have the conceptual tools for even conceiving such possibilities. But within his framework he did explicitly recognize that there were Jews, in large numbers, not accurately characterized, as to their religion, by the rabbinic writings at all. Then, so far as learning engaged with the religion of the Jews, not only the theology of some sages, the study of Judaism would have to address evidence of more than one Judaism.

Nor did Lieberman in that early time stand alone. Gershom Scholem's (vastly overrated) researches on Jewish mysticism in late antiquity demonstrated how both Talmudic and extra-Talmudic literature point toward the existence of Hellenistic themes, motifs, and symbols deep within the circles of "pious" Jews. Since the rabbinic literature scarcely accounts for the vitality of such themes within the life of Jewry, the existence of more than a single authoritative Judaism once more became a plausible hypothesis in the description, analysis, and interpretation of that religion. But Scholem's grasp of the rabbinic literature in its totality was superficial and conventional. His generative category was "Judaism." He drew no important conclusions from his own allegations, other than that the esoteric doctrines that surfaced in the Middle Ages were rooted in late antiquity. For historicistic positivism, that was not a trivial result. For scholarship on formative Judaism, Scholem led nowhere, with his facts celebrated out of all context. His entire contribution is now in the process of being dismantled and placed into storage. Moshe Idel, the great Israeli historian of religion, has shown Scholem's scholarship to be dated and, in the end, merely ideological.

It was Erwin R. Goodenough, whose major publications came out between 1920 and 1960, studying archaeological remains and Hellenistic literature, who was the first to state the obvious fact that archaeological evidence demanded interpretation within its own framework, as evidence of *a Judaism* – one with its own autonomy. Goodenough identified as distinct the Judaism formed among the circles in which the artifacts bearing pagan symbols, or symbols bearing Jewish values different from those associated with their original pagan setting, were used. Goodenough was the first explicitly to posit the existence of more than one Judaism. Goodenough's findings may be summarized in this way.

At the period between the first and sixth centuries, the manifestations of the Jewish religion were varied and complex, far more varied, indeed, than the extant Talmudic literature would have led us to believe. Besides the groups known from this literature, we have evidence that "there were widespread groups of loyal Jews who built synagogues and buried their dead in a manner strikingly different from that which the men represented by extant literature would have probably approved, and, in a manner motivated by myths older than those held by these men." The content of these myths may never be known with any great precision, but they suggest a Hellenistic-Jewish mystic mythology

far closer to the Qabbalah than to Talmudic Judaism. In a fairly limited
time before the advent of Islam, these groups dissolved. This is the plain
sense of the evidence brought by Goodenough, not a summary in any
sense of his discoveries, hypotheses, suggestions, or reconstruction of the
evidence into an historical statement. Clearly, he articulated for the first
time a fully exposed theory that there was more than a single Judaism in
the formative age.

Morton Smith, the fourth of the major figures of the 1950s and 1960s,
pointed out the striking convergence of the scholarly results of several
distinct inquiries, results based upon disparate sources and produced by
scholars who, though aware of one another's work, specialized in a
single body of evidence. But Smith did not then draw the proper
conclusion:

> [I]t is amazing how the evidence from quite diverse bodies of materials,
> studied independently by scholars of quite different backgrounds and
> temperaments, yields uniform conclusions which agree with the plain
> sense of these discredited passages. Scholem's study of the materials in
> the *hekhalot* tradition, for instance, has just led us to conclusions
> amazingly close to those reached by Goodenough from his study of the
> archaeological remains: to wit, the Hellenistic period saw the
> development of a Judaism profoundly shaped by Greco-oriental
> thought, in which mystical and magical...elements were very important.
> From this common background such elements were derived
> independently by the magical papyri, Gnosticism, Christianity, and
> Hellenistic and Rabbinic Judaism.

The integration of these bodies of evidence into a coherent picture of, if
not one Judaism, then multiple Judaisms, has yet to take place. But it is
clear that the history of Judaism in late antiquity will tell the story of
convergence and divergence.

But Smith's (characteristic) failure of interpretation – his strength
never lay in critical analysis – requiring the evidence to be harmonized
rather than analyzed, obscured the simple fact that each body of
evidence tells us what it tells us: about the people of whom it speaks, but
not (necessarily) about anybody else. Smith then marks the final chapter
in the one hundred fifty year story of the critical-historical reading of the
canonical (and other) sources about the Jews and their Judaism,
purporting to tell us pretty much what happened, what there was, and
assuming that, once we know what happened and what there was, we
can say what Judaism was (and, for Jews, is even now). Still, the demise
of the received paradigm took place not only because of the intellectual
failures of a generation of mere erudites, but also because new people,
working in different institutional settings, asked new questions and used
new methods in finding the answers. And this they did because they
found the received questions and methods insufficient.

This brings me from the general to the specific: What has been at stake in my own career? What do I think I have contributed in asking new questions and devising new methods for the study of the history of religion with special reference to Judaism? If I have to say in a single sentence, what it is about religion that after thirty years I am trying still to demonstrate through the case of Judaism, it is this: *religion is public and not personal. When we study religion, we analyze how people have identified urgent problems and solved them together.*

But religion is not merely public, something that we do together. Religion is the single most important force in the shaping of the world as we know it. Ours is an age that has given more compelling evidence for the vitality of religion than any prior age in the history of humanity. So my work has taken as its premise, but also has meant to demonstrate, that religion forms the foundation of the social order. Religion defines an independent variable for the interpretation of politics and culture. For those who, like me, believe that it is God who calls religion into being, so that, when we pray or (in my case) study the Torah or engage in acts of religious sanctification and service, it is in response to God who calls; the power of religion in the world today attests to the glory of God. But for those who deem religion a wholly this-worldly fact, a work of humanity alone, the proposition remains the same, though the explanation will certainly diverge. Religion explains the state of politics and culture and accounts for the formation of the social order.

2

The Documentary History of Judaism

During a long period in the history of scholarship on history of religion in general, and Judaism in particular, the premises of learning in the rabbinic literature of late antiquity joined new historical interest with a received theological conviction. The former wished to describe in context ideas that had formerly been assigned no context at all: they were "Torah" and now were to be the history of ideas. The latter maintained that the documents of the rabbinic corpus were essentially seamless and formed one vast Dual Torah, oral and written; and that all attributions were valid, so that if a given authority was supposed to have made a statement, he really made it. On the basis of that received conviction, imputing inerrancy to the attributions (as well as to the storytellers) just as had many generations of the faithful, but asking questions of context and development that were supposed to add up to history, the great figures of the first three-quarters of the twentieth century set forth their accounts of what they conceived to be Judaism in historical context, hence, the history of Judaism. This brings us to the era that reached its conclusion in the 1950s. When we investigate the history of the formative stage of the Judaism of the Dual Torah, what can we now learn from the generations of scholarship that began with Solomon Schechter and concluded with Ephraim E. Urbach?[1]

But what if we recognize that documentary formulations play a role in the representation of compositions, so that the compositors' formulation of matters takes a critical place in the making of the

---

[1]If I ignore lesser figures, such as Shmuel Safrai, Abraham Goldberg, Y. Gafni, Daniel R. Schwartz, and the like, it is because they have made no important contribution to historical scholarship and are not to be taken seriously in the way in which Schechter, Moore, and Urbach are. That seems to me to constitute a judgment that is no more than a common consensus among nearly all scholars in the field, and all of them outside of Jerusalem.

documentary evidence? And what if, further, we no longer assume the inerrancy of the Oral Torah's writings, so that attributions are no longer taken at face value, stories no longer believed unless there are grounds for disbelief (as the Jerusalem canard has it)? Then the fundamental presuppositions of the writing of Schechter, Moore, Kadushin, Urbach, and lesser figures prove null. And that fact bears in its wake the further problem: since we cannot take their answers at face value, can we pursue their questions any more? In my judgment, the answer is negative. The only reason nowadays to read Schechter, Moore, Kadushin, Urbach and others is to see what they have to say about specific passages upon which, episodically and unsystematically, they have comments to make. All work in the history of the formative age of the Judaism of the Dual Torah that treats documentary lines as null and attributions as invariably valid must be dismissed as a mere curiosity; a collection and arrangement of this and that, bearing no compelling argument or proposition to be dealt with by the new generation.[2]

---

[2]William Horbury, captiously reviewing my *Vanquished Nation, Broken Spirit* (*Epworth Review*, May, 1989), correctly observes: "Emotional attitudes form a traditional moral topic, and the recommendations on them in rabbinic ethics have often been considered, for example, in the *Rabbinic Anthology* of C. G. Montefiore and H. Loewe....This historical inquiry is closely related to the author's other work, and it is written on his own terms; he does not mention other writers on rabbinic ethics, and he gives no explicit criticism or development of modern study by others of the rabbinic passages and ideas with which he deals. He cannot be said to have fulfilled his obligation to his readers." Horbury does not seem to know my extensive writings on others who have worked on the formative history of Judaism, even though these have been collected and set forth in a systematic way, both as book reviews and as methodological essays, time and again. My *Ancient Judaism: Disputes and Debates* (Chico, 1986: Scholars Press for Brown Judaic Studies) is only one place in which I have indeed done just what Horbury asks, addressing Urbach and Moore and some of their most recent continuators in a systematic and thorough way. I am amazed that he can imagine I have not read the literature of my field; I not only have read and repeatedly criticized it, but I have done so in every accessible medium. His reviews of my work are simply uninformed and captious. His treatment of my *Incarnation of God* in *Expository Times*, which makes the same point in a more savage manner, shows the real problem; he does not find it possible to state more than the topic (the title!) of the book and cannot tell his readers what thesis or proposition is set forth in the book. Given those limitations of intellect, one can hardly find surprising his inability to grasp why Urbach, Schechter, Moore, Kadushin, and others by contemporary standards simply have nothing to teach us about the formative history of Judaism. Horbury wants us to do chemistry by appeal to not the oxygen but the phlogiston theory, and he wants geography to be carried out in accord with the convictions of the flat-earthers. But the latter have a better sense of humor about themselves.

Let me now reframe the question in a manner which will make clear the right way in which to work. For when we grasp how we must now investigate the formative history of Judaism, we shall also see why Schechter, Moore, and Urbach no longer compel attention for any serious and important purpose.

The question that demands a response before any historical issues can be formulated is this: How are we to determine the particular time and circumstance in which a writing took shape, and how shall we identify the generative problems, the urgent and critical questions, that informed the intellect of an authorship and framed the social world that nurtured that same authorship? Lacking answers to these questions, we find our work partial, and, if truth be told, stained by sterile academicism. Accordingly, the documentary method requires us to situate the contents of writings into particular circumstances, so that we may read the contents in the context of a real time and place. How to do so? I maintain that it is by reference to the time and circumstance of the closure of a document, that is to say, the conventional assignment of a piece of writing to a particular time and place, that we proceed outward from context to matrix.

Everyone down to Urbach, including Montefiore and Loewe, Schechter, Moore, and the rest, simply take at face value attributions of sayings to particular authorities and interpret what is said as evidence of the time and place in which the cited authorities flourished. When studying topics in the Judaism of the sages of the rabbinic writings from the first through the seventh centuries, people routinely cite sayings categorized by attribution rather than by document. That is to say, they treat as one group of sayings whatever is assigned to Rabbi X. This is without regard to the time of redaction of the documents in which those sayings occur or to similar considerations of literary context and documentary circumstance. The category defined by attributions to a given authority furthermore rests on the premise that the things given in the name of Rabbi X really were said by him. No other premise would justify resort to the category deriving from use of a name, that alone. Commonly, the next step is to treat those sayings as evidence of ideas held, if not by that particular person, then by people in the age in which the cited authority lived. Once more the premise that the sayings go back to the age of the authority to whom they are attributed underpins inquiry. Accordingly, scholars cite sayings in the name of given authorities and take for granted that those sayings were said by the authority to whom they were attributed and, of course, in the time in which that authority flourished. By contrast, in my method of the documentary study of Judaism, I treat the historical sequence of sayings only in accord with the order of the documents in which they first occur.

Let me expand on why I have taken the approach that I have, explain the way the method works, and then, as before, set forth an example of the method in action.[3]

---

[3]My example is drawn from a whole series of books in which I worked on the histories of specific conceptions or problems, formulated as I think correct, out of the sequence of documents. These are in the following works of mine:

The Idea of Purity in Ancient Judaism. The Haskell Lectures, 1972-1973. Leiden, 1973: E. J. Brill. [This was a most preliminary work, which made me aware of the problems to be addressed later on. The documentary theory of the history of ideas was worked out only in the earlier 1980s.]

Judaism and Story: The Evidence of The Fathers According to Rabbi Nathan. Chicago, 1990: University of Chicago Press.

The Foundations of Judaism. Method, Teleology, Doctrine. Philadelphia, 1983-1985: Fortress Press. I-III. I. *Midrash in Context. Exegesis in Formative Judaism.* Second printing: Atlanta, 1988: Scholars Press for Brown Judaic Studies.

The Foundations of Judaism. Method, Teleology, Doctrine. Philadelphia, 1983-1985: Fortress Press. I-III. II. *Messiah in Context. Israel's History and Destiny in Formative Judaism.* Second printing: Lanham, 1988: University Press of America. Studies in Judaism Series.

The Foundations of Judaism. Method, Teleology, Doctrine. Philadelphia, 1983-1985: Fortress Press. I-III. III. *Torah: From Scroll to Symbol in Formative Judaism.* Second printing: Atlanta, 1988: Scholars Press for Brown Judaic Studies.

The Foundations of Judaism. Philadelphia, 1988: Fortress. Abridged edition of the foregoing trilogy.

Vanquished Nation, Broken Spirit. The Virtues of the Heart in Formative Judaism. New York, 1987: Cambridge University Press. Jewish Book Club selection, 1987.

Editor: *Judaisms and Their Messiahs in the Beginning of Christianity.* New York, 1987: Cambridge University Press. [Edited with William Scott Green and Ernest S. Frerichs.]

Judaism in the Matrix of Christianity. Philadelphia, 1986: Fortress Press. British edition: Edinburgh: 1988, T. & T. Collins.

Judaism and Christianity in the Age of Constantine. Issues of the Initial Confrontation. Chicago, 1987: University of Chicago Press.

Judaism and Its Social Metaphors. Israel in the History of Jewish Thought. New York, 1988: Cambridge University Press.

The Incarnation of God: The Character of Divinity in Formative Judaism. Philadelphia, 1988: Fortress Press.

Edited: *The Christian and Judaic Invention of History.* [Edited with William Scott Green]. Atlanta, 1989: Scholars Press for American Academy of Religion. Studies in Religion Series. [All of the papers in this collection are worked out within the basic thesis of the documentary history of ideas.]

Since many sayings are attributed to specific authorities, why not lay out the sayings in the order of the authorities to whom they are attributed, rather than in the order of the books in which these sayings occur, which forms the documentary method for the description of the matrix of texts in context? It is because the attributions cannot be validated, but the books can. The first of the two principles by which I describe the matrix that defines the context in which texts are framed is that we compose histories of ideas of the Judaism of the Dual Torah in accord with the sequence of documents that, in the aggregate, constitute the corpus and canon of the Judaism of the Dual Torah. And those histories set forth dimensions of the matrix in which that Judaism, through its writings, is to be situated for broader purposes of interpretation. Documents reveal the system and structure of their authorships, and, in the case of religious writing, out of a document without named authors we may compose an account of the authorship's religion: a way of life, a worldview, a social entity meant to realize both. Read one by one, documents reveal the interiority of intellect of an authorship, and that inner-facing quality of mind inheres even when an authorship imagines it speaks outward, toward and about the world beyond. Even when set side by side, moreover, documents illuminate the minds of intersecting authorships, nothing more.

Then why not simply take at face value a document's *own* claims concerning the determinate situation of its authorship? Readers have already noted innumerable attributions to specific authorities. One obvious mode of determining the matrix of a text, the presently paramount way, as I said, is simply to take at face value the allegation that a given authority, whose time and place we may identify, really said what is attributed to him, and that if a writing says something happened, what it tells us is not what its authorship thought happened, but what really happened. That reading of writing for purposes of not only history, but also religious study, is in fact commonplace. It characterizes all accounts of the religion, Judaism, prior to mine, and it remains a serious option for all those outside of my school and circle.[4] Proof of that fact is to be shown, lest readers who find accommodation in more contemporary intellectual worlds, where criticism and the active intellect

---

[4]That is why people can still read Urbach or Moore as though we learned anything of historical and not merely ad hoc exegetical interest from their compilations of sayings under their various rubrics. In this regard Urbach's various asides are quite interesting, even though not a single account of the history and context of an idea can stand; and the straight historical chapters – for example, on the social role of sages, on the life of Hillel, on the history of the time – are not only intellectually vulgar, they are a travesty of scholarship, even for the time and within the premises in which they were written.

reign, doubt my judgment of competing methods and differing accounts. Accordingly, let me characterize the prevailing way of determining the historical and religious matrix of texts, and then proceed to explain my alternate mode for answering the question of what is to be learned, from within a piece of writing, about the religious world beyond.

In historical study, we gain access to no knowledge a priori. All facts derive from sources correctly situated, for example, classified, comprehensively and completely described, dispassionately analyzed, and evaluated. Nothing can be taken for granted. What we cannot show, we do not know. These simple dogmas of all historical learning derive not from this writer but go back to the very beginnings of Western critical historical scholarship, to the age of the Renaissance. But all historical and religious-historical scholarship on the documents of the Judaism of the Dual Torah in its formative age, except for mine and for that of a very few others, ignores the canons of criticism that govern academic scholarship. Everyone in the past and many even now take for granted that pretty much everything they read is true – except what they decide is not true.

They cannot and do not raise the question of whether an authorship knows what it is talking about, and they do not address the issue of the purpose of a text: historical or imaginative, for example. For them the issue always is history, namely, what really happened, and that issue was settled, so to speak, at Sinai: it is all true (except, on an episodic basis, what is not true, which the scholars somehow know instinctively). They exhibit the credulity characteristic of the believers, which in the circle of piety is called faith, and rightly so, but in the center of academic learning is mere gullibility. The fundamentalists in the Talmudic academies and rabbinical seminaries and Israeli universities take not only as fact but at face value everything in the holy books. "Judaism" is special and need not undergo description, analysis, and interpretation in accord with a shared and public canon of rules of criticism. "We all know" how to do the work, and "we" do not have to explain to "outsiders" either what the work is or why it is important. It is a self-evidently important enterprise in the rehearsal of information. Knowing these things the way "we" know them explains the value of knowing these things.

Scholarship formed on the premise that the sources' stories are to be believed at face value does not say so; rather, it frames questions that implicitly affirm the accuracy of the holy books, asking questions, for example, that can only be answered in the assumption that the inerrant Scriptures contain the answers – therefore, as a matter of process, do not err. By extension holy books that tell stories produce history through the paraphrase of stories into historical language: this is what happened, this is how it happened, and here are the reasons why it happened. If the Talmud says someone said something, he really said it, then and there. That premise moreover dictates their scholarly program, for it permits these faithful scholars to describe, analyze, and interpret events or ideas held in the time in which that person lived. Some of these would deny the charge, and all of them would surely point, in their writing, to evidence of a critical approach. But the premise remains the old gullibility. Specifically, the questions they frame to begin with rest on the assumption that the sources respond. The assumption that, if a story refers to a second-century rabbi, then the story tells us about the second century, proves routine. And that complete reliance merely on the allegations of sayings and stories constitutes perfect faith in the facticity of fairy tales.

The operative question facing anyone who proposes to translate writing into religion – that is, accounts of "Judaism," as Moore claims to give, or "the sages," that Urbach imagines he has made for us, is the historical one: How you know exactly what was said and done, that is, the history that you claim to report about what happened long ago? Specifically, how do you know he really said it? And if you do not know that he really said it, how can you ask the questions that you ask, which has as its premise the claim that you can say what happened or did not happen?

The wrong, but commonplace, method is to assume that if a given document ascribes an opinion to a named authority the opinion actually was stated in that language by that sage. On this assumption a much richer history of an idea, not merely of the literary evidences of that idea, may be worked out without regard only to the date of the document at hand. Within this theory of evidence, we have the history of what individuals thought on a common topic. I have already set forth the reason that we cannot proceed to outline the sequence of ideas solely on the basis of the sequence of the sages to whom ideas are attributed. We simply cannot demonstrate that a given authority really said what a document assigns to him. Let me list the range of uncertainty that necessitates this fresh approach, which I have invented.

First, if the order of the documents were fully sound and the contents representative of rabbinical opinion, then the result would be a history of the advent of the idea at hand and the development and articulation of that idea in formative Judaism. We should then have a fairly reliable picture of ideas at hand as these unfolded in orderly sequence. But we do not know that the canonical history corresponds to the actual history of ideas. Furthermore, we cannot even be sure that the order of documents presently assumed in scholarly convention is correct. Second, if a rabbi really spoke the words attributed to him, then a given idea would have reached expression within Judaism *prior* to the redaction of the document. Dividing things up by documents will tend to give a later date and thus a different context for interpretation to opinions held earlier than we can presently demonstrate. Third, although we are focusing upon the literature produced by a particular group, again we have no clear notion of what people were thinking outside of that group. We therefore do not know how opinions held by other groups or by the Jewish people in general came to shape the vision of rabbis. When, for example, we note that there also existed poetic literature and translations of Scriptures characteristic of the synagogue worship, we cannot determine whether the poetry and most translations spoke for rabbis or for some quite different group.

For these reasons I have chosen to address the contextual question within the narrow limits of the canon. That accounts for my formulation of the episteme as "the canonical history of ideas," and explains, also, why I have carefully avoided claiming that a given idea was broadly held only at a given time and place. All I allege is that a given document underscores the presence of an idea for that authorship – that alone. Obviously, if I could in a given formulation relate the appearance of a given idea to events affecting rabbis in particular or to the life of Israel in general, the results would be exceedingly suggestive. But since we do not know for whom the documents speak, how broadly representative they are, or even how comprehensive is their evidence about rabbis' views, we must carefully define what we do and do not know. So for this early stage in research, the context in which a given idea is described, analyzed, and interpreted is the canon. But this first step alone carries us to new territory. I hope that in due course others will move beyond the limits which, at the moment, seem to me to mark the farthest possible advance. Now let us turn to the specific case meant to illustrate the method.

Let me now explain in some greater detail the alternative, which I call the documentary history of ideas. It is a mode of relating writing to religion through history through close attention to the circumstance in which writing reached closure. It is accomplished, specifically, by assessing shifts exhibited by a sequence of documents and appealing to the generally accepted dates assigned to writings in explaining those shifts. In this way I propose to confront questions of cultural order, social system, and political structure, to which the texts respond explicitly and constantly. Confronting writings of a religious character, we err by asking questions of a narrowly historical character: what did X really say on a particular occasion, and why. These questions not only are not answerable on the basis of the evidence in hand. They also are trivial, irrelevant to the character of the evidence. What strikes me as I review the writings just now cited is how little of real interest and worth we should know, even if we were to concede the historical accuracy and veracity of all the many allegations of the scholars we have surveyed. How little we should know – but how much we should have *missed* if that set of questions and answers were to encompass the whole of our inquiry.

If we are to trace the unfolding, in the sources of formative Judaism, of a given theme or ideas on a given problem, the order in which we approach the several books, that is, components of the entire canon, gives us the sole guidance on sequence, order, and context, that we are apt to find. As is clear, we have no way of demonstrating that authorities to whom, in a given composition, ideas are attributed really said what is assigned to them. The sole fact in hand therefore is that the framers of a given document included in their book sayings imputed to named authorities. Are these dependable? Unlikely on the face of it. Why not? Since the same sayings will be imputed to diverse authorities by different groups of editors, of different books, we stand on shaky ground indeed if we rely for chronology upon the framers' claims of who said what. More important, attributions by themselves cannot be shown to be reliable.

What we cannot show we do not know.[5] Lacking firm evidence, for example, in a sage's own, clearly assigned writings, or even in writings redacted by a sage's own disciples and handed on among them in the discipline of their own community, we have for chronology only a single fact. It is that a document, reaching closure at a given time, contains the allegation that Rabbi X said statement Y. So we know that people at the time of the document reached closure took the view that Rabbi X said statement Y. We may then assign to statement Y a position, in the order of the sequence of sayings, defined by the location of the document in the order of the sequence of documents. The several documents' dates, as is clear, all constitute guesses. But the sequence explained in the prologue, Mishnah, Tosefta, Yerushalmi, Bavli for the exegetical writings on the Mishnah is absolutely firm and beyond doubt. The sequence for the exegetical collections on Scripture – Sifra, the Sifrés, Genesis Rabbah,

---

[5]It should be underlined that a British scholar, Hyam Maccoby, maintains exactly the opposite, alleging in a letter to the editor of *Commentary* and in various other writings that there is historical knowledge that we possess a priori. We must be thankful to him for making explicit the position of the other side. No historical scholarship known to me concurs with his position on a priori historical knowledge; all modern learning in history begins with sources, read *de novo*. But Maccoby has learned remarkably little from contemporary critical scholarship, which he declines to read or dismisses in a half-sentence; his work on problems in New Testament studies has been universally rejected by specialists in that field, as reviews of his writings on Paul and Jesus demonstrate.

Leviticus Rabbah, the Pesiqtas and beyond – is not entirely sure. Still the position of the Sifra and the two Sifrés at the head, followed by Genesis Rabbah, then Leviticus Rabbah, then Pesiqta deRab Kahana and Lamentations Rabbati and some related collections, seems likely.

What are the canonical main beams that sustain the history of ideas as I propose to trace that history? Three principal periods presently delineate the canonical sequence, the Mishnah's, in the first two centuries; the Yerushalmi's, in the next, ca. 200-400; and the Bavli's, in the third, ca. 400-600. The formative age of Judaism is the period marked at the outset by the Mishnah, taking shape from sometime before the Common Era and reaching closure at ca. 200 C.E., and at the end by the Talmud of Babylonia, ca. 600 C.E. In between these dates, two streams of writings developed, one legal, explaining the meaning of the Mishnah, the other theological and exegetical, interpreting the sense of Scripture. The high points of the former come with tractate Abot which is the Mishnah's first apologetic, the Tosefta, a collection of supplements ca. 300 C.E., the Talmud of the Land of Israel ca. 400 C.E., followed by the Babylonian Talmud. The latter set of writings comprise compositions on Exodus, in Mekhilta attributed to R. Ishmael and of indeterminate date, Sifra on Leviticus, Sifré on Numbers, and another Sifré, on Deuteronomy at a guess to be dated at ca. 300 C.E., then Genesis Rabbah ca. 400 C.E., Leviticus Rabbah ca. 425 C.E., and at the end, Pesiqta deRab Kahana, Lamentations Rabbati, and some other treatments of biblical books, all of them in the fifth or sixth centuries. The so-called Tannaitic Midrashim, Mekhilta, Sifra, the two Sifrés, form transitional documents, between the Mishnah and the Yerushalmi and its Midrash companions, Genesis Rabbah, Leviticus Rabbah, and Pesiqta deRab Kahana. Alongside the Bavli are its Midrash associates, Lamentations Rabbah, Song of Songs Rabbah, Esther Rabbah I, and Ruth Rabbah. These books and some minor related items together form the canon of Judaism as it had reached its definitive shape by the end of late antiquity.

If we lay out these writings in the approximate sequence in which – according to the prevailing consensus – they reached closure beginning with the Mishnah, the Tosefta, then Sifra and its associated compositions, followed by the Talmud of the Land of Israel, and alongside Genesis Rabbah and Leviticus Rabbah, then Pesiqta deRab Kahana and its companions, and finally the Talmud of Babylonia, we gain what I call "canonical history." This is, specifically, the order of the appearance of ideas when the documents, read in the outlined sequence, address a given idea or topic. The consequent history consists of the sequence in which a given statement on the topic at hand was made (early, middle, or late) in the unfolding of the canonical writings. To illustrate the process, what does the authorship of the Mishnah have to say on the theme? Then how does the compositor of Abot deal with it? Then the Tosefta's compositor's record comes into view, followed by the materials assembled in the Talmud of the Land of Israel, alongside those now found in the earlier and middle ranges of compilations of scriptural exegeses, and as always, the Talmud of Babylonia at the end. In the illustrative exercise that follows we shall read the sources in exactly the order outlined here. I produce a picture of how these sources treat an important principle of the Judaism of the Dual Torah We shall see important shifts and changes in the unfolding of ideas on the symbol under study.

So, in sum, this story of continuity and change rests upon the notion that we can present the history of the treatment of a topical program in the canonical writings of that Judaism. I do not claim that the documents represent the state of popular or synagogue opinion. I do not know whether the history of the idea in the unfolding official texts corresponds to the history of the idea among the people who stand behind those documents. Even less do I claim to speak about the history of the topic or idea at hand outside of rabbinical circles, among the Jewish nation at large. All these larger dimensions of the matter lie wholly beyond the perspective of this book. The reason is that the evidence at hand is of a particular sort and hence permits us to investigate one category of questions and not another. The category is defined by established and universally held conventions about the order in which the canonical writings reached completion. Therefore we trace the way in which matters emerge in the sequence of writings followed here.

We trace the way in which ideas were taken up and spelled out in these successive stages in the formation of the canon. Let the purpose of the exercise be emphasized. *When we follow this procedure, we discover how, within the formation of the rabbinical canon of writings, the idea at hand came to literary expression and how it was then shaped to serve the larger purposes of the nascent canonical system as a whole.* By knowing the place and uses of the topic under study within the literary evidences of the rabbinical system, we gain a better understanding of the formative history of that system. What do we not learn? Neither the condition of the people at large nor the full range and power of the rabbinical thinkers' imagination comes to the fore. About other larger historical and intellectual matters we have no direct knowledge at all. Consequently we claim to report only what we learn about the canonical literature of a system evidenced by a limited factual base. No one who wants to know the history of a given idea in all the diverse Judaisms of late antiquity, or the role of that idea in the history of all the Jews in all parts of the world in the first seven centuries of the Common Era will find it here.

In order to understand the documentary method we must again underline the social and political character of the documentary evidence presented. These are public statements, preserved and handed on because people have adopted them as authoritative. The sources constitute a collective, and therefore official, literature. All of the documents took shape and attained a place in the canon of the rabbinical movement as a whole. None was written by an individual in such a way as to testify to personal choice or decision. Accordingly, we cannot provide an account of the theory of a given individual at a particular time and place. We have numerous references to what a given individual said about the topic at hand. But these references do not reach us in the authorship of that person, or even in his language. They come to us only in the setting of a *collection* of sayings and statements, some associated with names, other unattributed and anonymous. The collections by definition were composed under the auspices of rabbinical authority – a school or a circle. They tell us what a group of people wished to preserve and hand on as authoritative doctrine about the meaning of the Mishnah and Scripture. The compositions reach us because the larger rabbinical estate chose to copy and hand them on. Accordingly, we know the state of doctrine at the stages marked by the formation and closure of the several documents.

We follow what references we find to a topic in accord with the order of documents just now spelled out. In this study we learn the order in which ideas came to expression in the canon. We begin any survey with the Mishnah, the starting point of the canon. We proceed systematically to work our way through tractate Abot, the Mishnah's first apologetic, then the Tosefta, the Yerushalmi, and the Bavli at the end. In a single encompassing sweep, we finally deal with the entirety of the compilations of the exegeses of Scripture, arranged, to be sure, in that order that I have now explained. Let me expand on the matter of my heavy emphasis on the order of the components of the canon. The reason for that stress is simple. We have to ask not only what documents viewed whole and all at once ("Judaism") tell us about our theme. In tracing the order in which ideas make their appearance, we ask about the components in sequence ("history of Judaism") so far as we can trace the sequence. Then and only then shall we have access to issues of *history*, that is, of change and development. If our theme makes its appearance early on in one form, so one set of ideas predominate in a document that reached closure in the beginnings of the canon and then that theme drops out of public discourse or undergoes radical revision in writings in later stages of the canon, that fact may make considerable difference. Specifically, we may find it possible to speculate on where, and why a given approach proved urgent, and also on the reasons that that same approach receded from the center of interest.

In knowing the approximate sequence of documents and therefore the ideas in them (at least so far as the final point at which those ideas reached formal expression in the canon), a second possibility emerges. What if – as is the case – we find pretty much the same views, treated in the same proportion and for the same purpose, yielding the same message, early, middle, and late in the development of the canon? Then we shall have to ask why the literature remains so remarkably constant. Given the considerable shifts in the social and political condition of Israel in the Land of Israel as well as in Babylonia over a period of more than four hundred years, that evident stability in the teachings for the effective life will constitute a considerable fact for analysis and interpretation. History, including the history of religion, done rightly thus produces two possibilities, both of them demanding sustained attention. Things change. Why? Things do not change. Why not? We may well trace the relationship between the history of ideas and the history of the society that holds those same ideas. We follow the interplay between society and system – worldview, way of life, addressed to a particular social group – by developing a theory of the relationship between contents and context, between the world in which people live and the world which people create in their shared social and imaginative life. When we can frame a theory of how a system in substance relates to its setting, of the interplay between the social matrix and the mode and manner of a society's worldview and way of life, then we may develop theses of general intelligibility, theories of why this, not that, of why, and why not and how come.

The story of continuity and change rests upon the notion that we can present the history of the treatment of a topical program in the canonical writings of that Judaism. I do not claim that the documents represent the state of popular or synagogue opinion. I do not know whether the history of the idea in the unfolding official texts corresponds to the history of the idea among the people who stand behind those documents. Even less do I claim to speak about the history of the topic or idea at hand outside of rabbinical circles, among the Jewish nation at large. All these larger dimensions of the matter lie wholly beyond the perspective of this book. The reason is that the evidence at hand is of a particular sort and hence permits us to investigate one category of questions and not another. The category is defined by established and universally held conventions about the order in which the canonical writings reached completion. Therefore we trace the way in which matters emerge in the sequence of writings followed here. We trace the way in which ideas were taken up and spelled out in these successive stages in the formation of the canon. When we follow this procedure, we discover how, within the formation of the rabbinical canon of writings, the idea at hand came to literary expression and how it was then shaped to serve the larger purposes of the nascent canonical system as a whole.

What do I conceive to be at stake in the documentary history of Judaism? It is to set forth the history of the formation of Judaism, as the canonical writings of late antiquity allow us to trace that history. Let me explain. Between 200 and 400 Judaism changed from a philosophy to a religion. In current work I explain the meaning of that simple sentence, starting with the subject, Judaism.[6] Defining the word *Judaism* in this

---

[6]Everything I say here concerning the movement from philosophy to religion to theology in the formation of the Judaic system of the Dual Torah, so far as it speaks of theology, is based on preliminary impressions and is purely speculative. By contrast, the monographic foundations for this account of the transformation of the Judaic system from philosophy to religion are nearly complete and certainly adequate to this task. The principal works are as follows:

A History of the Mishnaic Law of Purities. Leiden, 1977: Brill. XXI. *The Redaction and Formulation of the Order of Purities in the Mishnah and Tosefta.*

A History of the Mishnaic Law of Purities. Leiden, 1977: Brill. XXII. *The Mishnaic System of Uncleanness. Its Context and History.*

The Mishnah before 70. Atlanta, 1987: Scholars Press for Brown Judaic Studies. [Reprise of pertinent results of *A History of the Mishnah Law of Purities* Vols. III, V, VIII, X, XII, XIV, XVI, XVII, and XVIII.]

A History of the Mishnaic Law of Holy Things. Leiden, 1979: Brill. VI. *The Mishnaic System of Sacrifice and Sanctuary.*

A History of the Mishnaic Law of Women. Leiden, 1980: Brill. V. *The Mishnaic System of Women.*

A History of the Mishnaic Law of Appointed Times. Leiden, 1981: Brill. V. *The Mishnaic System of Appointed Times.*

A History of the Mishnaic Law of Damages. Leiden, 1985: Brill. V. *The Mishnaic System of Damages.*

Uniting the Dual Torah: Sifra and the Problem of the Mishnah. Cambridge and New York, 1989: Cambridge University Press.

Judaism. The Evidence of the Mishnah. Chicago, 1981: University of Chicago Press.

The Making of the Mind of Judaism. Atlanta, 1987: Scholars Press for Brown Judaic Studies.

The Economics of the Mishnah. Chicago, 1989: University of Chicago Press.

The Formation of the Jewish Intellect. Making Connections and Drawing Conclusions in the Traditional System of Judaism. Atlanta, 1988: Scholars Press for Brown Judaic Studies.

The Mishnah. An Introduction. Northvale, N.J., 1989: Jason Aronson.

context involves the understanding of a religion as an account of a system of the social order formed (whether in fact or in imagination) by the believers, an account portrayed in writing. The problem I address concerns the transformation by continuator documents of a Judaic system of the social order, fully set forth in its initial document. That problem therefore directs attention to systemic description, analysis, and interpretation of documentary evidence, for by comparing one set of writings with another I compare one system to another. This work is carried out in my *Transformation of Judaism. From Philosophy to Religion.*

Since the word *system* occurs throughout my account of the formation of Judaism, let me define it. Writings that are read all together, such as those of the unfolding canon of Judaism in late antiquity, are deemed to make a cogent and important statement. I call that encompassing, canonical picture a *system*, when it is composed of three necessary components: an account of a worldview, a prescription of a corresponding way of life, and a definition of the social entity that finds definition in the one and description in the other. When those three fundamental components fit together, they sustain one another in explaining the whole of a social order, hence constituting the theoretical account of a system.

Systems defined in this way work out a cogent picture, for those who make them up, of *how* things are correctly to be sorted out and fitted together, of *why* things are done in one way, rather than in some other, and of *who* they are that do things and understand matters in this particular way. When, as is commonly the case, people invoke God as the foundation for their worldview, maintaining that their way of life corresponds to what God wants of them, projecting their social entity in a

---

Rabbinic Political Theory: Religion and Politics in the Mishnah. Chicago, 1991: University of Chicago Press.

The Philosophical Mishnah. Volume I. *The Initial Probe.* Atlanta, 1989: Scholars Press for Brown Judaic Studies.

The Philosophical Mishnah. Volume II. *The Tractates' Agenda. From Abodah Zarah to Moed Qatan.* Atlanta, 1989: Scholars Press for Brown Judaic Studies.

The Philosophical Mishnah. Volume III. *The Tractates' Agenda. From Nazir to Zebahim.* Atlanta, 1989: Scholars Press for Brown Judaic Studies.

The Philosophical Mishnah. Volume IV. *The Repertoire.* Atlanta, 1989: Scholars Press for Brown Judaic Studies.

The Philosophy of Judaism. The First Principles. Under consideration by Johns Hopkins University Press and University of Illinois Press.

From Literature to Theology in Formative Judaism. Three Preliminary Studies. Atlanta, 1989: Scholars Press for Brown Judaic Studies.

particular relationship to God, then we have a religious system. When, finally, a religious system appeals as an important part of its authoritative literature or canon to the Hebrew Scriptures of ancient Israel or Old Testament, we have a Judaism.

Let me specify what I conceive to be at stake in this approach to the reading of the formation of the Judaism of the Dual Torah. I am trying to find out how to describe that "Judaism" beyond the specific texts, moving beyond the text and the context and toward the matrix of all of the canonical texts. What is it that each document takes for granted but no document spells out? To answer that question I have to describe the processes of category formation, to specify the categorical imperative in the description of a Judaism. That accounts for the focus on the re-formation of received categories and the formation of new ones, wholly congruent to the received ones but also entirely fresh, as well.

The categories that I bring to the study are those of the social order: philosophy or science, politics, and economics. These correspond to worldview, theory of the social entity, and way of life, or ethos, ethnos, and ethics. The reason it is legitimate to describe the categorical unfolding of Judaism within the categories of political economy is simple. The Mishnah, the foundation document, after Scripture, of the canonical corpus we study here, in point of fact sets forth a full account of the social order, to which philosophy, politics, and economics are integral, just as philosophy, politics, and economics are integral to the social order conceived by Greco-Roman philosophy in the tradition of Aristotle. These deal with the worldview (in philosophy), the way of life (in economics), and the definition of the social entity (in politics) of the (imagined, or real) social order portrayed in documents identified as canonical.

Then at stake in systemic description is the reading of written evidence as the evidence has been combined to form an authoritative statement. Then I ask, in the analysis at hand, what happened, in the unfolding of the canon, to these categories of description of the social order, the issues of the way of life, worldview, and definition of the social entity, that altogether form the social system imagined by the authors or authorships of authoritative writings? I know how to answer to that question.

These three inquiries of Greco-Roman political economy, philosophy, politics, and economics, set forth only the initial system of Judaism, the one to which the Mishnah attests. But that Judaism in many important ways hardly turned out wholly symmetrical with the final system of Judaism that emerged from the formative age and defined matters to the present day. The economics, politics, and philosophy of the initial formation of Judaism set the agenda and formed the court of appeal. But successors and continuators picked and chose, and, it follows, they framed a fresh definition for the social foundations of the world they proposed to invent. The philosophy, politics, and economics of the next phase in the formation of Judaism, seen on their own but also in relationship with the initial theories, will therefore demand sustained description, analysis, and interpretation. That explains why I know how the initial system was revised and adapted by later system makers. What is at stake, in all, is how intellectuals defined the rationalities of Judaism as a social composition: a theory of the society of Israel, the holy people of God.

Now to return to the definition of Judaism. By Judaism I mean a Judaic system, which is a cogent account of the social order, comprising a worldview, way of life, and theory of the social entity, "Israel," all together setting forth a response to a question deemed urgent and encompassing providing an answer found self-evidently valid. The Jews' long history has witnessed the formation of a variety of such Judaic systems. In the first seven centuries of the Common Era one such system, the one that has predominated since that time, took shape. That is the Judaic system the transformation of which is under discussion here.

The ultimate system of Judaism itself formed during those seven centuries in three distinct stages, marked in each case by the distinctive traits of the literature that reached closure at the end of each successive stage.[7] More to the point, each stage produced a Judaic system. Formed in the first two hundred years and represented by the Mishnah and its associated writings, the first is utterly free-standing. The second, taking shape from 200 to 400 and represented by the Talmud of the Land of Israel and its companions, is connected to the first but essentially distinct from it. The third, expressed in documents that reached closure between 400 and 600 within and around the Talmud of Babylonia, is connected to the second but in important traits distinct from it as well. These three systems, autonomous when viewed synchronically but connected when seen diachronically, ultimately, at the end of their formative age, formed a single, wholly and utterly continuous structure, that one we call Judaism. But in their successive stages of autonomy, then autonomy and connection, the three distinct systems may be classified, respectively, as philosophical, religious, and theological. Judaism then took shape in a passage from a philosophical, to a religious, and finally to a theological system, each one taking over and revising the definitive categories of the former and framing its own fresh, generative categories as well. The formative history of Judaism then is the story of the presentations and re-

---

[7]These are set forth presently.

presentations of categorical structures. In method it is the exegesis of taxonomy and taxic systems.

To begin with, then, the classification of types of systems – philosophical, religious, theological – requires explanation.

A philosophical system forms its learning inductively and syllogistically by appeal to the neutral evidence of the rules shown by the observation of the order of universally accessible nature and society.

A religious system frames its propositions deductively and exegetically by appeal to the privileged evidence of a corpus of writing deemed revealed by God.

A theological system imposes upon a religious one systematic modes of thought of philosophy, so in its message regularizing and ordering in a cogent and intellectually rigorous way the materials received from a religious system. The movement from the religious to the theological will involve the systematization and harmonization of the religious categories, their re-formation into a single tight and cogent statement. It is an initiative as radical, in its way, as the passage from the philosophical to religious formation is in its way. For the modes of thought, media of expression, and, as a matter of fact, categorical structure and system are reworked in the enterprise of turning a merely imputed order, imputed within the single heart of the faith, into a wholly public order, subject to sustained and cogent representation and expression, each component in its place and proper sequence, beginning, middle, and end. Religious conviction differs from theological proposition as do bricks and mortar from a building.

Religious and theological systems of course work over the same issues in ways that are common to themselves and that also distinguish them jointly from philosophical ones. But the rigorous task of forming of religious attitudes and convictions a cogent composition, a system and not merely a structure of beliefs, imposes on systems of the theological sort disciplines of mind and perception, modes of thought and media of expression, quite different from those that characterize the work of making a religious system. The connection is of course intimate, for a theological system succeeding and reshaping a religious one appeals to the same sources of truth in setting forth (often identical) answers to (ordinarily) the same urgent questions. But the theological type of system is different from the religious type in fundamental ways as well, for while there can be a religious system without theological order, there can be no theological system without a religious core. So much for the distinctions among types of systems.

In the transformation of the Judaic system from philosophical to religion in its basic character, the very raw materials, the categories themselves, undergo transformation. When a philosophical becomes a religious system, the categorical change yields not the reframing or re-formation or re-presentation. What happens is rather the fundamental revaluation of categories, which I call "counterpart categories," transvaluation and transformation – these comprise the history of religion, so far as history records connections, comparisons, and contrasts, between one thing and something else.

How do I know that these categorical transformations and reconsiderations have taken place in the systems in transition? The answer requires us to read literary evidence as testament to systemic formation. The evidence for systems of world construction, such as those with which we deal in the history of Judaism, derives from the correct description and analysis of the surviving writings of the formative age. These provide our evidence of how system builders chose to express their ideas (rhetoric), conceived that their ideas expressed cogent thought and formed intelligible statements to be shared by others (logic of cogent discourse), and formed the categories through which the facts attained sense and constituted orderly and systematic accounts of the world (topical, propositional program). All three together – the mode of discourse, the media of thought and expression, the message brought to representation through the particular rhetoric and logic at hand – prove accessible when we ask the documentary heritage of the system builders to point us toward the system expressed therein in detail. Now let me define the documentary evidence of Judaism, beginning with the Mishnah.

The evidence is canonical, because the canon recapitulates the system that animates the mentality of the framers of canonical writers and the authorities that adopted those writings for a single canonical composite. That canon in the case of the Judaism under study consisted of the Hebrew Scriptures of ancient Israel ("the Old Testament"), called in this Judaism the Written Torah, and a set of writings later on accorded the status of Torah as well and assigned origin at Sinai through a process of oral formulation and oral transmission, hence, the Oral Torah. Among those writings, the first beyond the Hebrew Scriptures. The first of those writings comprising the Oral Torah was the Mishnah, ca. 200; this document carried in its wake two sustained amplifications and extensions called Talmuds, the one produced in the Land of Israel, hence the Talmud of the Land of Israel, ca. 400, the other in Babylonia, in the Iranian Empire, hence the Talmud of Babylonia, ca. 600.

The other half of the Torah, the written part, served analogously and received a variety of sustained amplifications, called Midrash compilations. These were in three sets; the first, ca. 200-400, addressed the books of Exodus, Leviticus, Numbers, and Deuteronomy, in Mekhilta Attributed to R. Ishmael for Exodus, Sifra, for Leviticus, one Sifré to

Numbers, another Sifré, to Deuteronomy.[8] The second, ca. 400-500, took up the books of Genesis and Leviticus, in Genesis Rabbah and Leviticus Rabbah, and the latter begat Pesiqta deRab Kahana in its model. The third, ca. 500-600, addressed a lectionary cycle of the synagogue, dealing with the books of Lamentations (read on the ninth of Ab), Esther (read on Purim), Ruth (read on Pentecost), and Song of Songs (read on Passover), in Lamentations Rabbah, Esther Rabbah I (the first two chapters only), Ruth Rabbah, and Song of Songs Rabbah. The first of the three groups presents marks of transition and mediation from one system to the next; the second, Genesis Rabbah and Leviticus Rabbah, together with Pesiqta deRab Kahana, form a single circle with the Talmud of the Land of Israel, and the third, the final Rabbah compilations, belong together with the Talmud of Babylonia.

The documentary evidence sets forth a system of a very particular kind. I have already defined a system as a cogent account of the social order. From beginning to end, the Judaic systems defined as their problem the construction of a social world. Each, in succession, framed its categories for intelligible thought by appeal to the issues of the world framed by a particular ethnos, the social entity (the most neutral language I can find), which was called (an) "Israel," and every Judaic system would take as its task the definition of the social world of an Israel: the way of life or (broadly speaking) ethics, the worldview or ethos, and the account of the social entity or the "Israel" that realized in its shared and corporate being the ethics (again, broadly construed), and explained that ethos by appeal to the ethnos. So, as a matter of definition, a Judaic system is a system that derives its generative categories from the (theoretical) requirements of framing a social order: who are "we," what do we do together, and why are we the corporate body that we are, thus, ethnos, ethics, ethos. And that brings us back to the first of the great Judaic systems that in the end formed Judaism, the system to which the authorship of the Mishnah refer in framing their writing.

The Mishnah sets forth in the form of a law code an account of the world ("worldview"), a pattern for everyday and material activities and relationships ("way of life"), and a definition of the social entity

---

[8]In separate work I will position the so-called Tannaitic Midrashim in relationship to the two systems, the Mishnah's and the Yerushalmi's, or the philosophical and the religious. This will be *The Place of the So-called Tannaitic Midrashim* (Atlanta, 1992: Scholars Press for Brown Judaic Studies). The methodological premises of this study will be purely experimental: if this, then what happens? if that, then what happens? My advocacy will be limited to the correctness of the design of the experiment, which any interested colleague should be able to replicate.

("nation," "people," "us" as against "outsiders," "Israel") that realized that way of life and explained it by appeal to that worldview. Successor documents, closed two centuries later, addressed the Mishnah's system and recast its categories into a connected, but also quite revised, one. These documents attached themselves to the Mishnah, on the one side, and the Hebrew Scriptures, on the other, within the nascent theory that the one stood for the oral, the other, the written, revelation, or Torah, of God to Moses at Mount Sinai. The Talmud of the Land of Israel (hereinafter: the Yerushalmi, or Talmud of Jerusalem), formed around thirty-nine of the Mishnah's sixty-two tractates, and Genesis Rabbah and Leviticus Rabbah (joined by Pesiqta deRab Kahana), formed around the first and third books of Moses, respectively, along with some other documents, attest to a system that both extended and recast the categorical structure of the system for which the Mishnah stands, and also framed new categories within the same large-scale structure, involving way of life, worldview, and social entity, taken up in the Mishnah's system. The transformation of the one to the other stands for the movement from a philosophical to a religious mode of thinking. For the system to which the Mishnah as a document attests is essentially philosophical in its rhetorical, logical, and topical program; the successor system, fundamentally religious in these same principal and indicative traits of medium of intellect and mentality.

This system of the Mishnah designed the social order by an account of the principal components, a philosophy, an economics, and a politics, corresponding to worldview, way of life, and social entity. The philosophy explained how to think and identified the agenda for sustained thought and learning; the economics set forth a theory of rational action in the face of scarcity and in the increase and disposition of wealth; the politics laid out an account of precisely how power, encompassing legitimate violence, embodied in institutions and their staff, was to realize in everyday social transactions the social entity, "Israel." These categories in the successor documents, the Talmud of the Land of Israel for the Mishnah, the Midrash compilations Genesis Rabbah and Leviticus Rabbah together with Pesiqta deRab Kahana for Scripture, underwent revision, and, alongside, these same documents set forth their own categories for those served, initially, by philosophy, politics, and economics.

These general observations explain the task I propose, which is to characterize the basic traits of intellect of the system represented by the Mishnah and to compare and contrast that system with the one adumbrated by the Talmud of the Land of Israel, Genesis Rabbah, and Leviticus Rabbah with Pesiqta deRab Kahana. Our question, specifically, is simple: How shall we classify the Mishnah in its context? When we compare and contrast the Mishnah in its classification as to rhetoric and logic with the successor documents, do we find those later writings like the Mishnah or unlike it? If like, then of course we classify those documents as we have classified the Mishnah. But if unlike, then how – as a matter of hypothesis – may we classify the system represented by the successor writings? That is the work of comparison that seems to me to yield very interesting results indeed. Now, back to Schechter, Moore, and Urbach: Precisely what have they to say in reply to this question? In my view, the answer is, nothing at all, which is why we do not need to read them anymore.

3

The Three Stages in the Formation of Rabbinic Writings

Each of the score of documents that make up the canon of Judaism in late antiquity exhibits distinctive traits in logic, rhetoric, and topic, so that we may identify the purposes and traits of form and intellect of the authorship of that document. It follows that documents possess integrity and are not merely scrapbooks, compilations made with no clear purpose or aesthetic plan. But, as is well known, some completed units of thought – propositional arguments, sayings, and stories for instance – travel from one document to another. It follows that the several documents intersect through shared materials. Furthermore, writings that peregrinate by definition do not carry out the rhetorical, logical, and topical program of a particular document. In framing a theory to accommodate the facts that documents are autonomous but also connected through such shared materials, therefore, we must account for the history of not only the documents in hand but also the completed pieces of writing that move from here to there. We have at present no theory of the formation of the various documents of the rabbinic literature that derives from an inductive sifting of the evidence. Nor do we have even a theory as to the correct method for the framing of a hypothesis for testing against the evidence.

My theory on the literary history of the rabbinic canon posits three stages in the formation of writing. Moving from the latest to the earliest, one stage is marked by the definition of a document, its topical program, its rhetorical medium, its logical message. The document as we know it in its basic structure and main lines therefore comes at the end. It follows that writings that clearly serve the program of that document and carry the purposes of its authorship were made up in connection with the formation of *that* document. Another, and I think, prior stage is marked by the preparation of writings that do not serve the needs of a particular document now in our hands, but can have carried out the purposes of an authorship working on a document of a *type* we now have. The existing documents then form a model for defining other kinds of writings worked out to meet the program of a documentary authorship.

But there are other types of writings that in no way serve the needs or plans of any document we now have, and that, furthermore, also cannot find a place in any document of a type that we now have. These writings, as a matter of fact, very commonly prove peripatetic, traveling from one writing to another, equally at home in, or alien to, the program of the documents in which they end up. These writings therefore were carried out without regard to a documentary program of any kind exemplified by the canonical books of the Judaism of the Dual Torah. They form what I conceive to be the earliest in the three stages of the writing of the units of completed thought that in the aggregate form the canonical literature of the Judaism of the Dual Torah of late antiquity.

As a matter of fact, therefore, a given canonical document of the Judaism of the Dual Torah draws upon three classes of materials, and these were framed in temporal order. Last comes the final class, the one that the redactors themselves defined and wrote; prior is the penultimate class that can have served other redactors but did not serve these in particular; and earliest of all in the order of composition (at least, from the perspective of the ultimate redaction of the documents we now have) is the writing that circulated autonomously and served no redactional purpose we can now identify within the canonical documents.

I. The Correct Starting Point

In beginning the inquiry with the traits of documents seen whole, I reject the assumption that the building block of documents is the smallest whole unit of thought, the lemma, nor can we proceed in the premise that a lemma traverses the boundaries of various documents and is unaffected by the journey.[1] The opposite premise is that we start our work with the traits of documents as a whole, rather than with the traits of the lemmas of which documents are (supposedly) composed. In a variety of books I have set forth the documentary hypothesis for the analysis of the rabbinic literature of late antiquity.[2] But how shall we

---

[1]As a matter of fact, the identification of the lemma as the primary unit of inquiry rests upon the premise that the person to whom a saying is assigned really said that saying. That premise is untenable. But for the sake of argument, I bypass that still more fundamental flaw in the methodology at hand.

[2]Particularly *From Tradition to Imitation. The Plan and Program of Pesiqta deRab Kahana and Pesiqta Rabbati; Canon and Connection: Intertextuality in Judaism; Midrash*

proceed, if we take as our point of entry the character and conditions of the document, seen whole? And what are the results of doing so?

Having demonstrated beyond any doubt that a rabbinic text is a document, that is to say, a well-crafted text and not merely a compilation of this and that, and further specified in acute detail precisely the aesthetic, formal, and logical program followed by each of those texts, accordingly, I am able to move to the logical next step. That is to show that in the background of the documents that we have is writing that is *not* shaped by documentary requirements, writing that is not shaped by the documentary requirements of the compilations we now have, and also writing that is entirely formed within the rules of the documents that now present that writing. These then are the three kinds of writing that form, also, the three stages in the formation of the classics of Judaism.

II. Redaction and Writing
The Extreme Case of the Mishnah

My example of a document that is written down essentially in its penultimate and ultimate stages, that is, a document that takes shape within the redactional process and principally there, is, of course, the Mishnah. In that writing, the patterns of language, for example, syntactic structures, of the apodosis and protasis of the Mishnah's smallest whole units of discourse are framed in formal, mnemonic patterns. They follow a few simple rules. These rules, once known, apply nearly everywhere and form stunning evidence for the document's cogency. They permit anyone to reconstruct, out of a few key phrases, an entire cognitive unit, and even complete intermediate units of discourse. Working downward from the surface, therefore, anyone can penetrate into the deeper layers of meaning of the Mishnah. Then and at the same time, while discovering the principle behind the cases, one can easily memorize the whole by mastering the recurrent rhetorical pattern dictating the expression of the cogent set of cases. For it is easy to note the shift from one rhetorical pattern to another and to follow the repeated cases, articulated in the new pattern downward to its logical substrate. So syllogistic propositions, in the Mishnah's authors' hands, come to full expression not only in *what* people wish to state but also in *how* they choose to say it. The limits of rhetoric define the arena of topical articulation.

---

as Literature: The Primacy of Documentary Discourse; and *The Bavli and its Sources: The Question of Tradition in the Case of Tractate Sukkah;* as well as *The Talmud of the Land of Israel. 35. Introduction. Taxonomy;* and *Judaism. The Classic Statement. The Evidence of the Bavli.*

Now to state my main point in heavy emphasis: *the Mishnah's formal traits of rhetoric indicate that the document has been formulated all at once, and not in an incremental, linear process extending into a remote (mythic) past, (e.g., to Sinai).* These traits, common to a series of distinct cognitive units, are redactional, because they are imposed at that point at which someone intended to join together discrete (finished) units on a given theme. The varieties of traits particular to the discrete units and the diversity of authorities cited therein, including masters of two or three or even four strata from the turn of the first century to the end of the second, make it highly improbable that the several units were formulated in a common pattern and then preserved, until, later on, still further units, on the same theme and in the same pattern, were worked out and added. The entire indifference, moreover, to historical order of authorities and concentration on the logical unfolding of a given theme or problem without reference to the sequence of authorities, confirm the supposition that the work of formulation and that of redaction go forward together.

The principal framework of formulation and formalization in the Mishnah is the intermediate division rather than the cognitive unit. The least-formalized formulary pattern, the simple declarative sentence, turns out to yield many examples of acute formalization, in which a single distinctive pattern is imposed upon two or more (very commonly, groups of three or groups of five) cognitive units. While an intermediate division of a tractate may be composed of several such conglomerates of cognitive units, it is rare indeed for cognitive units formally to stand wholly by themselves. Normally, cognitive units share formal or formulary traits with others to which they are juxtaposed and the theme of which they share. It follows that the principal unit of formulary formalization is the intermediate division and not the cognitive unit. And what that means for our inquiry, is simple: we can tell when it is that the ultimate or penultimate redactors of a document do the writing. Now let us see that vast collection of writings that exhibit precisely the opposite trait: a literature in which, while doing some writing of their own, the redactors collected and arranged available materials.

III. When the Document Does Not Define the Literary Protocol: Stories Told But Not Compiled

Now to the other extreme. Can I point to a kind of writing that in no way defines a document now in our hands or even a type of document we can now imagine, that is, one that in its particulars we do not have but that conforms in its definitive traits to those that we do have? Indeed I can, and it is the writing of stories about sages and other exemplary figures. To show what might have been, I point to the simple fact that the final organizers of the Bavli, the Talmud of Babylonia had in hand a tripartite corpus of inherited materials awaiting composition into a final, closed document. First, the first type of material, in various states and stages of completion, addressed the Mishnah or took up the principles of laws that the Mishnah had originally brought to articulation. These the framers of the Bavli organized in accord with the order of those Mishnah-tractates that they selected for sustained attention. Second, they had in hand received materials, again in various conditions, pertinent to Scripture, both as Scripture related to the Mishnah and also as Scripture laid forth its own narratives. These they set forth as Scripture commentary. In this way, the penultimate and ultimate redactors of the Bavli laid out a systematic presentation of the two Torahs, the oral, represented by the Mishnah, and the written, represented by Scripture.

And, third, the framers of the Bavli also had in hand materials focused on sages. These in the received form, attested in the Bavli's pages, were framed around twin biographical principles, either as strings of stories about great sages of the past or as collections of sayings and comments drawn together solely because the same name stands behind all the collected sayings. These can easily have been composed into biographies. In the context of Christianity and of Judaism, it is appropriate to call the biography of a holy man or woman, meant to convey the divine message, a gospel.[3] This is writing that is utterly outside of the documentary framework in which it is now preserved; nearly all narratives in the rabbinic literature, not only the biographical ones, indeed prove remote from any documentary program exhibited by the canonical documents in which they now occur.

The Bavli as a whole lays itself out as a commentary to the Mishnah. So the framers wished us to think that whatever they wanted to tell us would take the form of Mishnah commentary. But a second glance indicates that the Bavli is made up of enormous composites, themselves closed prior to inclusion in the Bavli. Some of these composites – around

---

[3]I use the word "gospel" with a small *G* as equivalent to "didactic life of a holy man, portraying the faith." Obviously, the Christian usage, with a capital *G*, must maintain that there can be a Gospel only about Jesus Christ. Claims of uniqueness are, of course, not subject to public discourse. In the present context, I could as well have referred to lives of saints, since Judaism of the Dual Torah produced neither a gospel about a central figure nor lives of saints. Given the centrality of Moses "our rabbi," for example, we should have anticipated a "Gospel of Moses" parallel to the Gospels of Jesus Christ, and, lacking that, at least a "life of Aqiba," scholar, saint, martyr, parallel to the lives of various saints. We also have no autobiographies of any kind, beyond some "I"-stories, which themselves seem to me uncommon.

35 percent to 40 percent of Bavli's, if my sample is indicative[4] – were selected and arranged along lines dictated by a logic other than that deriving from the requirements of Mishnah commentary. The components of the canon of the Judaism of the Dual Torah prior to the Bavli had encompassed amplifications of the Mishnah, in the Tosefta and in the Yerushalmi, as well as the same for Scripture, in such documents as Sifra to Leviticus, Sifré to Numbers, another Sifré, to Deuteronomy, Genesis Rabbah, Leviticus Rabbah, and the like. But there was no entire document, now extant, organized around the life and teachings of a particular sage. Even the Fathers according to Rabbi Nathan, which contains a good sample of stories about sages, is not so organized as to yield a life of a sage, or even a systematic biography of any kind. Where events in the lives of sages do occur, they are thematic and not biographical in organization, for example, stories about the origins, as to Torah study, of diverse sages or death scenes of various sages. The sage as such, whether Aqiba or Yohanan ben Zakkai or Eliezer b. Hyrcanus, never in that document defines the appropriate organizing principle for sequences of stories or sayings. And there is no other in which the sage forms an organizing category for any material purpose.[5]

Accordingly, the decision that the framers of the Bavli reached was to adopt the two redactional principles inherited from the antecedent century or so and to reject the one already rejected by their predecessors, even while honoring it. [1] They organized the Bavli around the Mishnah. But [2] they adapted and included vast tracts of antecedent materials organized as scriptural commentary. These they inserted whole and complete, not at all in response to the Mishnah's program. But, finally, [3] while making provision for small-scale compositions built upon biographical principles, preserving both strings of sayings from a given master (and often a given tradent of a given master) as well as tales

---

[4]I compared Bavli and Yerushalmi tractates Sukkah, Sanhedrin, and Sotah, showing the proportion of what I call Scripture units of thought to Mishnah units of thought. See my *Judaism. The Classic Statement. The Evidence of the Bavli* (Chicago, 1986: University of Chicago Press).

[5]The occasion, in the history of Judaism, at which biography defines a generative category of literature, therefore also of thought, will therefore prove noteworthy. The model of biography surely existed from the formation of the Pentateuch, with its lines of structure, from Exodus through Deuteronomy, set forth around the biography of Moses, birth, call, career, death. And other biographies did flourish prior to the Judaism of the Dual Torah. Not only so, but the wall of the Dura synagogue highlights not the holy people so much as saints, such as Aaron and Moses. Accordingly, we must regard as noteworthy and requiring explanation the omission of biography from the literary genres of the canon of the Judaism of the Dual Torah. One obvious shift is marked by Hasidism, with its special interest in stories about saints and in compiling those stories.

about authorities of the preceding half millennium, they *never* created redactional compositions, of a sizable order, that focused upon given authorities. But sufficient materials certainly lay at hand to allow doing so.

We have now seen that some writings carry out a redactional purpose. The Mishnah was our prime example. Some writings ignore all redactional considerations we can identify. The stories about sages in the Fathers According to Rabbi Nathan for instance show us kinds of writing that are wholly out of phase with the program of the document that collects and compiles them. We may therefore turn to Midrash compilations and find the traits of writing that clearly are imposed by the requirements of compilation. We further identify writings that clearly respond to a redactional program, but not the program of any compilation we now have in hand. There is little speculation about the identification of such writings. They will conform to the redactional patterns we discern in the known compilations, but presuppose a collection other than one now known to us. Finally, we turn to pieces of writing that respond to no redactional program known to us or susceptible to invention in accord with the principles of defining compilation known to us.

IV. Pericopes Framed for the Purposes of the Particular Document in which They Occur

My analytical taxonomy of the writings now collected in various Midrash compilations point to not only three stages in the formation of the classics of Judaism. It also suggests that writing went on outside of the framework of the editing of documents, and also within the limits of the formation and framing of documents. Writing of the former kind then constituted a kind of literary work to which redactional planning proved irrelevant. But the second and the third kinds of writing responds to redactional considerations. So in the end we shall wish to distinguish between writing intended for the making of books – compositions of the first three kinds listed just now – and writing not in response to the requirements of the making of compilations.

The distinctions upon which these analytical taxonomies rest are objective and in no way subjective since they depend upon the fixed and factual relationship between a piece of writing and a larger redactional context.

[1] We know the requirements of redactors of the several documents of the rabbinic canon, because I have already shown what they are in the case of a large variety of documents. When, therefore, we judge a piece of writing to serve the program of the document in which that writing

occurs, it is not because of a personal impulse or a private and incommunicable insight, but because the traits of that writing self-evidently respond to the documentary program of the book in which the writing is located.

[2] When, further, we conclude that a piece of writing belongs in some other document than the one in which it is found, that too forms a factual judgment.

My example is a very simple one: writing that can serve only as a component of a commentary on a given scriptural book has been made up for the book in which it appears (or one very like it, if one wants to quibble). My example may derive from any of the ten Midrash compilations of late antiquity. Here is one among innumerable possibilities.

Sifré to Numbers

I:VII

1. A. "[The Lord said to Moses, 'Command the people of Israel that they put out of the camp every leper and every one having a discharge, and every one that is unclean through contact with the dead.] You shall put out both male and female, putting them outside the camp, that they may not defile their camp, in the midst of which I dwell'" (Gen. 5:1-4).
    B. I know, on the basis of the stated verse, that the law applies only to male and female [persons who are suffering from the specified forms of cultic uncleanness]. How do I know that the law pertains also to one lacking clearly defined sexual traits or to one possessed of the sexual traits of both genders?
    C. Scripture states, "...putting *them* outside the camp." [This is taken to constitute an encompassing formulation, extending beyond the male and female of the prior clause.]
    D. I know, on the basis of the stated verse, that the law applies only to those who can be sent forth. How do I know that the law pertains also to those who cannot be sent forth?
    E. Scripture states, "...putting them outside the camp." [This is taken to constitute an encompassing formulation, as before.]
    F. I know on the basis of the stated verse that the law applies only to persons. How do I know that the law pertains also to utensils?
    G. Scripture states, "...putting *them* outside the camp." [This is taken to constitute an encompassing formulation.]

I:VII

2. A. [Dealing with the same question as at 1.F,] R. Aqiba says, "'You shall put out both male and female, putting them outside the camp.' Both persons and utensils are implied."
    B. R. Ishmael says, "You may construct a logical argument, as follows:
    C. "Since man is subject to uncleanness on account of *negaim* ["plagues"], and clothing [thus: utensils] are subject to uncleanness

on the same count, just as man is subject to being sent forth [ostracism], likewise utensils are subject to being sent forth."

D. No, such an argument is not valid [and hence exegesis of the actual language of Scripture, as at A, is the sole correct route]. If you have stated the rule in the case of man, who imparts uncleanness when he exerts pressure on an object used for either sitting or lying, and, on which account, he is subject to ostracism, will you say the same rule of utensils, which do not impart uncleanness when they exert pressure on an object used for sitting and lying? [Clearly there is a difference between the uncleanness brought about by a human being from that brought about by an inanimate object, and therefore the rule that applies to the one will not necessarily apply to the other. Logic by itself will not suffice, and, it must follow, the proof of a verse of Scripture alone will suffice to prove the point.]

E. [No, that objection is not valid, because we can show that the same rule does apply to both an inanimate object and to man, namely] lo, there is the case of the stone affected with a *nega*, which will prove the point. For it does not impart uncleanness when it exerts pressure on an object used for sitting or lying, but it does require ostracism [being sent forth from the camp, a rule that Scripture itself makes explicit].

F. Therefore do not find it surprising that utensils, even though they in general do not impart uncleanness when they exert pressure on an object used for sitting or lying, are to be sent forth from the camp." [Ishmael's logical proof stands.]

I:VII
3. A. R. Yosé the Galilean says, "'You shall put out both male and female, putting them outside the camp, that they may not defile their camp, in the midst of which I dwell.'

B. "What marks as singular male and female is that they can be turned into a generative source of uncleanness [when they die and are corpses], and, it follows, they are to be sent forth from the camp when they become unclean [even while alive], so anything which can become a generative source of uncleanness will be subject to being sent forth from the camp.

C. "What is excluded is a piece of cloth less than three by three fingerbreadths, which in the entire Torah is never subject to becoming a generative source of uncleanness."

I:VII
4. A. R. Isaac says, "Lo, Scripture states, '[And every person that eats what dies of itself or what is torn by beasts, whether he is a native or a sojourner, shall wash his clothes and bathe himself in water and be unclean until the evening; they he shall be clean.] But if he does not wash them or bathe his flesh, he shall bear his iniquity' (Lev. 17:15-16).

B. "It is on account of failure to wash one's body that Scripture has imposed the penalty of extirpation.

C. "You maintain that it is on account of failure to wash one's body that Scripture has imposed the penalty of extirpation. But perhaps

Scripture has imposed a penalty of extirpation only on account of the failure to launder one's garments.

D. "Thus you may construct the argument to the contrary [*su eipas*]: if in the case of one who has become unclean on account of corpse uncleanness, which is a severe source of uncleanness, Scripture has not imposed a penalty merely because of failure to launder one's garments, as to one who eats meat of a beast that has died of itself, which is a minor source of uncleanness, it is a matter of reason that Scripture should not impose a penalty on the account of having failed to launder the garments."

Why do I maintain that the composition can serve only the document in which it occurs? The reason is that we read the verse in a narrow framework: what rule do we derive from the *actual* language at hand. No. 1 answers the question on the basis of an exegesis of the verse. No. 2 then provides an alternative proof. Aqiba provides yet another reading of the language at hand. Ishmael goes over the possibility of a logical demonstration. I find it difficult to see how Yosé's pericope fits in. It does not seem to me to address the problem at hand. He wants to deal with a separate issue entirely, as specified at C. No. 4 pursues yet another independent question. So Nos. 3, 4 look to be parachuted down. On what basis? No. 3 deals with our base verse. But No. 4 does not. Then what guided the compositors to introduce Nos. 1, 2, 3, and 4? Nos. 1, 2 deal with the exegesis of the limited rule at hand: how do I know to what classifications of persons and objects ostracism applies? No. 1 provides answers to questions, first, the classifications, then the basis for the rule. No. 2 introduces the second question: on what basis do we make our rule? The answer, as is clear, is Scripture, not unaided reason. Now at that point the issue of utensils emerges. So Yosé the Galilean's interest in the rule governing a utensil – a piece of cloth – leads to the intrusion of his item. And the same theme – the rule governing utensils, garments – accounts for the introduction of I:VII.4 as well. In sum, the redactional principle is clear: treat the verse, then the theme generated by the verse. Then this piece of writing can have been formed only for the purpose of a commentary to the book of Numbers: Sifré to Numbers is the only one we have. Q.E.D.

V. Pericopes Framed for the Purposes of a Particular Document But Not of a Type We Now Possess

A piece of writing that serves nowhere we now know may nonetheless conform to the rules of writing that we can readily imagine and describe in theory. For instance, a propositional composition, that runs through a wide variety of texts to make a point autonomous of all of the texts that are invoked, clearly is intended for a propositional document, one that (like the Mishnah) makes points autonomous of a given prior writing, for example, a biblical book, but that makes points that for one reason or another cohere quite nicely on their own. Authors of propositional compilations self-evidently can imagine that kind of redaction. We have their writings, but not the books that they intended to be made up of those writings. In all instances, the reason that we can readily imagine a compilation for that will have dictated the indicative traits of a piece of writing will prove self-evident: we have compilations of such a type, if not specific compilations called for by a given composition. A single example suffices. It derives from Sifra.

If the canon of Judaism included a major treatise or compilation on applied logic and practical reason, then a principal tractate, or set of tractates, would be devoted to proving that reason by itself cannot produce reliable results. And in that treatise would be a vast and various collection of sustained discussions, which spread themselves across Sifra and Sifré to Numbers and Sifré to Deuteronomy, the Yerushalmi and the Bavli, as well as other collections. Here is a sample of how that polemic has imposed itself on the amplification of Lev. 1:2 and transformed treatment of that verse from an exegesis to an example of an overriding proposition. It goes without saying that where we have this type of proof of the priority of Scripture over logic, or of the necessity of Scripture in the defining of generative taxa, the discussion serves a purpose that transcends the case, and on that basis I maintain the proposition proposed here. It is that there were types of collections that we can readily imagine but that were not made up. In this case, it is, as is clear, a treatise on applied logic, and the general proposition of that treatise is that reliable taxonomy derives only from Scripture.

Sifra Parashat Vayyiqra Dibura Denedabah Parashah 2

III.I

1. A. "Speak to the Israelite people [and say to them, 'When any (Hebrew: Adam) of you presents an offering of cattle to the Lord, he shall choose his offering from the herd or from the flock. If his offering is a burnt-offering from the herd, he shall offer a male without blemish; he shall offer it at the door of the tent of meeting, that he may be accepted before the Lord;] he shall lay [his hand upon the head of the burnt offering, and it shall be accepted for him to make atonement for him]'" (Lev. 1:2):

    B. "He shall lay his hand:" Israelites lay on hands, gentiles do not lay on hands.

    C. [But is it necessary to prove that proposition on the basis of the cited verse? Is it not to be proven merely by an argument of a logical order, which is now presented?] Now which measure [covering the applicability of a rite] is more abundant, the measure of wavings or the measure of laying on of hands?

D.   The measure of waving [the beast] is greater than the measure of laying on of hands.

E.   For waving [the sacrifice] is done to both something that is animate and something that is not animate, while the laying on of hands applies only to something that is animate.

F.   If gentiles are excluded from the rite of waving the sacrifice, which applies to a variety of sacrifices, should they not be excluded from the rite of laying on of hands, which pertains to fewer sacrifices? [Accordingly, I prove on the basis of reason the rule that is derived at A-B from the verse of Scripture.]

G.   [I shall now show that the premise of the foregoing argument is false:] [You have constructed your argument] from the angle that yields waving as more common and laying on of hands as less common.

H.   But take the other angle, which yields laying on of hands as the more common and waving as the less common.

I.   For the laying on of hands applies to all partners in the ownership of a beast [each one of whom is required to lay hands on the beast before it is slaughtered in behalf of the partnership in ownership of the beast as a whole],

J.   but the waving of a sacrifice is not a requirement that applies to all partners in the ownership of a beast.

K.   Now if I eliminate [gentiles' laying on of hands] in the case of the waving of a beast, which is a requirement applying to fewer cases, should I eliminate them from the requirement of laying on of hands, which applies to a larger number of cases?

L.   Lo, since a rule pertains to the waving of the sacrifice that does not apply to the laying on of hands, and a rule pertains to the laying on of hands that does not apply to the waving of the sacrifice, it is necessary for Scripture to make the statement that it does, specifically:

M.   "He shall lay his hand:" Israelites lay on hands, gentiles do not lay on hands.

The basic premise is that when two comparable actions differ, then the more commonly performed one imposes its rule upon further actions, the rule governing which is unknown. If, then, we show that action A is more commonly performed than action B, other actions of the same classification will follow the rule governing A, not the rule governing B. Then the correct route to overturn such an argument is to show that each of the actions, the rule governing which is known, differs from the other in such a way that neither the one nor the other can be shown to be the more commonly performed. Then the rule governing the further actions is not to be derived from the one governing the two known actions. The powerful instrument of analytical and comparative reasoning proves that diverse traits pertain to the two stages of the rite of sacrifice, the waving, the laying on of hands, which means that a rule pertaining to the one does not necessarily apply to the other. On account of that difference we must evoke the specific ruling of Scripture. The polemic in favor of Scripture, uniting all of the components into a single coherent argument, then insists that there really is no such thing as a genus at all, and Scripture's rules and regulations serve a long list of items, each of them *sui generis*, for discovering rules by the logic of analogy and contrast is simply not possible.

VI. Pericopes Framed for the Purposes Not Particular to a Type of Document Now in Our Hands

Some writings stand autonomous of any redactional program we have in an existing compilation or of any we can even imagine on the foundations of said writings. Compositions of this kind, as a matter of hypothesis, are to be assigned to a stage in the formation of classics prior to the framing of all available documents. For, as a matter of fact, all of our now exant writings adhere to a single program of conglomeration and agglutination, and all are served by composites of one sort, rather than some other. Hence we may suppose that at some point prior to the decision to make writings in the model that we now have but in some other model people also made up completed units of thought to serve these other kinds of writings. These persist, now, in documents that they do not serve at all well. And we can fairly easily identify the kinds of documents that they can and should have served quite nicely indeed. These, then, are the three stages of literary formation in the making of the classics of Judaism.

Of the relative temporal or ordinal position of writings that stand autonomous of any redactional program we have in an existing compilation or of any we can even imagine on the foundations of said writings we can say nothing. These writings prove episodic; they are commonly singletons. They serve equally well everywhere, because they demand no traits of form and redaction in order to endow them with sense and meaning. Why not? Because they are essentially free-standing and episodic, not referential and allusive. They are stories that contain their own point and do not invoke, in the making of that point, a given verse of Scripture. They are sayings that are utterly ad hoc. A variety of materials fall into this – from a redactional perspective – unassigned, and unassignable, type of writing. They do not belong in books at all. By that I mean, whoever made up these pieces of writing did not imagine that what he was forming required a setting beyond the limits of his own piece of writing; the story is not only complete in itself but could stand entirely on its own; the saying spoke for itself and required no nurturing context; the proposition and its associated proofs in no way was meant to draw nourishment from roots penetrating nutriments outside of its own literary limits.

Where we have utterly hermetic writing, able to define its own limits and sustain its point without regard to anything outside itself, we know that here we are in the presence of authorships that had no larger redactional plan in mind, no intent on the making of books out of their little pieces of writing. We may note that, among the "unimaginable" compilations is not a collection of parables, since parables rarely[6] stand free and never are inserted for their own sake. Whenever in the rabbinic canon we find a parable, it is meant to serve the purpose of an authorship engaged in making its own point; and the point of a parable is rarely, if ever, left unarticulated. Normally it is put into words, but occasionally the point is made simply by redactional setting. It must follow that, in this canon, the parable cannot have constituted the generative or agglutinative principle of a large-scale compilation. It further follows, so it seems to me, that the parable always takes shape within the framework of a work of composition for the purpose of either a large-scale exposition or, more commonly still, of compilation of a set of expositions into what we should now call the chapter of a book – that is to say, parables linked to purposes that transcend the tale that they tell (or even the point that the tale makes). Let me now give one example of what I classify as a free-standing piece of writing, one with no place for itself in accord with the purposes of compilers either of documents we now have in hand or of documents we can readily envisage or imagine. My example again derives from Sifra, although, as a matter of fact, every document of the canon yields illustrative materials for all three types of writing.

The issue of the relationship between the Mishnah and Scripture deeply engaged a variety of writers and compilers of documents. Time and again we have evidence of an interest in the scriptural sources of laws, or of greater consequence in the priority of Scripture in taxonomic inquiry. We can show large-scale compositions that will readily have served treatises on these matters. But if I had to point to a single type of writing that is quite commonplace in the compilations we do have, but *wholly* outside of the repertoire of redactional possibilities we have or can imagine, it must be a sustained piece of writing on the relationship of the Mishnah to Scripture. Such a treatise can have been enormous, not only because, in theory, every line of the Mishnah required attention. It is also because, in practice, a variety of documents, particularly Sifra, the two Sifrés, and the Talmuds, contain writing of a single kind, meant to amplify the Mishnah by appeal to Scripture (but never to amplify Scripture by appeal to the Mishnah!) It is perfectly clear that no one

---

[6]I should prefer to say "never," but it is easier to say what is in the rabbinic literature than what is never there.

imagined compiling a commentary to the Mishnah that would consist principally of proofs, of a sustained and well-crafted sort, that the Mishnah in general depends upon Scripture (even though specific and sustained proofs that the principles of taxonomy derive from Scripture are, as I said, susceptible of compilation in such treatises). How do we know that fact? It is because, when people did compile writings in the form of sustained commentaries to the Mishnah, that is to say, the two Talmuds, they did not focus principally upon the scriptural exegesis of the Mishnah; that formed only one interest, and, while an important one, it did not predominate; it certainly did not define the plan and program of the whole; and it certainly did not form a center of redactional labor. It was simply one item on a list of items that would be brought into relationship, where appropriate, with sentences of the Mishnah. And even then, it always was the intersection at the level of sentences, not sustained discourses, let alone with the Mishnah viewed whole and complete.

And yet – and yet if we look into compilations we do have, we find sizable sets of materials that can have been joined together with the Mishnah, paragraph by paragraph, in such a way that Scripture might have been shaped into a commentary to the Mishnah. Let me now give a sustained example of what might have emerged, but never did emerge, in the canonical compilations of Judaism. I draw my case from Sifra, but equivalent materials in other Midrash compilations as well as in the two Talmuds in fact are abundant. In boldface type are direct citations of Mishnah passages. I skip Nos. 2-12 because these are not germane to this part of my argument.

Sifra Parashat Behuqotai Parashah 3
CCLXX:I
1. A.   ["The Lord said to Moses, 'Say to the people of Israel, "When a man makes a special vow of persons to the Lord at your Valuation, then your Valuation of a male from twenty years old up to sixty years old shall be fifty shekels of silver according to the shekel of the sanctuary. If the person is a female, your Valuation shall be thirty shekels. If the person is from five years old up to twenty years old, your Valuation shall be for a male twenty shekels and for a female ten shekels. If the person is from a month old up to five years old, your Valuation shall be for a male five shekels of silver and for a female your Valuation shall be three shekels of silver. And if the person is sixty years old and upward, then your Valuation for a male shall be fifteen shekels and for a female ten shekels. And if a man is too poor to pay your Valuation, then he shall bring the person before the priest, and the priest shall value him; according to the ability of him who vowed the priest shall value him'" (Lev. 27:1-8).]

B. "Israelites take vows of Valuation, but gentiles do not take vows of Valuation [M. Ar. 1:2B].

C. "Might one suppose they are not subject to vows of Valuation?

D. "Scripture says, 'a man,'" the words of R. Meir.

E. Said R. Meir, "After one verse of Scripture makes an inclusionary statement, another makes an exclusionary statement.

F. "On what account do I say that gentiles are subject to vows of Valuation but may not take vows of Valuation?

G. "It is because greater is the applicability of the rule of subject to the pledge of Valuation by others than the applicability of making the pledge of Valuation of others [T. Ar. 1:1A].

H. "For lo, a deaf-mute, idiot, and minor may be subjected to vows of Valuation, but they are not able to take vows of Valuation [M. Ar. 1:1F]."

I. R. Judah says, "Israelites are subject to vows of Valuation, but gentiles are not subject to vows of Valuation [M. Ar. 1:2C].

J. "Might one suppose that they may not take vows of Valuation of third parties?

K. "Scripture says, 'a man.'"

L. Said R. Judah, "After one verse of Scripture makes an inclusionary statement, another makes an exclusionary statement.

M. "On what account do I say that gentiles are not subject to vows of Valuation but may take vows of Valuation?

N. "It is because greater is the applicability of the rule of pledging the Valuation of others than the applicability of being subject to the pledge of Valuation by others [T. Ar. 1:1C].

O. "For a person of doubtful sexual traits and a person who exhibits traits of both sexes pledge the Valuation of others but are not subjected to the pledge of Valuation to be paid by others" [M. Ar. 1:1D].

13. A. And how do we know that the sixtieth year is treated as part of the period prior to that year?

B. Scripture says, "from twenty years old up to sixty years old" —

C. this teaches that the sixtieth year is treated as part of the period prior to that year.

D. I know only that that is the rule governing the status of the sixtieth year. How do I know the rule as to assigning the fifth year, the twentieth year?

E. It is a matter of logic:

F. Liability is incurred when one is in the sixtieth year, the fifth year, and the twentieth year.

G. Just as the sixtieth year is treated as part of the period prior to that year,

H. so the fifth and the twentieth years are treated as part of the period prior to that year.

I. But if you treat the sixtieth year as part of the prior period, imposing a more stringent law [the Valuation requiring a higher fee before than after sixty],

J. shall we treat the fifth year and the twentieth year as part of the period prior to that year, so imposing a more lenient law in such cases [the Valuation being less expensive]?

K.   Accordingly, Scripture is required to settle the question when it refers repeatedly to "year,"

L.   thus establishing a single classification for all such cases:

M.   just as the sixtieth year is treated as part of the prior period, so the fifth and the twentieth years are treated as part of the prior period.

N.   And that is the rule, whether it produces a more lenient or a more stringent ruling [M. Ar. 4:4M-Q, with somewhat different wording].

14. A.   R. Eliezer says, "How do we know that a month and a day after a month are treated as part of the sixtieth year?

B.   "Scripture says, 'up...';

C.   "Here we find reference to 'up...,' and elsewhere we find the same. Just as 'up' used elsewhere means that a month and a day after the month [are included in the prior span of time], so the meaning is the same when used here. [M. Ar. 4:4R: R. Eleazar says, "The foregoing applies so long as they are a month and a day more than the years which are prescribed."]

15. A.   I know only that this rule applies after sixty. How do I know that the same rule applies after five or twenty?

B.   It is a matter of logic:

C.   One is liable to pay a pledge of Valuation if the person to be valued is older than sixty, and one is liable if such a one is older than five or older than twenty.

D.   Just as, if one is older than sixty by a month and a day, the person is as though he were sixty years of age, so if the one is after five years or twenty years by a month and a day, lo, these are deemed to be the equivalent of five or twenty years of age.

16. A.   "And if a man is too poor to pay your Valuation":

B.   this means, if he is too impoverished to come up with your Valuation.

17. A.   "Then he shall bring the person before the priest":

B.   this then excludes a dead person.

C.   I shall then exclude a corpse but not a dying person?

D.   Scripture says, "then he shall bring the person before the priest, and the priest shall value him" —

E.   one who is subject to being brought is subject to being valuated, and one who is not subject to being brought before the priest [such as a dying man] also is not subject to the pledge of Valuation.

18. A.   Might one suppose that even if someone said, "The Valuation of Mr. So-and-so is incumbent on me," and he died, the man should be exempt?

B.   Scripture says, "and the priest shall value him."

C.   That is so even if he is dead.

19. A.   "And the priest shall value him":

B.   This means that one pays only in accord with the conditions prevailing at the time of the Valuation.

20. A.   "According to the ability of him who vowed the priest shall value him":

B.   It is in accord with the means of the one who takes the vow, not the one concerning whom the vow is taken,

C.   whether that is a man, woman, or child.

D.   In this connection sages have said:

E.   **The estimate of ability to pay is made in accord with the status of the one who vows;**

F.   **and the estimate of the years of age is made in accord with the status of the one whose Valuation is vowed.**

G.   **And when this is according to the Valuations spelled out in the Torah, it is in accord with the status, as to age and sex, of the one whose Valuation is pledged.**

H.   **And the Valuation is paid in accordance with the rate prescribed at the time of the pledge of Valuation [M. Ar. 4:1A-D].**

21. A. "The priest shall value him:"

B.   This serves as the generative analogy covering all cases of Valuations, indicating that the priest should be in charge.

The program of the Mishnah and the Tosefta predominates throughout, for example, Nos. 1, 12, 13, 14-15. The second methodical inquiry characteristic of our authorship, involving exclusion and inclusion, accounts for pretty much the rest of this well-crafted discussion. Now we see a coherent and cogent discussion of a topic in accord with a program applicable to all topics, that trait of our document which so won our admiration. Thus Nos. 2-11, 17-20, involve inclusion, exclusion, or extension by analogy. I should offer this excellent composition as an example of the best our authorship has to give us, and a very impressive intellectual gift at that. The point throughout is simple. We know how the compilers of canonical writings produced treatments of the Mishnah. The one thing that they did not do was to create a scriptural commentary to the Mishnah. That is not the only type of writing lacking all correspondence to documents we have or can imagine, but it is a striking example.

VII. The Three Stages of Literary Formation

Now to return to my starting point, namely, those sizable selections of materials that circulated from one document to another and why I tend to think they were formed earlier than the writings particular to documents. The documentary hypothesis affects our reading of the itinerant compositions, for it identifies what writings are extra-documentary and nondocumentary and imposes upon the hermeneutics and history of these writings a set of distinctive considerations. The reason is that these writings serve the purposes not of compilers (or authors or authorships) of distinct compilations, but the interests of a another type of authorship entirely: one that thought making up stories (whether or not for collections) itself an important activity; or making up exercises on Mishnah-Scripture relationships; or other such writings as lie beyond the imagination of the compilers of the score of documents that comprise the canon. When writings work well for two or more documents, therefore, they must be assumed to have a literary history different from those that serve only one writing or one type of writing, and, also, demand a different hermeneutic.

My "three stages" in ordinal sequence correspond, as a matter of fact, to a taxic structure, that is, three types of writing. The first – and last in assumed temporal order – is writing carried out in the context of the making, or compilation, of a classic. That writing responds to the redactional program and plan of the authorship of a classic. The second, penultimate in order, is writing that can appear in a given document but better serves a document other than the one in which it (singularly) occurs. This kind of writing seems to me not to fall within the same period of redaction as the first. For while it is a type of writing under the identical conditions, it also is writing that presupposes redactional programs in no way in play in the ultimate, and definitive, period of the formation of the canon: when people did things this way, and not in some other. That is why I think it is a kind of writing that was done prior to the period in which people limited their redactional work and associated labor of composition to the program that yielded the books we now have.

The upshot is simple: whether the classification of writing be given a temporal or merely taxonomic valence, the issue is the same: have these writers done their work with documentary considerations in mind? I believe I have shown that they have not. Then where did they expect their work to makes its way? Anywhere it might, because, so they assumed, fitting in no where in particular, it found a suitable locus everywhere it turned up. But I think temporal, not merely taxonomic, considerations pertain.

The third kind of writing seems to me to originate in a period prior to the other two. It is carried on in a manner independent of all redactional considerations such as are known to us. Then it should derive from a time when redactional considerations played no paramount role in the making of compositions. A brief essay, rather than a sustained composition, was then the dominant mode of writing. My hypothesis is that people can have written both long and short compositions – compositions and composites, in my language – at one and the same time. But writing that does not presuppose a secondary labor of redaction, for example, in a composite, probably originated when authors or authorships did not anticipate any fate for their writing beyond their labor of composition itself.

Along these same lines of argument, this writing may or may not travel from one document to another. What that means is that the author or authorship does not imagine a future for his writing. What fits anywhere is composed to go nowhere in particular. Accordingly, what matters is not whether a writing fits one document or another, but whether, as the author or authorship has composed a piece of writing, that writing meets the requirements of any document we now have or can even imagine. If it does not, then we deal with a literary period in which the main kind of writing was ad hoc and episodic, not sustained and documentary.

Now extra- and nondocumentary kinds of writing seem to me to derive from either [1] a period prior to the work of the making of Midrash compilations and the two Talmuds alike; or [2] a labor of composition not subject to the rules and considerations that operated in the work of the making of Midrash compilations and the two Talmuds. As a matter of hypothesis, I should guess that nondocumentary writing comes prior to making any kind of documents of consequence, and extra-documentary writing comes prior to the period in which the specificities of the documents we now have were defined. That is to say, writing that can fit anywhere or nowhere is prior to writing that can fit somewhere but does not fit anywhere now accessible to us, and both kinds of writing are prior to the kind that fits only in what documents in which it is now located.

And given the documentary propositions and theses that we can locate in all of our compilations, we can only assume that the nondocumentary writings enjoyed, and were assumed to enjoy, ecumenical acceptance. That means, very simply, when we wish to know the consensus of the entire textual (or canonical) community[7] – I mean simply the people, anywhere and any time, responsible for everything we now have – we turn not to the distinctive perspective of documents, but the (apparently universally acceptable) perspective of the extra-documentary compositions. That is the point at which we should look for the propositions everywhere accepted but nowhere advanced in a distinctive way, the "Judaism beyond the texts" – or behind them.

Do I place a priority, in the framing of a hypothesis, over taxonomy or temporal order? Indeed I do. I am inclined to suppose that nondocumentary compositions took shape not only separated from, but in time before, the documentary ones did. My reason for thinking so is worth rehearsing, even though it is not yet compelling. The kinds of nondocumentary writing I have identified in general focus on matters of very general interest. These matters may be assembled into two very large rubrics: virtue, on the one side, reason, on the other. Stories about sages fall into the former category; all of them set forth in concrete form

---

[7] I prefer Brian Stock's "textual community," see his *Implications of Literacy* (Princeton, 1986: Princeton University Press).

the right living that sages exemplify. Essays on right thinking, the role of reason, the taxonomic priority of Scripture, the power of analogy, the exemplary character of cases and precedents in the expression of general and encompassing rules – all of these intellectually coercive writings set forth rules of thought as universally applicable, in their way, as are the rules of conduct contained in stories about sages, in theirs. A great labor of generalization is contained in both kinds of nondocumentary and extradocumentary writing. And the results of that labor are then given concrete expression in the documentary writings in hand; for these, after all, do say in the setting of specific passages or problems precisely what, in a highly general way, emerges from the writing that moves hither and yon, never with a home, always finding a suitable resting place.

Now, admittedly, that rather general characterization of the nondocumentary writing is subject to considerable qualification and clarification. But it does provide a reason to assign temporal priority, not solely taxonomic distinction, to the nondocumentary compositions. We can have had commentaries of a sustained and systematic sort on chronicles, on the one side, treatises on virtue, on the second, gospels, on the third – to complete the triangle. But we do not have these kinds of books.

In conclusion, let me confess that I wish our sages had made treatises on right action and right thought, in their own idiom to be sure, because I think these treatises will have shaped the intellect of generations to come in a more effective way than the discrete writings, submerged in collections and composites of other sorts altogether, have been able to do. Compositions on correct behavior made later on filled the gap left open by the redactional decisions made in the period under study; I do not know why no one assembled a Midrash on right action in the way in which, in Leviticus Rabbah and Genesis Rabbah, treatises on the rules of society and the rules of history were compiled. And still more do I miss those intellecually remarkable treatises on right thought that our sages can have produced out of the rich resources in hand: the art of generalization, the craft of comparison and contrast, for example. In this regard the Mishnah, with its union of (some) Aristotelian modes of thought and (some) neo-Platonic propositions forms the model, if a lonely one, for what can have been achieved, even in the odd and unphilosophical idiom of our sages.[8] The compositions needed for both kinds of treatises – and, as a matter of fact, many of them – are fully in hand. But no one made the compilations of them.

---

[8]This is fully explained in my *Philosophical Mishnah* (Atlanta, 1989: Scholars Press for Brown Judaic Studies) I-IV, and in my *The Philosophy of Judaism: The First Principles* (in press).

The books we do have not only preserve the evidences of the possibility of commentaries and biographies. More than that, they also bring to rich expression the messages that such books will have set forth. And most important, they also express in fresh and unanticipated contexts those virtues and values that commentaries and biographies (gospels) meant to bring to realization, and they do so in accord with the modes of thought that sophisticated reflection on right thinking has exemplifed in its way as well. So when people went about the work of making documents, they did something fresh with something familiar. They made cogent compositions, documents, texts enjoying integrity and autonomy. But they did so in such a way as to form of their distinct documents a coherent body of writing, of books, a canon, of documents, a system. And this they did in such a way as to say, in distinctive and specific ways, things that, in former times, people had expressed in general and broadly applicable ways.

4

Translating Rabbinic Documents: The Importance of an Analytical Reference System

In making my translations of the canon of the Judaism of the Dual Torah – Mishnah, Tosefta, two Talmuds, various Midrash compilations – I supply to the canonical writings a systematic and uniform reference system, corresponding, in the Bible, to the use of numbers for chapters and verses, for example, Gen. 1:12. Because of the failure of all prior translators as well as editors of critical versions of the received classics to provide a reference system, I found it necessary to re-translate all canonical writings of the Judaism of the Dual Torah that already had been presented in English, as well as to translate for the first time those many documents that were not in English. The reason, as I shall show here, is simply that no analytical work of any kind is possible without a reference system that identifies the parts of a large passage. Not only so, but in a bilingual document, readers must be told what language the original authors used. But until very recently, no translation differentiated one language from the other. Since, it is clear, colleagues engaged in the same work of translation of rabbinic canonical writings do not yet grasp why an analytical reference system of some kind is required, recent works in German and Spanish,[1] for instance, at best

---

[1]Spanish, for one example: *Midrás Exodo Rabbah I*, by Luis-Fernando Girón Blanc. Biblioteca Midrásica, 8. Valencia, Spain: Institución San Jerónimo, 1989. 190 pp. But the critical Hebrew text, of Exodus Rabbah used by the Spanish translation, that of A. Shinan, also has no analytical reference system that anyone can use. Not one [!] German "scientific" translation – Wewers's translation of the Talmud of the Land of Israel, for example – has recognized the requirement of a reference system to make possible further study of the translated documents, with the result that all we have in German is the contents of the Hebrew, but not the

numbering paragraphs, but, ordinarily, not doing even that, I propose to show what is at stake in a very simple exercise.

The problem goes beyond translation. No Hebrew language reprinting of the Talmud has ever made possible any sort of large-scale analytical work at all. Not only so, but I do not believe that any Hebrew edition, for example, a critical text, at which Israeli colleagues think they excel, attends to that minimum task. Giving page and line references hardly suffices, since these supply no signals, let alone visual evidence, on what is before us. Not only so, but – perhaps it was deemed more "authentic" because "traditional" – every current translation into various European languages fails to provide even the most minimal sigla, for example, indications of the smallest whole units of thought, sentences, paragraphs, completed expositions of a single idea, components of larger presentations of propositions, and the like – nothing, except page and line references (if that). No wonder the Bavli (among all writings) is (mis)represented as utterly confused, a hodgepodge of this and that, when, in fact, it is an orderly and well-disciplined construction. Accordingly, the whole of rabbinic literature has had to be retranslated in such a way as to indicate the individual components of a composition, for example, sentences, paragraphs, chapters or completed whole presentations of propositions. I have accomplished most of that task, out of an interest in not philology, let alone text criticism, but history of religion.

Only if the reader first meets an undifferentiated text, merely translated fairly literally, but in no way re-presented within the extant technology by which we organize information in a purposive manner, will the necessity of a differentiated text become self-evident. That is why, in what follows, I first present, without comment, a sizable abstract, marking each sentence off from the others only for the purpose of allowing the reader some sort of minimal access to what is said. I do not differentiate between Hebrew and Aramaic, and I do not include any signals on how a given sentence relates to what has gone before or to what is to follow. So I omit the signals that I have devised to ease the

---

construction or indications of the composition. Analytical scholarship on these documents is possible only within my, or some counterpart, reference system. Translators may maintain that analysis is not part of their work. But as soon as we who translate supply periods, commas, and quotation marks, we state what we conceive to be the elements of construction and composition. Then why not mark the sentences, one by one, so people can refer to them? And why not say what we conceive the "chapters" to be as well? I have done nothing more "radical" than was done by the printers who originally presented the Bible in printed form and added chapter and verse numbers. But, as is clear, I have had to do this work for the entirety of rabbinical literature of late antiquity.

reader's progress through the document, that is, not highlighting what the intended audience automatically will have grasped from shifts in language and other signals, articulated or implicit, in the flow of language. To facilitate some minimal intelligibility, to be sure, I do include quotation marks; many of the "modern, scientific" translations do not give even that mark.

Then, immediately afterward, I re-represent the entire passage, this time showing it as a differentiated set of citations and quotations from various sources (now, the passages of the Mishnah and Tosefta will be in boldface type). By giving Hebrew in plain type and Aramaic in italics, further, I differentiate the two languages and so drawing upon the signals that language choice delivers. I also display in indentation – further and further to the right hand column, as an item glosses a gloss, or provides an appendix to a gloss, or footnotes a footnote – what I conceive to be the secondary or subordinated discussions. As to the body of the materials, I differentiate what I conceive to be the smallest whole units of thought ("sentences") paragraph by paragraph, marking each with a letter for ready reference. I then identify what I conceive to be complete propositional formulations ("paragraphs") by marking a set of lettered "sentences" with Arabic numerals. Finally, I mark what I maintain are fully and exhaustively presented composites of propositions ("chapters") by a Roman number. Working from the whole to the parts, I move from a complete statement through the components of that statement to the smallest whole units of thought of which that statement is comprised.[2] A variety of issues is at stake in providing such an analytical reference system, inclusive of the signification of secondary and tertiary discourses by progressive indentation. In the present context, my discussion will then show how in presenting a vast corpus of material, and in fully providing the apparatus of information, not only the main points of proposition, evidence, and argument, the framers have followed a few simple rules, which a sensitive reader will have grasped after only minimal study.

Presenting the opening Mishnah paragraph and following Talmud of Babylonian Talmud tractate Abodah Zarah, folios 2A-3B, I first offer the whole, differentiated only by periods, sentence by sentence. All translations of all documents of rabbinic literature except for mine, wherever and whenever made, will follow this format (a glance at the

---

[2]I invented this reference system originally for my translation of the Mishnah, explaining its terms and categories, in *A History of the Mishnaic Law of Purities*. Leiden, 1977: Brill. XXI. *The Redaction and Formulation of the Order of Purities in the Mishnah and Tosefta*, which, to my knowledge, received not a single review.

fine translation published by Soncino Press, London, will validate my
claim on how translations represent the original of these pages):

> **Mishnah:** Before the festivals of gentiles for three days it is
> forbidden to do business with them, to lend anything to them or
> to borrow anything from them, to lend money to them or to
> borrow money from them, to repay them or to be repaid by
> them. R. Judah says, "They accept repayment from them,
> because it is distressing to him." They said to him, "Even though
> it is distressing to him now, he will be happy about it later."
> **Gemara:** Rab and Samuel [in dealing with the reading of the key
> word of the Mishnah, translated festival, the letters of which are
> 'aleph daled, rather than 'ayin daled, which means, calamity]:
> one repeated the formulation of the Mishnah as, "their festivals."
> And the other repeated the formulation of the Mishnah as "their
> calamities." The one who repeated the formulation of the
> Mishnah as "their festivals" made no mistake, and the one who
> repeated the formulation of the Mishnah as "their calamities"
> made no mistake. For it is written, "For the day of their calamity
> is at hand" (Deut. 32:15). The one who repeated the formulation
> of the Mishnah as "their festivals" made no mistake, for it is
> written, "Let them bring their testimonies that they may be
> justified" (Isa. 43:9). And as to the position of him who repeats
> the formulation of the Mishnah as "their festivals," on what
> account does he not repeat the formulation of the Mishnah to
> yield, "their calamities"? He will say to you, "'Calamity' is
> preferable [as the word choice when speaking of idolatry]." And
> as to the position of him who repeats the formulation of the
> Mishnah as "their calamities," on what account does he not
> repeat the formulation of the Mishnah to yield "their festivals"?
> He will say to you, "What causes the calamity that befalls them if
> not their testimony, so testimony is preferable!" And as to the
> verse, "Let them bring their testimonies that they may be
> justified" (Isa. 43:9), is this written with reference to gentiles? Lo,
> it is written in regard to Israel. For said R. Joshua b. Levi, "All of
> the religious duties that Israelites carry out in this world come
> and give testimony in their behalf in the world to come: 'Let
> them bring their witnesses that they may be justified' (Isa. 43:9),
> that is, Israel; 'and let them hear and say, It is truth' (Isa. 43:9) –
> this refers to gentiles." Rather, said R. Huna b. R. Joshua, "He
> who formulates the Mishnah to refer to their calamities derives
> the reading from this verse: 'They that fashion a graven image
> are all of them vanity, and their delectable things shall not profit,

and their own witnesses see not nor know' (Isa. 44:9)." As to the exposition [of the verse,"They that fashion a graven image are all of them vanity, and their delectable things shall not profit, and their own witnesses see not nor know" (Isa. 44:9)]: "In the age to come the Holy One, blessed be He, will bring a scroll of the Torah and hold it in his bosom and say, 'Let him who has kept himself busy with it come and take his reward.' Then all the gentiles will crowd together: 'All of the nations are gathered together' (Isa. 43:9). The Holy One, blessed be He, will say to them, 'Do not crowd together before me in a mob. But let each nation enter together with [2B] its scribes, 'and let the peoples be gathered together' (Isa. 43:9), and the word 'people' means 'kingdom': 'and one kingdom shall be stronger than the other' (Gen. 25:23)." But can there be a mob scene before the Holy One, blessed be He? Rather, it is so that from their perspective they not form a mob, so that they will be able to hear what he says to them. "The kingdom of Rome comes in first." How come? Because they are the most important. How do we know on the basis of Scripture they are the most important? Because it is written, "And he shall devour the whole earth and shall tread it down and break it into pieces" (Gen. 25:23), and said R. Yohanan, "This Rome is answerable, for its definition [of matters] has gone forth to the entire world [Mishcon: 'This refers to Rome, whose power is known to the whole world.']." And how do we know that the one who is most important comes in first? It is in accord with that which R. Hisda said. For said R. Hisda, "When the king and the community [await judgment], the king enters in first for judgment: 'That he maintain the case of his servant [Solomon] and [then] the cause of his people Israel' (1 Kgs. 8:59)." And how come? If you wish, I shall say it is not appropriate to keep the king sitting outside. And if you wish, I shall say that [the king is allowed to plea his case] before the anger of the Holy One is aroused." "The Holy One, blessed be He, will say to them, 'How have you defined your chief occupation?' They will say before him, 'Lord of the world, a vast number of marketplaces have we set up, a vast number of bathhouses we have made, a vast amount of silver and gold have we accumulated. And all of these things we have done only in behalf of Israel, so that they may define as their chief occupation the study of the Torah.' The Holy One, blessed be He, will say to them, 'You complete idiots! Whatever you have done has been for your own convenience. You have set up a vast number of marketplaces to be sure, but that was so as to set up whorehouses in them. The bathhouses were for your own pleasure. Silver and gold belong to me anyhow: "Mine is the silver and mine is the gold, says the Lord of hosts" (Hag. 2:8). Are there any among you who have been telling of "this," and "this" is only the Torah: "And this is the Torah that Moses set before the children of Israel' (Deut. 4:44)." So they will make their exit, humiliated. When the kingdom of Rome has made its exit, the kingdom of Persia enters afterward." How come? Because they are second in importance. And how do we know it on the basis of Scripture? Because it is written, "And behold, another beast, a second, like a bear" (Dan. 7:5), and in this connection R. Joseph repeated as a Tannaite formulation, "This refers to the Persians, who eat and drink like a bear, are obese like a bear, are shaggy like a bear, and are restless like a bear." The Holy One, blessed be He, will say to them, 'How have you defined your chief occupation?' They will say before him, 'Lord of the world, We have thrown up a vast number of bridges, we have conquered a vast number of towns, we have made a vast number of wars, and all of them we did only for Israel, so that they may define as their chief occupation the study of the Torah.' The Holy One, blessed be He, will say to them, 'Whatever you have done has been for your own convenience. You have thrown up a vast number of bridges to collect tolls, you have conquered a vast number of towns to collect the corvée, and, as to making a vast number of wars, I am the one who makes wars: "The Lord is a man of war" (Ex. 19:17). Are there any among you who have been telling of "this," and "this" is only the Torah: "And this is the Torah that Moses set before the children of Israel" (Deut. 4:44).' So they will make their exit, humiliated. But if the kingdom of Persia has seen that such a claim issued by the kingdom of Rome did no good whatsoever, how come they go in at all? They will say to themselves, "These are the ones who destroyed the house of the sanctuary, but we are the ones who built it." And so it will go with each and every nation." But if each one of them has seen that such a claim issued by the others did no good whatsoever, how come they go in at all? They will say to themselves, "Those two subjugated Israel, but we never subjugated Israel." And how come the two conquering nations are singled out as important and the others are not? It is because the rule of these will continue until the Messiah comes. "They will say to him, 'Lord of the world, in point of fact, did you actually give it to us and we did not accept it?'" But how can they present such an argument, since it is written, "The Lord came from Sinai and rose from Sier to them, he shined forth from Mount Paran" (Deut. 33:2), and further, "God comes from Teman" (Hab. 3:3). Now what in the world did he want in Seir, and what was he looking for in Paran? Said R. Yohanan, "This teaches that the Holy One, blessed be He, made the rounds of each and every nation and language and none accepted it, until he came to Israel, and they accepted it." Rather, this is what they say, "Did we accept it but then not carry it out?" But to this the rejoinder must be, "Why did you not accept it anyhow!" Rather, "This is what they say before him, 'Lord of the world, Did you hold a mountain over us like a cask and then we refused to accept it as you did to Israel, as it is written, "And they stood beneath the mountain" (Ex. 19:17).'" And [in connection with the verse, "And they stood beneath the mountain" (Ex. 19:17),] said R. Dimi bar Hama, "This teaches that the Holy One, blessed be He, held the mountain over Israel like a cask and said to them, 'If you accept the Torah, well and good, and if not, then there is where your grave will be.'" "Then the Holy One, blessed be He, will say to them, 'Let us make known what happened first: "Let them announce to us former things" (Isa. 43:9). As to the seven religious duties that you did accept, where have you actually carried them out?'" And how do we know on the basis of Scripture that they did not carry them out? R. Joseph formulated as a Tannaite statement, "'He stands and shakes the earth, he sees and makes the nations tremble' (Hab. 3:6): What did he see? He saw the seven religious duties that the children of Noah accepted upon themselves as obligations but never actually carried out. Since they did not carry out those obligations, he went and remitted their obligation." But then they benefited – so it pays to sin! Said Mar b. Rabina, [3A] "What this really proves is that even when they carry out those religious duties, they get no reward on that account." And they don't, don't they? But has it not been taught on Tannaite authority: R. Meir would say, "How on the basis of Scripture do we know that, even if it is a gentile, if he goes and takes up the study of the Torah as his occupation, he is equivalent to the high priest? Scripture states, 'You shall therefore keep my statutes and my ordinances, which, if a human being does them, one shall gain life through them' (Lev. 18:5). What is written is not 'priests' or 'Levites' or 'Israelites,' but rather, 'a human being.' So you have learned the fact that, even if it is a gentile, if he goes and takes up the study of the Torah as his occupation, he is equivalent to the high priest." Rather, what you learn from this is that they will not receive that reward that is coming to those who are commanded to do them and who carry them out, but rather, the reward that they receive will be like that coming to the one who is not commanded to do them and who carries them out anyhow. For said R. Hanina, "Greater is the one who is commanded and who carries out the religious obligations than the one who is not commanded but nonetheless carries out religious obligations."

"This is what the gentiles say before him, 'Lord of the world, Israel, who accepted it – where in the world have they actually carried it out?' The Holy One, blessed be He, will say to them, 'I shall bear witness concerning them, that they have carried out the whole of the Torah!' They will say before him, 'Lord of the world, is there a father who is permitted to give testimony concerning his son? For it is written, "Israel is my son, my firstborn" (Ex. 4:22).' The Holy One, blessed be He, will say to them, 'The heaven and the earth will give testimony in their behalf that they have carried out the entirety of the Torah.' They will say before him, 'Lord of the world, The heaven and earth have a selfish interest in the testimony that they give: 'If not for my covenant with day and with night, I should not have appointed the ordinances of heaven and earth' (Jer. 33:25).'" For said R. Simeon b. Laqish, "What is the meaning of the verse of Scripture, 'And there was evening, and there was morning, the sixth day' (Gen. 1:31)? This teaches that the Holy One, blessed be He, made a stipulation with all of the works of creation, saying to them, 'If Israel accepts my Torah, well and good, but if not, I shall return you to chaos and void.' That is in line with what is written: 'You did cause sentence to be heard from heaven, the earth trembled and was still' (Ps. 76:9). If 'trembling' then where is the stillness, and if stillness, then where is the trembling? Rather, to begin with, trembling, but at the end, stillness." "The Holy One, blessed be He, will say to them, 'Some of them may well come and give testimony concerning Israel that they have observed the entirety of the Torah. Let Nimrod come and give testimony in behalf of Abraham that he never worshipped idols. Let Laban come and give testimony in behalf of Jacob, that he never was suspect of thievery. Let the wife of Potiphar come and give testimony in behalf of Joseph, that he was never suspect of 'sin.' Let Nebuchadnessar come and give testimony in behalf of Hananiah, Mishael, and Azariah, that they never bowed down to the idol. Let Darius come and give testimony in behalf of Daniel, that he did not neglect even the optional prayers. Let Bildad the Shuhite and Zophar the Naamatite and Eliphaz the Temanite and Elihu son of Barachel the Buzite come and testify in behalf of Israel that they have observed the entirety of the Torah: "Let the nations bring their own witnesses, that they may be justified" (Isa. 43:9).' They will say to him, "Then give it to us to begin with, and let us carry it out.' The Holy One, blessed be He, will say to them, 'World class idiots! He who took the trouble to prepare on the eve of the Sabbath [Friday] will eat on the Sabbath, but he who took no trouble on the even of the Sabbath – what in the world is he going to eat on the Sabbath! Still, [I'll give you another chance.] I have a rather simple religious duty, which is called "the tabernacle." Go and do that one.'" But can you say any such thing? Lo, R. Joshua b. Levi has said, "What is the meaning of the verse of Scripture, 'The ordinances that I command you this day to do them' (Deut. 7:11)? Today is the day to do them, but not tomorrow; they are not to be done tomorrow; today is the day to do them, but not the day on which to receive a reward for doing them." Rather, it is that the Holy One, blessed be He, does not exercise tyranny over his creatures. And why does he refer to it as a simple religious duty? Because it does not involve enormous expense [to carry out that religious duty]. Forthwith every one of them will take up the task and go and make a tabernacle on his roof. But then the Holy, One, blessed be He, will come and make the sun blaze over them as at the summer solstice, and every one of them will knock down his tabernacle and go his way: 'Let us break their bands asunder and cast away their cords from us' (Ps. 23:3)." But lo, you have just said, "it is that the Holy One, blessed be He, does not exercise tyranny over his creatures"! It is because as to the Israelites, too – sometimes [3B] the summer solstice goes on to the festival of Tabernacles, and therefore they are bothered by the heat! But has not Raba stated, "One who is bothered [by the heat] is exempt from the obligation of dwelling in the tabernacle"? Granting that one may be exempt from the duty, is he going to go and tear the thing down? "Then the Holy One, blessed be He, goes into session and laughs at them: 'He who sits in heaven laughs' (Ps. 2:4)." Said R. Isaac, "Laughter before the Holy One, blessed be He, takes place only on that day alone." There are those who repeat as a Tannaite version this statement of R. Isaac in respect to that which has been taught on Tannaite authority: R. Yosé says, "In the coming age gentiles will come and convert." But will they be accepted? Has it not been taught on Tannaite authority: Converts will not be accepted in the days of the Messiah, just as they did not accept proselytes either in the time of David or in the time of Solomon? Rather, "they will make themselves converts, and they will put on phylacteries on their heads and arms and fringes on their garments and a mezuzah on their doors. But when they witness the war of Gog and Magog, he will say to them, 'How come you have come?' They will say, '"Against the Lord and against his Messiah."' For so it is said, 'Why are the nations in an uproar and why do the peoples mutter in vain' (Ps. 2:1). Then each one of them will rid himself of his religious duty and go his way: 'Let us break their bands asunder' (Ps. 2:3). Then the Holy One, blessed be He, goes into session and laughs at them: 'He who sits in heaven laughs' (Ps. 2:4)." Said R. Isaac, "Laughter before the Holy One, blessed be He, takes place only on that day alone." But is this really so? And has not R. Judah said Rab said, "The day is made up of twelve hours. In the first three the Holy One, blessed be He, goes into session and engages in study of the Torah; in the second he goes into session and judges the entire world. When he realizes that the world is liable to annihilation, he arises from the throne of justice and takes up a seat on the throne of mercy. In the third period he goes into session and nourishes the whole world from the horned buffalo to the brood of vermin. During the fourth quarter he laughs [and plays] with leviathan: 'There is leviathan, whom you have formed to play with' (Ps. 104:26)." [This proves that God does laugh more than on that one day alone.] Said R. Nahman bar Isaac, "With his creatures he laughs [everyday], but at his creatures he laughs only on that day alone."

That is what the page, without markings other than commas, periods and quotation marks yields. I shall argue that a proper reference system displays the cogency and well-crafted character of this piece of writing. But, at this point, anyone with the patience to have read the entire passage will by now have found utterly implausible my allegation that that page is at all coherent. And even were I to paragraph the column of words as the Soncino translation does, it would make little difference to that judgment. Long columns of undifferentiated words simply cannot be analyzed in any manner at all; the absence of a reference system renders the translation gibberish: we understand the sentences, but not the composition that they form.

Without further ado, we reconsider the entire passage, now differentiating the composites by Roman numerals, the compositions that form the components of the composites by Arabic numerals, the constitutive parts of the compositions by letters; the sources – Mishnah,

Tosefta from everything else – by different type faces; the two languages, Hebrew and Aramaic, by regular type and italics, respectively; and the text – the principal discourse – from footnotes and appendices by indenting and double and triple indenting the latter. In this way – through a simple and visually easily understood reference system – we see precisely what is in play in the page; my comments then will explain what our authors have done to give us everything they thought we had to know. We see that they followed a few simple rules, which we can discern and which guide us in reading their writing.

1:1

A. [2A] Before the festivals of gentiles for three days it is forbidden to do business with them.

B. (1) to lend anything to them or to borrow anything from them.

C. (2) to lend money to them or to borrow money from them.

D. (3) to repay them or to be repaid by them.

E. R. Judah says, "They accept repayment from them, because it is distressing to him."

F. They said to him, "Even though it is distressing to him now, he will be happy about it later."

I.1 A. [2A] Rab and Samuel [in dealing with the reading of the key word of the Mishnah, translated festival, the letters of which are 'aleph daled, rather than 'ayin daled, which means, calamity]:

B. *one repeated the formulation of the Mishnah as, "their festivals."*

C. *And the other repeated the formulation of the Mishnah as "their calamities."*

D. *The one who repeated the formulation of the Mishnah as "their festivals" made no mistake, and the one who repeated the formulation of the Mishnah as "their calamities" made no mistake.*

E. *For it is written, "For the day of their calamity is at hand" (Deut. 32:15).*

F. *The one who repeated the formulation of the Mishnah as "their festivals" made no mistake, for it is written, "Let them bring their testimonies that they may be justified" (Isa. 43:9).*

G. *And as to the position of him who repeats the formulation of the Mishnah as "their festivals," on what account does he not repeat the formulation of the Mishnah to yield, "their calamities"?*

H. *He will say to you, "'Calamity' is preferable [as the word choice when speaking of idolatry]."*

I. *And as to the position of him who repeats the formulation of the Mishnah as "their calamities," on what account does he not repeat the formulation of the Mishnah to yield "their festivals"?*

J. *He will say to you, "What causes the calamity that befalls them if not their testimony, so testimony is preferable!"*

K. *And as to the verse, "Let them bring their testimonies that they may be justified" (Isa. 43:9), is this written with reference to gentiles? Lo, it is written in regard to Israel.*

L. For said R. Joshua b. Levi, "All of the religious duties that Israelites carry out in this world come and give testimony in their behalf in the world to come: 'Let them bring their witnesses that they may be justified' (Isa. 43:9), that is, Israel; 'and let them hear and say, It is truth' (Isa. 43:9) – this refers to gentiles."

M Rather, said R. Huna b. R. Joshua, "He who formulates the Mishnah to refer to their calamities derives the reading from this verse: 'They that fashion a graven image are all of them vanity, and their delectable things shall not profit, and their own witnesses see not nor know' (Isa. 44:9)."

The foregoing, we see clearly, presents a beautifully balanced dispute form, and the form is used to provide a medium for presenting Mishnah text criticism: how are we to read the text of the paragraph before us. That classification presents no problems. We must now enter a much more difficult question because I maintain that, along with the classification of I.1, everything that is attached to I.1 in a continuous and ongoing manner goes along as a single composite, the whole put together in its own terms, but then utilized by the framer of the Talmud before us – folios 2A-5B – as a continuous (if in our perspective rather run-on) statement. It is obviously a composite. But I classify the entire composite all together and all at once, because it is more than a composite: it also is a composition. And the reason I see it as a coherent and cogent composition is that every item fits together with its predecessor and leads us without interruption to its successor, from the starting lines of I.1 to the concluding ones of I.32.

No. 1 has referred us to gentile idolatry and Israelite loyalty to the religious duties assigned to them by God. We now have a long exposition of the theme of gentile idolatry and perfidy. Everything that follows in I.2 serves as a play on the theme of I.1L-M! The unity of the whole of I.2 will be readily apparent because of the insets of gloss and expansion, and the further insets of the appendices to the gloss and expansion. We shall now see, through the device of indentations, how much in the expansion of the foregoing in fact serves as gloss, footnote, and appendix; recognizing that fact we see a rather well-crafted and cogent composite, made up of a principal composition – extending to the far left-hand margin – and a variety of subordinated compositions, moving off to the right in progressive indentations. And what we can see, visually, any well-endowed disciple of the document will readily have understood through his thoughtful reading of the document: this is primary, that is secondary and subordinate. In ages past the disciples will not have called what I indent "footnotes" or even "appendices." But they also will not have found confusing the glosses and supplements that, all together, give a full and rich account of any subject introduced in the primary discussion.

True, this is not how Plato and Aristotle set out their ideas; but the great philosophers also did not choose as the medium for writing down their ideas a commentary on a received text, in constant dialogue with yet another received text (the Mishnah, Scripture), with persistent attention to a variety of other received data, all to be provided in a complete and purposeful argument on a point of fundamental importance. They simply set forth a complete and purposeful argument in behalf of a proposition; the evidence and argument were recast by the philosophers into the language required for the proposition they wished to argue, whether in dialogue or in dialectical form. The character of the Judaic sages' system – the inheritance of revelation with which they proposed to enter dialogue – called forth a form that, in itself, expressed the character of the nurturing culture beyond.

L2   A.   R. Hanina bar Pappa, and some say, R. Simlai, gave the following exposition [of the verse,"They that fashion a graven image are all of them vanity, and their delectable things shall not profit, and their own witnesses see not nor know" (Isa. 44:9)]: "In the age to come the Holy One, blessed be He, will bring a scroll of the Torah and hold it in his bosom and say, 'Let him who has kept himself busy with it come and take his reward.' Then all the gentiles will crowd together: 'All of the nations are gathered together' (Isa. 43:9). The Holy One, blessed be He, will say to them, 'Do not crowd together before me in a mob. But let each nation enter together with [2B] its scribes, 'and let the peoples be gathered together' (Isa. 43:9), and the word 'people' means 'kingdom': 'and one kingdom shall be stronger than the other' (Gen. 25:23)."

    B.   *But can there be a mob scene before the Holy One, blessed be He? Rather, it is so that from their perspective they not form a mob, so that they will be able to hear what he says to them.*

    C.   [Resuming the narrative of A:] "The kingdom of Rome comes in first."

    D.   *How come? Because they are the most important. How do we know on the basis of Scripture they are the most important? Because it is written,* "And he shall devour the whole earth and shall tread it down and break it into pieces" (Gen. 25:23), *and said R. Yohanan,* "This Rome is answerable, for its definition [of matters] has gone forth to the entire world [Mishcon: 'This refers to Rome, whose power is known to the whole world.']."

    E.   *And how do we know that the one who is most important comes in first? It is in accord with that which R. Hisda said.*

    F.   For said R. Hisda, "When the king and the community [await judgment], the king enters in first for judgment: 'That he maintain the case of his servant [Solomon] and [then] the cause of his people Israel' (1 Kgs. 8:59)."

    G.   *And how come? If you wish, I shall say it is not appropriate to keep the king sitting outside. And if you wish, I shall say that [the king is allowed to plea his case] before the anger of the Holy One is aroused."*

H   [Resuming the narrative of C:] "The Holy One, blessed be He, will say to them, 'How have you defined your chief occupation?'

I   "They will say before him, 'Lord of the world, a vast number of marketplaces have we set up, a vast number of bathhouses we have made, a vast amount of silver and gold have we accumulated. And all of these things we have done only in behalf of Israel, so that they may define as their chief occupation the study of the Torah.'

J   "The Holy One, blessed be He, will say to them, 'You complete idiots!   Whatever you have done has been for your own convenience. You have set up a vast number of marketplaces to be sure, but that was so as to set up whorehouses in them. The bathhouses were for your own pleasure. Silver and gold belong to me anyhow: "Mine is the silver and mine is the gold, says the Lord of hosts" (Hag. 2:8). Are there any among you who have been telling of "this," and "this" is only the Torah: "And this is the Torah that Moses set before the children of Israel' (Deut. 4:44)." So they will make their exit, humiliated.

K   "When the kingdom of Rome has made its exit, the kingdom of Persia enters afterward."

L   *How come? Because they are second in importance. And how do we know it on the basis of Scripture? Because it is written, "And behold, another beast, a second, like a bear"* (Dan. 7:5), *and in this connection R. Joseph repeated as a Tannaite formulation,* "This refers to the Persians, who eat and drink like a bear, are obese like a bear, are shaggy like a bear, and are restless like a bear."

M   "The Holy One, blessed be He, will say to them, 'How have you defined your chief occupation?'

N   "They will say before him, 'Lord of the world, We have thrown up a vast number of bridges, we have conquered a vast number of towns, we have made a vast number of wars, and all of them we did only for Israel, so that they may define as their chief occupation the study of the Torah.'

O   "The Holy One, blessed be He, will say to them, 'Whatever you have done has been for your own convenience. You have thrown up a vast number of bridges to collect tolls, you have conquered a vast number of towns to collect the corvée, and, as to making a vast number of wars, I am the one who makes wars: "The Lord is a man of war" (Ex. 19:17). Are there any among you who have been telling of "this," and "this" is only the Torah: "And this is the Torah that Moses set before the children of Israel" (Deut. 4:44).' So they will make their exit, humiliated.

P.   *But if the kingdom of Persia has seen that such a claim issued by the kingdom of Rome did no good whatsoever, how come they go in at all?*

Q   *They will say to themselves, "These are the ones who destroyed the house of the sanctuary, but we are the ones who built it."*

R.   "And so it will go with each and every nation."

S   *But if each one of them has seen that such a claim issued by the others did no good whatsoever, how come they go in at all?*

T.   *They will say to themselves, "Those two subjugated Israel, but we never subjugated Israel."*

U.   *And how come the two conquering nations are singled out as important and the others are not?*

V.   *It is because the rule of these will continue until the Messiah comes.*

W.   "They will say to him, 'Lord of the world, in point of fact, did you actually give it to us and we did not accept it?'"

X.   *But how can they present such an argument, since it is written,* "The Lord came from Sinai and rose from Sier to them, he shined forth from Mount Paran" (Deut. 33:2), *and further,* "God comes from Teman" (Hab. 3:3). *Now what in the world did he want in Seir, and what was he looking for in Paran?* Said R. Yohanan, "This teaches that the Holy One, blessed be He, made the rounds of each and every nation and language and none accepted it, until he came to Israel, and they accepted it."

Y.   *Rather, this is what they say,* "Did we accept it but then not carry it out?"

Z.   *But to this the rejoinder must be,* "Why did you not accept it anyhow!"

AA.   Rather, "This is what they say before him, 'Lord of the world, Did you hold a mountain over us like a cask and then we refused to accept it as you did to Israel, as it is written, "And they stood beneath the mountain" (Ex. 19:17).'"

BB.   And [in connection with the verse, "And they stood beneath the mountain" (Ex. 19:17),] said R. Dimi bar Hama, "This teaches that the Holy One, blessed be He, held the mountain over Israel like a cask and said to them, 'If you accept the Torah, well and good, and if not, then there is where your grave will be.'"

CC.   "Then the Holy One, blessed be He, will say to them, 'Let us make known what happened first: "Let them announce to us former things" (Isa. 43:9). As to the seven religious duties that you did accept, where have you actually carried them out?'"

DD.   *And how do we know on the basis of Scripture that they did not carry them out?* R. Joseph formulated as a Tannaite statement, "'He stands and shakes the earth, he sees and makes the nations tremble' (Hab. 3:6): What did he see? He saw the seven religious duties that the children of Noah accepted upon themselves as obligations but never actually carried them out. Since they did not carry out those obligations, he went and remitted their obligation."

EE.   *But then they benefited – so it pays to sin!*

FF.   Said Mar b. Rabina, [3A] "What this really proves is that even when they carry out those religious duties, they get no reward on that account."

GG.   *And they don't, don't they? But has it not been taught on Tannaite authority:* R. Meir would say, "How on the basis of Scripture do we know that, even if it is a gentile, if he goes and takes up the study of the Torah as his occupation, he is equivalent to the high priest? Scripture states, 'You shall therefore keep my statutes and my ordinances, which, if a human being does them, one shall gain life through them' (Lev. 18:5). What is written is not 'priests' or 'Levites' or 'Israelites,' but rather, 'a human being.' So you have learned the fact that, even if it is a gentile, if he goes and takes up the study of the Torah as his occupation, he is equivalent to the high priest."

HH.   Rather, what you learn from this [DD] is that they will not receive that reward that is coming to those who are commanded to do them and who carry them out, but rather, the reward that they receive will be like that coming to the one who is not commanded to do them and who carries them out anyhow.

II.   For said R. Hanina, "Greater is the one who is commanded and who carries out the religious obligations than the one who is not commanded but nonetheless carries out religious obligations."

JJ.   [Reverting to AA:] "This is what the gentiles say before him, 'Lord of the world, Israel, who accepted it – where in the world have they actually carried it out?'

KK.   "The Holy One, blessed be He, will say to them, 'I shall bear witness concerning them, that they have carried out the whole of the Torah!'

LL.   "They will say before him, 'Lord of the world, is there a father who is permitted to give testimony concerning his son? For it is written, "Israel is my son, my firstborn" (Ex. 4:22).'

MM.   "The Holy One, blessed be He, will say to them, 'The heaven and the earth will give testimony in their behalf that they have carried out the entirety of the Torah.'

NN.   "They will say before him, 'Lord of the world, The heaven and earth have a selfish interest in the testimony that they give: 'If not for my covenant with day and with night, I should not have appointed the ordinances of heaven and earth' (Jer. 33:25).'"

OO.   *For said R. Simeon b. Laqish, "What is the meaning of the verse of Scripture, 'And there was evening, and there was morning, the sixth day' (Gen. 1:31)? This teaches that the Holy One, blessed be He, made a stipulation with all of the works of creation, saying to them, 'If Israel accepts my Torah, well and good, but if not, I shall return you to chaos and void.' That is in line with what is written: 'You did cause sentence to be heard from heaven, the earth trembled and was still' (Ps. 76:9). If 'trembling' then where is the stillness, and if stillness, then where is the trembling? Rather, to begin with, trembling, but at the end, stillness."*

PP.   [Reverting to MM-NN:] "The Holy One, blessed be He, will say to them, 'Some of them may well come and give testimony concerning Israel that they have observed the entirety of the Torah. Let Nimrod come and give testimony in behalf of Abraham that he never worshipped idols. Let Laban come and give testimony in behalf of Jacob, that he never was suspect of thievery. Let the wife of Potiphar come and give testimony in behalf of Joseph, that he was never suspect of 'sin.' Let Nebuchadnessar come and give testimony in behalf of Hananiah, Mishael, and Azariah, that they never bowed down to the idol. Let Darius come and give testimony in behalf of Daniel, that he did not neglect even the optional prayers. Let Bildad the Shuhite and Zophar the Naamatite and

Eliphaz the Temanite and Elihu son of Barachel the Buzite come and testify in behalf of Israel that they have observed the entirety of the Torah: "Let the nations bring their own witnesses, that they may be justified" (Isa. 43:9).'

QQ. 'They will say before him, 'Lord of the world, Give it to us to begin with, and let us carry it out.'

RR. 'The Holy One, blessed be He, will say to them, 'World class idiots! He who took the trouble to prepare on the eve of the Sabbath [Friday] will eat on the Sabbath, but he who took no trouble on the eve of the Sabbath – what in the world is he going to eat on the Sabbath! Still, [I'll give you another chance.] I have a rather simple religious duty, which is called "the tabernacle." Go and do that one.'"

SS. *But can you say any such thing? Lo, R. Joshua b. Levi has said, "What is the meaning of the verse of Scripture, 'The ordinances that I command you this day to do them' (Deut. 7:11)? Today is the day to do them, but not tomorrow; they are not to be done tomorrow; today is the day to do them, but not the day on which to receive a reward for doing them."*

TT. Rather, it is that the Holy One, blessed be He, does not exercise tyranny over his creatures.

UU. *And why does he refer to it as a simple religious duty? Because it does not involve enormous expense [to carry out that religious duty].*

VV. "Forthwith every one of them will take up the task and go and make a tabernacle on his roof. But then the Holy One, blessed be He, will come and make the sun blaze over them as at the summer solstice, and every one of them will knock down his tabernacle and go his way: 'Let us break their bands asunder and cast away their cords from us' (Ps. 23:3)."

WW. But lo, you have just said, "it is that the Holy One, blessed be He, does not exercise tyranny over his creatures"!

XX. *It is because as to the Israelites, too – sometimes [3B] the summer solstice goes on to the festival of Tabernacles, and therefore they are bothered by the heat!*

YY. But has not Raba stated, "One who is bothered [by the heat] is exempt from the obligation of dwelling in the tabernacle"?

ZZ. *Granting that one may be exempt from the duty, is he going to go and tear the thing down?*

AAA [Continuing from UU:] "Then the Holy One, blessed be He, goes into session and laughs at them: 'He who sits in heaven laughs' (Ps. 2:4)."

BBB. Said R. Isaac, "Laughter before the Holy One, blessed be He, takes place only on that day alone."

CCC. *There are those who repeat as a Tannaite version this statement of R. Isaac in respect to that which has been taught on Tannaite authority:*

DDD. R. Yosé says, "In the coming age gentiles will come and convert."

EEE. *But will they be accepted? Has it not been taught on Tannaite authority: Converts will not be accepted in the days of the*

Messiah, just as they did not accept proselytes either in the time of David or in the time of Solomon?

FFF.   Rather, "they will make themselves converts, and they will put on phylacteries on their heads and arms and fringes on their garments and a mezuzah on their doors. But when they witness the war of Gog and Magog, he will say to them, 'How come you have come?' They will say, '"Against the Lord and against his Messiah."' For so it is said, 'Why are the nations in an uproar and why do the peoples mutter in vain' (Ps. 2:1). Then each one of them will rid himself of his religious duty and go his way: 'Let us break their bands asunder' (Ps. 2:3). Then the Holy One, blessed be He, goes into session and laughs at them: 'He who sits in heaven laughs' (Ps. 2:4)."

GGG.   Said R. Isaac, "Laughter before the Holy One, blessed be He, takes place only on that day alone."

HHH.   But is this really so? And has not R. Judah said Rab said, "The day is made up of twelve hours. In the first three the Holy One, blessed be He, goes into session and engages in study of the Torah; in the second he goes into session and judges the entire world. When he realizes that the world is liable to annihilation, he arises from the throne of justice and takes up a seat on the throne of mercy. In the third period he goes into session and nourishes the whole world from the horned buffalo to the brood of vermin. During the fourth quarter he laughs [and plays] with leviathan: 'There is leviathan, whom you have formed to play with' (Ps. 104:26)." [This proves that God does laugh more than on that one day alone.]

III.   Said R. Nahman bar Isaac, "With his creatures he laughs [everyday], but at his creatures he laughs only on that day alone."

The shift from language to language signals the presence of a sotto voce observation, a gloss, or a footnote. The movement from the main point to an indented composition does not obliterate the character of the whole as a well-crafted composite – a unity from start to finish.

That the whole of the foregoing constitutes a single essay is readily apparent. When the continuing discussion set forth by Hanina bar Pappa or Simlai is interrupted with a gloss, that is readily apparent. To show how that glossing process in our terms would form a footnote, I indent what I conceive to be footnotes. The interesting point comes at CCC, where we have an appendix to BBB. That is to say, the footnote, BBB, completes the foregoing statement, AAA. Then the additional information is added not to the basic text but to the gloss; it is not filler, the information is valued. But the insertion clearly adds nothing to the basic text – hence it is relegated to an appendix, which, in our technical age, we should simply place at the end of a book. But then HHH forms a footnote to an appendix, therefore is indented still further. The two pages of the Talmud of Babylonia presented here therefore are seen, through a proper reference system, to form a coherent and well-crafted essay, text and notes, in which a clear and present proposition governs from beginning to end.[3]

---

[3]I do not claim mine is the best of all possible reference systems, but I have yet to find any alternative one at all – let alone one that provides as much information about the original for analytical purposes as does mine.

BIBLIOGRAPHY

A list of my translations of the canonical writings, all following the reference system just now described, follows. The differentiation of Hebrew and Aramaic through different type faces began only in my most current translations of the Talmud of Babylonia. It made possible my *Language as Taxonomy. The Rules for Using Hebrew and Aramaic in the Babylonian Talmud.* Atlanta, 1990: Scholars Press for South Florida Studies in the History of Judaism.

A History of the Mishnaic Law of Purities. Leiden, 1974-1977: Brill. I-XXII.

I.	*Kelim. Chapters One through Eleven.* 1974.
II.	*Kelim. Chapters Twelve through Thirty.* 1974.
III.	*Kelim. Literary and Historical Problems.* 1974.
IV.	*Ohalot. Commentary.* 1975.
V.	*Ohalot. Literary and Historical Problems.* 1975.
VI.	*Negaim. Mishnah Tosefta.* 1975.
VII.	*Negaim. Sifra.* 1975.
VIII.	*Negaim. Literary and Historical Problems.* 1975.
IX.	*Parah. Commentary.* 1976.
X.	*Parah. Literary and Historical Problems.* 1976.
XI.	*Tohorot. Commentary,* 1976.
XII.	*Tohorot. Literary and Historical Problems.* 1976.
XIII.	*Miqvaot. Commentary.* 1976.
XIV,	*Miqvaot. Literary and Historical Problems.* 1976.
XV.	*Niddah. Commentary.* 1976.
XVI.	*Niddah. Literary and Historical Problems.* 1976.
XVII.	*Makhshirin.* 1977.
XVIII.	*Zabim.* 1977.
XIX.	*Tebul Yom. Yadayim.* 1977.
XX.	*Uqsin. Cumulative Index, Parts I-XX.* 1977.

The Tosefta. Translated from the Hebrew. New York, 1977-1980: Ktav. II-VI.

II.	*The Tosefta. Translated from the Hebrew. Second Division. Moed.*
III.	*The Tosefta. Translated from the Hebrew. Third Division. Nashim.*
IV.	*The Tosefta. Translated from the Hebrew. Fourth Division. Neziqin.*
V.	*The Tosefta. Translated from the Hebrew. Fifth Division. Qodoshim.*
VI.	*The Tosefta. Translated from the Hebrew. Sixth Division. Tohorot.* Second printing: Atlanta, 1990: Scholars Press for *South Florida Studies in the History of Judaism.* With a new preface.

Edited: *The Tosefta. Translated from the Hebrew. I. The First Division (Zeraim).* New York, 1985: Ktav.

A History of the Mishnaic Law of Holy Things. Leiden, Brill: 1979. I-VI.
I.   *Zebahim. Translation and Explanation.*
II.   *Menahot. Translation and Explanation.*
III.   *Hullin, Bekhorot. Translation and Explanation.*
IV.   *Arakhin, Temurah. Translation and Explanation.*
V.   *Keritot, Meilah, Tamid, Middot, Qinnim. Translation and Explanation.*

A History of the Mishnaic Law of Women. Leiden, Brill: 1979-1980. I-V.
I.   *Yebamot. Translation and Explanation.*
II.   *Ketubot. Translation and Explanation.*
III.   *Nedarim, Nazir. Translation and Explanation.*
IV.   *Sotah, Gittin, Qiddushin. Translation and Explanation.*

A History of the Mishnaic Law of Appointed Times. Leiden, Brill: 1981-1983. I-V.
I.   *Shabbat. Translation and Explanation.*
II.   *Erubin, Pesahim. Translation and Explanation.*
III.   *Sheqalim, Yoma, Sukkah. Translation and Explanation.*
IV.   *Besah, Rosh Hashshanah, Taanit, Megillah, Moed Qatan, Hagigah. Translation and Explanation.*

A History of the Mishnaic Law of Damages. Leiden, Brill: 1983-1985. I-V.
I.   *Bava Qamma. Translation and Explanation.*
II.   *Bava Mesia. Translation and Explanation.*
III.   *Bava Batra, Sanhedrin, Makkot. Translation and Explanation.*
IV.   *Shebuot, Eduyyot, Abodah Zarah, Abot, Horayyot. Translation and Explanation.*

The Mishnah. A New Translation. New Haven and London, 1987: Yale University Press. Second printing: 1990. Paperbound edition: 1991.

The Talmud of the Land of Israel. A Preliminary Translation and Explanation. Chicago: University of Chicago Press: 1982-1989. IX-XII, XIV-XV, XVII-XXXV.
XXXIV   *Horayot. Niddah.* 1982.
XXXIII *Abodah Zarah.* 1982.
XXXII. *Shebuot.* 1983.
XXXI.   *Sanhedrin. Makkot.* 1984.
XXX.   *Baba Batra.* 1984.
XXIX.   *Baba Mesia.* 1984.
XXVIII *Baba Qamma.* 1984.

XXVII. *Sotah.* 1984.
XXVI. *Qiddushin.* 1984.
XXV. *Gittin.* 1985
XXIV. *Nazir.* 1985.
XXIII. *Nedarim* 1985.
XXII. *Ketubot.* 1985.
XXI. *Yebamot.* 1986.
XX. *Hagigah. Moed Qatan* 1986.
XIX. *Megillah.* 1987.
XVIII. *Besah. Taanit.* 1987.
XVII. *Sukkah.* 1988.
XV. *Sheqalim.* 1990.
XIV. *Yoma.* 1990.
XII. *Erubin.* 1990.
XI. *Shabbat.* 1991.
X. *Orlah. Bikkurim.* 1991.
IX. *Hallah.* 1991.

Torah from Our Sages: Pirke Avot. A New American Translation and Explanation. Chappaqua, 1983: Rossel. Paperback edition: 1987.

The Talmud of Babylonia. An American Translation. Chico, 1984-1985: Scholars Press for Brown Judaic Studies.

I. *Tractate Berakhot.*
VI. *Tractate Sukkah.*
XVII. *Tractate Sotah.*
XXIII.A *Tractate Sanhedrin. Chapters I-III.*
XXIII.B *Tractate Sanhedrin. Chapters IV-VIII.*
XXIII.C *Tractate Sanhedrin. Chapters IX-XI.*
XXXII. *Tractate Arakhin.*

The Talmud of Babylonia. An American Translation. Atlanta, 1990: Scholars Press for Brown Judaic Studies.

XXI.A. *Tractate Bava Mesia. Introduction. Chapters One and Two.*
XXI.B. *Tractate Bava Mesia. Chapters Three and Four.*
XXI.C. *Tractate Bava Mesia. Chapters Five and Six.*
XXI.D. *Tractate Bava Mesia. Chapters Seven through Ten.*
XXV.A. *Tractate Abodah Zarah. Chapters One and Two.*
XXV.B. *Tractate Abodah Zarah. Chapters Three, Four, and Five.*
XXXI.A. *Tractate Bekhorot. Chapters One through Four.*
XXXI.B. *Tractate Bekhorot. Chapters Five through Nine.*
XXXIII. *Tractate Temurah.*
XXXIV. *Tractate Keritot.*
XXXVI.A *Tractate Niddah. Chapters One through Three.*

XXXVI.B *Tractate Niddah. Chapters Four through Ten.*

The Talmud of Babylonia. An American Translation. Atlanta, 1991: Scholars Press for Brown Judaic Studies.
XXVIII.A.   *Tractate Zebahim. Chapters One through Three.*
XXVIII.B.   *Tractate Zebahim. Chapters Four through Seven.*
XXVIII.C.   *Tractate Zebahim. Chapters Eight through Ten.*

Judaism and Scripture: The Evidence of Leviticus Rabbah. Chicago, 1986: University of Chicago Press.

Genesis Rabbah. The Judaic Commentary on Genesis. A New American Translation. Atlanta, 1985: Scholars Press for Brown Judaic Studies. I. *Genesis Rabbah. The Judaic Commentary on Genesis. A New American Translation. Parashiyyot One through Thirty-Three. Genesis 1:1-8:14.*

Genesis Rabbah. The Judaic Commentary on Genesis. A New American Translation. Atlanta, 1985: Scholars Press for Brown Judaic Studies. II. *Genesis Rabbah. The Judaic Commentary on Genesis. A New American Translation. Parashiyyot Thirty-Four through Sixty-Seven. Genesis 8:15-28:9.*

Genesis Rabbah. The Judaic Commentary on Genesis. A New American Translation. Atlanta, 1985: Scholars Press for Brown Judaic Studies. III. *Genesis Rabbah. The Judaic Commentary on Genesis. A New American Translation. Parashiyyot Sixty-Eight through One Hundred. Genesis 28:10-50:26.*

Sifra. The Judaic Commentary on Leviticus. A New Translation. The Leper. Leviticus 13:1-14:57. Chico, 1985: Scholars Press for Brown Judaic Studies. [With a section by Roger Brooks.] Based on *A History of the Mishnaic Law of Purities. VI. Negaim. Sifra.*

Sifré to Numbers. An American Translation. I. 1-58. Atlanta, 1986: Scholars Press for Brown Judaic Studies.

Sifré to Numbers. An American Translation. II. 59-115. Atlanta, 1986: Scholars Press for Brown Judaic Studies. [III. *116-161*: William Scott Green].

The Fathers According to Rabbi Nathan. An Analytical Translation and Explanation . Atlanta, 1986: Scholars Press for Brown Judaic Studies.

Pesiqta deRab Kahana. An Analytical Translation and Explanation. I. 1-14. Atlanta, 1987: Scholars Press for Brown Judaic Studies.

Pesiqta deRab Kahana. An Analytical Translation and Explanation. II. 15-28. With an Introduction to Pesiqta deRab Kahana. Atlanta, 1987: Scholars Press for Brown Judaic Studies.

From Tradition to Imitation. The Plan and Program of Pesiqta deRab Kahana and Pesiqta Rabbati. Atlanta, 1987: Scholars Press for Brown Judaic Studies. A fresh translation of Pesiqta Rabbati *Pisqaot* 1-5, 15.

Sifré to Deuteronomy. An Analytical Translation. Atlanta, 1987: Scholars Press for Brown Judaic Studies. I. *Pisqaot One through One Hundred Forty-Three. Debarim, Waethanan, Eqeb, Re'eh.*

Sifré to Deuteronomy. An Analytical Translation. Atlanta, 1987: Scholars Press for Brown Judaic Studies. II. *Pisqaot One Hundred Forty-Four through Three Hundred Fifty-Seven. Shofetim, Ki Tese, Ki Tabo, Nesabim, Ha'azinu, Zot Habberakhah.*

Sifra. An Analytical Translation. Atlanta, 1988: Scholars Press for Brown Judaic Studies. I. *Introduction* and *Vayyiqra Dibura Denedabah* and *Vayiqqra Dibura Dehobah.*

Sifra. An Analytical Translation. Atlanta, 1988: Scholars Press for Brown Judaic Studies. II. *Sav, Shemini, Tazria, Negaim, Mesora,* and *Zabim.*

Sifra. An Analytical Translation. Atlanta, 1988: Scholars Press for Brown Judaic Studies. III. *Aharé Mot, Qedoshim, Emor, Behar,* and *Behuqotai.*

Mekhilta Attributed to R. Ishmael. An Analytical Translation. Atlanta, 1988: Scholars Press for Brown Judaic Studies. I. *Pisha, Beshallah, Shirata, and Vayassa.*

Mekhilta Attributed to R. Ishmael. An Analytical Translation. Atlanta, 1988: Scholars Press for Brown Judaic Studies. II. *Amalek, Bahodesh, Neziqin, Kaspa, and Shabbata.*

Lamentations Rabbah. An Analytical Translation. Atlanta, 1989: Scholars Press for Brown Judaic Studies.

Esther Rabbah I. An Analytical Translation. Atlanta, 1989: Scholars Press for Brown Judaic Studies.

Ruth Rabbah. An Analytical Translation. Atlanta, 1989: Scholars Press for Brown Judaic Studies.

Song of Songs Rabbah. An Analytical Translation. Volume One. *Song of Songs Rabbah to Song Chapters One through Three.* Atlanta, 1990: Scholars Press for Brown Judaic Studies.

Song of Songs Rabbah. An Analytical Translation. Volume Two. *Song of Songs Rabbah to Song Chapters Four through Eight.* Atlanta, 1990: Scholars Press for Brown Judaic Studies.

Part One
HISTORY OF RELIGION

5

Analogical-Contrastive Thinking and the Problem of Dialectical Thought Or: When Is a List a Series?

Entire chapters of the Bavli work in detail on accumulating evidence in behalf of a single, unarticulated but always stipulated, proposition. The Babylonian Talmud's exposition of Mishnah-tractate Zebahim 5:1-2 – Bavli Zebahim 47B-52B – in a systematic and amazingly orderly way sets forth principles of comparison and contrast within the discipline of dialectical thinking. There we find beneath the surface – but not very far – the issue of the dialectics of analogical-contrastive thought. That is, the question facing us is the logic of a series. The authors of the chapter are trying to show the logic, and limits, of a series: if A=B and B=C, then does A=C, and, if so, why? and if not, why not? To state matters in words rather than symbols, if we say something equals something else, what more are we saying, that is, what is the implication of the claim of equivalency? In its interest in finding the connection to Scripture of a rule that is set forth by the Mishnah, the Bavli's treatment of M. Zeb. 5:1-2 presents this metaproposition that encompasses numerous specific propositions: How do we make connections between rules and their point of origin? Every time we ask, What is the source [in Scripture] for this statement, we find an answer that is left to stand. So one fundamental and ubiquitous metaproposition of the Bavli may be set forth in this language:

1. It is important to link laws that occur in one source to those that occur in another;
2. Among the compilations [components of "the one whole Torah of Moses, our rabbi," in later mythic language] that enjoy canonical status [in our language], the premier is Scripture;

3. So whenever we find a statement of a rule in the Mishnah and ask for its source, the implicit criterion of success will be, "the rule is founded on language of Scripture, properly construed";

4. So, consequently, the proposition implicit in numerous propositions, common to them all and holding them all together, is this: all rules cohere, and the point of origin of nearly all of them is the written part of the Torah revealed by God to Moses at Sinai.

The particular document in which the rules now circulate does not place into a hierarchy the various rules because they all are one; but the reason they all are one is that nearly all of them find a point of origin in the written part of the Torah; and every single one of them is harmonious in principle with each of the others – once we identify the principle implicit in the cases that make up the law. Now if we asked the framers of the Mishnah their judgment upon these allegations of one of the metapropositional planks of the platform of the Bavli, they will have found surprising only our inquiry. For, while not common or characteristic of Mishnaic discourse, each of these traits can be located therein. The Mishnah's framers sometimes explicitly cite a verse of Scripture in support of the law; they occasionally undertake the exegesis of a verse of Scripture in order to discover the law; they know the distinction between rulings of the Torah and rulings of scribes, the latter standing a cut below the former; and their heirs, in undertaking vast exercises of linkage of the Mishnah to Scripture in such documents as Sifra to Leviticus and Sifré to Deuteronomy, engage in a persistent and compelling demonstration of the same metapropositional program, point by point. And yet we cannot then assign to the authorship of our chapter (and the numerous other chapters in which a principal, recurrent concern and point of generative tension is the link of the law contained in the Mishnah or other Tannaite compilations to the law (contained in Scripture and its particular wording) merely the task of saying explicitly what the framers of the Mishnah occasionally said and commonly implied.

For there is a second metaproposition in our chapter, one so profound as to demand for itself priority over all other questions and answers. It addresses the issue of the nature and structure of thought. When we understand that issue, we shall see the remarkable intellectual achievement of the authorship of the Bavli's reading of Mishnah-tractate Zebahim 5:1-2. At stake in this appreciation of what they have accomplished is the demonstration that metapropositions in the Bavli are not only particular to the problem of the documentary provenance of rules – Scripture forms the basis of nearly all rules; all rules harmonize, at their foundations in abstract principles, with all other rules. The metapropositional program turns out, as I shall now show through a reprise of the pertinent propositions of the Bavli's reading of Mishnah-tractate Zebahim 5:1-2, to be so abstract as vastly to transcend rules and their generalizations and harmonies, rising to the height of principles of thought that guide the intellect in contemplation of all being and all reality.

To grasp the metapropositional program that, in my view, defines the stakes of discourse, let me specify what I conceive to be the counterpart program, pertaining to not connecting rules to Scripture, but rather, connecting principle to (consequent) principle: how thought really takes place, which is, not in a stationary pool but in a moving stream. To state the result up front: the Mishnah portrays all things at rest, a beautifully composed set in stasis, a stage on which nothing happens. The Bavli portrays all things in motion, a world of action, in which one thing leads to some other, and nothing stands still. All of this is accomplished in a shift in the received mode of thought, and the shift is set forth in the metaproposition, fully exposed, in the reading of two paragraphs of the Mishnah. We now consider what I conceive to be the counterpart program to the one that, in my view, the Bavli's sages inherited from the Mishnah and spelled out in tedious and unending particulars. To understand what is fresh and important in the Bavli's metapropositional program concerning the nature of thought, we have to call to mind what they inherited, for what they did was to impose the stamp of their own intellect upon the intellectual heritage that the Mishnah had provided for them.

To set forth the basic theory of the framers of the Mishnah on how thought takes place, which is to say, how we may understand things and know them, we must recall a simple fact. The Mishnah teaches the age-old method of scientific thought through comparison and contrast. Like things follow like rules, unlike things, the opposite rules, and the task of thought is to show what is like something else and therefore follows the rule that governs that something else, or what is unlike something else and therefore follows the opposite of the rule that governs that something else. So the Mishnah's mode of thought establishes connections between and among things and does so, as is clear, through the method of taxonomy, comparison and contrast, list making of like things, yielding the rule that governs all items on the list.

List making places on display the data of the like and the unlike and implicitly (ordinarily, not explicitly) then conveys the rule. The Mishnah is then a book of lists, with the implicit order, the nomothetic traits of a monothetic order, dictating the ordinarily unstated general and encompassing rule. And all this why? It is in order to make a single statement, endless times over, and to repeat in a mass of tangled detail precisely the same fundamental judgment. The framers of the Mishnah appeal solely to the traits of things. List making then defines a way of proving propositions through classification, so establishing a set of shared traits that form a rule which compels us to reach a given conclusion. Probative facts derive from the classification of data, all of which point in one direction and not in another. A catalogue of facts, for example, may be so composed that, through the regularities and indicative traits of the entries, the catalogue yields a proposition. A list of parallel items all together point to a simple conclusion; the conclusion may or may not be given at the end of the catalogue, but the catalogue – by definition – is pointed. All of the catalogued facts are taken to bear self-evident connections to one another, established by those pertinent shared traits implicit in the composition of the list, therefore also bearing meaning and pointing through the weight of evidence to an inescapable conclusion. The discrete facts then join together because of some trait common to them all. This is a mode of classification of facts to lead to an identification of what the facts have in common and – it goes without saying, an explanation of their meaning.

What is at stake in the making of lists, that is, the formation of classes of things, is the comparison and contrast of one class of things with some other, yielding at the end the account of the hierarchization of all classes of things in correct sequence and grade. The following abstract shows us through the making of connections and the drawing of conclusions the propositional and essentially philosophical mind that animates the Mishnah and makes explicit what that authorship always wants to know: the relationships, in hierarchical order, between classes of things. In the following passage, drawn from Mishnah-tractate Sanhedrin Chapter Two, the authorship wishes to say that Israel has two heads, one of state, the other of cult, the king and the high priest, respectively, and that these two offices are nearly wholly congruent with one another, with a few differences based on the particular traits of each. Broadly speaking, therefore, our exercise is one of setting forth the genus and the species. The genus is head of holy Israel. The species are king and high priest. Here are the traits in common and those not shared, and the exercise is fully exposed for what it is, an inquiry into the rules that govern, the points of regularity and order, in this minor matter, of political structure. My outline, imposed in boldface type, makes the point important in this setting. We deal with Mishnah-tractate Sanhedrin Chapter Two:

I.   The rules of the high priest: subject to the law, marital rites, conduct in bereavement

2:1   A.   A high priest judges, and [others] judge him;

       B.   gives testimony, and [others] give testimony about him;

C.	performs the rite of removing the shoe [Deut. 25:7-9], and [others] perform the rite of removing the shoe with his wife.
D.	[Others] enter levirate marriage with his wife, but he does not enter into levirate marriage,
E.	because he is prohibited to marry a widow.
F.	[If] he suffers a death [in his family], he does not follow the bier.
G.	"But when [the bearers of the bier] are not visible, he is visible; when they are visible, he is not.
H.	"And he goes with them to the city gate," the words of R. Meir.
I.	R. Judah says, "He never leaves the sanctuary,
J.	"since it says, '*Nor shall he go out of the sanctuary*' (Lev. 21:12)."
K.	And when he gives comfort to others
L.	the accepted practice is for all the people to pass one after another, and the appointed [prefect of the priests] stands between him and the people.
M.	And when he receives consolation from others,
N.	all the people say to him, "Let us be your atonement."
O.	And he says to them, "May you be blessed by Heaven."
P.	And when they provide him with the funeral meal,
Q.	all the people sit on the ground, while he sits on a stool.

II. **The rules of the king: not subject to the law, marital rites, conduct in bereavement**

2:2	A.	The king does not judge, and [others] do not judge him;
	B.	does not give testimony, and [others] do not give testimony about him;
	C.	does not perform the rite of removing the shoe, and others do not perform the rite of removing the shoe with his wife;
	D.	does not enter into levirate marriage, nor [does his brother] enter levirate marriage with his wife.
	E.	R. Judah says, "If he wanted to perform the rite of removing the shoe or to enter into levirate marriage, his memory is a blessing."
	F.	They said to him, "They pay no attention to him [if he expressed the wish to do so]."
	G.	[Others] do not marry his widow.
	H.	R. Judah says, "A king may marry the widow of a king.
	I.	"For so we find in the case of David, that he married the widow of Saul,
	J.	"For it is said, '*And I gave you your master's house and your master's wives into your embrace*' (2 Sam. 12:8)."
2:3	A.	[If] [the king] suffers a death in his family, he does not leave the gate of his palace.
	B.	R. Judah says, "If he wants to go out after the bier, he goes out,
	C.	"for thus we find in the case of David, that he went out after the bier of Abner,
	D.	"since it is said, '*And King David followed the bier*' (2 Sam. 3:31)."
	E.	They said to him, "This action was only to appease the people."
	F.	And when they provide him with the funeral meal, all the people sit on the ground, while he sits on a couch.

III. **Special rules pertinent to the king because of his calling**

2:4   A   [The king] calls out [the army to wage] a war fought by choice on the instructions of a court of seventy-one.

B   He [may exercise the right to] open a road for himself, and [others] may not stop him.

C.   The royal road has no required measure.

D   All the people plunder and lay before him [what they have grabbed], and he takes the first portion.

E   *"He should not multiply wives to himself"* (Deut. 17:17) – only eighteen.

F.   R Judah says, "He may have as many as he wants, so long as they *do not entice him* [to abandon the Lord (Deut. 7:4)]."

G   R. Simeon says, "Even if there is only one who entices him [to abandon the Lord] – lo, this one should not marry her."

H.   If so, why is it said, "He should not multiply wives to himself"?

I.   Even though they should be like Abigail (1 Sam. 25:3).

J   *"He should not multiply horses to himself"* (Deut. 17:16) – only enough for his chariot.

K   *"Neither shall he greatly multiply to himself silver and gold"* (Deut. 17:16) – only enough to pay his army.

L.   *"And he writes out a scroll of the Torah for himself"* (Deut. 17:17)

M   When he goes to war, he takes it out with him; when he comes back, he brings it back with him; when he is in session in court, it is with him; when he is reclining, it is before him,

N   as it is said, *"And it shall be with him, and he shall read in it all the days of his life"* (Deut. 17:19).

2:5   A   [Others may] not ride on his horse, sit on his throne, handle his scepter.

B   And [others may] not watch him while he is getting a haircut, or while he is nude, or in the bathhouse,

C   since it is said, *"You shall surely set him as king over you"* (Deut. 17:15) – that reverence for him will be upon you.

The subordination of Scripture to the classification scheme is self-evident. Scripture supplies facts. The traits of things – kings, high priests – dictate classification categories on their own, without Scripture's dictate.

The philosophical cast of mind is amply revealed in this essay, which in concrete terms effects a taxonomy, a study of the genus, national leader, and its two species, [1] king, [2] high priest: how are they alike, how are they not alike, and what accounts for the differences. The premise is that national leaders are alike and follow the same rule, except where they differ and follow the opposite rule from one another. But that premise also is subject to the proof effected by the survey of the data consisting of concrete rules, those systemically inert facts that here come to life for the purposes of establishing a proposition. By itself, the fact that, for example, others may not ride on his horse, bears the burden of no systemic proposition. In the context of an argument constructed for nomothetic, taxonomic purposes, the same fact is active and weighty. The whole depends upon three premises: [1] the importance of comparison and contrast, with the supposition that [2] like follows the like, and the unlike follows the opposite, rule; and [3] when we classify, we also hierarchize, which yields the argument from hierarchical classification: if this, which is the lesser, follows rule X, then that, which is the greater, surely should follow rule X. And that is the whole sum and substance of the logic of *Listenwissenschaft* as the Mishnah applies that logic in a practical way.

If I had to specify a single mode of thought that established connections between one fact and another, it is in the search for points in common and therefore also points of contrast. We seek connection between fact and fact, sentence and sentence in the subtle and balanced rhetoric of the Mishnah, by comparing and contrasting two things that are like and not alike. At the logical level, too, the Mishnah falls into the category of familiar philosophical thought. Once we seek regularities, we propose rules. What is like another thing falls under its rule, and what is not like the other falls under the opposite rule. Accordingly, as to the species of the genus, so far as they are alike, they share the same rule. So far as they are not alike, each follows a rule contrary to that governing the other. So the work of analysis is what produces connection, and therefore the drawing of conclusions derives from comparison and contrast: the *and*, the *equal*. The proposition, then, that forms the conclusion concerns the essential likeness of the two offices, except where they are different, but the subterranean premise is that we can explain both likeness and difference by appeal to a principle of fundamental order and unity.

To make these observations concrete, we turn to the case at hand. The important contrast comes at the outset. The high priest and king fall into a single genus, but speciation, based on traits particular to the king, then distinguishes the one from the other. Now if I further had to set forth what I conceive to form the deepest conviction at the most profound layers of thought, it is that things set in relationship always stand in that same relationship. The work of making connections and drawing conclusions produces results that are fixed and final. If we establish a connection between one set of things and another, that connection forms the end of matters – that, and not a series, by which the connection between A and B serves as a guide to a movement from C to A via B, that is, as we shall now see, the formation of not a connection but a series of things that are connected only to one another, but not to other components of the same series – which is to say, a series.

To put matters very simply, if A is like B, and B is like C, then is C like A? And if – as the received logic of the age insists! – we entertain the possibility of a series, then, and much more to the point, *precisely what are the rules of connection that form the links of the results of comparison and contrast?*

In other words, in the aftermath of classification comes not hierarchization but movement, this thing in relationship to that, that in relationship to the other, all things in movement, nothing at rest. So, if a series is possible, then how is a series composed? That is the question answered by the Bavli, the question no one in the Mishnah asked because the Mishnah's framers contemplated a world at rest, and the Bavli's, a world in motion.

In so stating, I have leapt over each of the necessary stages of my exposition. So let us begin from the beginning. Now that the Mishnah's position is in hand, we revert to my claim that the Bavli's own statement in the chapter under discussion concerns the nature of thought. Let us first of all review the points that are made, and the sequence in which they are set forth. We begin with the point of intersection:

1. It is important to know how to connect rules to Scripture.
2. The principles that govern the making of connections to Scripture are those that govern making connections not between words and words ("the hermeneutical principles") but rather between one thing and something else, that is, defining a genus and its species; so when we know how to compare and contrast, find what is like something else and what is different from something else, we know how to conduct the passage from rules to Scripture.
3. Exegetical rules tell us how to form classes of things in relationship to Scripture.
4. Dialectical rules tell us how to move from one class of things to another class of things.

To state matters simply: What makes a list into a series? And how are we supposed to effect that transformation – that movement? Step 2 then marks the point of departure, and Steps 3 and 4 denote the remarkable shift in the passage. We go not only from rule to generalization, or from case to principle. That, to be sure, takes place and forms an everywhere-present metaproposition, as the tedium of the remainder of the chapter showed us. Rather, we go from thinking about things and their connections (comparison and contrast) to thinking about thought itself. So what I have represented as the rules of dialectical thinking – not merely argument! – turn out to tell us how thought happens; the Bavli's reading of Mishnah-tractate Zebahim 5:1-2 forms a fundamental exercise of thought about thinking.

When we review the principal steps in the sustained and unfolding inquiry as the Bavli's commentary on M. Zeb. 5:1-2 unfolds, we realize that, in particulars and in detail, the framers of the passage have set forth a profound essay on thought. In the terms just now given, if A=B, and B=C, then does A=C? Is a series possible? Are there limits to the extension of a series? And on what basis do we construct a series? Do the media of linkage between A and B, that is, A=B, have to be the same as those that link B to C, for C to stand in the series that A has begun? These abstract questions have to become concrete before the sense of matters will emerge. So let us now review what the chapter has already told us: the sequence of points that represent the inquiry into the making of connections, which is to say, the Bavli's metapropositional statement on the character of a series. For it is the series, first this, then that, finally the third thing, and the rules that govern the movement from this, to that, to the third thing, that defines what is the center of deep thought in the Bavli's reading of the specified Mishnah paragraphs. I cite the pertinent language of my translation of the text,[1] where necessary restating what has already been given in the context of the exposition of the text, but I do not then repeat all of the text.. The stages in the argument of the Talmud now are identified and repeated, as marked by boldface capital letters. The argument is astonishing for its sustained quality; it moves in an inexorable course, rigorously insisting on settling one question before raising the next, and consequent one.

A. II.2. E.[2]   That answer is satisfactory for him who takes the view that one may indeed derive a rule governing a prior subject from one that is given later on, but from the perspective of him who denies that fact, what is to be said?

The opening question contains the entirety of what is to follow: the conviction that anterior to conclusions and debates on fixed propositions is a premise, and the premise concerns not issues but thought itself. For what is before us is not a hermeneutical principle that guides the exegesis of Scripture, the movement from a rule back to a scriptural formulation deemed to pertain. It is a rule of how to think. And the issue is explicit: does thought flow, or does it stand still? Does it flow backward from conclusion to a conclusion already reached? In the context of the document at hand, the issue is one of arrangements of words, that is, a

---

[1]This is published as *The Talmud of Babylonia. An American Translation*. Atlanta, 1991: Scholars Press for Brown Judaic Studies. XXVIII.B. *Tractate Zebahim. Chapters Four through Eight.*

[2]The reference system used in that translation is indicated; the Roman numeral, II, represents the starting point of the treatment of a Mishnah sentence; the Arabic number, 2, represents the second complete and exhaustive treatment of a subject or presentation of a proposition; the letter, E, denotes the fifth whole unit of thought ("sentence") of that presentation.

literary and therefore an exegetical question. That is, then, the proposition. But the metaproposition is otherwise, though that is not yet explicit.

B. II.2. J.   But this is the reason for the position of rabbis, who declare one exempt [from having to present a suspensive guilt-offering in the case of a matter of doubt regarding acts of sacrilege]: they derive a verbal analogy to a sin-offering based on the appearance of the word "commandments" with reference to both matters.

   N   They take the view that one may not derive from an argument by analogy established through the use of a word in common only a limited repertoire of conclusions [but once the analogy is drawn, then all of the traits of one case apply to the other].

Here is an issue not of exegesis, therefore of hermeneutics, but of the rules of right thinking: thinking about thought. And what it concerns, as I have suggested in context, is how we establish not classes of things but linkage between and among classes of things. Let me state the centerpiece in simple words but with heavy emphasis: *since I make connections through analogy and contrast, may I proceed to make connections beyond the limits of the original connection? And the answer is, I must proceed, because thought does not come to rest. Comparison and contrast yield connections, which then govern.*

In the language before us, once I draw an analogy, do all traits of the two classes of things that have been linked through analogy – of necessity only partial, since were the analogy entire, both classes would constitute a single class! – pertain to each class? In the present context, what we establish is the anonymous, therefore the governing rule. The norm is that once we draw an analogy, the connection established by the (mere) analogy takes over, so that we treat as analogous traits not covered by the analogy at all. The analogy establishes the connection; but then the movement of thought is such that the connection is deemed to have established a new class of things, all of them subject to one rule. The movement – the dialectic – therefore is not a mere trait of argument, "if you say this, I say that," but a trait of thought: if this is the result of step A, then step B is to be taken – out from, without regard to, the limitations of step A. Thought, then, is continuous, always in motion, and that metaproposition states in the most abstract terms possible the prior and generative metaproposition that, when we compare classes of things, the comparison initiates a process that transcends the limits of comparison. That is to say, again with emphasis, *we can effect a series.*

C. II.2. S.   *One authority maintains that proof supplied by analogy [here: the analogy sustained by the use of "and" to join the two subjects] takes priority, and the other party maintains that the proof supplied by the*

> *demonstration of a totality of congruence among salient traits takes*
> *precedence. Rabbis prefer the latter, Aqiba the former position.]*

T.   *Not at all! All parties concur that proof supplied by analogy [here:*
     the analogy sustained by the use of "and" to join the two subjects]
     takes priority. But rabbis in this context will say to you that the rule
     governing the subject treated below derives from the rule governing
     the subject treated above, so that the guilt-offering must be worth at
     least two silver shekels. This is established so that you should not
     argue that the doubt cannot be more stringent than the matter of
     certainty, and just as where there is certainty of having committed a
     sin, one has to present a sin-offering that may be worth even so little
     as a sixth of a zuz in value, so if there is a matter of doubt, the guilt-
     offering worth only a sixth of a zuz would suffice.

Once the connection is made, linking an earlier rule (in Scripture's
orderly exposition) to a later one, then the connection is such that
movement is not only forward but backward. We have established not a
connection between one thing and something else, but a series that can
encompass a third thing and a fourth thing, onward – but with, or
without formal limit? This principle of right thinking that the hypothesis
of the series requires is revealed by Scripture, as is made explicit once
more in the following:

D. III.1   I.   *...And should you say that if Scripture had not included the matter,*
                 we should have reached the same conclusion by argument for analogy,
                 then if that is the case, we can infer by analogy also the rule on laying
                 *on of hands....*The main point here is that, once an analogy
                 serves, it serves everywhere an analogy can be drawn; there is
                 no a priori that limits the power of an analogy to govern all like
                 cases.

A series is possible once the work of thought moves beyond contrast and
analogy. And it is the rule of right thought that, once we have
established a comparison and a contrast, that fact validates drawing
conclusions on other aspects of the classes of things that have been
connected through the comparison and contrast – analogical-contrastive
thinking is then not static but in motion. Is the motion perpetual? Not at
all, for Scripture, for its part, has the power to place limits on a series.

E. IV.2. B.   If a matter was covered by an encompassing rule but then was
                 singled out for some innovative purpose, you have not got the
                 right to restore the matter to the rubric of the encompassing
                 rule unless Scripture itself explicitly does so. [That means that
                 the encompassing rule does not apply to an item that Scripture,
                 for its own purposes, has singled out. The upshot is that the
                 identified item is now exceptional in some aspect, so it is no
                 longer subject to a common rule governing all other items in
                 context; then the limits of analogy are set by Scripture's
                 treatment of the items of a series. It is worthwhile reviewing
                 the pertinent example:]

The series is subjected to limits, if an item in the sequence of connections that forms the series proves exceptional: this is connected to that, that to the other thing, but the other thing is other in some other way, so there the series ends.

H   *If [you claim that the purpose of the verse is as stated and not to teach that doing the rite at the north is indispensable, as originally proposed,] then Scripture should have stated only the rule governing the rite for the one healed from the skin ailment but not the earlier version of the rule.*

I   *Quite so – if we take the view that when something becomes the subject of a new law, it cannot then be covered by an encompassing rule that otherwise would apply, while the encompassing rule still can be derived from that special case. But if we take the view that when something becomes the subject of a new law, then it cannot be covered by an encompassing rule that otherwise would apply, and the encompassing rule also cannot be derived from that special place, then the law [Lev. 7:1-10, indicating that the guilt-offering must be killed in the north] is needed for its own purpose!*

J.   *Since Scripture has restored the matter to the rubric of the encompassing rule explicitly, that restoration has taken place.*

K.   *Said Mar Zutra b. R. Mari to Rabina, "But why not say, when Scripture restored the matter to the rubric of the encompassing rule, that was solely in regard to having to present the blood and the sacrificial parts on the altar, since the priest is necessary to perform that rite. But as to slaughtering the animal, which does not have to be done by a priest, that does not have to be done at the northern side of the altar?"*

L.   *[He said to him,]* "If so, Scripture should say simply, 'for it is like the sin-offering.' Why say, 'or the guilt-offering, like the sin-offering'? *It is to teach, let it be like other guilt-offerings [that must be slaughtered at the northern side of the altar]."* Here again, therefore, the issue is the limits of analogy, how these are determined.

F.   IV.4.   A   *Raba said, "[The proposition that that which is derived on the basis of a verbal analogy does not in turn go and impart a lesson by means of a verbal analogy] derives from the following proof:*

We go over familiar ground. Raba takes the view that a series is simply not possible. Others allege that if we connect one class of things to some other by means, for example, of a verbal analogy, then making that same connection once again, where another verbal analogy connects the second class of things to yet a third, is not correct. Scripture shows that verbal analogies do not validate the making of series, and this is shown in an explicit way:

B.   *"It is written, 'As is taken off from the ox of the sacrifice of peace-offerings' (Lev. 4:10) [namely, the sacrificial parts of the anointed priest's bullock brought for a sin-offering] – now for what purpose is this detail given? That the lobe of the liver and the two kidneys are to be burned on the altar [as is the case with those of the sin-offering], that fact is specified in the body of the verse itself. But the purpose is to intimate that the burning of the lobe of the liver and the two kidneys of the he-goats brought as sin-offerings for idolatry are to be derived by analogy from the bullock of the community brought on account of an inadvertent sin. That law is not explicitly stated in the passage on the bullock that is brought for an inadvertent sin, but is derived from the rule governing the bullock of the anointed priest. 'As is taken off' is required so that it might be treated as something written in that very passage [on the bullock of inadvertence, being superfluous in its own context], not as something derived on the basis of a verbal analogy that does not in turn go and impart a lesson by means of a verbal analogy."*

To repeat my exposition of this matter: I have two items, A and B. I claim that B is like A, therefore the rule governing A applies also to B. Now I turn forward, to C. C is not analogous to A; there are no points of congruence or (in the exegetical formulation that our authors use) verbal intersection. But C is like B. It is like B because there is an analogy by reason of verbal intersection (the same word being used in reference to C and B.) The question is, may I apply to C, by reason of the verbal intersection between C and B, the lesson that I have learned in regard to B only by reason of B's similarity by reason of congruence, not verbal intersection, to A? Can a conclusion that is derived on the basis of a verbal analogy go and impart a lesson by reason of analogy to a third item? Raba now maintains that that is not the case. But the matter has gone in the other direction: a series is possible. But if a series is possible, then what limits are to be placed on the media by which a series is effected?

G IV.5. A Now it is a fact that that which is derived on the basis of a verbal analogy does in turn go and impart a lesson by means of a verbal analogy, *whether demonstrated in the manner of Raba or in the manner of Rabina.*

Now we revert to our basic issue: the validity of a series. Here we move into as yet unexplored ground, which is the basis for my claim that the order of problems is dictated by an interest in a systematic presentation of the rules of right thinking. We have been exposed to the case in favor of a series: once the analogy makes the connection, then all traits of the things connected are brought into relationship with all other such traits. Scripture then provides one limit to the length of a series: a series cannot be infinite. But there is another limit proposed, and it is not scriptural but substantive, in the nature of things, a trait of thought itself. Here is the point at which I find this sustained exposition of thinking about thought simply remarkable.

> B.   Is it the rule, however, that *that which is derived on the basis of a*
>   *verbal analogy may in turn go and impart a lesson by means of an*
>   *argument on the basis of congruence?* [Freedman: Thus the law
>   stated in A is applied to B by analogy. Can that law then be
>   applied to C because of congruence between B and C?]

We have proved one point. It bears a consequence. We go on to the
consequence. The mode of thought is dialectical not only in form, but
also in substance: if A, then B. If B, then what about C? It is one thing to
have shown that if B is like A, and C, unlike A, is rendered comparable to
B by a verbal analogy. But then may I take the next step and draw into
the framework of B and C, joined by verbal analogy and assigned a
common rule by B's congruent analogy to A, also D, E, F, and G, that is,
other classes of things joined to C by verbal analogy – but not necessarily
the same verbal analogy that has joined C to B? That indeed is the
obvious next step to be taken, and it is now taken. It is taken in the
simple words just now given, and the same point is now going to be
made, in a systematic way, for each medium by which classes of things
are formed and then connected to one another. Analogical-contrastive
thinking, therefore, is not static but always in motion, since, once a
connection is made, other connections made follow. If we make a
connection between A and B on the basis of one set of shared traits, we
may proceed to make a connection between C and A, via B, on the basis
of traits shared by B and C but not by A and C. Not only so, but the
same mode of thought extends to the media of connection. If I connect A
to B by verbal analogy, I may connect B to other classes of things, for
example, C, D, E, by other media of connection, for instance, verbal
analogy connects A to B, and an argument based on congruent connects
B to C, and backward to A; and an argument a fortiori may connect C to
D, and backward to A and B – series without end, or series that ends only
in the dictates of revelation, the ultimate arbiter of the classification and
hierarchy of all things. What is truly impressive in what follows is the
rigorous order by which each possibility is raised in its turn, the
connections fore and aft, such that the framer of the whole not only
makes his point in words, but also illustrates it in his own representation
of matters: a series is not only possible, it is also compelling. So we see as
we move forward, now with no need for further exposition, from H to M.

H   IV.6.   A   That which is learned by a verbal analogy may in turn go and
                    impart a rule by an argument a fortiori .

L   IV.7.   A   Can that which is learned by verbal analogy established in turn
                    go and impart a rule by an analogy based on the congruence of
                    other shared traits [but not verbal ones in context]? Once more
                    to review: we have now linked B to C via a verbal analogy. C
                    stands in relationship to other classes of things, but not for the

same reason that it stands in relationship to B, that is, through other than verbal analogical relationships. It forms a relationship a fortiori, for instance, with D, E, and F. If something applies to C, the lesser, it surely should apply to D, the greater. So now we want to know the permissible grounds for drawing relationships – comparisons and contrasts – of classes of things. So on what basis do we move from species to species and uncover the genera of which they form a part (if they do form a part)? Is it only verbal correspondence or intersection, as has been implicit to this point? Or are there more abstract bases for the same work of genus construction (in our language: category formation and re-formation)?

J. IV.8.   A   Can a rule that is derived by analogy based on the congruence of other shared traits [but not verbal ones in context] turn around and teach a lesson through an analogy based on verbal analogy?

K. IV.9.   A   Can a rule that is derived by an analogy based on the congruence of other shared traits [but not verbal ones in context] turn around and teach a lesson?

L. IV.10 A   Can a rule that is derived by an analogy based on the congruence of other shared traits [but not verbal ones in context] go and teach a lesson through an argument a fortiori?

M. IV.10 F.   If an argument deriving from an analogy based on verbal congruence, which cannot go and, by an argument based on verbal congruence, impart its rule to some other class – *as has been shown by either Raba's or Rabina's demonstration* – nonetheless can go and by an argument a fortiori impart its rule to some other class – *as has been shown by the Tannaite authority of the household of R. Ishmael* – then a rule that is derived by an argument based on analogy based on other than verbal congruence, which can for its part go and impart its lesson by an argument based on an analogy resting on verbal congruity which is like itself– *as has been shown by Rami bar Hama* – surely can in turn teach its lesson by an argument a fortiori to yet another case!

So at stake throughout is the question of how a series is composed: the media for the making of connections between one thing and something else (that is, one class of things and some other class of things, in such wise that the rules governing the one are shown by the analogy to govern the other as well). We want to know not only that a connection is made, but how it is made. And some maintain that if the connection is made between one thing and something else by means, for example, of a verbal analogy dictated by Scripture's wording, then a connection between that something else and a third thing must also be made in a manner consistent with the initial medium of connection, verbal analogy. It cannot be made by means of some other medium of connection. But the paramount position is otherwise: dialectics affect not only argument but thought itself because connections are made through all media by which connections are made. We now reach the end of the matter, in a set of ultimately theoretical issues:

N IV.11. A. Can a rule that is derived by an analogy based on the congruence of other shared traits [but not verbal ones in context] go and teach a lesson through an argument constructed by analogy based on the congruence of other of other shared traits among two or more classifications of things?

     B. *That question must stand.*

Q IV.12. A. Can a rule derived by an argument a fortiori go and teach a rule established through analogy of verbal usage?

     B. The affirmative derives from an argument a fortiori:

     C. If an argument deriving from an analogy based on points of other than verbal congruence, which cannot go and, by an argument based on verbal congruence, impart its rule to some other class – *as has been shown by either R. Pappa's demonstration,* – then a rule that is derived by an argument a fortiori, which can be derived by an argument based on the shared verbal traits of two things, – *as has been shown by the Tannaite authority of the house of R. Ishmael* – surely should be able to impart its rule to another classification of things by reason of an argument based on a verbal analogy!

     D. *That position poses no problems to one who takes the view that R. Pappa's case has been made. But for one who takes the view that R. Pappa's case has not been made, what is to be said?*

     E. *The question then must stand.*

P. IV.13. A. Can a rule that is derived by an argument a fortiori go and teach a lesson through an argument based on the congruence of other shared traits [but not verbal ones in context]?

     B. The affirmative derives from an argument a fortiori:

     C. If an argument deriving from an analogy based on points of other than verbal congruence, which cannot be derived from an argument based on verbal congruence, impart its rule to some other class – *as has been shown by R. Yohanan's demonstration* – can go and teach a lesson by an argument based on an analogy established through other-than-verbal traits, *as has been shown by Rami bar Hama* – a rule based on an argument a fortiori, which can be derived by an argument based on an analogy resting on verbal coincidence, surely should be able to impart its rule to another classification of things by reason of an argument based on an other-than-verbal analogy!

Q IV.14. A. Can a rule based on an argument a fortiori turn around and teach a lesson through an argument based on an argument a fortiori?

     B. Indeed so, and the affirmative derives from an argument a fortiori:

C. If an argument deriving from an analogy based on points of other-than-verbal congruence, which cannot be derived from an argument based on verbal congruence, imparts its rule to some other class – *as has been shown by R. Yohanan's demonstration,* – can go and teach a lesson by an argument a fortiori, as we have just pointed out, then an argument that can be derived from an analogy based on verbal congruence – *as has been shown by the Tannaite authority of the household of R. Ishmael* – surely should be able to impart its rule by an argument a fortiori!

D. But would this then represent what we are talking about, namely, a rule deriving from an argument a fortiori that has been applied to another case by means of an argument a fortiori? Surely this is nothing more than a secondary derivation produced by an argument a fortiori!

E. Rather, argue in the following way:

F. Indeed so, and the affirmative derives from an argument a fortiori:

G. If an argument based on an analogy of a verbal character cannot be derived from another such argument based on an analogy between two classes of things that rests upon a verbal congruence – *in accordance with the proofs of either Raba or Rabina* – nonetheless can then go and impart its lesson by an argument a fortiori – *in accordance with the proof of the Tannaite authority of the household of R. Ishmael* – then an argument a fortiori, which can serve to transfer a lesson originally learned through an argument based upon verbal congruence, *in accordance with the proof of the Tannaite authority of the household of R. Ishmael* – surely should be able to impart its lesson to yet another classification of things through an argument a fortiori.

H. And this does represent what we are talking about, namely, a rule deriving from an argument a fortiori that has been applied to another case by means of an argument a fortiori.

R. IV.15. A. Can a rule based on an argument a fortiori turn around and teach a rule through an argument constructed on the basis of shared traits of an other-than-verbal character among two classifications of things?

C. *But that is not so. For even if we concede that that is the case there, then still the rule derives from the act of slaughter of unconsecrated beasts [Freedman].*

S. IV.16 A. Can a rule derived by an argument based on shared traits of an other-than-verbal character shared among two classes of things then turn around and teach a lesson by an argument based on an analogy of a verbal character, an analogy not of a verbal character, an argument a fortiori, or an argument based on shared traits?

B. *Solve at least one of those problems by appeal to the following:*

C. On what account have they said that if blood of an offering is left overnight on the altar, it is fit? Because if the sacrificial parts are kept overnight on the altar, they are fit. And why if the sacrificial parts are kept overnight on the altar are they fit? Because if the meat of the offering is kept overnight on the altar it is fit. [Freedman: Thus the rule governing the sacrificial parts is derived by an appeal to an argument based on shared traits of an other-than-verbal character shared among two classes of things, and that rule in turn is applied to the case of the blood by another such argument based on shared traits of an other-than-verbal character shared among two classes of things.]

D.   What about the rule governing meat that is taken outside of the Temple court? [If such meat is put up on the altar, it is not removed therefrom. Why so?]

E.   Because meat that has been taken out of the Holy Place is suitable for a high place.

M.   [Reverting to C-E:] Now can an analogy be drawn concerning something that has been disposed of in the proper manner for something that has not been disposed of in the proper manner? [If the sacrificial parts are kept overnight, they are not taken off the altar, and therefore the meat kept overnight is fit; but the meat may be kept overnight, while the sacrificial parts may not. So, too, when the Temple stood, the flesh might not be taken outside, but where there was no Temple and only high places, the case is scarcely analogous!]

N.   *The Tannaite authority for this rule derives it from the augmentative sense, extending the rule, deriving from the formulation,* "This is the Torah of the burnt-offering" (Lev. 6:2). [Freedman: The verse teaches that all burnt-offerings, even with the defects catalogued here, are subject to the same rule and do not get removed from the altar once they have been put there; the arguments given cannot be sustained but still support that proposition.].

The movement from point to point, first things first, second things in sequence, is so stunning in the precise logic of the order of issues – we must know A before we can contemplate asking about B – that only a brief review is called for.

We have shown that we may move from a class of things joined to another through analogy based on congruence, that is, from A to B, onward to other classes of things joined to the foregoing by verbal analogy or intersection, that is, from B to C and beyond. But can we then move from C, linked to B via verbal analogy, to D, linked to C, but not to A or B, by congruence, for example, comparable and shared traits of a salient order? The issue then, is may we move forward to further classes of things by moving "backward," to a principle of linkage of classes that has served to bring us to this point, in other words, reversing the course of principles of linkage? What our framers then want to know is a very logical question: are there fixed rules that govern the order or sequence by which we move from one class of things to another, so that, if we propose to link classes of things, we can move only from A to B by one principle (comparison and contrast of salient traits), and from B to C by a necessarily consequent and always second principle (verbal intersection); then we may move (by this theory) from C to D only by verbal intersection but not by appeal to congruence. Why not? Because, after all, if C is linked to B only by verbal intersection but not by congruence, bearing no relationship to A at all, then how claim that D stands in a series begun at A, if it has neither verbal connection, nor, as a matter of fact, congruence to link it to anything in the series. What is clear in this reprise is that the issue is drawn systematically, beginning to end. By simply seeing the sequence of questions, we grasp the whole: the program, the method, the order, all dictated by the inner requirements of sustained inquiry into the logic of comparison and contrast, read as a dialectical problem. The upshot may be stated now in a very few words.

A list is never a list, it is always part of a series; thought moves but does not come to rest. That metaproposition comes to formal expression at the very surface of discourse, in the ever-flowing movement of argument of the Talmud itself. That is why the framers of the Bavli never leave the Mishnah alone, allowing its formal perfection and its serene expositions of the classification of things to stand still. Rather they insist on exploring the connections among classifications of things – the connections that in their character and even in their function turn out to shift and change. The dialectic of connection takes the place of the hierarchization that, for the framers of the Mishnah, everything is deemed satisfactorily to portray connection in some one, set way.

The metapropositional program contributed by the Bavli's framers concerns how series are made, which is to say, whether connections yield static or dynamic results, which is to say, at the deepest layers of intellect, how thought happens. Now, at the end, we ask the framers of the Mishnah to address the question before us. And in answer, they give us silence. So we know that here we hear what is distinctive to, and the remarkable discovery of, the authorship of the Bavli. Since, it is clear, that discovery has taken place within the words of the Written Torah, and, since their deepest metaproposition maintained that the words of the Written Torah are the words of God to Moses, our rabbi, at Sinai, – the words, not just the gist – we have to conclude with what I conceive to be the bedrock of the metapropositional program before us: the Torah teaches us not only what God said, but how God thinks. We know how God thinks because the Torah reveals not only God's word, but also God's wording of God's word. And from the rules of language we move upward to the rules of logical and coherent expression; from there still higher, to rules of logical and cogent thought; and from there, upward to the rules of logic themselves. When God revealed not only the Torah, but the exact wording of the Torah, God taught us the most profound and abstract principles of how to think about thought. That claim forms the foundation of the analysis of M. Zeb. 5:1-2 at Bavli Zebahim 47B-52B. When we understand the Torah rightly, we engage in thinking about thought. And that is how we know God: thinking about thought. So Spinoza perhaps was not so heretical after all.

6

Systemic Integration and Theology: The Concept of *Zekhut* in Formative Judaism

A single conception forms the integrating centerpiece of the theology of the Judaism of the Dual Torah, the conception of *zekhut*, to be defined presently. *Zekhut* is the power of the powerless, the riches of the disinherited, the valuation and valorization of the will of those who have no right to will. In the context of Christian Palestine, Jews found themselves on the defensive, their ancestry called into question, their supernatural standing thrown into doubt, their future denied. They called themselves "Israel," and the land, "the Land of Israel," but what power did they possess, legitimately, if need be through violence, to assert their claim to form "Israel"? And, with the Holy Land passing into the hands of others, what scarce resource did they own and manage, to take the place of that measure of value that now no longer was subjected to their rationality? Asserting a politics in which all violence was illegitimate, an economics in which nothing tangible, even real property in the Holy Land,[1] had value, the system through its counterpart categories made a single, simple, and sufficient statement.

---

[1] A test of this interpretation is whether or not in the provenance of Babylonia stories are told about the equivalence of owning land and studying the Torah. That is to say, if studying the Torah is represented as outweighing owning real estate in Babylonia as much as in the Land of Israel, then something is awry with my results here. But if a survey, for example, of the Talmud of Babylonia, shows that, in the context of Babylonia and not the Land of Israel, stories of the superiority of Torah study over land ownership do not occur, then that would form a fair confirmation of my point of insistence here. This test of falsification will be carried on in the context of the next phase of my *oeuvre*, which will bring me deep into the Babylonian part of the canon of the Dual Torah.

The concept *zekhut* integrates the Judaic system of the Dual Torah as that system emerges in the pages of the Talmud of the Land of Israel and associated Midrash compilations. So far as, in systemic integration, everything can be located in some one thing, it is *zekhut* that contains the system and expresses its main points. The word *zekhut* bears a variety of meanings, as Jastrow summarizes the data,[2] and the pertinence of each possible meaning is to be determined in context: [1] acquittal, plea in favor of the defendant; [2] doing good, blessing; [3] protecting influence of good conduct, merit; [4] advantage, privilege, benefit. The first meaning pertains solely in juridical (or metaphorically juridical) contexts; the second represents a very general and imprecise use of the word, since a variety of other words bears the same meaning. Only the third and the fourth meanings pertain, since they are particular to this word, on the one side, and also religious, on the other. That is to say, only through using the word *zekhut* do authors of compositions and authorships of composites express the sense given at No. 3.

My simple definition emphasizes "heritage" because the advantages or privileges conferred by *zekhut* may be inherited and also passed on; it stresses "entitlements" because advantages or privileges always, invariably result from receiving *zekhut* from ancestors or acquiring it on one's own; and I use the word "virtue" to refer to those supererogatory acts that demand a reward because they form matters of choice, the gift of the individual and his or her act of free will, an act that is at the same time [1] uncompelled, for example, by the obligations imposed by the Torah, but [2] also valued by the Torah. *Zekhut* bears the capacity to unite the generations in a heritage of entitlements; *zekhut* is fundamentally a historical category and concept, in that, like all historical systems of thought, it explains the present in terms of the past, and the future in terms of the present.

Because *zekhut* is something one may receive as an inheritance, out of the distant past, *zekhut* imposes upon the definition of the social entity, "Israel," a genealogical meaning. It furthermore imparts a distinctive character to the definitions of way of life. So the task of the political component of a theory of the social order, which is to define the social entity by appeal to empowerment, and of the economic component, which is to identify scarce resources by specification of the rationality of right management, is accomplished in a single word, which stands for a conception, a symbol, and a myth. All three components of this religious theory of the social order turn out to present specific applications, in

---

[2]Marcus Jastrow, *A Dictionary of the Targumim, The Talmud Bavli and Yerushalmi, and the Midrashic Literature* (repr. New York, 1950: Pardes Publishing House, Inc.), p. 398.

context, for the general conception of *zekhut*. For the first source of *zekhut* derives from the definition of Israel as family; the entitlements of supernatural power deriving from virtue then are inherited from Abraham, Isaac, and Jacob. The second source is personal: the power one can gain for one's own heirs, moreover, by virtuous deeds. *Zekhut* deriving from either source is to be defined in context: what can you do if you have *zekhut* that you cannot do if you do not have *zekhut*, and to whom can you do it. The answer to that question tells you the empowerment of *zekhut*.

The word *zekhut* has been given the confusing translation of "merit," promiscuously referring to pretty much anything that one gets *not* by one's own merit or just desserts at all, but despite what one has done. Scripture, for example, knows that God loves Israel because he loved the patriarchs (Deut. 4:37); the memory or deeds of the righteous patriarchs and matriarchs appears in a broad range of contexts, for example, "Remember your servants, Abraham, Isaac, and Jacob" (Ex. 32:13), for Moses, and "Remember the good deeds of David, your servant" (2 Chr. 6:42), for David. At stake throughout is giving people what they do not merit, to be sure. But in these contexts, "remembering" what X did as an argument in behalf of favor for Y does not invoke the word *zekhut*, and the context does not require use of that word either.[3] Accordingly, our problem of definition requires limitation to precise usages of a given word. Were we to propose to work our way back from situations that seem to exhibit conceptual affinities to the concept represented by the word under consideration, cases, for instance, in which someone appeals to what is owing the fathers in behalf of the children, we shall not accomplish the goal at hand, which is one of definition of a word that bears a very particular meaning, and, more to the point, carries out a highly critical systemic role.

Zekhut stands for the empowerment, of a supernatural character that derives from the virtue of one's ancestry or from one's own virtuous deeds of a very particular order. No single word in English bears the same meaning, nor can I identify a synonym for *zekhut* in the canonical writings in the original either. The difficulty of translating a word of systemic consequence with a single word in some other language (or in the language of the system's documents themselves) tells us we deal with what is unique, beyond comparison, and therefore beyond contrast and

---

[3]God's "remembering" is the principal point in the scriptural situations adduced as evidence for the ancient origins of the concept of *zekhut*. Then the other part of the same concept, that there are deeds I may do that gain *zekhut* for myself, is excluded, and hence *zekhut* as it is revealed in the systemic sources is not represented in the scriptural ones.

comprehension. A mark that we have found our way to the systemic center is that we cannot easily translate with a single English equivalent the word that identifies what we conceive to define the system's critical tension and generative concept. What is most particular to, distinctive of, the systemic structure and its functioning requires definition through circumlocution, such as, "the heritage of virtue and its consequent entitlements."[4] The word *zekhut* for the successor system forms the systemic counterpart to the mythologoumenon of the resurrection of Jesus Christ, unique son of God, for important Christianities.

A further mark of the systemic importance accorded to *zekhut* is that even though a man was degraded, one action sufficed to win for him that heavenly glory to which rabbis in lives of Torah study aspired. The mark of the system's integration around *zekhut* lies in its insistence that all Israelites, not only sages, could gain *zekhut* for themselves (and their descendants). A single remarkable deed, exemplary for its deep humanity, sufficed to win for an ordinary person the *zekhut* that elicits supernatural favor enjoyed by some rabbis on account of their Torah study. The centrality of *zekhut* in the systemic structure and the critical importance of the heritage of virtue together with its supernatural entitlements therefore emerge in a striking claim. Even though a man was degraded, one action sufficed to win for him that heavenly glory to which rabbis in general aspired.

The rabbinical storyteller to whom we shall listen identifies with this lesson. In all three instances that follow, defining what the individual must do to gain *zekhut*, the point is that the deeds of the heroes of the story make them worthy of having their prayers answered, which is a mark of the working of *zekhut*. It is deeds beyond the strict requirements of the Torah, and even the limits of the law altogether, that transform the hero into a holy man, whose holiness served just like that of a sage marked as such by knowledge of the Torah. The following stories should not be understood as expressions of the mere sentimentality of the clerks concerning the lower orders, for they deny in favor of a single action of surpassing power sages' lifelong devotion to what the sages held to be the highest value, knowledge of the Torah:

---

[4]The commonly used single word, "merit," does not apply, but "merit" bears the sense of reward for carrying out an obligation, for example, by doing such and such, he merited so and so. *Zekhut*, by contrast, commonly refers to acts of supererogatory free will, and therefore while such acts are meritorious in the sense of being virtuous (by definition), they are not acts that one owes but that one gives. And the rewards that accumulate in response to such actions are always miraculous or supernatural or signs of divine grace, for instance, an unusually long life, the power to prevent a dilapidated building from collapsing.

Y. Taanit 1:4

I. F. A certain man came before one of the relatives of R. Yannai. He said to him, "Rabbi, attain *zekhut* through me [by giving me charity]."

G. He said to him, "And didn't your father leave you money?"

H. He said to him, "No."

I. He said to him, "Go and collect what your father left in deposit with others."

J. He said to him, "I have heard concerning property my father deposited with others that it was gained by violence [so I don't want it]."

K. He said to him, "You are worthy of praying and having your prayers answered."

The point of K, of course, is self-evidently a reference to the possession of entitlement to supernatural favor, and it is gained, we see, through deeds that the law of the Torah cannot require but must favor: what one does on one's own volition, beyond the measure of the law. Here I see the opposite of sin. A sin is what one has done by one's own volition beyond all limits of the law. So an act that generates *zekhut* for the individual is the counterpart and opposite: what one does by one's own volition that also is beyond all requirements of the law.

L. A certain ass driver appeared before the rabbis [the context requires: in a dream] and prayed, and rain came. The rabbis sent and brought him and said to him, "What is your trade?"

M. He said to them, "I am an ass driver."

N. They said to him, "And how do you conduct your business?"

O. He said to them, "One time I rented my ass to a certain woman, and she was weeping on the way, and I said to her, 'What's with you?' and she said to me, 'The husband of that woman [me] is in prison [for debt], and I wanted to see what I can do to free him.' So I sold my ass and I gave her the proceeds, and I said to her, 'Here is your money, free your husband, but do not sin [by becoming a prostitute to raise the necessary funds].'"

P. They said to him, "You are worthy of praying and having your prayers answered."

The ass driver clearly has a powerful lien on Heaven, so that his prayers are answered, even while those of others are not. What did he do to get that entitlement? He did what no law could demand: impoverished himself to save the woman from a "fate worse than death."

Q. In a dream of R. Abbahu, Mr. Pentakaka ["Five sins"] appeared, who prayed that rain would come, and it rained. R. Abbahu sent and summoned him. He said to him, "What is your trade?"

R. He said to him, "Five sins does that man [I] do every day, [for I am a pimp:] hiring whores, cleaning up the theater, bringing home their garments for washing, dancing, and performing before them."

S. He said to him, "And what sort of decent thing have you ever done?"

T. He said to him, "One day that man [I] was cleaning the theater, and a woman came and stood behind a pillar and cried. I said to her, 'What's with you?' And she said to me, 'That woman's [my] husband is in prison, and I wanted to see what I can do to free him,' so I sold my bed and cover, and I gave the proceeds to her. I said to her, 'Here is your money, free your husband, but do not sin.'"

U. He said to him, "You are worthy of praying and having your prayers answered."

Q moves us still further, because the named man has done everything sinful that one can do, and, more to the point, he does it every day. So the singularity of the act of *zekhut*, which suffices if done only one time, encompasses its power to outweigh a life of sin – again, an act of *zekhut* as the mirror image and opposite of sin. Here again, the single act of saving a woman from a "fate worse than death" has sufficed.

V. A pious man from Kefar Imi appeared [in a dream] to the rabbis. He prayed for rain and it rained. The rabbis went up to him. His householders told them that he was sitting on a hill. They went out to him, saying to him, "Greetings," but he did not answer them.

W. He was sitting and eating, and he did not say to them, "You break bread too."

X. When he went back home, he made a bundle of faggots and put his cloak on top of the bundle [instead of on his shoulder].

Y. When he came home, he said to his household [wife], "These rabbis are here [because] they want me to pray for rain. If I pray and it rains, it is a disgrace for them, and if not, it is a profanation of the Name of Heaven. But come, you and I will go up [to the roof] and pray. If it rains, we shall tell them, 'We are not worthy to pray and have our prayers answered.'"

Z. They went up and prayed and it rained.

AA. They came down to them [and asked], "Why have the rabbis troubled themselves to come here today?"

BB. They said to him, "We wanted you to pray so that it would rain."

CC. He said to them, "Now do you really need my prayers? Heaven already has done its miracle."

DD. They said to him, "Why, when you were on the hill, did we say hello to you, and you did not reply?"

EE. He said to them, "I was then doing my job. Should I then interrupt my concentration [on my work]?"

FF. They said to him, "And why, when you sat down to eat, did you not say to us, 'You break bread too'?"

GG. He said to them, "Because I had only my small ration of bread. Why would I have invited you to eat by way of mere flattery [when I knew I could not give you anything at all]?"

HH. They said to him, "And why when you came to go down, did you put your cloak on top of the bundle?"

II. He said to them, "Because the cloak was not mine. It was borrowed for use at prayer. I did not want to tear it."

JJ. They said to him, "And why, when you were on the hill, did your wife wear dirty clothes, but when you came down from the mountain, did she put on clean clothes?"

KK. He said to them, "When I was on the hill, she put on dirty clothes, so that no one would gaze at her. But when I came home from the hill, she put on clean clothes, so that I would not gaze on any other woman."

LL. They said to him, "It is well that you pray and have your prayers answered."

The pious man of V, finally, enjoys the recognition of the sages by reason of his lien upon Heaven, able as he is to pray and bring rain. What has so endowed him with *zekhut*? Acts of punctiliousness of a moral order: concentrating on his work, avoiding an act of dissimulation, integrity in the disposition of a borrowed object, his wife's concern not to attract other men and her equal concern to make herself attractive to her husband. None of these stories refers explicitly to *zekhut*; all of them tell us about what it means to enjoy not an entitlement by inheritance but a lien accomplished by one's own supererogatory acts of restraint.

In its integrating power, *zekhut* integrates what has been differentiated. *Zekhut* here serves to hold together learning, virtue, and supernatural standing, by explaining how Torah study transforms the learning man. The Mishnah's focus upon hierarchical classification, with its demonstration of the upward-reaching unity of all being, gives way to a different, and more compelling proposition: the unity of all being within the heritage of *zekhut*, to be attained equally and without differentiation in all the principal parts of the social order. The definition of *zekhut* therefore carries us to the heart of the integrating and integrated religious system of Judaism.

What we shall now see is that *zekhut*, an entirely available idea, had been systemically tangential to the philosophical Judaism, and only now – in the Talmud of the Land of Israel and related writings – proved itself systemically critical. That fact will accomplish the twin tasks facing anyone who claims to describe the connections between two historically related systems, represented by a single canon. Specifically, showing that *zekhut* was both available and systemically inert will both prove the connectedness of the two systems, and also show how the successor system transformed the first. That is to say, the system builders represented by the Talmud of the Land of Israel, Genesis Rabbah, Leviticus Rabbah, and Pesiqta deRab Kahana made their own choices within their inheritance. Their system consequently defined its own categories and accomplished through its own medium the integration of its systemic components, the counterpart categories.[5]

At M. San. 4:1, 5:4, 5:5, and 6:1 we find *zekhut* in the sense of "acquittal," as against conviction; at M. Ket. 13:6 the sense is, "right," as in "right of ownership;" at M. Git. 8:8 the sense is not "right of ownership" in a narrow sense, but "advantage," in a broader one of prerogative: "It is not within the power of the first husband to render void the right of the second." These usages of course bear no point in common with the sense of the word later on. But the evidence of the Mishnah seems to me to demonstrate that the sense of *zekhut* paramount in the successor documents is not original to them. The following usage at M. Qid. 4:14 seems to me to invite something very like the sense that I have proposed here. So states M. Qid. 4:14E-I:

> R. Meir says, "A man should always teach his son a clean and easy trade. And let him pray to him to whom belong riches and possessions. For there is no trade which does not involve poverty or wealth. For poverty does not come from one's trade, nor does wealth come from one's trade. But all is in accord with a man's *zekhut*."

Quite how to translate our keyword in this passage is not self-evident. The context permits a variety of possibilities. The same usage seems to me to be located at M. Sot. 3:4, 3:5, and here there is clear indication of the presence of a conception of an entitlement deriving from some source other than one's own deed of the moment:

Mishnah-tractate Sotah 3:4

E.   There is the possibility that *zekhut* suspends the curse for one year, and there is the possibility that *zekhut* suspends the curse for two years, and there is the possibility that *zekhut* suspends the curse for three years.

F.   On this basis Ben Azzai says, "A man is required to teach Torah to his daughter.

G.   "For if she should drink the water, she should know that [if nothing happens to her], *zekhut* is what suspends [the curse from taking effect]."

---

[5]In my *Judaism: The Evidence of the Mishnah*, pp. 230-286, I have asked and answered in terms of the power of intentionality as the medium of classification the question of what holds the system together, and in the counterpart study of the philosophical system of Judaism attested by the Mishnah, *The Mishnah as Philosophy*, I have identified the integrating and generative problematic, that of hierarchical classification. These two answers seem to me cogent with one another, even though the one appeals to psychological, the other to philosophical considerations.

Mishnah-tractate Sotah 3:4

A   R. Simeon says, "*Zekhut* does not suspend the effects of the bitter water.

B   "And if you say, '*Zekhut* does suspend the effects of the bitter water,' you will weaken the effect of the water for all the women who have to drink it.

C   "And you give a bad name to all the women who drink it who turned out to be pure.

D   "For people will say, 'They are unclean, but *zekhut* suspended the effects of the water for them.'"

E   Rabbi says, "*Zekhut* does suspend the effects of the bitter water. But she will not bear children or continue to be pretty. And she will waste away, and in the end she will have the same [unpleasant] death."

Now if we insert for *zekhut* at each point, "the heritage of virtue and its consequent entitlements" (thus: "For people will say, 'They are unclean, but *zekhut* suspended the effects of the water for them,'" then, "For people will say, 'They are unclean, but the heritage of virtue and its consequent entitlements suspended the effects of the water for them'"), we have good sense. That is to say, the woman may not suffer the penalty to which she is presumably condemnable, not because her act or condition (for example, her innocence) has secured her acquittal or nullified the effects of the ordeal, but because she enjoys some advantage extrinsic to her own act or condition. She may be guilty, but she may also possess a benefice deriving by inheritance, hence, heritage of virtue, and so be entitled to a protection not because of her own, but because of someone else's action or condition.

That meaning may be sustained by the passage at hand, even though it is not required by it; still, it seems to me plausible that the word *zekhut* in the Mishnah bears not only a juridical but a religious sense. But, if, as I think, it does, that usage is not systemically critical, or even very important. If we search the pages of the Mishnah for places in which, absent the word *zekhut*, the conception at hand is present, we find none – not one. For example, there simply is no reference to gaining *zekhut* through doing one's duty, for example, in reciting the *Shema* or studying the Torah, and references to studying the Torah, for instance, at M. Peah 1:1, do not encompass the conception that, in doing so, one gains an advantage or entitlement for either one's own descendants or for all Israel. On that basis we are on firm ground in holding the twin positions [1] that the word bore, among its meanings, the one important later on, and also [2] that the word played no systemic role, in the philosophical system adumbrated by the Mishnah, commensurate with the importance accorded to the word and its sense in the religious system that took shape and came to expression in the successor writings.[6]

The evidence of tractate Abot is consistent with that of the Mishnah. The juridical sense of zekhut occurs at 1:6, "Judge everybody as though to be acquitted," more comprehensibly translated, "And give everybody the benefit of the doubt," forming a reasonably coherent fit with the usages important in Mishnah-tractate Sanhedrin. In Abot, however, we have clear evidence for the sense of the word that seems to me demanded later on. At M. Abot 2:2 we find the following:

Tractate Abot 2:2

C. "And all who work with the community – let them work with them for the sake of Heaven.

D. "For the [1] zekhut of their fathers strengthens them, and their [fathers'] [2] righteousness stands forever.

E. "And as for you, I credit you with a great reward, as if you had done [all of the work required by the community on your own merit alone]."

Here there is no meaning possible other than that I have given above: "the heritage of virtue and its consequent entitlements." The reference to an advantage that one gains by reason of inheritance out of one's fathers' righteousness is demanded by the parallel between zekhut of clause [1] and righteousness of clause [2]. Whatever the conceivable ambiguity of the Mishnah, none is sustained by the context at hand, which is explicit in language and pellucid in message. That the sense is exactly the same as the one I have proposed is shown at the following passages, which seem to me to exhibit none of the possible ambiguity that characterized the usage of zekhut in the Mishnah:

Tractate Abot 5:18

A. He who causes zekhut to the community never causes sin.

---

[6]A rapid review of the Tosefta's usages of the word zekhut suffices, since there are no surprises. Juridical usages are at these passages: T. Git. 1:5 (zekhut in the sense of an advantage or a benefit); Sanhedrin 1:8, 3:3, 9:1, 2, 3, 4, 10:11; T. Qid. 1:13. An indeterminate sense of zekhut in the sense of "advantage" or "entitlement," without a clear definition of what one must do or why one gains a benefit therefrom, is at T. Pe. 1:2, T. Yoma 5:12=T. Ta. 4:9 (zekhut in contrast to disadvantage or liability, conceivably a juridical usage). The sense, "by reason of the claim..." or "the entitlement of..." seems to me justified in context at T. M.S. 5:27, 29, T. Sot. 11:10, and T. B.B. 7:9. Overall, I do not find here anything as decisive as what we see in tractate Abot, though the case may be made that some of the Tosefta's passages use the word in the same sense as is revealed in that tractate. In the balance, nonetheless, I judge that a full-scale review of Tosefta's usages would not greatly change the results just now given for the Mishnah.

B. And he who causes the community to sin – they never give him a sufficient chance to attain penitence.

Here the contrast is between causing *zekhut* and causing sin, so *zekhut* is the opposite of sin. The continuation is equally clear that a person attained *zekhut* and endowed the community with *zekhut*, or sinned and made the community sin:

C. Moses attained *zekhut* and bestowed *zekhut* on the community.
D. So the *zekhut* of the community is assigned to his [credit],
E. as it is said, "He executed the justice of the Lord and his judgments with Israel" (Deut. 33:21).
F. Jeroboam sinned and caused the community to sin.
G. So the sin of the community is assigned to his [debit],
H as it is said, "For the sins of Jeroboam which he committed and wherewith he made Israel to sin" (1 Kgs. 15:30).

The appropriateness of interpreting the passage in the way I have proposed will now be shown to be self-evident. All that is required is to substitute for *zekhut* the proposed translation:

C. Moses attained the heritage of virtue and bestowed its consequent entitlements on the community.
D. So the heritage of virtue and its entitlements enjoyed by the community are assigned to his [credit],

The sense then is simple. Moses through actions of his own (of an unspecified sort) acquired *zekhut*, which is the credit for such actions that accrued to him and bestowed upon him certain supernatural entitlements; and he for his part passed on as an inheritance that credit, a lien on Heaven for the performance of these same supernatural entitlements: *zekhut*, pure and simple.

If we may now define *zekhut* as the initial system explicated in tractate Abot has used the word, we must pay close attention to the antonymic structure before us. The juridical opposites are guilty as against innocent, the religious ones, as we have now seen, sin as against the opposite of sin. That seems to me to require our interpreting *zekhut* as [1] an action, as distinct from a (mere) attitude; that [2] is precisely the opposite of a sinful one; it is, moreover, an action that [3] may be done by an individual or by the community at large, and one that [4] a leader may provoke the community to do (or not do). The contrast of sin to *zekhut* requires further attention. Since, in general, two classes that are compared to begin with, if different, must constitute opposites, the ultimate definition of *zekhut* requires us to ask how *zekhut* is precisely the opposite of sin. For one thing, as we recall, Scripture is explicit that the burden of sins cannot be passively inherited, willy-nilly, but, to form a heritage of guilt, must be actively accepted and renewed; the children cannot be made to suffer for the sins of the parents, unless they repeat them. Then *zekhut*, being a mirror image, can be passively inherited, not by one's own merit[7] but by one's good fortune alone. But what constitute these *actions* that form mirror images of sins? Answers to that critical question must emerge from the systemic documents before us, since they do not occur in those of the initial system.

That simple fact, too, attests to the systemic centrality of *zekhut*: it defines a principal point of exegesis. For the question left open by the Mishnah's merely episodic, and somewhat opaque, reference to the matter and the incomplete evidence provided by its principal apologetic's representation as well, alas, is the critical issue. Precisely what actions generate *zekhut*, and which ones do not? To find answers to those questions, we have to turn to the successor documents, since not a single passage in the Mishnah or in tractate Abot provides me with information on the matter of what I must do to secure for myself or my descendents a lien upon Heaven, that is, an entitlement to supernatural favor and even action of a miraculous order.

We turn first to the conception of the *zekhut* that has been accumulated by the patriarchs and been passed on to Israel, their children. The reason is that the single distinctive trait of *zekhut*, as we have seen it to this point, is its transitive quality: one need not earn or merit the supernatural power and resource represented by the things you can do if you have *zekhut* but cannot do if you do not have it. One can inherit that entitlement from others, dead or living. Moses not only attains *zekhut* but he also imparts *zekhut* to the community of which he is leader, and the same is so for any Israelite. That conception is broadened in the successor documents into the deeply historical notion of *zekhut avot*, empowerment of a supernatural character to which Israel is entitled by reason of what the patriarchs and matriarchs in particular did long ago. That conception forms the foundation for the paramount sense of

---

[7]Indeed, the conception of "merit" is so alien to the concept of *zekhut*, which one enjoys whether or not one personally has done something to merit it, that I am puzzled on how "merit" ever seemed to anyone to serve as a translation of the word *zekhut*. If I can inherit the entitlements accrued by my ancestors, then these entitlements not only cannot be classed as merited (by me), they must be classed as a heritage bestowed by others and not merited by me at all. And, along these same lines, the *zekhut* that I gain for myself may entitle me to certain benefits, but it may also accrue to the advantage of the community in which I live (as is made explicit by Abot for Moses' *zekhut*) and also of my descendants. The transitive character of *zekhut*, the power we have of receiving it from others and handing it on to others, serves as the distinctive trait of this particular entitlement, and, it must follow from that definitive characteristic, *zekhut* is the opposite of merit, as I said, and its character is obscured by the confusion created through that long-standing and conventional, but wrong translation of the word.

zekhut in the successor system: the Israel possesses a lien upon Heaven by reason of God's love for the patriarchs and matriarchs, his appreciation for certain things they did, and his response to those actions not only in favoring them but also in entitling their descendants to do or benefit from otherwise unattainable miracles. *Zekhut*, as we noted earlier, explains the present – particularly what is odd and unpredictable in the present – by appeal to the past, and hence forms a distinctively historical conception.

Within the historically grounded metaphor of Israel as a family expressed by the conception of *zekhut avot*, Israel was a family, the children of Abraham, Isaac, and Jacob, or children of Israel, in a concrete and genealogical sense. Israel hence fell into the genus, family, as the particular species of family generated by Abraham and Sarah. The distinguishing trait of that species was that it possessed the inheritance, or heritage, of the patriarchs and matriarchs, and that inheritance, consisting of *zekhut*, served the descendants and heirs as protection and support. It follows that the systemic position of the conception of *zekhut* to begin with lies in its power to define the social entity, and hence, *zekhut* (in the terms of the initial category formation, the philosophical one) forms a fundamentally political conception[8] and only secondarily an economic and philosophical one.

But *zekhut* serves, in particular, that counterpart category that speaks of not legitimate but illegitimate violence, not power but weakness. *Zekhut* is the power of the weak. People who through their own merit and capacity can accomplish nothing, but through what others do for them in leaving a heritage of *zekhut*, or have done for them, can accomplish miracles. And, not to miss the stunning message of the triplet of stories cited above, *zekhut* also is what the weak and excluded and despised can do that outweighs in power what the great masters of the Torah have accomplished. In the context of a system that represents Torah as supernatural, that claim of priority for *zekhut* represents a

---

[8]And that political definition of the systemic role and function of *zekhut* is strengthened by the polemical power of the concept vis-à-vis the Christian critique of Israel after the flesh. The doctrine of the *zekhut* of the ancestors served as a component of the powerful polemic concerning Israel. Specifically, that concrete, historical Israel, meaning for Christian theologians "Israel after the flesh," in the literature before us manifestly and explicitly claimed fleshly origin in Abraham and Sarah. The extended family indeed constituted precisely what the Christian theologians said: an Israel after the flesh, a family linked by genealogy. The heritage then became an inheritance, and what was inherited from the ancestors was a heavenly store, a treasure of *zekhut*, which protected the descendants when their own *zekhut* proved insufficient. The conflict is a political one, involving the legitimacy of the power of the now-Christian empire, denied by this "Israel," affirmed by the other one.

considerable transvaluation of power, as much as of value. And, by the way, *zekhut* also forms the inheritance of the disinherited: what you receive as a heritage when you have nothing in the present and have gotten nothing in the past, that scarce resource that is free and unearned but much valued. So let us dwell upon the definitive character of the transferability of *zekhut* in its formulation, *zekhut abot*, the *zekhut* handed on by the ancestors, the transitive character of the concept and its standing as a heritage of entitlements.

It is in the successor documents that the concept of *zekhut* is joined with *avot*, referring to the patriarchs (rarely, also the matriarchs), that is, the *zekhut* that has been left as Israel's family inheritance by the patriarchs or ancestors, yielding the very specific notion, defining the systemic politics, its theory of the social entity, of Israel not as a (mere) community (for example, as in tractate Abot's reference to Moses's bestowing *zekhut* upon the community) but as a family, with a history that takes the form of a genealogy, precisely as Genesis has represented that history.[9] Now *zekhut* was joined to the metaphor of the genealogy of patriarchs and matriarchs and served to form the missing link, explaining how the inheritance and heritage were transmitted from them to their heirs. Consequently, the family, called "Israel," could draw upon the family estate, consisting of the inherited *zekhut* of matriarchs and patriarchs in such a way as to benefit today from the heritage of yesterday. This notion involved very concrete problems. If "Israel, the family" sinned, it could call upon the "*zekhut*" accumulated by Abraham and Isaac at the binding of Isaac (Genesis 22) to win forgiveness for that sin. True, "fathers will not die on account of the sin of the sons," but the children may benefit from the *zekhut* of the forebears. That concrete expression of the larger metaphor imparted to the metaphor a practical consequence, moral and theological, that was not at all neglected.

A survey of Genesis Rabbah proves indicative of the character and use of the doctrine of *zekhut* because that systematic reading of the book of Genesis dealt with the founders of the family and made explicit the definition of Israel as family. What we shall see is that *zekhut* draws in its wake the notion of the inheritance of an ongoing (historical) family, that of Abraham and Sarah, and *zekhut* worked itself out in the moments of

---

[9]And it is by no means an accident, therefore, that Genesis was one of the two pentateuchal books selected by the system builders for their Midrash exegesis. The systemic centrality of *zekhut* accounts for their selection. In my *Judaism and Scripture*, pp. 94-125, I have accounted for the selection of the book of Leviticus, an explanation that accords in a striking way with the one pertaining to Genesis. That means that any system analysis must explain why one scriptural book, and not some other, has been chosen for the Midrash compilation(s) that that system sets forth alongside its Mishnah amplification.

crisis of that family in its larger affairs. So the Israelites later on enjoy enormous *zekhut* through the deeds of the patriarchs and matriarchs. That conception comes to expression in what follows:

Genesis Rabbah LXXVI

V.2 A "...for with only my staff I crossed this Jordan, and now I have become two companies":

B. R. Judah bar Simon in the name of R. Yohanan: "In the Torah, in the Prophets, and in the Writings we find proof that the Israelites were able to cross the Jordan only on account of the *zekhut* achieved by Jacob:

C. "In the Torah: '...for with only my staff I crossed this Jordan, and now I have become two companies.'

D. "In the prophets: 'Then you shall let your children know, saying, "Israel came over this Jordan on dry land"' (Josh. 4:22), meaning our father, Israel.

E. "In the Writings: 'What ails you, O you sea, that you flee? You Jordan, that you burn backward? At the presence of the God of Jacob' (Ps. 114:5ff.)."

Here is a perfect illustration of my definition of *zekhut* as an entitlement I enjoy by reason of what someone else – an ancestor – has done; and that entitlement involves supernatural power. Jacob did not only leave *zekhut* as an estate to his heirs. The process is reciprocal and ongoing. *Zekhut* deriving from the ancestors had helped Jacob himself:

Genesis Rabbah LXXVII

III.3 A "When the man saw that he did not prevail against Jacob, [he touched the hollow of his thigh, and Jacob's thigh was put out of joint as he wrestled with him]" (Gen. 32:25):

B. Said R. Hinena bar Isaac, "[God said to the angel,] 'He is coming against you with five "amulets" hung on his neck, that is, his own *zekhut*, the *zekhut* of his father and of his mother and of his grandfather and of his grandmother.

C. "'Check yourself out, can you stand up against even his own *zekhut* [let alone the *zekhut* of his parents and grandparents].'

D. "The matter may be compared to a king who had a savage dog and a tame lion. The king would take his son and sick him against the lion, and if the dog came to have a fight with the son, he would say to the dog, 'The lion cannot have a fight with him, are you going to make out in a fight with him?'

E. "So if the nations come to have a fight with Israel, the Holy One, blessed be He, says to them, 'Your angelic prince could not stand up to Israel, and as to you, how much the more so!'"

The collectivity of *zekhut*, not only its transferability, is illustrated here as well: what an individual does confers *zekhut* on the social entity. It is, moreover, a matter of the legitimate exercise of supernatural power. And the reciprocity of the process extended in all directions.

Accordingly, what we have in hand is first and foremost a matter of the exercise of legitimate violence, hence a political power. The conception of the *zekhut* of the patriarchs is explicit, not general. It specifies what later benefit to the heir, Israel the family, derived from which particular action of a patriarch or matriarch.

Genesis Rabbah XLIII

VIII.2 A. "And Abram gave him a tenth of everything" (Gen. 14:20):

B. R. Judah in the name of R. Nehorai: "On the strength of that blessing the three great pegs on which the world depends, Abraham, Isaac, and Jacob, derived sustenance.

C. "Abraham: 'And the Lord blessed Abraham in *all* things' (Gen. 24:1) on account of the *zekhut* that 'he gave him a tenth of *all* things' (Gen. 14:20).

D. "Isaac: 'And I have eaten of *all*' (Gen. 27:33), on account of the *zekhut* that 'he gave him a tenth of *all* things' (Gen. 14:20).

E. "Jacob: 'Because God has dealt graciously with me and because I have all' (Gen. 33:11) on account of the *zekhut* that 'he gave him a tenth of *all* things' (Gen. 14:20).

Genesis Rabbah XLIII

VIII.3 A. Whence did Israel gain the *zekhut* of receiving the blessing of the priests?

B. R. Judah said, "It was from Abraham: '*So* shall your seed be' (Gen. 15:5), while it is written in connection with the priestly blessing: '*So* shall you bless the children of Israel' (Num. 6:23)."

C. R. Nehemiah said, "It was from Isaac: 'And I and the lad will go *so* far' (Gen. 22:5), therefore said the Holy One, blessed be He, '*So* shall you bless the children of Israel' (Num. 6:23)."

D. And rabbis say, "It was from Jacob: '*So* shall you say to the house of Jacob' (Ex. 19:3) (in line with the statement, '*So* shall you bless the children of Israel' (Num. 6:23)."

No. 2 links the blessing at hand with the history of Israel. Now the reference is to the word "all," which joins the tithe of Abram to the blessing of his descendants. Since the blessing of the priest is at hand, No. 3 treats the origins of the blessing. The picture is clear. "Israel" constitutes a family as a genealogical and juridical fact. It inherits the estate of the ancestors. It hands on that estate. It lives by the example of the matriarchs and patriarchs, and its history exemplifies events in their lives. And *zekhut* forms that entitlement that one generation may transmit to the next, in a way in which the heritage of sin is not to be transmitted except by reason of the deeds of the successor generation. The good that one does lives onward, the evil is interred with the bones.

To conclude this brief survey of how the systemic writings express the concept of *zekhut* as the medium of historical existence, that is, the *zekhut* deriving from the patriarchs or *zekhut abot*, let me present a statement of the legitimate power – sufficient to achieve salvation, which, in this context, always bears a political dimension, of imparted by the *zekhut* of the ancestors. That *zekhut* will enable them to accomplish the political goals of Israel: its attaining self-rule and avoiding government by gentiles. This statement appeals to the binding of Isaac as the source of the *zekhut*, deriving from the patriarchs and matriarchs, which will in the end lead to the salvation of Israel. What is important here is that the *zekhut* that is inherited joins together with the *zekhut* of one's own deeds; one inherits the *zekhut* of the past, and, moreover, if one does what the progenitors did, one not only receives an entitlement out of the past, one secures an entitlement on one's own account. So the difference between *zekhut* and sin lies in the sole issue of transmissibility:

Genesis Rabbah LVI

II.5 A Said R. Isaac, "And all was on account of the *zekhut* attained by the act of prostration.

B "Abraham returned in peace from Mount Moriah only on account of the *zekhut* owing to the act of prostration: '...and we will worship [through an act of prostration] and come [then, on that account] again to you' (Gen. 22:5).

C "The Israelites were redeemed only on account of the *zekhut* owing to the act of prostration: And the people believed...then they bowed their heads and prostrated themselves' (Ex. 4:31).

D "The Torah was given only on account of the *zekhut* owing to the act of prostration: 'And worship [prostrate themselves] you afar off' (Ex. 24:1).

E "Hannah was remembered only on account of the *zekhut* owing to the act of prostration: 'And they worshipped before the Lord' (1 Sam. 1:19).

F. "The exiles will be brought back only on account of the *zekhut* owing to the act of prostration: 'And it shall come to pass in that day that a great horn shall be blown and they shall come that were lost...and that were dispersed...and they shall worship the Lord in the holy mountain at Jerusalem' (Isa. 27:13).

G "The Temple was built only on account of the *zekhut* owing to the act of prostration: 'Exalt you the Lord our God and worship at his holy hill' (Ps. 99:9).

H "The dead will live only on account of the *zekhut* owing to the act of prostration: 'Come let us worship and bend the knee, let us kneel before the Lord our maker' (Ps. 95:6)."

The entire history of Israel flows from its acts of worship ("prostration") beginning with that performed by Abraham at the binding of Isaac. Every sort of advantage Israel has ever gained came about through that act of worship done by Abraham and imitated thereafter. Israel constitutes a family and inherits the *zekhut* laid up as a treasure for the descendants by the ancestors. It draws upon that *zekhut* but, by doing the deeds they did, it also enhances its heritage of *zekhut* and leaves to the descendants greater entitlement than they would enjoy by reason of their own actions. But their own actions – here, prostration in worship – generate *zekhut* as well.

Accordingly, as I claimed at the outset, *zekhut* may be personal or inherited. The *zekhut* deriving from the prior generations is collective and affects all Israel. But one's own deeds can generate *zekhut* for oneself, with the simple result that *zekhut* is as much personal as it is collective. Specifically, Jacob reflects on the power that Esau's own *zekhut* had gained for Esau. He had gained that *zekhut* by living in the Land of Israel and also by paying honor and respect to Isaac. Jacob then feared that, because of the *zekhut* gained by Esau, he, Jacob, would not be able to overcome him. So *zekhut* worked on its own; it was a credit gained by proper action, which went to the credit of the person who had done that action. What made the action worthy of evoking Heaven's response with an act of supernatural favor is that it was an action not to be required but if done to be rewarded, an act of will that cannot be coerced but must be honored.

For if we now ask, what are the sorts of deeds that generate *zekhut*, we realize that those deeds produce a common result of gaining for their doer, as much as for the heirs of the actor, an entitlement for Heavenly favor and support when needed. And that fact concerning gaining and benefiting from *zekhut* brings us to the systemic message to the living generation, its account of what now is to be done. And that message proves acutely contemporary, for its stress is on the power of a single action to create sufficient *zekhut* to outweigh a life of sin. Then the contrast between sin and *zekhut* gains greater depth still. One sin of sufficient weight condemns, one act of *zekhut* of sufficient weight saves; the entire issue of entitlements out of the past gives way, then, when we realize what is actually at stake.

We recall that Torah study is one – but only one – means for an individual to gain access to that heritage, to get *zekhut*. There are other equally suitable means, and, not only so, but the merit gained by Torah study is no different from the merit gained by acts of a supererogatory character. If one gets *zekhut* for studying the Torah, then we must suppose there is no holy deed that does not generate its share of *zekhut*. But when it comes to specifying the things one does to get *zekhut*, the documents before us speak of what the Torah does not require but does recommend: not what we are commanded to do in detail, but what the right attitude, formed within the Torah, leads us to do on our own volition:

Y. Taanit 3:11

IV. C.   There was a house that was about to collapse over there [in Babylonia], and Rab set one of his disciples in the house, until they had cleared out everything from the house. When the disciple left the house, the house collapsed.

D.   And there are those who say that it was R. Adda bar Ahbah.

E.   Sages sent and said to him, "What sort of good deeds are to your credit [that you have that much merit]?"

F.   He said to them, "In my whole life no man ever got to the synagogue in the morning before I did. I never left anybody there when I went out. I never walked four cubits without speaking words of Torah. Nor did I ever mention teachings of Torah in an inappropriate setting. I never laid out a bed and slept for a regular period of time. I never took great strides among the associates. I never called my fellow by a nickname. I never rejoiced in the embarrassment of my fellow. I never cursed my fellow when I was lying by myself in bed. I never walked over in the marketplace to someone who owed me money.

G.   "In my entire life I never lost my temper in my household."

H.   This was meant to carry out that which is stated as follows: "I will give heed to the way that is blameless. Oh when wilt thou come to me? I will walk with integrity of heart within my house" (Ps. 101:2).

What I find striking in this story is that mastery of the Torah is only one means of attaining the merit that enabled the sage to keep the house from collapsing. The question at E provides the key, together with its answer at F.

For what the sage did to gain such remarkable merit is not to master such-and-so many tractates of the Mishnah. Nor does the storyteller refer to carrying out the commandments of the Torah as specified. It was rather acts of that expressed courtesy, consideration, restraint. These acts, which no specification can encompass in detail, produced the right attitude, one of gentility, that led to gaining merit. Acts rewarded with an entitlement to supernatural power are self-abnegation or the avoidance of power over others – not taking great strides among the associates, not using a nickname, not rejoicing in the embarrassment of one's fellow, not singling out one's debtor – and the submission to the will and the requirement of self-esteem of others.

Here, in a moral setting, we find the politics replicated: the form of power that the system promises derives from the rejection of power that the world recognizes – legitimate violence replaced by legitimation of the absence of the power to commit violence or of the failure to commit violence. Not exercising power over others, that is, the counterpart politics, moreover, produced that scarcest of all resources, supernatural favor, by which the holy man could hold up a tottering building. Here, then, we find politics and economics united in the counterpart category formed of *zekhut*: the absence of power yielding supernatural power, the valuation of the intangible, Torah, yielding supernatural power. It was, then, that entitlement to supernatural favor that formed the systemic center.

The system through *zekhut* speaks to everybody, Jew and gentile, past and present and future; *zekhut* therefore defines the structure of the cosmic social order and explains how it is supposed to function. It is the encompassing quality of *zekhut*, its pertinence to past and future, high and low, rich and poor, gifted and ordinary, that marks as the systemic statement the message of *zekhut*, now fully revealed as the conception of reciprocal response between Heaven and Israel on earth, to acts of devotion beyond the requirements of the Torah but defined all the same by the Torah. As Scripture had said, God responds to the faith of the ancient generations by supernatural acts to which, on their own account, the moderns are not entitled, hence a heritage of entitlement. But those acts, now fully defined for us, can and ought to be done, also, by the living generation, and, as a matter of fact, there is none today, at the time of the system builders, exempt from the systemic message and its demands: even steadfastness in accomplishing the humble work of the everyday and the here and now.

The systemic statement made by the usages of *zekhut* speaks of relationship, function, the interplay of humanity and God. One's store of *zekhut* derives from a relationship, that is, from one's forebears. That is one dimension of the relationships in which one stands. *Zekhut* also forms a measure of one's own relationship with Heaven, as the power of one person, but not another, to pray and so bring rain attests. What sort of relationship does *zekhut*, as the opposite of sin, then posit? It is not one of coercion, for Heaven cannot force us to do those types of deeds that yield *zekhut*, and that, story after story suggests, is the definition of a deed that generates *zekhut*: doing what we ought to do but do not have to do. But then, we cannot coerce Heaven to do what we want done either, for example, by carrying out the commandments. These are obligatory, but do not obligate Heaven.

Whence, then, our lien on Heaven? It is through deeds of a supererogatory character – to which Heaven responds by deeds of a supererogatory character: supernatural favor to this one, who through deeds of ingratiation of the other or self-abnegation or restraint exhibits the attitude that in Heaven precipitates a counterpart attitude, hence generating *zekhut*, rather than to that one, who does not. The simple fact that rabbis cannot pray and bring rain, but a simple ass driver can, tells the whole story. The relationship measured by *zekhut* – Heaven's response by an act of uncoerced favor to a person's uncoerced gift, for example, act of gentility, restraint, or self-abnegation – contains an element of unpredictability for which appeal to the *zekhut* inherited from ancestors accounts. So while I cannot coerce Heaven, I can through *zekhut* gain acts of favor from Heaven, and that is by doing what Heaven cannot require of me. Heaven then responds to my attitude in carrying out my duties – and more than my duties. That act of pure disinterest – giving the woman my means of livelihood – is the one that gains for me Heaven's deepest interest.

So *zekhut* forms the political economy of the religious system of the social order put forward by the Talmud of the Land of Israel, Genesis Rabbah, Leviticus Rabbah, and related writings. Here we find the power that brought about the transvaluation of value, the reversal of the meaning of power and its legitimacy. *Zekhut* expresses and accounts for the economic valuation of the scarce resource of what we should call moral authority. *Zekhut* stands for the political valorization of weakness, that which endows the weak with a power that is not only their own but their ancestors'. It enables the weak to accomplish goals through not their own power, but their very incapacity to accomplish acts of violence – a transvaluation as radical as that effected in economics. And *zekhut* holds together both the economics and the politics of this Judaism: it makes the same statement twice.

7

The Two Vocabularies of Symbolic Discourse in Judaism

In some of the canonical writings of the Judaism of the Dual Torah we find lists of different things joined with the words, "another matter." These different things cohere in two ways. First, all of them address the same verse of Scripture. Second, each of these other matters in its way proves to make the same statement as all the others. Appeal is made to what we shall see is a standard and fixed repertoire of things – events, named persons, objects or actions or attitudes. As these things combine and recombine, a thing appearing here next to one thing, there next to another, they appear to serve, as words serve, to make statements. Strung out in one selection of the larger vocabulary of symbols, they then say this, and in another set of choices made out of the same larger repertoire, they say that. How do people know which things to choose for which statement? Why combine this with that? These are the questions I bring to the examination of the numerous sets of "another matter" composites, scattered throughout the canonical literature. Along these same lines a restricted repertoire of persons, events, and objects is portrayed in synagogue art, mosaics, frescoes, carvings, and the like. Were we to compose a list of things that might have been chosen, it would prove many times longer than the list of things that in fact were selected and represented by the synagogue artists. Do these, too, make a statement, and if they do, how are we to discern what it is?[1]

---

[1] I review the findings of my *Symbol and Theology in Judaism* (Minneapolis, 1991: Fortress Press).

I. One Symbolic Language or Two?

In asking the literary and artistic evidence to tell us about shared convictions of a common Judaism attested for in late antiquity in both written and iconic representation, how are we to proceed? It is, first, by identifying the sort of evidence that serves. We limit our analysis to this public and official evidence: in literature, what anonymous, therefore genuine, authorities accepted as the implicit message of canonical and normative writings, on the one hand, in art, what synagogue communities accepted as the tacit message of the symbols in the presence of which they addressed God, on the other. Excluded then are expressions deriving from individuals, for example, letters or private writings, ossuaries and sarcophagi, which can have spoken for everyone, but assuredly spoke only for one person.

Second, within public evidence, what do we identify as potential evidence for a shared vocabulary, common to evidence in both media, written and iconic, and shared among all sponsors – artists and patrons, authors, authorships, and authorities of canonical collections alike? The answer must be, the evidence provided by symbolic discourse, which is the only kind of discourse that can be shared between iconic and literary expressions. By definition, iconic evidence does not utilize the verbal medium, and, it goes without saying, our documents are not illustrated and never were. But the two bodies of publicly accepted and therefore authoritative evidence on the symbolic structure of Judaism deliver their messages in the same way. So constant reference to a set of what we must classify as not facts but symbols will turn up evidence for a shared vocabulary.

We wish to bring the restricted iconic vocabulary of the synagogue into juxtaposition, for purposes of comparison and contrast, with that of the canonical books. What we want to know is first, whether the same symbols occur in both media of expression, literary and artistic. Second, we ask whether the same messages are set forth in the two media, or whether the one medium bears one message, the other a different message. If, as I claim, symbolic discourse in the fifth and sixth centuries took place in Judaic expression in both synagogues and among sages, the one in iconic, the other in written form, we naturally wonder whether the symbols were the same, and whether the discourse was uniform. To frame the question in simple terms: were the same people saying the same things in different media, verbal and iconic, or were different people saying different things in different media? At the present, elementary stage in our reading of the symbolic discourse, we cannot expect to reach a final answer to that question. But the outlines of an answer even now will emerge when we compare the symbolic language of synagogue iconography with the symbolic language framed in verbal terms in the rabbinic Midrash compilations.

Effecting that comparison, of course, requires us to frame in the same medium the two sets of symbols. But which medium – the visual (in our imagination at least) or the verbal? If it is to be the verbal, then we have to put into words the symbolic discourse portrayed for us on the walls and floors of synagogues. That is to say, we have to set forth in a manner parallel to symbolic discourse in words the symbols of the *etrog* and *lulab*, *shofar*, and *menorah*. And we have to do so in accord with the rhetoric forms that sustain symbolic discourse in verbal media. But by definition that cannot be done. First, symbolic discourse in verbal form requires us to identify and parse a verse of Scripture. But which verse for the items at hand? Second, we should require a clear notion of the meanings of the iconic symbols. But among the possible meanings, for example, for the *shofar* – the New Year and Day of Atonement, Abraham binding Isaac on the altar, the coming of the Messiah, Moriah and the Temple – which are we to choose? And, third, since the symbolic discourse in iconic form obviously joins the *etrog* and *lulab*, *shofar*, and *menorah*, translating the three (or four) into words demands a theory about what those symbols mean when they are joined in order, arrangement, and context. What do the symbols mean together that they do not mean when apart? The key is why certain combinations yield meaning, others, gibberish (Moses and Sennacherib on the same list, for example). Since we do not have that key for symbolic discourse in iconic form, we had best consider the alternative.

Since we cannot meet any one of those three conditions, we take the other road, which is open. That is, we must proceed to translate into visual images (in our imagination) the symbols in verbal form that we have. Here, by definition, we have access to the context defined by a parsed verse of Scripture. We have a fairly explicit statement of the meanings imputed to the symbols, that is, the use in communication that is made of them. And, finally, the combinations of symbols for symbolic discourse are defined for us by our documents – again by definition. So we can turn to written evidence and ask whether, in verbal form, symbolic discourse seems to converge with the counterpart discourse in the iconic medium.

II. Connections, Iconic and Verbal

To repeat: the key to a symbolic code must explain what connects with one thing but not with another, and how correct connections bear meaning, incorrect ones, gibberish. Now to carry forward that notion, we ask whether a single key will serve to decipher the code of symbolic discourse that governs symbols in both verbal and iconic form. The answer to that lies on the surface, in the connections that people made between and among symbols. If we find the same connections in both verbal and literary symbolic discourse, we may not know what message (if any) is supposed to be communicated, but we have solid grounds for thinking that a single code governs discourse in both media. On the other hand, if we find no combinations of the same symbols in both media of symbolic discourse, then we have no reason to suppose that a single key will explain what connects one thing with some other, or why one thing connects with this other, but not with that other. So the first test of whether or not we have a single discourse in two media or two distinct discourses, symbolic in both cases, but differentiated by media, is whether or not we find the same combination of symbols in both writing and iconography. We take as our test case symbols we now know are very commonly connected, the *etrog* and *lulab, shofar,* and *menorah.* Our question is simple: when in writing people refer to the *lulab* or to the *shofar,* do they forthwith think also of the *menorah* and *shofar,* along with the *lulab,* or the *lulab* and *menorah,* along with the *shofar*? Or do they think of other things – or of nothing? As a matter of fact, they think of other things, but not, in the case of the *lulab,* of the *menorah* and *shofar;* and not, in the case of the *shofar,* of the *lulab* and *menorah.* So the combinations that people make in writing are not of the same symbols as the combinations that people make iconically. In combination with these things that in iconic form clearly connect with one thing and not some other, they think of other things.[2]

To satisfy ourselves that the distinctive combination of symbols – the *etrog* and *lulab, shofar,* and *menorah* – does not occur in the literary form of discourse (whether symbolic or otherwise) I present a brief account of how the Midrash compilations treat two of the three items, the first and second. Here we shall see that the persistent manipulation of the three symbols as a group finds no counterpart in writing. The connections are different.

We begin with the *lulab* and ask whether representation of that symbol provokes discourse pertinent, also, to the symbols of the *shofar* and of the *menorah,* or even only of the *menorah.* The answer is negative. Other matters, but not those matters, are invoked. Leviticus Rabbah

---

[2]I state categorically that in no case of symbolic discourse in verbal form that I have examined do we find the combinations of the *etrog* and *lulab, shofar,* and *menorah.* I have taken the more difficult problem, therefore, of moving beyond the specific evidence of discourse of a symbolic character and treating propositional discourse as well.

Parashah XXX treats the festival of Tabernacles (*Sukkot*), the sole point in the liturgical calendar at which the *etrog* and *lulab* pertain. The base verse that is treated is Lev. 23:39-40: "You shall take on the first day the fruit of goodly trees, branches of palm trees and boughs of leafy trees and willows of the brook," and that statement is taken to refer, specifically, to the *lulab*. When sages read that verse, they are provoked to introduce the consideration of Torah study; the opening and closing units of the pertinent unit tell us what is important:

Leviticus Rabbah XXX

I.1   A   "[On the fifteenth day of the seventh month, when you have gathered in the produce of the land, you shall keep the feast of the Lord seven days....] And you shall take on the first day [the fruit of goodly trees, branches of palm trees and boughs of leafy trees and willows of the brook, and you shall rejoice before the Lord your God for seven days]" (Lev. 23:39-40).

        B   R. Abba bar Kahana commenced [discourse by citing the following verse]: "Take my instruction instead of silver, [and knowledge rather than choice gold]" (Prov. 8:10).

        C   Said R. Abba bar Kahana, "Take the instruction of the Torah instead of silver.

        D   "'Why do you weigh out money? Because there is no bread' (Isa. 55:2).

        E   "'Why do you weigh out money to the sons of Esau [Rome]? [It is because] "there is no bread," because you did not sate yourselves with the bread of the Torah.

        F.   "'And [why] do you labor? Because there is no satisfaction' (Isa. 55:2).

        G   "'Why do you labor while the nations of the world enjoy plenty? 'Because there is no satisfaction,' that is, because you have not sated yourselves with the wine of the Torah.

        H   "For it is written, 'Come, eat of my bread, and drink of the wine I have mixed'" (Prov. 9:5).

I.6   A   Said R. Abba bar Kahana, "On the basis of the reward paid for one act of 'taking,' you may assess the reward for [taking] the palm branch [on the festival of Tabernacles].

        B.   "There was an act of taking in Egypt: 'You will take a bunch of hyssop' (Ex. 12:22).

        C.   "And how much was it worth? Four *manehs*.

        D.   "Yet that act of taking is what made Israel inherit the spoil at the Sea, the spoil of Sihon and Og, and the spoil of the thirty-one kings.

        E.   "Now the palm branch, which costs a person such a high price, and which involves so many religious duties – how much the more so [will a great reward be forthcoming on its account]!"

        F.   Therefore Moses admonished Israel, saying to them, "And you shall take on the first day..." (Lev. 23:40).

Whatever the sense of *lulab* to synagogue artists and their patrons, the combination with the *etrog, menorah,* and *shofar* was critical; nothing in these words invokes any of those other symbols. What would have led us to suppose some sort of interchange between iconic and verbal symbols? If we had an association, in iconic combinations, of the Torah shrine and the *etrog* and *lulab,* we might have grounds on which to frame the hypothesis that some sort of association – comparison, contrast for instance – between the symbols of the festival of Tabernacles and Torah study was contemplated. Here there is no basis for treating the iconic symbols as convergent with the manipulation of those same symbols in propositional discourse. It suffices to say that nowhere in Leviticus Rabbah Parashah XXX do we find reason to introduce the other iconic symbols.

What about the *shofar?* If we speak of that object, do we routinely introduce the *etrog, lulab, menorah?* The answer is negative. We introduce other things, but not those things. Pesiqta deRab Kahana *pisqa* XXIII addresses the New Year as described at Lev. 23:24: "In the seventh month on the first day of the month you shall observe a day of solemn rest, a memorial proclaimed with blast of trumpets." The combination of judgment and the end of days is evoked in the following. I give two distinct statements of the same point, to show that it is in context an important motif.

Pesiqta deRab Kahana XXIII

II.2   A   *For I will make a full end of all the nations* (Jer. 30:11): As to the nations of the world, because they make a full end (when they harvest even the corner) of their field, concerning them Scripture states: *I will make a full end of all the nations among whom I scattered you.*

       B   But as to Israel, because they do not make a full end (when they harvest, for they leave the corner) of their field, therefore: *But of you I will not make a full end* (Jer. 30:11).

       C   *I will chasten you in just measure, and I will by no means leave you unpunished* (Jer. 30:11). I shall chasten you through suffering in this world, so as to leave you unpunished in the world to come.

       D.   When?

       E.   *In the seventh month, [on the first day of the month]* (Lev. 23:24).

Pesiqta deRab Kahana XXIII

V.1   A   R. Jeremiah commenced [discourse by citing the following verse]: "*The wise man's path of life leads upward, that he may avoid Sheol beneath* (Prov. 15:24).

       B   "*The path of life*: The path of life refers only to the words of the Torah, for it is written, as it is written, *It is a tree of life* (Prov. 3:18).

       C   "Another matter: *The path of life*: The path of life refers only to suffering, as it is written, *The way of life is through rebuke and correction* (Prov. 6:23).

D. *"[The wise man's path]...leads upward* refers to one who looks deeply into the Torah's religious duties, [learning how to carry them out properly].

E. "What, then, is written just prior to this same matter (of the New Year)?

F. *"When you harvest your crop of your land, you will not make a full end of the corner of your field* (Lev. 23:22).

G. "The nations of the world, because they make a full end when they harvest even the corner of their field, [and the rest of the matter is as is given above: *I will make a full end of all the nations among whom I have driven you* (Jer. 30:11). But Israel, because they do not make a full end when they harvest, for they leave the corner of their field, therefore, *But of you I will not make a full end* (Jer. 30:11). *I will chasten you in just measure, and I will by no means leave you unpunished* (Jer. 30:11)." When? *In the seventh month, on the first day of the month, [you shall observe a day of solemn rest, a memorial proclaimed with blast of trumpets]* (Lev. 23:24)].

What is now linked is Israel's leaving the corner of the field for the poor, Lev. 23:22, the connection between that verse and the base verse here is what is expounded. Then there is no evocation of the *menorah* or the *lulab* and *etrog* – to state the obvious. We can explain what is combined, and we also can see clearly that the combination is deliberate. That means what joined elsewhere but not here bears another message but not this one. An elaborate investigation of the role of *lulab* and *etrog, shofar* and *menorah* in the literary evidence of the Midrash compilations hardly is required to demonstrate what we now know: we find no evidence of interest in the combination of those items in literary evidence.

III. One Version of a Symbolic Structure of Judaism: Symbols in Verbal Form

Now that we have identified the iconic representations that form, if not a system, at least a structure – items that occur together in a given manner – let me set forth one example of what I conceive to be a fine statement of the symbolic structure of Judaism as symbols in verbal form set forth in such a structure. This will serve as an example of the kinds of symbols we find in general in symbolic discourse in verbal form.[3] Our further experiments will then draw on the symbolic repertoire that a single passage – counterpart to a single synagogue – has supplied. The character of the passage will explain why I have chosen it as representative:

---

[3]A reference to the materials gathered in *Symbol and Theology in Judaism*, Chapters Four through Seven will suffice to show that what follows is reasonably proposed as representative.

Genesis Rabbah LXX

VIII.2   A.   "As he looked, he saw a well in the field":

        B.   R. Hama bar Hanina interpreted the verse in six ways [that is, he divides the verse into six clauses and systematically reads each of the clauses in light of the others and in line with an overriding theme:

        C.   "'As he looked, he saw a well in the field': this refers to the well [of water in the wilderness, Num. 21:17].

        D.   "'...and lo, three flocks of sheep lying beside it': specifically, Moses, Aaron, and Miriam.

        E.   "'...for out of that well the flocks were watered': for from there each one drew water for his standard, tribe, and family."

        F.   "And the stone upon the well's mouth was great":

        G.   Said R. Hanina, "It was only the size of a little sieve."

        H   [Reverting to Hama's statement:] "'...and put the stone back in its place upon the mouth of the well': for the coming journeys. [Thus the first interpretation applies the passage at hand to the life of Israel in the wilderness.]

VIII.3   A.   "'As he looked, he saw a well in the field': refers to Zion.

        B.   "'...and lo, three flocks of sheep lying beside it': refers to the three festivals.

        C   "'....for out of that well the flocks were watered': from there they drank of the Holy Spirit.

        D.   "'...The stone on the well's mouth was large': this refers to the rejoicing of the house of the water drawing."

        E   Said R. Hoshaiah, "Why is it called 'the house of the water drawing'? Because from there they drink of the Holy Spirit."

        F.   [Resuming Hama b. Hanina's discourse:] "'...and when all the flocks were gathered there': coming from 'the entrance of Hamath to the brook of Egypt' (1 Kgs. 8:66).

        G   "'...the shepherds would roll the stone from the mouth of the well and water the sheep': for from there they would drink of the Holy Spirit.

        H   "'...and put the stone back in its place upon the mouth of the well': leaving it in place until the coming festival. [Thus the second interpretation reads the verse in light of the Temple celebration of the festival of Tabernacles.]

VIII.4   A.   "'...As he looked, he saw a well in the field': this refers to Zion.

        B.   "'...and lo, three flocks of sheep lying beside it': this refers to the three courts, concerning which we have learned in the Mishnah: **There were three courts there, one at the gateway of the Temple Mount, one at the gateway of the courtyard, and one in the chamber of the hewn stones** [M. San. 11:2].

        C.   "'...for out of that well the flocks were watered': for from there they would hear the ruling.

        D.   "The stone on the well's mouth was large': this refers to the high court that was in the chamber of the hewn stones.

        E   "'...and when all the flocks were gathered there': this refers to the courts in session in the Land of Israel.

F. "'...the shepherds would roll the stone from the mouth of the well and water the sheep': for from there they would hear the ruling.

G. "'...and put the stone back in its place upon the mouth of the well': for they would give and take until they had produced the ruling in all the required clarity." [The third interpretation reads the verse in light of the Israelite institution of justice and administration.]

VIII.5 A. "'As he looked, he saw a well in the field': this refers to Zion.

B. "'...and lo, three flocks of sheep lying beside it': this refers to the first three kingdoms [Babylonia, Media, Greece].

C. "'...for out of that well the flocks were watered': for they enriched the treasures that were laid up in the chambers of the Temple.

D. "'...The stone on the well's mouth was large': this refers to the merit attained by the patriarchs.

E. "'...and when all the flocks were gathered there': this refers to the wicked kingdom, which collects troops through levies over all the nations of the world.

F. "'...the shepherds would roll the stone from the mouth of the well and water the sheep': for they enriched the treasures that were laid up in the chambers of the Temple.

G. "'...and put the stone back in its place upon the mouth of the well': in the age to come the merit attained by the patriarchs will stand [in defense of Israel].' [So the fourth interpretation interweaves the themes of the Temple cult and the domination of the four monarchies.]

VIII.6 A. "'As he looked, he saw a well in the field': this refers to the Sanhedrin.

B. "'...and lo, three flocks of sheep lying beside it': this alludes to the three rows of disciples of sages that would go into session in their presence.

C. "for out of that well the flocks were watered': for from there they would listen to the ruling of the law.

D. "'...The stone on the well's mouth was large': this refers to the most distinguished member of the court, who determines the law decision.

E. "'...and when all the flocks were gathered there': this refers to disciples of the sages in the Land of Israel.

F. "'...the shepherds would roll the stone from the mouth of the well and water the sheep': for from there they would listen to the ruling of the law.

G. "'...and put the stone back in its place upon the mouth of the well': for they would give and take until they had produced the ruling in all the required clarity." [The fifth interpretation again reads the verse in light of the Israelite institution of legal education and justice.]

VIII.7 A. "'As he looked, he saw a well in the field': this refers to the synagogue.

B. "'...and lo, three flocks of sheep lying beside it': this refers to the three who are called to the reading of the Torah on weekdays.

C. "'...for out of that well the flocks were watered': for from there they hear the reading of the Torah.

D.   "'...The stone on the well's mouth was large': this refers to the impulse to do evil.

E.   "'...and when all the flocks were gathered there': this refers to the congregation.

F.   "'...the shepherds would roll the stone from the mouth of the well and water the sheep': for from there they hear the reading of the Torah.

G.   "'...and put the stone back in its place upon the mouth of the well': for once they go forth [from the hearing of the reading of the Torah] the impulse to do evil reverts to its place." [The sixth and last interpretation turns to the twin themes of the reading of the Torah in the synagogue and the evil impulse, temporarily driven off through the hearing of the Torah.]

Genesis Rabbah LXX

IX.1

A.   R. Yohanan interpreted the statement in terms of Sinai:

B.   "'As he looked, he saw a well in the field': this refers to Sinai.

C.   "'...and lo, three flocks of sheep lying beside it': these stand for the priests, Levites, and Israelites.

D.   "'...for out of that well the flocks were watered': for from there they heard the Ten Commandments.

E.   "'...The stone on the well's mouth was large': this refers to the Presence of God."

F.   "...and when all the flocks were gathered there":

G.   R. Simeon b. Judah of Kefar Akum in the name of R. Simeon: "All of the flocks of Israel had to be present, for if any one of them had been lacking, they would not have been worthy of receiving the Torah."

H.   [Returning to Yohanan's exposition:] "'...the shepherds would roll the stone from the mouth of the well and water the sheep': for from there they heard the Ten Commandments.

I.   "'...and put the stone back in its place upon the mouth of the well': 'You yourselves have seen that I have talked with you from Heaven' (Ex. 20:19)."

The six themes read in response to the verse cover (1) Israel in the wilderness, (2) the Temple cult on festivals with special reference to Tabernacles, (3) the judiciary and government, (4) the history of Israel under the four kingdoms, (5) the life of sages, and (6) the ordinary folk and the synagogue. The whole is an astonishing repertoire of fundamental themes of the life of the nation, Israel: at its origins in the wilderness, in its cult, in its institutions based on the cult, in the history of the nations, and, finally, in the twin social estates of sages and ordinary folk, matched by the institutions of the master disciple circle and the synagogue. The vision of Jacob at the well thus encompassed the whole of the social reality of Jacob's people, Israel. Yohanan's exposition adds what was left out, namely, reference to the revelation of the Torah at Sinai. The reason I have offered the present passage as a fine instance of symbolic discourse is now clear. If we wished a catalogue of the kinds of topics addressed in passages of symbolic, as distinct from propositional, discourse, the present catalogue proves compendious and complete. Our next experiment is now possible.

IV. Symbolic Discourse in Iconic and in Verbal Form: Convergence or Divergence?

A simple set of indicators will now permit us to compare the character of symbolic discourse in verbal form with that in iconic form. The question is now a simple one. Let us represent the Judaism – way of life, worldview, theory of who or what is "Israel"? – set forth by symbolic discourse in iconic form effected by the *lulab* and *etrog*, *shofar*, and *menorah*. Let us further represent the Judaism set forth by symbolic discourse in verbal form, treating as exemplary a discourse that will appeal to visual images appropriate to the themes of Israel in the wilderness, the Temple cult, the judiciary and government, Israel under the four kingdoms and at the end of time, the life of sages, ordinary folk and the synagogue. How do these statements relate?

The shared program will cover the standard topics that any symbolic structure of representing a religion should treat: holy day, holy space, holy word, holy man (or: person), and holy time or the division of time.

	ICONIC SYMBOLS	VERBAL SYMBOLS
Holy day	New Year/Tabernacles/Hanukkah	
	Tabernacles/Pentecost/Passover	
Holy space	Temple	Temple/Zion
Holy man/person	No evidence	The sage and disciple
Holy time	Messiah *(shofar)*	Four kingdoms/Israel's rule
Holy event	Not clear	Exodus from Egypt

The important point of convergence is unmistakable: holy space for both symbolic structures is defined as the Temple and Mount Zion. That is hardly surprising; no Judaic structure beyond 70 ignored the Temple, and all Judaisms, both before and after 70, found it necessary to deal in some way with, to situate themselves in relationship to, that paramount subject. So the convergence proves systemically inert, indeed trivial.

Whether or not we classify the treatment of holy time as convergent or divergent is not equally obvious to me. Both structures point toward the end of time; but they speak of it differently. So far as the *shofar* means to refer to the coming of the Messiah, the gathering of the exiles, and the restoration of the Temple, as, in the synagogue liturgy, it does, then the iconic representation of the messianic topic and the verbal representation of the same topic diverge. For the latter, we see in our case and in much of the evidence surveyed earlier, frames the messianic topic in terms of Israel's relationship with the nations, and the principal interest is in Israel's rule over the world as the fifth and final monarchy. That theme is repeated in symbolic discourse in verbal form, and, if the *shofar* stands in synagogue iconography for what the synagogue liturgy says, then the message, if not an utterly different one, is not identical with that delivered by symbols in verbal form. So here matters are ambiguous.

The unambiguous points of divergence are equally striking. The most important comes first. Symbolic discourse in verbal form privileges the three festivals equally and utterly ignores Hanukkah. So far as the *menorah* stands for Hanukkah – and in the literary evidence, the association is firm – we may suppose that, just as the *lulab* and *etrog* mean to evoke Tabernacles, and the *shofar*, the New Year and Day of Atonement, so the *menorah* speaks of Hanukkah. Then we find a clear and striking divergence. That the *menorah* serves, also, as an astral symbol is well established, and if that is the fact, then another point of divergence is registered. In symbolic discourse in verbal form I find not one allusion to an astral ascent accessible to an Israelite, for example, through worship or Torah study. A survey of the cited passages yields not a trace of the theme of the astral ascent.

The second point of divergence seems similarly unambiguous. Critical to the symbolic vocabulary of the rabbinic Midrash compilations is study of the Torah, on the one side, and the figure of the sage and disciple, on the other. I do not find in the extant literary sources a medium for identifying the figure of the sage and the act of Torah study with the symbols of the *lulab, etrog, shofar,* or *menorah*. Quite to the contrary, the example given above from Leviticus Rabbah counterpoises the *lulab* with words of Torah. The fact that these are deemed opposites, with the former not invoking, but provoking, the latter, by itself means little. But it does not sustain the proposition that the combined symbols before us, the *lulab, etrog, shofar,* and *menorah,* somehow mean to speak of Torah study and the sage.

Thus far we see marks of convergence and also of divergence. What happens if we present a sizable repertoire of the combinations of symbols in verbal form that we find in Song of Songs Rabbah? We wonder whether a sizable sample of combinations of symbols in verbal form intersects, or even coincides, with the simple vocabulary, in combination, paramount in iconic representations of symbolic discourse in synagogues. A list drawn from combinations of symbols in verbal form found in Song of Songs Rabbah must include the following items:

Joseph, righteous men, Moses, and Solomon;

patriarchs as against princes, offerings as against merit, and Israel as against the nations; those who love the king, proselytes, martyrs, penitents;

first, Israel at Sinai; then Israel's loss of God's presence on account of the golden calf; then God's favoring Israel by treating Israel not in accord with the requirements of justice but with mercy;

Dathan and Abiram, the spies, Jeroboam, Solomon's marriage to Pharaoh's daughter, Ahab, Jezebel, Zedekiah;

Israel is feminine, the enemy (Egypt) masculine, but God the father saves Israel the daughter;

Moses and Aaron, the Sanhedrin, the teachers of Scripture and Mishnah, the rabbis;

the disciples; the relationship among disciples, public recitation of teachings of the Torah in the right order; lections of the Torah;

the spoil at the Sea = the Exodus, the Torah, the Tabernacle, the ark;

the patriarchs, Abraham, Isaac, Jacob, then Israel in Egypt, Israel's atonement and God's forgiveness;

the Temple where God and Israel are joined, the Temple is God's resting place, the Temple is the source of Israel's fecundity;

Israel in Egypt, at the Sea, at Sinai, and subjugated by the gentile kingdoms, and how the redemption will come;

Rebecca, those who came forth from Egypt, Israel at Sinai, acts of loving kindness, the kingdoms who now rule Israel, the coming redemption;

fire above, fire below, meaning heavenly and altar fires; Torah in writing, Torah in memory; fire of Abraham, Moriah, bush, Elijah, Hananiah, Mishael, and Azariah;

the Ten Commandments, show fringes and phylacteries, recitation of the *Shema* and the Prayer, the tabernacle and the cloud of the Presence of God, and the *mezuzah;*

the timing of redemption, the moral condition of those to be redeemed, and the past religious misdeeds of those to be redeemed;

Israel at the Sea, Sinai, the Ten Commandments; then the synagogues and schoolhouses; then the redeemer;

the Exodus, the conquest of the Land, the redemption and restoration of Israel to Zion after the destruction of the first Temple, and the final and ultimate salvation;

the Egyptians, Esau and his generals, and, finally, the four kingdoms;

Moses' redemption, the first, to the second redemption in the time of the Babylonians and Daniel;

the litter of Solomon: the priestly blessing, the priestly watches, the Sanhedrin, and the Israelites coming out of Egypt;

Israel at the Sea and forgiveness for sins effected through their passing through the Sea; Israel at Sinai; the war with Midian; the crossing of the Jordan and entry into the Land; the house of the sanctuary; the priestly watches; the offerings in the Temple; the Sanhedrin; the Day of Atonement;

God redeemed Israel without preparation; the nations of the world will be punished, after Israel is punished; the nations of the world will present Israel as gifts to the royal messiah, and here the base verse refers to Abraham, Isaac, Jacob, Sihon, Og, Canaanites;

the return to Zion in the time of Ezra, the Exodus from Egypt in the time of Moses;

the patriarchs and with Israel in Egypt, at the Sea, and then before Sinai;

Abraham, Jacob, Moses;

Isaac, Jacob, Esau, Jacob, Joseph, the brothers, Jonathan, David, Saul, man, wife, paramour;

Abraham in the fiery furnace and Shadrach, Meshach, and Abednego, the Exile in Babylonia, now with reference to the return to Zion.

Now let us ask ourselves some very simple questions: is there a single combination of symbols in verbal form in this catalogue that joins the same symbols as are combined in the symbolic vocabulary in iconic form that we have identified? No, not a single combination coincides. Is there a paramount role assigned to Tabernacles at all? No, in this catalogue the principal holy day must be Passover, commemorating the Exodus, which occurs throughout, and not Tabernacles, commemorating the life in the wilderness, which occurs not at all. Is there a single set of symbols in verbal form that can be served by the *shofar*? No, not one. Whatever the sense or meaning that we assign to the *shofar*, if the *shofar* stands for Isaac on the altar with Abraham ready to give him up, if it stands for the New Year and Day of Atonement, or if it stands for the coming of the Messiah and the ingathering of the exiles, makes no difference.

On the list before us, I see no point at which the *shofar* in any of these senses will have served uniquely well or even served at all. Whatever the sense of the *menorah*, whether invoking Hanukkah or an astral ascent, makes no difference; it is not a useful symbol, in verbal form, for any of the combinations before us; it cannot have served in a single recombinant statement. The *lulab* and *etrog* so far as I can see can have claimed no place, in verbal form, in any of our combinations. While, therefore, at certain points the symbolic discourse in verbal form surely intersects with the same mode of discourse in iconic form, in the aggregate, symbolic discourse represented in one medium bears one set of symbols – singly or in combination! – and symbolic discourse in another medium appeals to a quite different set of symbols altogether.

V. What Is at Stake in Analyzing Symbolic Discourse?

The divergent vocabularies utilized for symbolic discourse point toward divergent symbolic structures: two Judaisms, one of them represented by the symbolic discourse in verbal form of the rabbinic Midrash compilations, the other by symbolic discourse in iconic form represented by the synagogue ornamentation. That conclusion[4] calls into question the possibility of describing, on the basis of the written and archaeological evidence, a Judaism that is attested, in one way or another, by all data equally; a Judaism to which all data point; a Judaism that is implicit in or presupposed by, all data. If there were such a uniform and encompassing Judaic structure, sufficiently commodious to make a place for diverse Judaisms, then it is at the level of symbolic discourse that we should find evidence for its description. For in the preverbal evidence of symbols should emerge messages, at least significations, that can be expressed in the diverse ways that verbal discourse makes possible (and may even require). But, as we have now seen, when we compare the symbols that reach us in two distinct forms, the verbal and the iconic, we find ourselves at an impasse. The verbal symbols serve in one way, the iconic in another, and while they occasionally converge, the points of convergence are few, those of divergence, overwhelming.

---

[4]Goodenough's work led to precisely the same conclusion. But the proposition that "Judaism" was diverse, meaning that there was more than a single normative Judaism, has been implicit, if not entirely conventional, even from the late 1940s. The most effective and important statement of the divergence of literary and iconic evidence in general emerged in the earliest volumes of Goodenough's *Jewish Symbols in the Greco-Roman Period*. The recognition that that divergence pointed toward more than a single Judaic system or Judaism, and the specification of the meaning of that fact, derive principally from my *oeuvre*.

At stake in these observations is whether we can locate evidence that, beyond any text or artifact, a body of thought – a religious system, encompassing a worldview, way of life, and theory of the social group that held the one and realized the other – circulated. What is this "Judaism" to which my hypothesis makes reference? It is, as a matter of working hypothesis, that set of conceptions and convictions that the generality of Jews took for granted, but that no particular group of Jews made distinctively its own. It is the Judaism that all writings, all art, presupposes. And at stake in this analysis of the repertoire of symbols is, Can we claim that a single such structure served to sustain all Judaisms? Is there such a unitary, single, and harmonious "symbolic structure of Judaism" at all? That body of thought, that Judaism – perhaps formed of one Judaism out of many, perhaps identified as what is essential throughout, perhaps defined as the least common denominator among all evidence, is then alleged to be presupposed in all documents and by all artifacts. The answer to that question is simple. No evidence permits us to describe that one Judaism. So far as we are limited to the demonstration made possible by evidence – for example, sources, whether in writing or in iconic or other material form, the kind of evidence that is most general, fundamental, and susceptible of homogenization – the picture is clear and one-sided.

Now some who posit a "Judaism" of which we are informed appeal not to evidence (for example of a given period) but to an a priori: they maintain that there is one Judaism by definition and without demonstration that informs all Judaisms, or to which all Judaisms refer or give testimony. Some scholars just now claim that there is a "Judaism out there," beyond any one document, to which in some way or other all documents in various ways and proportions are supposed to attest.[5]

---

[5]One statement of the matter derives from the British medievalist, Hyam Maccoby. Writing in the symposium, "The Mishnah: Methods of Interpretation," *Midstream*, October, 1986, p. 41, he states:

Neusner argues that since the Mishnah has its own style and program, nothing outside it is relevant to explaining it. This is an obvious fallacy. The Mishnah, as a digest, in the main, of the legal...aspect of rabbinic Judaism, necessarily has its own style and program. But to treat it as something intended to be a comprehensive compendium of the Oral Torah is simply to beg the question. Neusner does not answer the point, put to him by E. P. Sanders and myself, that the liturgy being presupposed by the Mishnah, is surely relevant to the Mishnah's exegesis. Nor does he answer the charge that he ignores the aggadic material within the Mishnah itself, for example, Abot; or explain why the copious aggadic material found in roughly contemporaneous works should be regarded as irrelevant. Instead he insists that he is right to

They even know how to describe that Judaism even though no document and no artifact on its own attests to its character. And that Judaism – which I label, the "Judaism out there," that is, prior to, encompassing all documents, each with its own distinctive representation of a Judaic system, which I label a "Judaism in here" is readily defined. Indeed, that Judaism beyond, or beside, all evidences and data is such as to impose its judgment upon our reading of every sentence, every paragraph, every

---

carry out the highly artificial project of deliberately closing his eyes to all aggadic material, and trying to explain the Mishnah without it.

Maccoby exhibits a somewhat infirm grasp of the nature of the inquiry before us. If one starts with the question, "What does the authorship of this book mean to say, when read by itself and not in light of other, *later* writings?" then it would be improper to import into the description of the system of the Mishnah in particular (its "Judaism" – hence "Judaism: The evidence of the Mishnah") conceptions not contained within its pages. Tractate Abot, for one instance, cites a range of authorities who lived a generation beyond the closure of the (rest of the) Mishnah and so is ordinarily dated to about 250, with the Mishnah dated to about 200. On that basis how one can impute to the Mishnah's system conceptions first attaining closure half a century later I do not know. To describe the Mishnah, for example, as a part of "rabbinic Judaism" is to invoke the premise that we know, more or less on its own, just what this "rabbinic Judaism" is and says. But what we cannot show we do not know. And, as a matter of established fact, many conceptions dominant in the final statements of rabbinic Judaism to emerge from late antiquity play no material role whatsoever in the system of the Mishnah, or, for that matter, of Tosefta and Abot. No one who has looked for the conception of "the Oral Torah" in the Mishnah or in the documents that succeeded it, for the next two hundred years, will understand why Maccoby is so certain that the category of Oral Torah, or the myth of the Dual Torah, applies at all. For the mythic category of "Oral Torah" makes its appearance, so far as I can discern, only with the Yerushalmi and not in any document closed prior to that time, although a notion of a revelation over and above Scripture – not called "Oral Torah" to be sure – comes to expression in Abot. Implicitly, moreover, certain sayings of the Mishnah itself, for example, concerning rulings of the Torah and rulings of sages, may contain the notion of a secondary tradition, beyond revelation. But that tradition is not called "the Oral Torah," and I was disappointed to find that even in the Yerushalmi the mythic statement of the matter, so far as I can see, is lacking. It is only in the Bavli, for example, in the famous story of Hillel and Shammai and the convert at B. Shab. 30B-31A, that the matter is fully explicit. Now, if Maccoby maintains that the conception circulated in the form in which we know it, for instance, in the Yerushalmi in truncated form or in the Bavli in complete form, he should supply us with the evidence for his position. As I said, what we cannot show we do not know. And most secular and academic scholarship concurs that we have no historical knowledge a priori, though in writing Maccoby has indeed in so may words maintained that we do. In fact the documents of formative Judaism do yield histories of ideas, and not every idea can be shown to have taken part in the statement of each, let alone all, of the documents. But those who appeal to a Judaism out there, before and beyond all of the documents, ignore that fact.

book.[6] Now if such evidence is to be located, then nonverbal data such as we have examined should have provided it, for here, by definition, in symbols, we should have been able to demonstrate that, whatever verbal explanations people attached to symbols, a fundamentally uniform symbolic structure served all Judaisms that our evidence attests.

---

[6]Commenting on this debate with Maccoby and Sanders, William Scott Green says, Sanders "reads rabbinic texts by peering through them for the ideas (presumably ones Jews or rabbis believed) that lie beneath them." This runs parallel to Maccoby's criticism of my "ignoring" a variety of conceptions I do not find in the Mishnah. Both Maccoby and Sanders, in my view, wish to discuss what *they* think important and therefore to ignore what the texts themselves actually talk about, as Green says, "the materials that attracted the attention and interest of the writers" (Personal letter, January 17, 1985). In my original review I pointed out that Sanders' categories ignore what the texts actually say and impose categories the Judaic-rabbinic texts do not know. Sanders, in Green's judgment, introduces a distinct premise:

> For Sanders, the religion of Mishnah lies unspoken beneath its surface; for Neusner it is manifest in Mishnah's own language and preoccupations (William Scott Green in his Introduction, *Approaches to Ancient Judaism* (Chicago, 1980: Scholars Press for Brown Judaic Studies II), p. xxi.

Generalizing on this case, Green further comments in those more general terms that bring us into a debate on the nature of religion and culture, and that larger discourse lends importance to what, in other circumstances, looks to be a mere academic argument. Green writes as follows:

> The basic attitude of mind characteristic of the study of religion holds that religion is certainly in your soul, likely in your heart, perhaps in your mind, but never in your body. That attitude encourages us to construe religion cerebrally and individually, to think in terms of beliefs and the believer, rather than in terms of behavior and community. The lens provided by this prejudice draws our attention to the intense and obsessive belief called "faith," so religion is understood as a state of mind, the object of intellectual or emotional commitment, the result of decisions to believe or to have faith. According to this model, people have religion but they do not do their religion. Thus we tend to devalue behavior and performance, to make it epiphenomenal, and of course to emphasize thinking and reflecting, the practice of theology, as a primary activity of religious people....The famous slogan that "ritual recapitulates myth" follows this model by assigning priority to the story and to peoples' believing the story, and makes behavior simply an imitation, an aping, a mere acting out.

Now as we reflect on Green's observations, we of course recognize what is at stake. It is the definition of religion, or, rather, what matters in or about religion, emerging from one reading of Protestant theology and Protestant religious experience. But in these pages, only a limited aspect of the larger debate is at issue.

Now to test the proposition that there was one Judaism nourishing all Judaisms, I have proposed to find out whether we may discern *the* symbolic system or structure upon which all Judaic systems relied, with which every system contended (each in its own way to be sure), and, above all, to which all Jews responded. If we had been able to show that a single symbolic vocabulary and a single syntax and grammar of symbolic discourse served in all extant testimonies to all Judaisms – iconic, literary evidence alike, then we should have begun to pursue the problem of defining that Judaism through the principles of symbolic discourse.

Why choose the symbolic data? Because, it seems to me, it is through the study of what is inchoate and intuitive, a matter of attitude and sentiment and emotion rather than of proposition and syllogism, therefore through the analysis of symbolic structure, that we should be able to discern and set forth the things on which everyone agreed. As a matter of hypothesis, that is the repertoire of conventions and accepted facts that made possible the characteristic disagreements, small and fundamental alike, that until now have required us in studying the formation of Judaism in the first seven centuries of the Common Era [=A.D.] to describe diverse Judaisms and not a single Judaism. All our evidence derives from Judaisms, however, which is to say, every piece of writing speaks for a particular authorship, every work of art met the specifications of a single artist and patron. True, the writings resort to conventions, for instance, the entirety of the Scriptures of ancient Israel known as the Old Testament (for Christianity) or the Written Torah (for Judaism). Admittedly, the artists and their patrons implicitly accepted whatever restrictions they recognized, made their selections, as to both themes and representational conventions, from whatever repertoire they deemed self-evident.

Why give privilege to symbolic discourse rather than the propositional kind? Consider the alternative. Were we to have compiled a list of facts we must suppose everyone knew, the truths everyone affirmed, we should still not have an answer to the question of the character of normative theological statements which all known parties affirmed. True, in the canonical literature of the Judaism of the Dual Torah, for one example, we are able to list matters of fact, bearing profound meaning, that all authorships of all documents affirm, but that serve to deliver the particular message of none of them in particular. Beyond that important, indeed paramount, corpus of literary evidence for Judaism, moreover, we may take note of beliefs and practices implicit in buildings set aside for cultic purposes – Temple and synagogue before 70, synagogue afterward – and take for granted that, whatever characterized as special one place or group, all Jews everywhere came to synagogues to do pretty much the same thing, such as say prayers and read the Torah. But our task is not only or mainly to outline the range of agreement, the consensus of practice and belief, that characterized all those Jews represented by the evidence now in our hands. For much that people affirmed was commonplace, and facts, by themselves, do not give us the outlines of a vivid religious system. We saw a case in point when we found that both symbolic vocabularies appealed to the Temple in one way or another. But that proved an inert fact, when we proceeded to see the symbolic vocabulary of Song of Songs Rabbah, which proved to have nothing in common with the symbolic vocabulary that dominated in the provenance of synagogue life.

That observation draws us to another initiative in the description of this single prior Judaism, of which we are informed a priori: What are the facts that mattered to everybody, that delivered the same message in behalf of everybody? That is a different question, since it introduces the consideration of consequence. We hardly need to demonstrate that all Jews took as fact the miraculous exodus from Egypt or the giving of the Torah by God to Moses at Sinai. But any supposition that those facts meant the same thing to everybody, that all Judaic systems through the same facts made the same statement, not only is unfounded, but also is unlikely. Facts that serve a particular system in a particular way – the revelation of the Torah at Sinai to convey the systemically emblematic myth of the Dual Torah, for instance, in the Judaism of the Dual Torah we call rabbinic – by definition do not serve any other system in that same way. So when we want to know about consequence, we inquire into facts that mattered in all systems in the same way; those are the facts that tell us about the religious and cultural system as a whole that we call Judaism, not a Judaic system or the aggregate of Judaic systems, but simply Judaism, encompassing, ubiquitous, universal, and, as a matter of fact, particular also to every circumstance and system.

A shared symbolic vocabulary can have overcome a further difficulty, namely, the very particular context to which the evidence in hand attests. The evidence we have, deriving as it does from particular synagogues or distinct books or sets of books, by its nature tells us about not the general but the specific: this place, for synagogues, that authorship, for compilers of books, that authority, for decisors of canonical composites. One authorship then makes the points important to it in its context, for its purpose – by nature, therefore, not merely informative but polemical. And another authorship will speak of what matters in its setting. Drawing two or more documents together not uncommonly yields the impression of different people talking about different things to different people. So, too, with the art of synagogues: it is by definition local and particular because a given synagogue, however it may conform to conventions of architecture and decoration that we discern throughout, still attests only to what its community – the people who paid for the building, directed its construction and decoration, and contentedly worshiped within it for centuries – desired. If we were to collect all the statements of all the books and homogenize them, we should produce a hodgepodge of contradictions and – more to the point – nonsequiturs. And if we were to combine all the representations on all the walls and floors of all the synagogues of late antiquity, what we should have would be a list of everything everywhere. In both cases, the labor of collecting and arranging everything about everything from everywhere yields uninterpretable, indeed, unintelligible facts.

Our task – to define the kind of evidence that forms the *lingua franca* of all documents and all iconic evidence alike – then demanded attention to symbolic discourse. By definition, then, documentary evidence read propositionally will not serve, because that kind of evidence excludes the mute but eloquent message of art, such as we have in abundance. The artistic evidence by itself cannot be read at all, since in its nature it communicates other than propositions and through other than syllogistic media. Arrangements of figures, to be sure, tell stories, and narrative art can be read as to its tale. But the sense and meaning the tale is meant to convey appeals to representation, and that, by definition, forms a distinctive medium for communication in other than verbal ways.

VI. The Way Forward: Symbolic Discourse and the Description of the Theology of the Dual Torah

The theology of the Judaism of the Dual Torah that took shape in late antiquity comes to expression not only in propositional but also in symbolic discourse.[7] The "another matter" construction, constitutes a play on what I have been calling theological "things" – names, places, events, actions deemed to bear theological weight and to affect attitude and action. The play is worked out by a reprise of available materials, composed in some fresh and interesting combination. When three or more such theological "things" are combined, they form a theological structure, and, viewed all together, all of the theological "things" in a

---

[7]At this point I cannot claim that the principal or the preferred medium is symbolic discourse, but my instinct tells me that that is the case. However, what is required is the analysis of theological discourse in a given, important document and the comparison of what is said in propositional discourse, what in analytical, what in symbolic, and what in narrative. When we have classified and compared the media for theological expression in a given document in which theology forms a principal theme or topic, we shall be able to proceed with this discussion, which is tangential to the argument of this book.

given document constitute the components of the entire theological structure that the document affords. The propositions portrayed visually, through metaphors of sight, or dramatically, through metaphors of action and relationship, or in attitude and emotion, through metaphors that convey or provoke feeling and sentiment, when translated into language prove familiar and commonplace. The work of the theologian in this context is not to say something new or even persuasive, for the former is unthinkable by definition, the latter unnecessary in context. It is rather to display theological "things" in a fresh and interesting way, to accomplish a fresh exegesis of the canon of theological "things."

Until now, in my judgment, we have had no method of description of theology in the canonical writings of the Judaism of the Dual Torah that is both coherent with the character of the documents and also cogent with the tasks of theological description. By theological description I mean the account of the principles and ideas concerning God's relationship with Israel (for we speak of a Judaism) that form the foundation and substrate of the thought that comes to expression in a variety of canonical writings. The problem has been the character of the documents and their mode of theological discourse. It is not that the writers speak only in concrete terms; we could readily move from their detail to our abstraction and speak in general terms about the coherence of prevailing principles of a theological order.

The problem has been much more profound. We face a set of writings that clearly mean to tell us about God and God's relationship to Israel, and Israel and Israel's relationship to God. The authorships a priori exhibit the conviction that the thoughts of the whole are cogent and coherent, since they prove deeply concerned to identify contradiction, disharmony, and incoherence, and remove it.[8] But we have not known how to find the connections between what they have written and the structure or system of thought that leads them to say, in detail, the things that they say. In working out a theory of the symbolic discourse, I hope to make possible the description of the symbolic structure set forth by that discourse, and, thereby, I further mean to open the way to the description of the theology.

The reason that I think we must begin with the elementary analysis of how discourse proceeds is simple. The kind of evidence before us offers little alternative. When we propose to describe the theological system to which a piece of well-crafted writing testifies, our task is easy

---

[8]To prove that proposition, I need merely to point to the Talmud of Babylonia, the triumph of the Judaism of the Dual Torah and its definitive and complete statement.

when the writing to begin with discusses in syllogistic logic and within an appropriate program of propositions what we conceive to be theological themes or problems. Hence – it is generally conceded – we may legitimately translate the topically theological writings of Paul, Augustine, or Luther into the systematic and coherent theologies of those three figures, respectively: finding order and structure in materials of a cogent theological character. But what about a literature that to begin with does not set forth theological propositions in philosophical form, even while using profoundly religious language for self-evidently religious purposes? And how shall we deal with a literature that conducts theological thought without engaging in analytical inquiry in the way in which the philosophers and theologians of Christianity have done, and did in that period?

Surely the canonical literature of this Judaism testifies to an orderly structure or system of thought, for the alternative is to impute to the contents of those writings the status of mere episodic and unsystematic observations about this and that. True, profound expressions of piety may exhibit the traits of intellectual chaos and disorder, and holy simplicity may mask confusion. But, as I have already stressed, such a description of the rabbinic literature of late antiquity, which I call the canon of the Judaism of the Dual Torah, defies the most definitive and indicative traits of the writings. These are order, system, cogency, coherence, proportion, fine and well-crafted thought.

To begin with, we have to justify the theological inquiry, through analysis of symbolism, into literature that self-evidently does not conform to the conventions of theological discourse to which Western civilization in its Greco-Roman heritage and Christian (and, as a matter of fact, Muslim) civilization in its philosophical formulation has made us accustomed. The Muslim and Christian theological heritage, formulated within the conventions of philosophical argument, joined by a much smaller Judaic theological corpus to be sure, does not allow us to read as a theological statement a single canonical writing of the Judaism of the Dual Torah of late antiquity. So if the literary canons of Western theology are to govern, then to begin with the literature of Judaism in its formative age by definition can present no theological order and system at all.

But that proposition on the face of it hardly proves compelling. For it is difficult for us to imagine a mental universe so lacking in structure, form, and order as to permit everything and its opposite to be said about God, to imagine a God so confused and self-contradictory as to yield a revelation lacking all cogency and truly unintelligible.[9] The very premises of all theology – that there is order, structure, and composition, proportion, and form, in God's mind, which in fact is intelligible to us through the medium of revelation properly construed – a priori render improbable the hypothesis that the canonical writings of the Judaism of the Dual Torah violate every rule of intelligible discourse concerning the principal and foundation of all being. If, after all, we really cannot speak intelligibly about God, the Torah, holy Israel, and what God wants of us, then why write all those books to begin with?

While theology may comprise propositions well-crafted into a cogent structure, about fundamental questions of God and revelation, the social entity that realizes that revelation, the attitudes and deeds that God, through revelation, requires of humanity, there is another way entirely. Theology – the structure and system, the perception of order and meaning of God, in God, through God – these may make themselves known otherwise than through the media of thought and expression that yield belief that theology can deliver its message to and through sentiment and emotion, heart as much as mind; it can be conviction as much as position, and conviction for its part also is orderly, proportioned, compelling of mind and intellect by reason of right attitude, rather than right proposition or position. That is to say, theology may set forth a system of thought in syllogistic arguments

---

[9]As a matter of fact, the great Zoroastrian theologians of the ninth century criticized Judaism (and other religions) on just this point, see my "Zoroastrian Critique of Judaism," reprinted in my *History of the Jews in Babylonia* (Leiden, 1969: E. J. Brill) 4:403-423. But not a single Judaic thinker, whether a philosopher or a theologian, whether in the Islamic philosophical tradition or the Western theological and philosophical tradition, has ever entertained the proposition that the God who gave the Torah is confused and arbitrary; and why should anyone have thought so, when, after all, the entire dynamic of Judaic thought embodied within the great halakhic tradition from the Yerushalmi and Bavli forward has aimed at the systematization, harmonization and ordering of confusing, but never confused, facts of the Torah. There is, therefore, no possibility of finding in the Judaism of the Dual Torah the slightest hint of an unsystematic system, an atheological corpus of thought. True, a fixed truth of the theological system known as *die Wissenschaft des Judenthums* has maintained that "Judaism has no theology," but that system knew precisely what it meant by "Judaism," even while never explaining what it might mean by the "theology" that that "Judaism" did not have. But that is a problem of description, analysis, and interpretation for those who take an interest in the system of thought that underpins "Jewish scholarship" and Reform Judaism in particular, that is, specialists in the history of ideas in the nineteenth century, and of the nineteenth century in the twentieth century. These are not statements of fact that must be taken into account in describing, analyzing, and interpreting documents of the Judaism of the Dual Torah.

concerning the normative truths of the worldview, social entity, and way of life of a religious system. But theology may speak in other than dynamic and compelling argument, and theologians may accomplish their goal of speaking truth about God through other than the statements made by language and in conformity with the syntax of reasoned thought.

Theology may also address vision and speak in tactile ways; it may utilize a vocabulary of not proposition but opaque symbol (whether conveyed in visual or verbal media), and through portraying symbol, theology may affect attitude and emotion, speak its truth through other media than those of philosophy and proposition. From the time of Martin Buber's *Two Types of Faith*, now nearly four decades ago, people have understood that this other type of theology, the one that lives in attitude and sentiment and that evokes and demands trust, may coexist, or even compete, with the philosophical type to the discourse of which, in general, we are accustomed. Since, as a matter of fact, in the canonical writings of the Judaism of the Dual Torah we do not have a single sustained theological treatise, while we do have a monument to a faith that is choate and subject to fully accessible expression, we must teach ourselves how to describe the theology of the Judaism of the Dual Torah out of its fully exposed and complete, systemic documents, and, as we shall see, one way of doing so lies in the analysis of symbolism. Some documents utilize certain forms to make theological statements in symbolic discourse, the recombinant symbolic ones such as that which we have now examined. These documents communicate through symbolic discourse. They therefore point toward the symbolic structure that, for the Judaism of the Dual Torah, constitutes the theological statement and message.

Now that we recognize the mode of discourse that serves as one principal medium of theological speech, understanding that at stake was the portrayal of God in relationship to Israel, and Israel in relationship to God, rather than dialectical analysis of propositions concerning that relationship and the demonstration thereof, we may begin the task of the description of the theology of the Judaism of the Dual Torah – and even contemplate the further task, the theological description of the Judaism of the Dual Torah. Each thing will take place in its turn – God willing.

8

The Role of Scripture in the Torah: Is Judaism a "Biblical Religion"?

I. Writing with Scripture in Judaism and Christianity

Judaism inherits and makes its own the Hebrew Scriptures of ancient Israel, just as does Christianity. And just as Christianity rereads the entire heritage of ancient Israel in the light of "the resurrection of Jesus Christ," so Judaism understands the Hebrew Scriptures as only one part, the written one, of "the one whole Torah of Moses, our rabbi." So the Old Testament forms no model for a single piece of writing in the rabbinic canon, by contrast to the situation in the library found at Qumran, where imitation of the scriptural psalms and other writings proved common. But what does that simple fact mean when we wish to understand the role of the Scriptures of ancient Israel in Judaism? While the writings of ancient Israel, which Judaism knows as "the Written Torah," formed a principal component of the Torah, these writings were both differentiated but also made into an integral part of a single autonomous statement of a determinate logic and cogency. So Judaism is not a "biblical religion," but the Torah of Judaism encompasses the Hebrew Scriptures of ancient Israel – a very different thing. That fact explains why the Old Testament provided no model for writers within the framework of rabbinic Judaism.

The received Scriptures formed an instrumentality for the expression of a writing bearing its own integrity and cogency, appealing to its own conventions of intelligibility, and, above all, making its own points. Any notion therefore that the authorships of Judaism proposed a systematic exegesis of Scripture conducted in terms of the original or historical program of Scripture, or appealed to Scripture for validation or vindication of doctrine or practice perceived as independent of Scripture, distorts the character of the discourse of Judaism.[1] Scripture formed part of the Torah. The authorships of Judaism, particularly in late antiquity, also participated in the discourse and statement of the Torah. They did not write *about* Scripture, they wrote *with* Scripture, for Scripture supplied the syntax and grammar of their thought, hence, "writing with Scripture." But then, Judaism cannot be classified as "a biblical religion," because Judaism – the Torah – utilized the Hebrew Scriptures (which in context means "the Bible") for whatever purposes authors formed on their own. The conception that Judaism continues and paraphrases and restates the original message of the Hebrew Scriptures derives from narrowly apologetic motives and is no more defensible than the Christian-theological claim that forms its counterpart and comes to expression in the titles of the parts of the Bible, Old Testament, New Testament.

The Judaism of the Dual Torah, oral and written, which people ordinarily mean when they speak of "Judaism," commonly makes its appearance as a "biblical religion." That is to say, people ordinarily take for granted that that Judaism (like all other Judaisms) appeals for validation to the Hebrew Scriptures or Old Testament. Consequently, we tend to compare Judaism to Christianity, regarding both of them, each in its own way, as biblical: appealing to Scripture, whether the Written Torah (Judaism) or the Old Testament (Christianity). But when we adopt such a perspective upon the two great religions of the European West and its overseas diaspora in the Western hemisphere, we treat as distinct and independent what for both religions forms part of an integrated whole. That is to say, we see Scripture (Written Torah, Old Testament) not as part of an integral revelation, in which each part illuminates all others (Oral Torah, New Testament). Rather, we address one part on its

[1]That is the argument of Daniel Boyarin, for one very current example, in his *Intertextuality and the Reading of Midrash* (Indiana Studies in Biblical Literature. Bloomington & Indianapolis: Indiana University Press, 1990). The apologetic point of the work is clear: "What in the Bible's text might have motivated this gloss on this verse?" He states at the end (p. 128), "Midrash is best understood as a continuation of the literary activity which engendered the Scriptures themselves." This sounds suspiciously like the familiar claim that Midrash says what Scripture really means, and that *is* the theology of some Orthodox Judaisms. In this book the literary critical frosting covers a stale but kosher cake. When we read Boyarin's analysis of passage after passage, we know pretty much what we knew before we read his analysis. The publisher's blurb holds: "the best, most cogent and intelligent attempt to date to apply insights from modern literary criticism to the interpretation of midrash." But Indiana University Press appears to have forgotten its own publication of a far more original and compelling work, José Faur, *Golden Doves with Silver Dots* (Bloomington: Indiana University Press, 1986).

own, ignoring the perspective of faith altogether. But if we read the Written Torah/Old Testament distinct from the Oral Torah/New Testament, what we do is deny the fundamental conviction of the faith of Judaism or Christianity.

We do just that when we describe as exegetical ("midrashic") the relationship of the Oral to the Written Torah or the New to the Old Testament. That is to say, we deem one document to be essentially autonomous of the other, then establishing its relationship to the other through processes of rereading and reinterpretation. On that basis we develop the conception that the original scriptures (again: Written Torah/Old Testament) enjoy an existence independent of the faith and the synagogue or church that preserve them. These original scriptures bear an autonomous meaning, determined by the criteria of initial context and historical circumstance, and that meaning stands in judgment, so to speak, upon the meanings imputed to these scriptures by the Judaism of the Dual Torah or by the Christianity of the Bible, Old and New Testaments alike. Viewed historically, the collection of writings we know as the Hebrew Scriptures or Old Testament obviously bear meaning determined by the original setting and intent of authors or authorships (individual, collective writers).

But that meaning never made a profound impact, prior to the nineteenth century, upon the reception and reading of the Israelite Scriptures. What did make its mark was the uses of those Scriptures for the makers of the Judaism of the Dual Torah, on the one side, and the Christianity we now know as Orthodox: the Christianity of the Bible, Old and New Testaments, on the other. And what mattered to those system builders concerned the revelation of God as they received it: the Torah of Moses, our rabbi, for the Judaism of the Dual Torah, the person of Jesus Christ, God incarnate, for Christianity. To those protean conceptions, Scripture served, as did all else, as testimony and testament. It formed part of a larger, wholly cogent statement. It served important purposes in the formation and expression of that statement. But it constituted a subordinated and merely instrumental entity, not the court of last appeal and final judgment, not the ultimate source of truth and validation, except – of course – after the fact. The fact found expression in the figure of the sage, in the model of Moses, our rabbi, or in the person, as the Church received him, of Christ Jesus.

People commonly suppose that when Judaic or Christian authorships turned to Israelite Scripture, it was in search of prooftexts. The relationship was exegetical or eisegetical. The representation of either religion as forming an essentially exegetical relationship to Israelite writings, however, vastly distorts the nature of that religion. When Judaic and Christian authorships proposed to compose their statements, they of course appealed to Scripture. But it was an appeal to serve a purpose defined not by Scripture but by the faith – the Judaic or Christian system – under construction and subject to articulation. Scripture formed a dictionary, providing a vast range of permissible usages of intelligible words. Scripture did not dictate the sentences that would be composed through the words found in that (limited) dictionary. Much as painters paint with a palette of colors, authorships wrote with Scripture. The paint is not the picture. Matthew's Gospel of Jesus is not (merely) a reprise of Isaiah. But the picture cannot be painted without the pigments on the palette, and Matthew's Gospel cannot have been created without the verses of Isaiah and other prophetic passages that provided Matthew's framework for the Gospel story of Jesus Christ. And when the Church in its first three centuries framed its Scriptures, – as everybody knows – it received the Israelite writings because of the Church's reading of those writings. It spoke through those writings. It appealed to their facts. It responded, in the formation of its imagination and metaphoric reality, to those writings. Its life and being were nourished by those writings. But the Church came first, then the Scriptures, and, ultimately, the Bible, Old and New Testaments forming one complete and wholly harmonious, seamless statement and document. And so it was with the Judaism of the Dual Torah, in its framework and within its inner logic and discipline.

What follows from these propositions is clear. If we wish to understand the place and power of the Israelite Scriptures in the Judaism of the Dual Torah and in the writings of nascent Christianity, we must begin by freeing ourselves of one conception and exploring the implications of another. The negative is this: we must abandon any notion of a perceived distinction between the Oral and the Written Torahs, or between the New and Old Testaments. The positive is that we must see the two Torahs as the one whole Torah of Moses, our rabbi. We must see the two Testaments as "the Bible." The negative: we cannot take for granted that the appearance of a verse of the Israelite Scriptures in a rabbinic composition or a New Testament writing serves a single, determinate purpose, for example, as a "prooftext," as a source of vindication or validation for a statement a later author wishes to prove. The positive: we have to undertake an inductive inquiry into the uses and authority of the received scriptures of ancient Israel, allowing diverse documents to provide, each its own indication of where and how the inherited, authoritative writings serve the purposes of an author or authorship.

The founders of Judaism engaged in dialogue with the Scriptures of ancient Israel. They turned to Scripture not for prooftexts, let alone for pretexts, to say whatever they wanted, anyhow, to say. They used

Scripture as an artist uses the colors on the palette, expressing ideas through and with Scripture as the artists paints with those colors and no others. This reading of the ways in which the Judaic sages read Scripture insists on two propositions. Sages created within a limited and well-defined vocabulary of thought, contrary to the conception that these same sages engaged in an essentially indeterminate and unlimited process of thought. They appealed to Scripture not merely for prooftexts as part of an apologia but for a far more original and sustained mode of discourse. Verses of Scripture served not merely to prove but to instruct. Israelite Scripture constituted not merely a source of validation but a powerful instrument of profound inquiry.

It follows that the category, "prooftexts," does not correspond to the role and authority of Scripture in the Torah. It is supposed that people settled questions by discovering a verse to demonstrate what they wished to say, with the further implication, within Judaic and Christian apologetics of the present century, of an original and determinate meaning of a Scripture, perceived as complete and autonomous, that validates, historically, the claim of the faith. That second premise, of course, imputes conceptions discovered only in modern times. We all recognize, of course, that ancient Israel no more testified to the Oral Torah, now written down in the Mishnah and later rabbinic writings, than it did to Jesus as the Christ. In both cases, religious circles within Israel of later antiquity reread the entire past in the light of their own conscience and convictions. They took for granted that the Torah and the contents of their conscience and convictions coalesced. Hence the conception that Scripture formed a court of last appeal, an authoritative criterion established out of a completed past, contradicts the situation of intellect and faith in which the authorships of the Judaism at hand endured. True, the Written Torah formed a distinct and always distinguished corpus of writing.[2]

---

[2]The distinction between the authority of Scripture and the authority of scribes, for example, forms a commonplace. But that distinction did not bear the sense that has commonly been assigned to it, that the Written Torah and the Oral Torah constituted distinct entities, separated from one another by centuries. The Judaism of the Dual Torah reached the firm conclusion that the two media in which the Torah was received accomplished the formulation and transmission of one whole Torah. Accordingly, the relationship between the Torah that derived from one medium, the written, and the Torah that derived from another medium, the oral, requires close analysis. That relationship cannot be imputed on the basis of a misunderstanding of the weight and implications of the distinction between the two media.

II. Defining a "Biblical Religion"

While the framers of Judaism as we know it received as divinely revealed ancient Israel's literary heritage, they picked and chose as they wished what would serve the purposes of the larger system they undertook to build. Since the Judaism at hand first reached literary expression in the Mishnah, a document in which Scripture plays a subordinate role, the founders of that Judaism clearly made no pretense at tying up to scriptural prooftexts or at expressing in the form of scriptural commentary the main ideas they wished to set out. Accordingly, Judaism rests only asymmetrically upon the foundations of the Hebrew Scriptures, and Judaism is not alone or mainly "the religion of the Old Testament."

Since Judaism is not "the religion of the Old Testament," we cannot take for granted or treat as predictable or predetermined the entry of the Hebrew Scriptures into the system of Judaism at hand. That is why we must ask exactly how the Scriptures did enter the framework of Judaism. In what way, when, and where, in the unfolding of the canon of Judaism, were they absorbed and recast, and how did they find the distinctive role they were to play from late antiquity onward? That question points toward the larger issue, namely, the place and use of Scripture in the Judaism of the Dual Torah. Once we realize that "Scripture" in the Judaism of the Dual Torah formed (merely) one component of the Torah, everything changes. Scripture loses its autonomous standing and its paramount authority and becomes one more medium for God's revealing the Torah to Israel. And other writings enter the status of that same revelation. When that shift takes place – as it does for Judaism as well as for Christianity, each within its own logic – then what of the Written Torah/Old Testament? That is what is at stake in the recognition that authorships of ancient Judaism wrote with Scripture and proposed the result to form part of the Torah.

When the Judaism of the Dual Torah had defined its matrix of myth and rite – a system of worldview and way of life focused on a particular social group – then that Judaism attained its independent voice, its inner structure and logic. At that moment – but only then – Scripture for its part also would assume its position as source of truth and proof for all (autonomously framed, independently reached) propositions. In the nature of things Scripture could form a focus of discourse only when discourse itself had expressed determinants autonomous of both the Mishnah and also Scripture – determinants, or propositions prior to all else. To revert to the operative myth, it is only when the Torah had reached full expression as an autonomous entity of logic that the (mere) components of Torah – Scripture, the Mishnah, and associated writings alike – found their proper place and proportion.

Let me take as my example the character of Scripture in the Midrash compilation, Leviticus Rabbah.[3] In Leviticus Rabbah we see how statements become intelligible not contingently, that is, on the strength of an established text, but a priori, that is, on the basis of a deeper logic of meaning, an independent principle of rhetorical intelligibility. The reason we say so is simple. Leviticus Rabbah is topical, not exegetical. Each of its thirty-seven *parashiyyot* pursues its given topic and develops points relevant to that topic. It is logical, in that (to repeat) discourse appeals to an underlying principle of composition and intelligibility, and that logic inheres in what is said. Logic is what joins one sentence to the next and forms the whole into paragraphs of meaning, intelligible propositions, each with its place and sense in a still larger, accessible system. Because of logic one mind connects to another, public discourse becomes possible, debate on issues of general intelligibility takes place, and an anthology of statements about a single subject becomes a composition of theorems about that subject. Accordingly, with Leviticus Rabbah rabbis take up the problem of saying what they wish to say not in an exegetical, but in a syllogistic and freely discursive logic and rhetoric.

To appreciate what was new, let us rapidly review the prior pattern of how people wrote both with and without Scripture. To seek, through biblical exegesis, to link the Mishnah to Scripture, detail by detail, represented a well-trodden and firmly packed path. Sifra, an exegetical study of Leviticus as rabbis read the document, shows what could be done.[4] The exegetes there cite a passage of the Mishnah verbatim and show that only through Scriptural exegesis, not through the processes of

---

[3]See my studies of Leviticus Rabbah in the following three monographs: *Judaism and Scripture: The Evidence of Leviticus Rabbah* (Chicago, 1986: University of Chicago Press); *The Integrity of Leviticus Rabbah. The Problem of the Autonomy of a Rabbinic Document* (Chico, 1985: Scholars Press for Brown Judaic Studies); *Comparative Midrash: The Plan and Program of Genesis Rabbah and Leviticus Rabbah* (Atlanta, 1986: Scholars Press for Brown Judaic Studies).

[4]*Sifra. An Analytical Translation* (Atlanta, 1988: Scholars Press for Brown Judaic Studies). I. *Introduction* and *Vayyiqra Dibura Denedabah* and *Vayiqqra Dibura Dehobah; Sifra. An Analytical Translation* (Atlanta, 1988: Scholars Press for Brown Judaic Studies). II. *Sav, Shemini, Tazria, Negaim, Mesora*, and *Zabim; Sifra. An Analytical Translation* (Atlanta, 1988: Scholars Press for Brown Judaic Studies). III. *Aharé Mot, Qedoshim, Emor, Behar*, and *Behuqotai*; and the two monographs based on that analytical translation, *Uniting the Dual Torah: Sifra and the Problem of the Mishnah* (Cambridge and New York, 1989: Cambridge University Press), and *Sifra in Perspective: The Documentary Comparison of the Midrashim of Ancient Judaism* (Atlanta, 1988: Scholars Press for Brown Judaic Studies).

reason, can we reach the correct law. Scripture exegesis by rabbis also was a commonplace, as Genesis Rabbah indicates. Leviticus Rabbah was the first major rabbinic composition to propose to make topical and discursive statements, not episodically, as in Sifré to Deuteronomy, but systematically and in a disciplined framework. Not merely a phrase-by-phrase or verse-by-verse exegesis of a document, whether the Mishnah or a book of Scripture itself, Leviticus Rabbah takes a new road.

The framers of that composition undertook to offer propositions, declarative sentences (so to speak), in which, not through the exegesis of verses of Scripture in the order of Scripture but through an order dictated by their own sense of the logic of syllogistic composition, they would say what they had in mind. To begin with, they laid down their own topical program, related to, but essentially autonomous of, that of the book of Leviticus. Second, in expressing their ideas on these topics, they never undertook simply to cite a verse of Scripture and then to claim that that verse states precisely what they had in mind to begin with. Accordingly, through rather distinctive modes of expression, the framers said what they wished to say in their own way – just as had the authors of the Mishnah itself. True, in so doing, the composers of Leviticus Rabbah treated Scripture as had their predecessors. That is to say, to them as to those who had gone before, Scripture provided a rich treasury of facts.

III. Writing with Scripture in a Biblical Religion

How, very concretely, do the framers of Leviticus Rabbah accomplish that "writing with Scripture" of which we have spoken? The paramount and dominant exegetical construction in Leviticus Rabbah is the base-verse/intersecting-verse exegesis. In this construction, a verse of Leviticus is cited (hence: base verse), and another verse, from such books as Job, Proverbs, Qohelet, or Psalms, is then cited (hence: intersecting verse). The latter, not the former, is subjected to detailed and systematic exegesis. But the exegetical exercise ends up by leading the intersecting verse back to the base verse and reading the latter in terms of the former. In such an exercise, what in fact do we do? We read one thing in terms of something else. To begin with, it is the base verse in terms of the intersecting verse. But it also is the intersecting verse in other terms as well – a multiple layered construction of analogy and parable. The intersecting verse's elements always turn out to stand for, to signify, to speak of, something other than that to which they openly refer. If water stands for Torah, the skin disease for evil speech, the reference to something for some other thing entirely, then the mode of thought at hand is simple. One thing symbolizes another, speaks not of itself but of some other thing entirely.

How shall we describe this mode of thought? It seems to me we may call it an as-if way of seeing things. That is to say, it is as if a common object or symbol really represented an uncommon one. Nothing says what it means. Everything important speaks metonymically, elliptically, parabolically, symbolically. All statements carry deeper meaning, which inheres in other statements altogether. The profound sense, then, of the base verse emerges only through restatement within and through the intersecting verse – as if the base verse spoke of things that, on the surface, we do not see at all. Accordingly, if we ask the single prevalent literary construction to testify to the prevailing frame of mind, its message is that things are never what they seem. All things demand interpretation. Interpretation begins in the search for analogy, for that to which the thing is likened, hence the deep sense in which all exegesis at hand is parabolic. It is a quest for that for which the thing in its deepest structure stands.

Exegesis as we know it in Leviticus Rabbah (and not only there, since in the context of this article, Leviticus Rabbah is meant only as exemplary) consists in an exercise in analogical thinking – something is like something else, stands for, evokes, or symbolizes that which is quite outside itself. It may be the opposite of something else, in which case it conforms to the exact opposite of the rules that govern that something else. The reasoning is analogical or it is contrastive, and the fundamental logic is taxonomic. The taxonomy rests on those comparisons and contrasts we should call, as we said, metonymic and parabolic. In that case what lies on the surface misleads. What lies beneath or beyond the surface – there is the true reality, the world of truth and meaning. To revert to the issue of taxonomy, the tracts that allow classification serve only for that purpose. They signify nothing more than that something more.

How shall we characterize people who see things this way? They constitute the opposite of ones who call a thing as it is. Self-evidently, they have become accustomed to perceiving more – or less – than is at hand. Perhaps that is a natural mode of thought for the Jews of this period (and not then alone), so long used to calling themselves God's first love, yet now seeing others with greater worldly reason claiming that same advantaged relationship. Not in mind only, but still more, in the politics of the world, the people that remembered its origins along with the very creation of the world and founding of humanity, that recalled how it alone served, and serves, the one and only God, for more than three hundred years had confronted a quite different existence. The radical disjuncture between the way things were and the way Scripture said things were supposed to be – and in actuality would some day become – surely imposed an unbearable tension. It was one thing for the slave born to slavery to endure. It was another for the free man sold into slavery to accept that same condition. The vanquished people, the nation that had lost its city and its temple, that had, moreover, produced another nation from its midst to take over its Scripture and much else could not bear too much reality. That defeated people will then have found refuge in a mode of thought that trained vision to see other things otherwise than as the eyes perceived them. Among the diverse ways by which the weak and subordinated accommodate to their circumstance, the one of iron-willed pretense in life is most likely to yield the mode of thought at hand: things never are, because they cannot be, what they seem.

IV. The Role of Scripture: Paradigm of Renewal and Reconstruction

Everyone has always known that Jews read Scripture. Every system of Judaism has done so. But why did they do so? What place did Scripture take in the larger systems of reality presented by various Judaisms? Why one part of Scripture rather than some other, and why read it in one way rather than another? These questions do not find ready answers in the mere observation that Jews read Scripture and construct Judaisms out of it. Nor is that observation one of a predictable and necessary pattern, since some of the documents of the rabbinic canon did not focus upon Scripture or even find it necessary to quote Scripture a great deal. The Mishnah, Tosefta, and important units of discourse of both Talmuds, for example, did not express their ideas in the way in which people who "read Scripture" ought to. They make use of Scripture sparingly, only with restraint adducing proofs for propositions even when these are based upon scriptural statements. So the paramount and dominant place accorded to Scripture in Leviticus Rabbah and documents like it cannot pass without comment and explanation.

Exactly what can we say for the position of Scripture in this composition in particular, and what did Scripture contribute? We ask first about the use of Scripture in the mode of thought at hand: where, why, and how did Scripture find its central place in the minds of people who thought in the way in which the framers of our document did? The answer is that Scripture contributed that other world that underlay this one. From Scripture came that other set of realities to be discovered in the ordinary affairs of the day. Scripture defined the inner being, the mythic life, that sustained Israel. The world is to be confronted as if things are not as they seem, because it is Scripture that tells us how things always are – not one time, in the past only, not one time, in the future only, but now and always. So the key to the system is what happens to, and through, Scripture. The lock that is opened is the deciphering of the code by which people were guided in their denial of one thing and recognition and affirmation of the presence of some other. It was not general, therefore mere lunacy, but specific, therefore culture.

To spell this out: the mode of thought pertained to a particular set of ideas. People did not engage ubiquitously and individually in an ongoing pretense that things always had to be other than they seemed. Had they done so, the Jewish nation would have disintegrated into a collectivity of pure insanity. The insistence on the as-if character of reality collectively focused upon one, and only one, alternative existence. All parties (so far as we know) entered into and shared that same and single interior universe. It was the one framed by Scripture. What happens in Leviticus Rabbah (and, self-evidently, in other documents of the same sort)? Reading one thing in terms of something else, the builders of the document systematically adopted for themselves the reality of the Scripture, its history and doctrines. They transformed that history from a sequence of one-time events, leading from one place to some other, into an ever-present mythic world. No longer was there one Moses, one David, one set of happenings of a distinctive and never-to-be-repeated character. Now whatever happens, of which the thinkers propose to take account, must enter and be absorbed into that established and ubiquitous pattern and structure founded in Scripture. It is not that biblical history repeats itself. Rather, biblical history no longer constitutes history as a story of things that happened once, long ago, and pointed to some one moment in the future. Rather it becomes an account of things that happen every day – hence, an ever-present mythic world, as we said.

A rapid glance at the work of the authorships of Leviticus Rabbah or Sifré to Deuteronomy (or any of their fellows) tells us that Scripture supplies the document with its structure, its content, its facts, its everything. But a deeper analysis also demonstrates that Scripture never provides the document with that structure, contents, and facts, that it now exhibits. Everything is reshaped and reframed. Whence the paradox? Scripture as a whole does not dictate the order of discourse, let alone its character. Just as the Talmudic authors destroyed the wholeness of the Mishnah and chose to take up its bits and pieces, so the exegetical writers did the same to Scripture. In our document they chose in Leviticus itself a verse here, a phrase there. These then presented the pretext for propositional discourse commonly quite out of phase with the cited passage. Verses that are quoted ordinarily shift from the meanings they convey to the implications they contain, speaking – as we have made clear – about something, anything, other than what they seem to be saying.

So the as-if frame of mind brought to Scripture brings renewal to Scripture, seeing everything with fresh eyes. And the result of the new vision was a re-imagining of the social world envisioned by the document at hand, we mean, the everyday world of Israel in its Land in that difficult time. For what the sages now proposed was a reconstruction of existence along the lines of the ancient design of Scripture as they read it. What that meant was that, from a sequence of one-time and linear events, everything that happened was turned into a repetition of known and already experienced paradigms, hence, once more, a mythic being. The source and core of the myth, of course, derive from Scripture – Scripture reread, renewed, reconstructed along with the society that revered Scripture.

So, to summarize, the mode of thought that dictated the issues and the logic of the document, telling the thinkers to see one thing in terms of something else, addressed Scripture in particular and collectively. And thinking as they did, the framers of the document saw Scripture in a new way, just as they saw their own circumstance afresh, rejecting their world in favor of Scripture's, reliving Scripture's world in their own terms. That, incidentally, is why they did not write history, an account of what was happening and what it meant. It was not that they did not recognize or appreciate important changes and trends reshaping their nation's life. They could not deny that reality. In their apocalyptic reading of the dietary and leprosy laws, they made explicit their close encounter with the history of the world as they knew it. But they had another mode of responding to history. It was to treat history as if it were already known and readily understood. Whatever happened had already happened. How so? Scripture dictated the contents of history, laying forth the structures of time, the rules that prevailed and were made known in events. Self-evidently, these same thinkers projected into Scripture's day the realities of their own, turning Moses and David into rabbis, for example. But that is how people think in that mythic, enchanted world in which, to begin with, reality blends with dream, and hope projects onto future and past alike how people want things to be.

The upshot is that the mode of thought revealed by the literary construction under discussion constitutes a rather specific expression of a far more general and prevailing way of seeing things. The literary form in concrete ways says that the entirety of the biblical narrative speaks to each circumstance, that the system of Scripture as a whole not only governs, but comes prior to, any concrete circumstance of that same Scripture. Everything in Scripture is relevant everywhere else in Scripture. It must follow, the Torah (to use the mythic language of the system at hand) defines reality under all specific circumstances. Obviously we did not have to come to the specific literary traits of the document at hand to discover those prevailing characteristics of contemporary and later documents of the rabbinic canon. True, every exercise in referring one biblical passage to another expands the range of discourse to encompass much beyond the original referent. But that is a commonplace in the exegesis of Scripture, familiar wherever midrash exegesis was undertaken, in no way particular to rabbinic writings.

V. Writing with Scripture and Rewriting Scripture

Scripture proves paramount on the surface, but subordinated in the deep structure of the logic of Leviticus Rabbah and the other Midrash compilations. Why so? Because Scripture enjoys no autonomous standing, for example, as the sole source of facts. It does not dictate the order of discussion. It does not (by itself) determine the topics to be taken up, since its verses, cited one by one in sequence, do not tell us how matters will proceed. Scripture, moreover, does not allow us to predict what proposition a given set of verses will yield. On the contrary, because of the insistence that one verse be read in light of another, one theme in light of another, augmentative one, Leviticus Rabbah (and the related writings) prohibits us from predicting at the outset, merely by reading a given verse of Scripture, the way in which a given theme will be worked out or the way in which a given proposition will impart a message through said theme.

What does it mean, then, to write with Scripture? The order of Scripture does not govern the sequence of discourse, the themes of Scripture do not tell us what themes will be taken up, the propositions of Scripture about its stated themes, what Scripture says, in its context, about a given topic, do not define the propositions of Leviticus Rabbah about that topic. The upshot is simple. Scripture contributes everything and nothing. It provides the decoration, the facts, much language. But whence the heart and soul and spirit? Where the matrix, where source? The editors, doing the work of selection, making their points through juxtaposition of things not otherwise brought into contact with one another – they are the ones who speak throughout. True, the voice is the voice of Scripture. But the hand is the hand of the collectivity of the sages, who are authors speaking through Scripture. If, moreover, Scripture contributes facts, so too do the ones who state those ineluctable truths that are expressed in parables, and so too do the ones who tell stories, also exemplifying truths, about great heroes and villains. No less, of course, but, in standing, also no more than these, Scripture makes its contribution along with other sources of social truth.

Greek science focused upon physics. Then the laws of Israel's salvation serve as the physics of the sages. But Greek science derived facts and built theorems on the basis of other sources besides physics; the philosophers also, after all, studied ethnography, ethics, politics, and history. For the sages at hand, along these same lines, parables, exemplary tales, and completed paragraphs of thought deriving from other sources (not to exclude the Mishnah, Tosefta, Sifra, Genesis Rabbah and such literary compositions that had been made ready for the Talmud of the Land of Israel) – these too make their contribution of data subject to analysis. All of these sources of truth, all together, were directed toward the discovery of philosophical laws for the understanding of Israel's life, now and in the age to come.

Standing paramount and dominant, Scripture contributed everything but the main point. That point comes to us from the framers of Midrash compilations such as Leviticus Rabbah – from them alone. So far as Leviticus Rabbah transcends the book of Leviticus – and that means, in the whole of its being – the document speaks for the framers, conveys their message, pursues their discourse, makes the points they wished to make. For they are the ones who made of Leviticus, the book, Leviticus Rabbah, that greater Leviticus, the document that spoke of sanctification but, in its augmented version at hand, meant salvation. As closely related to the book of Leviticus as the New Testament is to the Old, Leviticus Rabbah delivers the message of the philosophers of Israel's history.

We have emphasized that Leviticus Rabbah carries a message of its own, which finds a place within, and refers to, a larger system. The method of thought and mode of argument act out a denial of one reality in favor of the affirmation of another. That dual process of pretense at the exegetical level evokes the deeper pretense of the mode of thought of the larger system, and, at the deepest layer, the pretense that fed Israel's soul and sustained it. Just as one thing evokes some other, so does the rabbinic system overall turn into aspects of myth and actions of deep symbolic consequence what to the untutored eye were commonplace deeds and neutral transactions. So, too, the wretched nation really enjoyed God's special love.

Now what are the commonplace traits of Scripture in this other, new context altogether?

1. Scripture, for one thing, forms a timeless present, with the affairs of the present day read back into the past and the past into the present, with singular events absorbed into Scripture's paradigms.
2. Scripture is read whole and atomistically. Everything speaks to everything else, but only one thing speaks at a time.

3. Scripture is read as an account of a seamless world, encompassing present and past alike, and Scripture is read atemporally and ahistorically.

All of these things surprise no one; they have been recognized for a very long time. What is new here is the claim to explain why these things are so, we mean, the logic of the composition that prevails, also, when Scripture comes to hand.

1. Scripture is read whole, because the framers pursue issues of thought that demand all data pertain to all times and all contexts. The authors are philosophers, looking for rules and their verification. Scripture tells stories, to be sure. But these exemplify facts of social life and national destiny: the laws of Israel's life.
2. Scripture is read atomistically, just as is the Mishnah, because each of its components constitutes a social fact, ever relevant to the society of which it forms a part, with that society everywhere uniform.
3. Scripture is read as a source of facts pertinent to historical and contemporary issues alike, because the issues at hand when worked out will indicate the prevailing laws, the rules that apply everywhere, all the time, to everyone of Israel.

Accordingly, there is no way for Scripture to be read except as a source of facts about that ongoing reality that forms the focus and the center of discourse, the life of the unique social entity, Israel. But the simple logic conveyed by the parable also contributes its offering of facts. The simple truth conveyed by the tale of the great man, the exemplary event of the rabbinic sage, the memorable miracle – these too serve as well as facts of Scripture. The several truths therefore stand alongside and at the same level as the truths of Scripture, which is not the sole source of rules or cases. The facts of Scripture stand no higher than those of the parable, on the one side, or of the tale of the sage, on the other. Why not? Because to philosophers and scientists, facts are facts, whatever their origin or point of application.

What we have in the Torah's use of Scripture, therefore, is the result of the mode of thought not of prophets or historians, but of philosophers and scientists. The framers propose not to lay down, but to discover, rules governing Israel's life. We state with necessary emphasis: as we find the rules of nature by identifying and classifying facts of natural life, so we find rules of society by identifying and classifying the facts of Israel's social life. In both modes of inquiry we make sense of things by bringing together like specimens and finding out whether they form a species, then bringing together like species and finding out whether they form a genus – in all, classifying data and identifying the rules that make possible the classification.

That sort of thinking lies at the deepest level of list-making, which is work of offering a proposition and facts (for social rules) as much as a genus and its species (for rules of nature). Once discovered, the social rules of Israel's national life of course yield explicit statements, such as that God hates the arrogant and loves the humble. The readily assembled syllogism follows: if one is arrogant, God will hate him, and if he is humble, God will love him. The logical status of these statements, in context, is as secure and unassailable as the logical status of statements about physics, ethics, or politics, as these emerge in philosophical thought. What differentiates the statements is not their logical status – as sound, scientific philosophy – but only their subject matter, on the one side, and distinctive rhetoric, on the other.

So rabbinic writings are anything but an exegetical exercise. We err if we are taken in by the powerful rhetoric of our documents, which resort so ubiquitously to the citation of biblical verses and, more important, to the construction, out of diverse verses, of a point transcendent of the cited verses. At hand is not a canon comprising exegetical compositions at all, nor even verses of Scripture read as a corpus of prooftexts. We have, rather, statements that stand by themselves, each document formed in its own terms and separate from Scripture, and that makes it points only secondarily, along the way, by evoking verses of Scripture to express and exemplify those same points. We miss the main point if we posit that Scripture plays a definitive or even central role in providing the program and agenda for the framers of Leviticus Rabbah. Their program is wholly their own. But of course Scripture then serves their purposes very well indeed.

So, too, their style is their own. Scripture merely contributes to an aesthetic that is at once pleasing and powerful for people who know Scripture pretty much by heart. But in context the aesthetic too is original. The constant invocation of scriptural verses compares with the place of the classics in the speech and writing of gentlefolk of an earlier age, in which the mark of elegance was perpetual allusion to classical writers. No Christian author of the age would have found alien the aesthetic at hand. So while the constant introduction of verses of Scripture provides the wherewithal of speech, these verses serve only as do the colors of the painter. The painter cannot paint without the oils. But the colors do not make the painting. The painter does. As original and astonishing as is the aesthetic of the Mishnah, the theory of persuasive rhetoric governing Leviticus Rabbah produces a still more amazing result.

VI. A Fond Farewell to the Notion of [1] Judaism as a (Mere) Paraphrase of the Hebrew Scriptures and of [2] Scripture as (Mere) Source of (Mere) Prooftexts

We may say that (again by way of example) Leviticus Rabbah provides an exegesis of the book of Leviticus just as much as the school of Matthew provides an exegesis of passages cited in the book of Isaiah. Yet, we must reiterate at the end, Leviticus serves as something other than a source of prooftexts. It is not that at all. And that is the important fact we mean to prove. What is new in Leviticus Rabbah's encounter with Scripture emerges – and that document stands for others in the canon of the Judaism of the Dual Torah – when we realize that, for former Israelite writers, Scriptures do serve principally as a source of prooftexts. That certainly is the case for the school of Matthew, for one thing, and also for the Essene writers whose library survived at Qumran, for another. The task of Scripture for the authors of the Tosefta, Sifra, Genesis Rabbah, and the Talmud of the Land of Israel emerged out of a single need. That need was to found the creations of the new age upon the authority of the old. Thus the exegetical work consequent upon the Mishnah demanded a turning to Scripture. From that necessary and predictable meeting, exegetical work on Scripture itself got under way, with the results so self-evident in most of the exegetical compositions on most of the Pentateuch, including Leviticus, accomplished in the third and fourth centuries. None of this in fact defined how Scripture would reach its right and proper place in the Judaism of the Talmuds and exegetical compositions. It was Leviticus Rabbah that set the pattern, and its pattern would predominate for a very long time. The operative rules would be these:

1. From Leviticus Rabbah onward, Scripture would conform to paradigms framed essentially independent of Scripture.
2. From then onward, Scripture was made to yield paradigms applicable beyond the limits of Scripture.

In these two complementary statements we summarize the entire argument concerning the uses of Scripture in the Torah of formative Judaism. The heart of the matter lies in laying forth the rules of life – of Israel's life and salvation. These rules derive from the facts of history, as much as the rules of the Mishnah derive from the facts of society (and, in context, the rules of philosophy derive from the facts of nature). Scripture then never stands all by itself. Its exalted position at the center of all discourse proves contingent, never absolute. That negative result of course bears an entirely affirmative complement. Judaism is not the religion of the Old Testament because Judaism is Judaism. Scripture enters Judaism because Judaism is the religion of "the one whole Torah of Moses, our rabbi," and part of that Torah is the written part, Scripture. But that whole Torah, viewed whole, is this: God's revelation of the rules of life: creation, society, history alike.

Obviously, every Judaism would be in some way a scriptural religion. But the sort of scriptural religion a given kind of Judaism would reveal is not to be predicted on the foundations of traits of Scripture in particular. One kind of Judaism laid its distinctive emphasis upon a linear history of Israel, in a sequence of unique, one-time events, all together yielding a pattern of revealed truth, from creation, through revelation, to redemption. That kind of Judaism then would read Scripture for signs of the times and turn Scripture into a resource for apocalyptic speculation. A kind of Judaism interested not in one-time events of history but in all-time rules of society, governing for all time, such as the kind at hand, would read Scripture philosophically and not historically. That is, Scripture would yield a corpus of facts conforming to rules. Scripture would provide a source of paradigms, the opposite of one-time events.

So no, Judaism of the Dual Torah is not a "biblical religion," because the system of the Dual Torah does not recapitulate the canon of the Old Testament, but selects what it finds useful within that canon.[5] True enough, many kinds of Judaism would find their definitive propositions in Scripture and build upon them. But while all of Scripture was revealed and authoritative, for each construction of a system of Judaism only some passages of Scripture would prove to be relevant. Just as the framers of the Mishnah came to Scripture with a program of questions and inquiries framed essentially among themselves, one which turned out to be highly selective, so did their successors who made up Leviticus Rabbah and its companions. What they brought was a mode of thought, a deeply philosophical and scientific quest, and an acute problem of history and society. In their search for the rules of Israel's life and salvation, they found answer not in the one-time events of history but in paradigmatic facts, social laws of salvation. It was in the mind and imagination of the already philosophical authors of the Rabbah-Midrash compilations that Scripture came to serve – as did nature, as did everyday life and its parables, all together – to reveal laws everywhere and always valid.

[5]This is a point sadly missed by H. Maccoby in his critique of my reading of the Red Cow (and much else). See Chapter Fifteen, below.

9

The Role of History:
Is Judaism a "Historical Religion"?

The writing of history – narrative of things that have happened, propositions deriving from events, their order and significance – provides one reliable guide to the course of the history of Judaism. Whether or not people wrote history at all, and if they did, the purpose they imputed to events and their sequence, differentiate one Judaism – a Judaic system comprising a worldview, way of life, and account of the social entity, "Israel" – from another. Some Judaisms have set forth elaborate accounts of history, others have treated events as episodic and anecdotal and merely exemplary, drawing no large pictures of connected events and making slight effort to derive meaning and religious truth from those connections. The differentiation of one Judaism from another, therefore, may play off the indicative trait supplied by the religious and theological uses of history that define one Judaism but not some other. Since all Judaisms (by definition) appeal to the Hebrew Scriptures of ancient Israel (a.k.a, "the Old Testament," "the Written Torah," "Tanakh"), that work of differentiation and classification, moreover, gains perspective against a shared reference point among them all. And because the ancient Scriptures themselves present their systemic statement through a remarkable, sustained historical narrative, with a beginning, a middle, and an end, and since such books as Genesis, Exodus, Numbers, Deuteronomy-Joshua-Judges-Samuel-Kings, as well as the whole of the prophetic writings, insist on the priority of events, viewed as connected and probative, history forms a native category of the first Judaic system, the pentateuchal one.

That fact makes all the more surprising the formation, in centuries beyond the closure of the Pentateuch by Ezra in ca. 450 B.C., of Judaisms that found in historical thinking no hermeneutic, in historical events no heuristic challenge, and in the large view of the message and meaning of history no materials of theological consequence, let alone of probative value. In the pages of this anthology, a variety of papers underline the fact that history served as a source of mere "hagiography with footnotes," or as a source of paradigms, not differentiated and singular events. The character of the Judaism that nurtured medieval and early modern thought on history and history writing explains why that fact indeed is not at all surprising. And when, in modern times, modern Jewish historiography emerged, that development signaled a new Judaism aborning – connected to, but essentially not continuous with, the ahistorical Judaism of the Dual Torah that reached its authoritative statement in the Talmud of Babylonia and that shaped the antihistorical thinking of its continuator systems, the Judaisms that flourished, paramount, from then to nearly the present day and that continue to occupy the center stage of Judaism even now.

So if we ask whether or not the Judaism of the Dual Torah is to be classified as a historical religion, to find the succinct answer to that question is simple. When we know how Judaism *classifies* events, we shall have the answer to the question of defining events – a perfectly routine procedure in the natural history of ideas. So, too, when we know how Judaism *utilizes* events, assessing with accuracy, and on the basis of a vast and characteristic kind of writing, the heuristic value, the probative standing, of events, we once again shall have our answer. While the Judaism of the Dual Torah makes ample use of the Old Testament in its account of itself, in the end, the canon of the Dual Torah – written and oral, encompassing the two Talmuds and various Midrash compilations – appealed to events but produced very little history. There is no counterpart, for example, to Eusebius, none to Augustine. We should expect that the canon of heirs to the deuteronomic historians would encompass narrative history, but it does not. We should expect to find therein accounts of events of not only times past but also the present explained by the past, but we do not. We should go in search of the description of one-time, unique happenings – events in the conventional sense – but, if we did, we should return disappointed. The result will be quite opposite. When we read matters properly, we shall find out how to read. For the archaeology of texts uncovers abstract structure in the identification and explication of the concrete event.

If we ask ourselves, then, how the Judaic invention of history served the larger systemic interests of the Judaism that reverted to historical thinking, the answer is by no means the one we should anticipate. Specifically, that Judaism utilized events, but produced no history, and the precise character of the Judaic utilization of history requires definition. The answer, not surprisingly, is that history served at the altar of theology – and, as a matter of fact, did not take a principal part in that service. We see that fact with great clarity when we ask ourselves what exactly does Judaism mean by "events"? For, until our own time, "events" formed the raw material of history, the source of probative evidence of propositions, the pattern that, all together and all at once, pointed to that truth that history proved. When, therefore, we can say how the Judaism of the canon of the Dual Torah defined and utilized events, we shall have a clear picture of the theological uses to which, in Judaism, history was put.

In the canonical literature of the Judaism of the Dual Torah, formed between the second and the seventh centuries and authoritative to this day, events find their place, within the science of learning of *Listenwissenschaft* that characterizes this literature, along with sorts of things that, for our part, we should not characterize as events at all. It follows that the Judaism of the canon in no way appeals to history as a sequence of ordered events, yielding a clear truth and meaning, in the way, for instance, that history in the deuteronomic sequence of Deuteronomy, Joshua, Judges, Samuel, and Kings forms a sequence of events that comprise history. In canonical Judaism, by contrast, events have no autonomous standing; events are not unique, each unto itself; events have no probative value on their own; and events are not to be strung together as explanations for how things are. In this writing, philosophical and scientific, rather than (in the aggregate) historical and theological, events form cases, along with a variety of other cases, making up lists of things that, in common, point to or prove one thing.

Not only so, but events do not make up their own list at all, and this is what I found rather curious when I first noted that fact. That is to say, just as in the canon of Judaism of the Dual Torah is not a single piece of writing of sustained narrative, something we might call history as Josephus or the Deuteronomists wrote history, so we have only episodically and then unsustainedly the representation of events as merely exemplary, never probative by reason of connection and sequence and order. Events therefore do not form components of an independent variable, and history constitutes no independent variable. Events will appear on – form components of – the same list as persons, places, things. That means that events not only have no autonomous standing on their own, but also that events constitute no species even within a genus, the historical order. For persons, places, and things in our way of thinking do not belong on the same list as events; they are not of the same order. Within the logic of our own minds, we cannot classify the city, Paris, within the same genus as the event, the declaration of the rights of man, for instance, nor is Sinai of the same order of things as the Torah.

What, then, are we to make of a list that encompasses within the same taxic composition events and things? One such list made up of events, persons, and places, is as follows: [1] Israel at the Sea; [2] the ministering angels; [3] the tent of meeting; [4] the eternal house [=the Temple]; [5] Sinai. That mixes an event (Israel redeemed at the Sea), a category of sensate being (angels), a location (tent of meeting, Temple), and then Sinai, which can stand for a variety of things but in context stands for the Torah. In such a list an event may or may not stand for a value or a proposition, but it does not enjoy autonomous standing; the list is not defined by the eventfulness of events and their meaning, the compilation of matters of a single genus or even a single species (tent of meeting, eternal house, are the same species here). The notion of event as autonomous, even unique, is quite absent in this taxonomy.

Another such list moves from events to other matters altogether, finding the whole subject to the same metaphor, hence homogenized. First come the events that took place at these places or with these persons: Egypt, the Sea, Marah, Massah and Meribah, Horeb, the wilderness, the spies in the Land, Shittim, for Achan/Joshua and the conquest of the Land. Now that mixture of places and names clearly intends to focus on particular things that happened, and hence, were the list to which I refer to conclude at this point, we could define an event for Judaism as a happening that bore consequence, taught a lesson or exemplified a truth; in the present case, an event matters because of the mixture of rebellion and obedience. But there would then be no doubt that "event" formed a genus unto itself, and that a proper list could not encompass both events, defined conventionally as we should, and also other matters altogether.

But the literary culture at hand, this textual community proceeds, in the same literary context, to the following items: [1] the Ten Commandments; [2] the show fringes and phylacteries; [3] the *Shema* and the Prayer; [4] the tabernacle and the cloud of the Presence of God in the world to come. Why we invoke, as our candidates for the metaphor at hand, the Ten Commandments, show fringes and phylacteries, recitation of the *Shema* and the Prayer, the tabernacle and the cloud of the Presence of God, and the *mezuzah*, seems to me clear from the very catalogue. These reach their climax in the analogy between the home and the tabernacle, the embrace of God and the Presence of God. So the whole is meant to list those things that draw the Israelite near God and make the Israelite cleave to God. And to this massive catalogue, events are not only exemplary – which historians can concede without difficulty – but also subordinated.

They belong on the same list as actions, things, persons, places, because they form an order of being that is not to be differentiated between events (including things that stand for events) and other cultural artifacts altogether. A happening is no different from an object, in which case "event" serves no better, and no worse, than a hero, a gesture or action, recitation of a given formula, or a particular locale, to establish a truth. It is contingent, subordinate, instrumental. I can think of no more apt illustration of Geertz's interesting judgment cited by Sahlin, that "an event is a unique actualization of a general phenomenon, a contingent realization of the cultural pattern." And why find that fact surprising, since all history comes to us in writing, and it is the culture that dictates how writing is to take place; that is why history can only paraphrase the affirmations of a system, and that is why events recapitulate in acute and concrete ways the system that classifies one thing that happens as event, but another thing is not only not an event but is not classified at all. In the present instance, an event is not at all eventful; it is merely a fact that forms part of the evidence for what is, and what is eventful is not an occasion at all, but a condition, an attitude, a perspective and a viewpoint. Then, it is clear, events are subordinated to the formation of attitudes, perspectives, viewpoints – the formative artifacts of not history in the conventional sense but culture in the framework of Sahlin's generalization, "history is culturally ordered, differently so in different societies, according to meaningful schemes of things."

To make more concrete the evidence on which I have drawn to join the public discussion, let me refer to one important compilation of lists, of the sixth century A.D., contemporary with the Talmud of Babylonia, a compilation of exegesis of Song of Songs called Song of Songs Rabbah.[1] That compilation presents a reading of the Song of Songs as a metaphorization of God's relationship of intense love for Israel, and Israel's relationship of intense love for God. In that document we find sequences, or combinations, of references to Old Testament persons, events, actions, and the like. These bear the rhetorical emblem, "another matter," in long lists of composites of well-framed compositions.[2] Each

---

[1]My translation and analysis of the document are in the following: *Song of Songs Rabbah. An Analytical Translation.* Volume One. *Song of Songs Rabbah to Song Chapters One through Three.* Atlanta, 1990: Scholars Press for Brown Judaic Studies; *Song of Songs Rabbah. An Analytical Translation.* Volume Two. *Song of Songs Rabbah to Song Chapters Four through Eight.* Atlanta, 1990: Scholars Press for Brown Judaic Studies; and *The Midrash Compilations of the Sixth and Seventh Centuries: An Introduction to the Rhetorical, Logical, and Topical Program. IV. Song of Songs Rabbah.* Atlanta, 1990: Scholars Press for Brown Judaic Studies.

[2]I estimate that approximately 80 percent of the document in bulk is comprised of "another matter" compositions. The list in this form defines the paramount rhetorical medium and logical structure of the document.

entry on a given list will be represented as "another matter," meaning, another interpretation of reading of a given verse in the Song of Songs. As a matter of fact, however, that "other matter," one following the other, turns out to be the same matter in other terms.   These constructions form lists out of diverse entries.   When in Song of Songs Rabbah we have a sequence of items alleged to form a taxon, that is, a set of things that share a common taxic indicator, of course what we have is a list.   The list presents diverse matters that all together share, and therefore also set forth, a single fact or rule or phenomenon. That is why we can list them, in all their distinctive character and specificity, on a common catalogue of "other things" that pertain all together to one thing.

Since, on these lists, we find classified within a single taxon events, persons, places, objects and actions, it is important to understand how they coalesce.[3] The rhetoric is the key indicator, since it is objective and superficial.   When we find the rhetorical formula, "another matter," that is, *davar aher*, what follows says the same thing in other words, or at least something complementary and necessary to make some larger point. That is why I insist the constructions form lists.   William Scott Green states the matter, in his analysis of a single passage, in these words:

> Although the interpretations in this passage are formally distinguished from one another...by the disjunctive device *davar aher* ("another interpretation"), they operate within a limited conceptual sphere and a narrow thematic range....Thus rather than "endless multiple meanings," they in fact ascribe to the words "doing wonders" multiple variations of a single meaning....By providing multiple warrant for that message, the form effectively restricts the interpretive options.[4]

When we have a sequence of *davar-aher* passages forming a *davar-aher* construction, the message is cumulative, and the whole as a matter of fact forms a sum greater than that of the parts; it will then be that accumulation that guides us to what is implicit yet fundamental in the exact sense: at the foundation of matters; there is where we should find

---

[3]The archaeological evidence of ancient synagogues yields counterpart "lists," that is to say, recurrent groups of iconic symbols that appear together, but with no other items, from one synagogue to another, for example, the ram's horn, the palm branch, the candelabrum, are commonly grouped, but no other iconic symbols then appear in groups or what we should call "iconic lists."   I have compared the iconic lists with the "another matter lists" in *Theology and Symbol in Judaism.* Minneapolis, 1990: Fortress Press.

[4]In Jacob Neusner with William Scott Green, *Writing with Scripture. The Authority and Uses of the Hebrew Bible in the Torah of Formative Judaism* (Minneapolis, 1989: Fortress Press), p. 19.

that system, order, proportion, cogency that all together we expect a theology to impart to discrete observations about holy matters.

In general, "another matter" signals "another way of saying the same thing": or the formula bears the sense, "these two distinct things add up to one thing," with the further proviso that both are necessary to make one point that transcends each one. Not only so, but in Song of Songs Rabbah the fixed formula of the *davar-aher compilation* points toward fixed formulas of theological thought: sets of coherent verbal symbols that work together. These "other things" encompass time, space, person and object, action and attitude, and join them all together, for instance, David, Solomon, Messiah at the end of time; this age, the age to come; the Exodus from Egypt, Sinai, the age to come all may appear together within a single list. Let me give a single example of the list that makes it possible to redefine "event" into a category of quite ahistorical valence.

Chapter Five. Song of Songs Rabbah to Song 1:5

V.i.1	A	"I am very dark, but comely, [O daughters of Jerusalem, like the tents of Kedar, like the curtains of Solomon]" (Song 1:5):
	B.	"I am dark" in my deeds.
	C.	"But comely" in the deeds of my forebears.
V.2	A.	"I am very dark, but comely":
	B.	Said the Community of Israel, "'I am dark' in my view, 'but comely' before my Creator."
	C.	For it is written, "Are you not as the children of the Ethiopians to Me, O children of Israel, says the Lord" (Amos 9:7):
	D.	"as the children of the Ethiopians" – in your sight.
	E.	But "to Me, O children of Israel, says the Lord."
V.3	A.	Another interpretation of the verse, "I am very dark": in Egypt.
	B.	"But comely": in Egypt.
	C.	"I am very dark" in Egypt: "But they rebelled against me and would not hearken to me" (Ezek. 20:8).
	D.	"But comely" in Egypt: with the blood of the Passover-offering and circumcision, "And when I passed by you and saw you wallowing in your blood, I said to you, In your blood live" (Ezek. 16:6) – in the blood of the Passover.
	E.	"I said to you, In your blood live" (Ezek. 16:6) – in the blood of the circumcision.
V.4	A.	Another interpretation of the verse, "I am very dark": at the sea, "They were rebellious at the sea, even the Red Sea" (Ps. 106:7).
	B.	"But comely": at the sea, "This is my God and I will be comely for him" (Ex. 15:2) [following Simon's rendering of the verse].
V.5	A.	"I am very dark": at Marah, "And the people murmured against Moses, saying, What shall we drink" (Ex. 15:24).
	B.	"But comely": at Marah, "And he cried to the Lord and the Lord showed him a tree, and he cast it into the waters and the waters were made sweet" (Ex. 15:25).
V.6	A.	"I am very dark": at Rephidim, "And the name of the place was called Massah and Meribah" (Ex. 17:7).

B. "But comely": at Rephidim, "And Moses built an altar and called it by the name "the Lord is my banner" (Ex. 17:15).

V.7 A "I am very dark": at Horeb, "And they made a calf at Horeb" (Ps. 106:19).

B. "But comely": at Horeb, "And they said, All that the Lord has spoken we will do and obey" (Ex. 24:7).

V.8 A "I am very dark": in the wilderness, "How often did they rebel against him in the wilderness" (Ps. 78:40).

B. "But comely": in the wilderness at the setting up of the tabernacle, "And on the day that the tabernacle was set up" (Num. 9:15).

V.9 A "I am very dark": in the deed of the spies, "And they spread an evil report of the land" (Num. 13:32).

B. "But comely": in the deed of Joshua and Caleb, "Save for Caleb, the son of Jephunneh the Kenizzite" (Num. 32:12).

V.10 A "I am very dark": at Shittim, "And Israel abode at Shittim and the people began to commit harlotry with the daughters of Moab" (Num. 25:1).

B. "But comely": at Shittim, "Then arose Phinehas and wrought judgment" (Ps. 106:30).

V.11 A "I am very dark": through Achan, "But the children of Israel committed a trespass concerning the devoted thing" (Josh. 7:1).

B. "But comely": through Joshua, "And Joshua said to Achan, My son, give I pray you glory" (Josh. 7:19).

V.12 A. "I am very dark": through the kings of Israel.

B. "But comely": through the kings of Judah.

C. If with my dark ones that I had, it was such that "I am comely," all the more so with my prophets.

V:ii.5 A [As to the verse, "I am very dark, but comely," R. Levi b. R. Haita gave three interpretations:

B. "'I am very dark:' all the days of the week.

C. "'But comely': on the Sabbath.

D. "'I am very dark:' all the days of the year.

E. "'But comely': on the Day of Atonement.

F. "'I am very dark:' among the Ten Tribes.

G. "'But comely': in the tribe of Judah and Benjamin.

H. "'I am very dark:' in this world.

I. "'But comely': in the world to come."

The contrast of dark and comely yields a variety of applications; in all of them the same situation that is the one also is the other, and the rest follows in a wonderfully well-crafted composition. What is the repertoire of items? Dark in deeds but comely in ancestry; dark in my view but comely before God; dark when rebellious, comely when obedient, a point made at Nos. 3, for Egypt, 4, for the Sea, and 5 for Marah, 6, for Massah and Meribah, 7 for Horeb, 8 for the wilderness, 9 for the spies in the Land, 10 for Shittim, 11 for Achan/Joshua and the conquest of the Land, 12 for Israel and Judah. But look what follows: the week as against the Sabbath, the weekdays as against the Day of Atonement, the Ten Tribes as against Judah and Benjamin, this world as against the world to come. Whatever classification these next items demand for themselves, it surely will not be that of events. Indeed, if by event we mean something that happened once, as in "once upon a time," then Sabbath as against weekday, Day of Atonement as against ordinary day form a different category; the Ten Tribes as against Judah and Benjamin constitute social entities, not divisions of time; and this age and the age to come form utterly antihistorical taxa altogether.

Events not only do not form a taxon, they also do not present a vast corpus of candidates for inclusion into some other taxon. The lists in the document at hand form selections from a most limited repertoire of candidates. If we were to catalogue all of the exegetical repertoire encompassed by *davar-aher* constructions in this document, we should not have a very long list of candidates for inclusion in any list. And among the candidates, events are few indeed. They encompass Israel at the Sea and at Sinai, the destruction of the first Temple, the destruction of the second Temple, events as defined by the actions of some holy men such as Abraham, Isaac, and Jacob (treated not for what they did but for who they were), Daniel, Mishael, Hananiah and Azariah, and the like. It follows that the restricted repertoire of candidates for taxonomic study encompasses remarkably few events, remarkably few for a literary culture that is commonly described as quintessentially historical!

Then what taxic indicator dictates which happenings will be deemed events and which not? What are listed throughout are not data of nature or history but of theology: God's relationship with Israel, expressed in such facts as the three events, the first two in the past, the third in the future, namely, the three redemptions of Israel, the three patriarchs, and holy persons, actions, events, what-have-you. These are facts that are assembled and grouped; in Song of Songs Rabbah the result is not propositional at all, or, if propositional, then essentially the repetition of familiar propositions through unfamiliar data. What we have is a kind of recombinant theology, in which the framer ("the theologian") selects from a restricted repertoire a few items for combination, sometimes to make a point (for example, the contrast of obedient and disobedient Israel we saw just now), sometimes not. What is set on display justifies the display: putting this familiar fact together with that familiar fact in an unfamiliar combination constitutes what is new and important in the list; the consequent conclusion one is supposed to draw, the proposition or rule that emerges – these are rarely articulated and never important. True, the list in Song of Songs Rabbah may comprise a rule, or it may substantiate a proposition or validate a claim; but more often than not, the effect of making the list is to show how various items share a single taxic indicator, which is to say, the purpose of the list is to make the list. The making of connections among ordinarily not-connected things is then one outcome of *Listenwissenschaft*. What I find engaging in *davar-aher constructions* is the very variety of things that, on one list or another, can be joined together – a list for its own sake. What we have is a kind of subtle restatement, through an infinite range of possibilities, of the combinations and recombinations of a few essentially simple facts (data). It is as though a magician tossed a set of sticks this way and that, interpreting the diverse combinations of a fixed set of objects. The propositions that emerge are not the main point; the combinations are.

That seems to me an important fact, for it tells me that the culture at hand has defined for itself a repertoire of persons and events and conceptions (for example, Torah study), holy persons, holy deeds, holy institutions, presented candidates for inclusion in *davar-aher* constructions, and the repertoire, while restricted and not terribly long, made possible a scarcely limited variety of lists of things with like taxic indicators. That is to say, the same items occur over and over again, but there is no pattern to how they recur. By a pattern I mean that items of the repertoire may appear in numerous *davar-aher* constructions or not; they may keep company with only a fixed number of other items, or they may not. Most things can appear in a *davar-aher* composition with most other things.

The upshot is simple. List making is accomplished within a restricted repertoire of items that can serve on lists; the list making then presents interesting combinations of an essentially small number of candidates for the exercise. But then, when making lists, one can do pretty much anything with the items that are combined; the taxic indicators are unlimited, but the data studied, severely limited. And that fact returns us to our starting point, the observations on history as a cultural artifact that form the premise for the study of history within the archaeology of knowledge. In fact, in Judaism history serves the theological sciences and therefore cannot be said to constitute history in any ordinary sense at all; but that is a trivial and obvious observation. More to the point, history, in the form of events, contributes to a rather odd way of conducting theological science.

For, forming part of the *davar-aher* construction, history constitutes one among a variety of what I call, for lack of more suitable language at this point, theological "things,"[5] – names, places, events, actions deemed

---

[5]I find myself at a loss for a better word choice and must at this stage resort to the hopelessly inelegant, "'theological' things," to avoid having to repeat the formula that seems to me to fit the data, namely, "names, places, events, actions deemed to bear theological weight and to affect attitude and action." Still, better a simple Anglo-Saxon formulation than a fancy German or Greek or Latin one. And Hebrew, whether Mishnaic or modern, simply does not serve for analytical work

to bear theological weight and to affect attitude and action. The play is worked out by a reprise of available materials, composed in some fresh and interesting combination. When three or more such theological "things" – whether person, whether event, whether action, whether attitude – are combined, they form a theological structure, and, viewed all together, all of the theological "things" in a given document constitute the components of the entire theological structure that the document affords. The propositions portrayed visually, through metaphors of sight, or dramatically, through metaphors of action and relationship, or in attitude and emotion, through metaphors that convey or provoke feeling and sentiment, when translated into language prove familiar and commonplace. The work of the theologian in this context is not to say something new or even persuasive, for the former is unthinkable by definition, the latter unnecessary in context. It is rather to display theological "things" in a fresh and interesting way, to accomplish a fresh exegesis of the canon of theological "things."

The combinations and recombinations defined for us by our document form events into facts, sharing the paramount taxic indicators of a variety of other facts, comprising a theological structure within a larger theological structure: a reworking of canonical materials. An event is therefore reduced to a "thing," losing all taxic autonomy, requiring no distinct indicator of an intrinsic order. It is simply something else to utilize in composing facts into knowledge; the event does not explain, it does not define, indeed, it does not even exist within its own framework at all. Judaism by "an event" means, in a very exact sense, nothing in particular. It is a component in a culture that combines and recombines facts into structures of its own design, an aspect of what I should call a culture that comes to full expression in recombinant theology.

We have been prepared for such a result by Jonathan Z. Smith, who has made us aware of the critical issue of the recombinancy of a fixed canon of "things" in his discussion of sacred persistence, that is, "the rethinking of each little detail in a text, the obsession with the significance and perfection of each little action." In the canonical literature of Judaism, these minima are worked and reworked, rethought and recast in some other way or order or combination – but always held to be the same thing throughout. In this context I find important Smith's statement:

> An almost limitless horizon of possibilities that are at hand...is arbitrarily reduced...to a set of basic elements....Then a most intense

---

except when thought conceived in some other language is translated back into that language, should anyone be interested.

ingenuity is exercised to overcome the reduction...to introduce interest and variety. This ingenuity is usually accompanied by a complex set of rules.[6]

The possibilities out of which the authorship of our exemplary document has made its selections are limited not by the metaphorical potential of the Song of Songs (!) but by the contents of the Hebrew Scriptures.

For every Abraham, Isaac, and Jacob that we find, there are Job, Enoch, Jeroboam, or Zephaniah, whom we do not find; for every Sea/Sinai/entry into the Land that we do find, there are other sequences, for example, the loss of the ark to the Philistines and its recovery, or Barak and Deborah, that we do not find. Ezra figures, Haggai does not; the Assyrians play a minor role, Nebuchadnezzar is on nearly every page. Granted, Sinai must enjoy a privileged position throughout. But why prefer Shadrach, Meshach, and Abednego, Hananiah, Mishael, and Azariah, over other trilogies of heroic figures? So the selection is an act of choice, a statement of culture in miniature. But once restricted through this statement of choice, the same selected theological "things" then undergo combination and recombination with other theological things, the counterpart to Smith's "interest and variety." If we know the complex set of rules in play here, we also would understand the system that makes this document not merely an expression of piety but a statement of a theological structure: orderly, well-composed and proportioned, internally coherent and cogent throughout.

The canonical, therefore anything but random, standing of events forms a brief chapter in the exegesis of a canon. That observation draws us back to Smith, who observes:

> the radical and arbitrary reduction represented by the notion of canon and the ingenuity represented by the rule-governed exegetical enterprise to apply the canon to every dimension of human life is that most characteristic, persistent, and obsessive religious activity....The task of application as well as the judgment of the relative adequacy of particular applications to a community's life situation remains the indigenous theologian's task; but the study of the process, particularly the study of comparative systematics and exegesis, ought to be a major preoccupation of the historian of religions.[7]

Smith speaks of religion as an "enterprise of exegetical totalization," and he further identifies with the word "canon" precisely what we have identified as the substrate and structure of the list. If I had to define an event in this canonical context, I should have to call it merely another

---

[6] "Sacred Persistence: Towards a Redescription of Canon," in William Scott Green, ed., *Approaches to Ancient Judaism* 1978, 1:11-28. Quotation: p. 15.
[7] Ibid., p. 18.

theological thing: something to be manipulated, combined in one way or in another, along with other theological things.

Have we access to other examples of cultures that define for themselves canonical lists of counterparts to what I have called "theological things"? Indeed, defining matters as I have, I may compare the event to a fixed object in a diviner's basket of the Ndembu, as Smith describes that divinatory situation:

> Among the Ndembu there are two features of the divinatory situation that are crucial to our concern: the diviner's basket and his process of interrogating his client. The chief mode of divination consists of shaking a basket in which some twenty-four fixed objects are deposited (a cock's claw, a piece of hoof, a bit of grooved wood,...withered fruit, etc.). These are shaken in order to winnow out' truth from falsehood' in such a way that few of the objects end up on top of the heap. These are 'read' by the diviner both with respect to their individual meanings and their combinations with other objects and the configurations that result.[8]

In Song of Songs Rabbah, Abraham, Isaac, Jacob, or the Sea and Sinai, or Hananiah, Mishael, and Azariah, are the counterpart to the cock's claw and the piece of hoof. The event, in Judaism, is the counterpart to a cock's claw in the Ndembu culture. Both will be fixed, but will combine and recombine in a large number of different ways. But then what of "the lessons of history," and how shall we identify the counterpart to historical explanation? I find the answer in the Ndembu counterpart, the mode of reading "the process of interrogating the client"? Again Smith:

> The client's situation is likewise taken into account in arriving at an interpretation. Thus...there is a semantic, syntactic, and pragmatic dimension to the "reading." Each object is publicly known and has a fixed range of meanings....The total collection of twenty-four objects is held to be complete and capable of illuminating every situation....What enables the canon to be applied to every situation or question is not the number of objects....Rather it is that, prior to performing the divination, the diviner has rigorously question his client in order to determine his situation with precision.....It is the genius of the interpreter to match a public set of meanings with a commonly known set of facts...in order to produce a quite particular plausibility structure which speaks directly to his client's condition, which mediates between that which is public knowledge and the client's private perception of his unique situation.[9]

That concludes our inquiry, since it draws us to the task of the exegesis of exegesis. Events then form a problem of exegesis, in which, from what a culture defines as a consequential happening, we find our way back to the system and structure that that culture means to form. The theology

---

[8]Smith, p. 25.
[9]Smith, p. 25.

of this Judaism – that is to say, our account of the worldview that comes to expression within this literary culture and textual community – will take shape within the exegesis of that exegesis.

The upshot is that in an exact sense, "event" has no meaning at all in Judaism, since Judaism forms culture through other than historical modes of organizing existence. Without the social construction of history, there also is no need for the identification of events, that is, individual and unique happenings that bear consequence, since, within the system and structure of Judaism, history forms no taxon, assuredly not the paramount one, and, it must follow, no happening is unique, and, on its own, no event bears consequence. These statements rest upon modes of the analysis of history as the fabrication of culture, including a religious culture, and require us to review the recent formation of thought on history as culturally ordered, and on the event as "contingent realization of the cultural pattern," for it is only in that context that we may make sense, also, of the representation of both history and its raw materials, events, in Judaism in its definitive canon.

It follows that, when the Judaism of the Dual Torah invented history, it not only did so for its own purposes, but it also undertook the work within its own distinctive idiom of thought and expression. And, as we have seen, idiom did not yield the kind of history writing that, even in that day and age, others nearby undertook. The initial definition of history turns out to have been remarkably congruent to that of what we today classify as social science: the search not for the unique but the exemplary, the inquiry into not the particular but the general, the quest for generalization concerning the social order, rather than the search for the unusual and the different that marked one component of the social order as an event, the other as routine.

The history that the Judaism of the Dual Torah invented in the fourth century therefore differs radically from the history that, in general, people assume ancient Judaism, in the pages of the Hebrew Scriptures for instance, invoked. History served the cause of theological truth, but it was never the source of theological truth. The Torah set forth the truth; history, if truth be told, was not needed to prove any element of the truth that the Torah revealed. History was subordinate, not probative; at best exemplary, but never normative. That conception of history draws us far from the contemporary one. For some time now in the West we have called upon history to serve as arbiter of truth, history as mediator of sensibility and source of explanation. But before its own entry into the Western intellect, in the nineteenth and twentieth centuries, Judaism knew nothing of that other use of history, so different from its own.

Indeed, these honored roles in the court of intellect came to history only in the formative centuries of our own civilization. We should, after all, have to trace the path back to the Protestant Reformation, with its insistence on the priority of historical fact, deriving from a mythic age of perfection, in dictating the legitimacy of social reality in the present moment. Renewed in the romantic reentry into historical discourse, this same preference for history as a medium of organizing the everyday and explaining it characterized the formation of the historical sciences in the nineteenth century: history proves, history teaches, the verdict of history, the lessons of history – these and other accepted formulations bear the single message. Cutting through the detritus and sediment of the long centuries of increment and accumulation, therefore appealing not to *Listenwissenschaft*, but to a different, more autonomous kind of judgment altogether, for the logic of their discourse, the Reformation theologians and the nineteenth century German historians who were their secular continuators, identified history, the record of what happened (in this case) in Scripture, as the instrument for the validation of reform. Reform, then, would accomplish the renewal of times past, times perfect, appealing therefore to the court of appeal formed by history. Describing "Judaism" as a historical religion therefore classifies what was philosophical as historical, a religion that sought the rules of the social order in regularity as one that appealed to the singular and the extraordinary. But history is of more than one kind, in religion as much as in the life of intellect, and the kind of history that Judaism invented in the fourth century and carried on from then to the nineteenth finds more in common with modes of thought familiar to us today, in the social scientific reconsideration of the meaning of historical knowledge, than with the Protestant theological appeal to history as a source of validation of reform, as the source of Reformation.

Turning toward the future, we do well to reflect on the subordination of history by Judaism in light of the current recognition that history forms a discourse of contemporary taste and judgment, events become eventful only because we make them so, and, in all, history is culturally ordered, and events are defined and identified as statements of an intensely contemporary perception. It follows, we now understand, that all histories are the creation of an eternal present, that is, those moments in which histories are defined and distinguished, in which events are identified and assigned consequence, and in which sequences of events, "this particular thing happened here and therefore...," are strung together, pearls on a string, to form ornaments of intellect. And, with that understanding well in hand, fully recognizing that history is one of the grand fabrications of the human intellect, facts not discovered but invented, explanations that themselves form cultural indicators of how things are in the here and now, we find ourselves no longer historians of ideas of history, or analysts of the history of culture, let alone practitioners of the dread narrative history that makes of historical writing a work of elegant imagination. We find ourselves, rather, archaeologists, working from the surface, that is known, through the detritus of the unknown, in quest of a material understanding of a reality that is not known but for its artifacts, not susceptible of explanation and understanding except in categories and terms that are defined by those same artifacts. And that quest is, we all recognize, not a very smooth one.

Today we understand that events in particular, and history in general, form cultural indicators. Accomplishing the analysis of events for what they teach us about the culture that identifies a given happening as eventful, neglecting some other as inconsequential or routine, is important. In the vast canon of the two Talmuds and the Midrash compilations that took shape in late antiquity, the first seven centuries A.D., under the title, the Oral Torah, history was invented within Judaism for the distinctive purposes of Judaism: it was not a general thing, and was never meant to be. That labor of rewriting and recasting of one thing in light of something else that produced the Judaism of the Dual Torah forms a rich set of cases in cultural transformation, in the determination, by a system, of its own past, in the identification, within a system, of its own resources. For, after all, while a system speaks through its canon, and while theologians commonly read the canon to describe the system, in point of fact it is the canon that recapitulates the system, the system that speaks, in detail to be sure, through the canon. History forms part of not the system but merely the canon. So the writing of history defines a critical category for the study of the history of Judaic religions systems – Judaisms. Not only so, but since, as we noted at the outset, the generative and principal Judaic system, the pentateuchal one, makes its statement wholly within the idiom of historiography, we may say that history defines a native category of Judaism. When we have produced so contradictory a result – history as a native category of the initial Judaic system, history as essentially irrelevant to the dominant Judaic system that rests, if asymmetrically, upon that initial system – we have reached the threshold of a new century of research. We have come as far as we can within the received episteme. The revolution that began in the 1950s has reached its natural conclusion.

10

How is "Eternity" To Be Understood in the Theology of Judaism? An Exercise in Comparative Theology

The canonical books of Judaism, to which we turn for the definition of theological categories and doctrines, rarely set forth ideas in the form of abstractions and generalizations, with the result that understanding any generative theological categories requires the philological exegesis of texts.[1] In the case of the Judaic canon, the pertinent texts are the those of the Torah, written and oral. When we turn to the Written Torah, which the West knows as the Old Testament, and to the Oral Torah, which Judaism assembles out of the Mishnah, the two Talmuds, the Midrash compilations of the formative age, our work only begins. For we have also to determine for ourselves what words, in the canonical writings, stand for, or refer us to, the counterpart category that our Christian and Greek philosophical heritage has conferred upon us. When, as we shall see, we ask ourselves about how the classical theology of Judaism conceives of "eternity," we therefore engage in a prior inquiry into what we mean by "eternity" and how in the Judaic canon's substrate of theology we may locate the counterpart language for that meaning. Not only so, but we have further to find out in what context thought takes place on the category, "eternity": when and why is discourse on eternity precipitated in the canonical theology of Judaism? And when not?

When we understand how "eternity" is conceived within the theology of Judaism, what we learn concerns not "eternity" but the theology of Judaism – and we learn, also that the philosophical and theological world of the West that defines "eternity" in the way that it

---

[1]Address to a conference at Institut de philosophie Arts et Sciences Humaines Université de Tours, France, October 19, 20, 1990.

does likewise appeals to what is not a universal, but only a native category. In medieval terms, what we set forth in the framework of a realistic composition turns out to form a nominalist construct: an episode in a culture, not a universal in a philosophy everywhere pertaining.

Like all abstractions, "eternity" with its counterpart and opposite, "time," proves to be a category distinctively native to the philosophical system that deems the matter constitutive. Neither "time" nor "eternity" in fact defines a generative category in the canonical documents of the oral Torah, upon which I shall focus. These standing by themselves are invariably contingent, instrumental, never autonomous and taxonomic. "Time" may be holy or profane, but then the native categories are the sacred and the ordinary, and "time," like a variety of categories that in other systems of thought prove independent variables, turns out to be dependent and merely acted upon. The constitutive categories, "holy," "ordinary," utilize a variety of data, including the passage of time, to register whatever it is that they wish to say. And, since, by definition, the same is so of "eternity," the counterpart, complement, and opposite of time, it is clear that our task – how do people deliver their message concerning "eternity," when does the question of "eternity" arise, and how are we to define what they conceived when they spoke of "eternity" – that task proves somewhat more complicated than a mere lexical inquiry would suggest.

When we attempt to find, in some other setting, the right vocabulary to guide us to those canonical writings of Judaism in which the category proves definitive, we note how what we put forward as abstract, general, universal in its power to classify and define, turns out the opposite. The categories, "eternity" and "time," emerge as not ubiquitous structures of systems of thought put forth here and there and everywhere: universal categories. Rather, we see them as concrete, specific, and entirely particular to the writings that (as a matter of fact) imagine the category to be self-evident and universal. That paradox of our Christian and Hellenistic heritage of philosophical thinking, justly proud of its capacity to make something general and susceptible to sustained analysis out of anything particular and distinctive to a given cultural and intellectual circumstance, disconcerts. And well it should, since much of Western philosophy has turned out to incapacitate us in our encounter with the thought of other worlds, besides our own, and even of different worlds within our own.

If I had then to specify those traits that characterize "eternity" when we use the category in general, I should identify these as necessary: age without end; age without change; time beyond time as we know it; time past time that is authentic and meaningful, perfect because unchanging; the age of perfection in which truth flourishes and true life is lived. Then the counterpart, complement, and opposite, "time," must be an age that will end; an age that is differentiated and subject to change; time that is awaiting for meaning to emerge, significance to be established. Then the contrast is between the inauthentic and meaningless age, and the authentic and meaningful one; the age that is differentiated, changing, and contingent and the age that is undifferentiated (hence, beyond time), permanent (beyond change), and absolute. The proposed contrast is hardly subjective, since any dictionary, in any Western language, is likely to give for eternal the synonyms of unceasing, unending, lasting, permanent, perpetual, undying, as against ephemeral, evanescent, momentary, passing, temporary, transient – and so forth.

If this definition of the conception of eternity and time prove acceptable, then we shall find reason to wonder whether, in the theology of the Judaism of the Dual Torah in particular, there is a conception of "eternity" in contrast to "time" that corresponds in any important way to the meanings and usages of the categories, "eternity" and "time" that characterize Western philosophical and theological thought. What we shall see, in a single important case, is that when, in Western thought, particularly Christian theological thought, we have a right to expect to find "eternity" as an age that is beyond differentiation, in the Judaic theology adumbrated by a critical canonical document of the Dual Torah, the Mishnah, "eternity" proves differentiated just as much as is "time." But then that must mean, as we understand "eternity," there is no eternity in Judaism.

Having shaded over from the canon of the Judaism of the Dual Torah to a single canonical document, the Mishnah, I have to ask for a definition of "eternity" deriving from a Christian writing of a roughly contemporary period and type. The Mishnah speaks of concrete things, so the Christian counterpart must be of not a philosophical and abstract but a specific and concrete character. Among many candidates, one in which I find important reflection on the nature of the "age to come" or "eternity" is the Revelation to John. And since the Mishnah reached closure at ca. A.D. 200, drawing on materials that took shape over the preceding hundred years or so, I turn to the Revelation to John, for it is generally assigned to the end of the first century. There we find a vision of the coming age, the end of time as it is known. Here we find a fair point of intersection, for, as we shall see in a moment, both the Mishnah's and John of Patmos's treatment of "eternity" appeals for the media of thought and expression to highly mythic and pictorial language. Here is the vision of eternity:

> a new heaven and a new earth, for the first heaven and the first earth had passed away...behold the dwelling of God is with men. He shall dwell with them, and they shall be his people, and God himself will be

with them; he will wipe away every tear from their eyes, and death shall
be no more, neither shall there be mourning nor crying nor pain any
more, for the former things have passed away (Revelation 21:1-4).

Now the great philosophical theologians of Christianity in antiquity will
have framed their doctrine of eternity in the language of abstraction and
generalization that they spoke so fluently; but they will have found their
doctrine of eternity in terms entirely congruent to this vision, with its
stress on the permanence of eternity, on the radical shift from now to
then, from here to there. And, we see, when we find a vision and a
doctrine of eternity, what precipitates discourse is deep thought on the
nature of now in light of what is coming: time and eternity, death and life
beyond, an utter change in the nature of being. Very rapidly we shall
observe that, were the great philosophical theologians of Judaism, when
they came along in the Middle Ages, to have framed in their language of
abstraction and generalization what we shall find in the Mishnah, they
would have had reason to formulate doctrines of not eternity but the
social order. But in making such an observation I have moved ahead of
my argument.

Let me ask, first of all, what in imagination of the authors of the
Mishnah will precipitate discourse on issues of eternity, life after death,
and the world to come? The answer is not life after death and eternity,
but the social order of Israel, the holy people. That is to say, when the
political structure and system that the Mishnah sets forth proposes to
express the theory of its teleology, it does so by recourse to the language
eternity and the world to come and life after death; its account of the
theory of power over the nation, Israel, appeals in the end to the
conception of an entire nation outliving the grave. The set,
eternity/time, defines not a free-standing but a contingent category.
What is independent, autonomous, and generative is the category, Israel,
the holy people. Then eternity will be conceived as a variable, and it
serves discourse, where and when it does, solely in relationship to – not
time but – Israel. And "Israel" forms a category different in not species
but genus: Israel is a social and a political entity, eternity/time are
temporal/historical categories. If in the Christian discourse undertaken
by John of Patmos, eternity/time form a category that is an independent
variable – and the contrast between now and then forms the sub-
structure and foundation of that writing, in Judaism these constitute not
an independent variable at all, and, therefore, they form a category of a
different classification of categories altogether, species of a genus, not *sui
generis* at all. And the counterpart category – one that in this system,
Judaism, is free-standing and independent and *sui generis* – is Israel (and
its counterpart, the gentiles).

It follows, as we shall now see, that in Judaism, eternity is conceived as a dependent variable, dependent wholly in relationship to the independent variable, Israel/nations. And that calls into question whether Judaism in its classical statement sets forth a conception of eternity in the way that Christianity and philosophy in their classical statements set forth a conception of eternity. For, as I have now underlined, how can we compare a category that defines with one that is defined, or one that is autonomous with one that is subordinate? In Judaism the category, eternity, forms a subordinated detail of a political structure, not a temporal grid. And that simple, but fundamental fact, makes us wonder whether, in Judaism, there is a conception of eternity that can correspond with that of philosophy and Christianity, since what is subordinate also will prove differentiated, impermanent, and not absolute but relative. But if by "eternity" we mean what is permanent, absolute, enduring, authentic, whole and complete, then in Judaism there is something else than eternity that will meet the definition of eternity, that is, that exhibits those indicative traits that, as a matter of fact, make eternity "eternal."

This is stated very simply in the opening lines of the protracted account of who gets, and who does not get, a share in the world to come. The importance of the passage requires us to consider it in full detail. The passage has as its topic eternity: life of the world to come. And it forms, as a matter of fact, also the single most important political statement in the Mishnah; and it is quintessentially a political statement, about the state of the people, Israel, and about the state that they create, complete with the program of sanctions, spelled out in Mishnah-tractate Sanhedrin, of which the following comes as the climactic formulation:[2]

Mishnah-tractate Sanhedrin 10:1A-B

A.   All Israelites have a share in the world to come,

B.   as it is said, *Your people also shall be all righteous, they shall inherit the land forever; the branch of my planting, the work of my hands, that I may be glorified* (Isa. 60:21).

The prooftext at B bears a definition of the world to come, with its reference to [1] the land, to [2] permanent possession of the land, to [3] Israel's possession of the land as God's doing. Here then is the world to come: locativity attained at the end, the fulfillment of a utopian politics in some one place. True, that one place is not of this world at all. It finds its boundaries not in space but in time and space joined in union with God. It constitutes life eternal in the land of Israel under God's protection.

---

[2]I have dealt with this matter more systematically in my *Rabbinic Political Theory: Religion and Politics in the Mishnah* (Chicago, 1991: University of Chicago Press).

But, as we see, this offers a vision of eternity that is, as a matter of fact, deeply political in its essence. For the system's teleology speaks of a political entity, this people forming a nation, that is, "Israel," with its system of penalties and sanctions, that is, its politics, located in a particular place, the "land," and a permanent possession of enduring life in that community, that "people" that is "your people" and "righteous." True, too, the principle is static, not dynamic. No matter what happens now or in the short term, and without regard to who does or does not do what is expected, all Israel has a share in that coming world. Clearly, we have here a politics of eternity, not a politics of time at all. But that judgment is rapidly given nuance, and, with the nuance, the politics of eternity looks suspiciously worldly: there is change, impermanence, and things prove remarkably relative.

In eternity everybody will get that "world to come" that is comprised by none other than the "Israel" of the here and now. What makes the statement a doctrine of eternity? Well, first of all, the introduction of life without death, that is, life beyond death: eternal life. Israelites then – beyond time, hence by definition, in eternity – will never die and (by way of definition) they will always possess the sanctified territory in which God does God's planting. No wonder that – in the law of the Mishnah – death at the hands of the earthly court or extirpation by the Heavenly court prove ephemeral; everybody, that is, every Israelite, will live forever pretty much in the place and in the manner of the present, except that all will be righteous, none will die, and God will secure the society and state of that unending present coming in the indeterminate future.

Some actions permanently exclude a person from ongoing existence, from life beyond the grave:

M. 10:1C-G

C.	And these are the ones who have no portion in the world to come:
D.	(1) He who says the resurrection of the dead is a teaching which does not derive from the Torah, (2) and the Torah does not come from Heaven; and (3) an Epicurean.
E.	R. Aqiba says, "Also, he who reads in heretical books,
F.	"and he who whispers over a wound and says, *I will put none of the diseases upon you which I have put on the Egyptians, for I am the Lord who heals you* (Ex. 15:26)."
G.	Abba Saul says. "Also: he who pronounces the divine Name as it is spelled out."

Clearly, the true mortal sins comprise doctrinal violations directed against God. These include, for example, denying the resurrection of the dead as a teaching of the Torah. Such a denial effectively denies the world to – come and what one denies one cannot have. As for denying that the Torah comes from God, practicing the sin of Epicureanism, reading heretical books, using God's name in healing, or expressing God's ineffable name, these form mere concretizations of the same species of sin. Unlike sins or crimes committed against other human beings – or even against the law of the Torah and the social order – these sins or crimes directly and immediately engage God. They misuse God's name, deny God's Torah, and above all and first of all, reject the view that God has provided life as the permanent condition of creation. Why should my utterances in these matters make so profound a difference, overriding all other crimes or sins? Because in misusing God's name and in denying the Torah, the Israelite places his or her will over the will of God in an explicit and articulated way.

The various forms of blasphemy that provoke political penalties that happen to take place in eternity but can take place in time – that is, whether from Heaven or on earth – deny that the human being is like God – if the Torah does not teach that the human being gets "the world to come," which is to say, lives beyond the grave, then the Torah does not represent the human being as like God, who lives forever. These two notions unite into a single sanction: denying eternal life for the human being means rejecting the image of God as it defines human beings, and, species of the same genus of crime and sin, misusing the name or the image of God provokes the same odious penalty. What motivates the politics is the issue of death or life. And eternity then forms a motivation for politics, at the service of the social order.

No wonder, then, that those who have no access to "the world to come," in this context, in light of the definitive prooftext, to eternal life beyond the grave, require specification. Kings and commoners, prophets and ordinary people, all are listed, with their crimes or sins alongside. The kings are those who caused Israel to sin. Then come entire political entities, complete communities, "the generation of the flood," "the generation of Babel," "the men of Sodom." These are gentiles, but not individuals. They are political entities, and what these have in common is that as entire communities, they form counterparts to Israel as a whole nation.[3] They rebelled against God, so they lost eternal life. Then come individual Israelites, too.[4]

---

[3]Gentiles considered as individuals, not part of political entities, do not come under consideration. The sins or crimes that deny a person the world to come all pertain to beliefs or actions of Israelites (as M. 10:1D1, 2, and E make clear). The ethnic venue of "Epicurean" is not so self-evident as the others; I take it the sense is that it is an Israelite who maintains Epicurean beliefs or attitudes. The context surely requires that view.

[4]Once more it seems to me that Israelites are treated as persons whose individual actions bear consequence, while gentiles are not.

Which Israelites lose the world to come? The counterpart to rejecting God is rejecting the Land. In light of the definitive prooftext with which we began, that hardly presents a surprise. The spies who rejected the land have lost their portion in the world to come. So, too, have the generation of the wilderness, which did not believe and trust. Clearly, then, the counterpart to the kings who made Israel sin and the gentiles who warred against God, are the Israelites who rejected the Land, on the one side, or who rejected God, on the other.

M. 10:2

A.   Three kings and four ordinary folk have no portion in the world to come.

B.   Three kings: Jeroboam, Ahab, and Manasseh.

C.   R. Judah says, "Manasseh has a portion in the world to come,

D.   'since it is said, *And he prayed to him and he was entreated of him and heard his supplication and brought him again to Jerusalem into his kingdom* (2 Chr. 33:13)."

E.   They said to him, "To his kingdom he brought him back, but to the life of the world to come he did not bring him back."

F.   Four ordinary folk: Balaam, Doeg, Ahitophel, and Gahazi.

M. 10:3

I.

A.   The generation of the flood has no share in the world to come,

B.   and they shall not stand in the judgment,

C.   since it is written, *My spirit shall not judge with man forever* (Gen. 6:3) –

D.   neither judgment not spirit.

II.

E.   The generation of the dispersion has no share in the world to come,

F.   since it is said, *So the Lord scattered them abroad from up there upon the face of the whole earth* (Gen. 11:8).

G.   *So the Lord scattered them abroad* – in this world.

H.   *And the Lord scattered them from there* – in the world to come.

III.

I.   The men of Sodom have no portion in the world to come,

J.   since it is said, *Now the men of Sodom were wicked and sinners against the Lord exceedingly* (Gen. 13:13) –

K.   *Wicked* – in this world,

L.   *And sinners* – in the world to come.

M.   But they will stand in judgment.

N.   R. Nehemiah says, "Both these and those will not stand in judgment,

O.   "for it is said, *Therefore the wicked shall not stand in judgment, not sinners in the congregation of the righteous* (Ps. 1:5) –

P.   *"Therefore the wicked shall not stand in judgment* – this refers to the generation of the flood.

Q.   *"Nor sinners in the congregation of the righteous* – this refers to the men of Sodom."

R.   They said to him, "They will not stand in the congregation of the righteous, but they will stand in the congregation of the sinners."

IV.
S.   The spies have no portion in the world to come,

T.   as it is said, *Even those men who brought up an evil report of the land died by the plague before the Lord* (Num. 14:37) –

U.   *Died* – in this world.

V.   *By the plague* – in the world to come.

V.
W.   (1) "The generation of the wilderness has no portion in the world to come and will not stand in judgment,

X.   "for it is written, *In this wilderness they shall be consumed and there they shall die* (Num. 14:25)," the words of R. Aqiba.

Y.   R. Eliezer says, "Concerning them it says, *Gather my saints together to me, those that have made a covenant with me by sacrifice* (Ps. 50:5)."

Z.   (2) "The party of Korah is not destined to rise up,

AA.   "for it is written, *And the earth closed upon them* – in this world.

BB.   *"And they perished from among the assembly* – in the world to come," the words of R. Aqiba.

CC.   And R. Eliezer says, "Concerning them it says, *The Lord kills and resurrects, brings down to Sheol and beings up again* (1 Sam. 2:6)."

DD.   (3) "The ten tribes are not destined to return,

EE.   "since it is said, *And he cast them into another land, as on this day* (Deut. 29:28). Just as the day passes and does not return, so they have gone their way and will not return," the words of R. Aqiba.

FF.   R. Eliezer says, "Just as this day is dark and then grows light, so the ten tribes for whom it now is dark – thus in the future it is destined to grow light for them."

From historical, we turn to contemporary political entities, communities acting all together in such a way as to lose their eternal life. What follows identifies a city, that is, a political entity, that has no portion in the world to come. It explains how collective punishment is applied.

Mishnah-tractate Sanhedrin 10:4

A.   The townsfolk of an apostate town have no portion in the world to come,

B.   as it is said, *Certain base fellows have gone out from the midst of thee and have drawn away the inhabitants of their city* (Deut. 13:14).

C.   And they are not put to death unless (1) those who misled the [town] come from that same town and from that same tribe,

D.   and unless (2) the majority is misled,

E.   and unless (3) men did the misleading.

F.   [If] (1) women or children misled them,
G.   or if (2) a minority of the town was misled,
H.   or if (3) those who misled the town came from outside of it,
I.   lo, they are treated as individuals [and not as a whole town],
J.   and they [thus] require [testimony against them] by two witnesses,
         and a statement of warning, for each and every one of them.
K.   This rule is more strict for individuals than for the community:
L.   for individuals are put to death by stoning.
M.   Therefore their property is saved.
N.   But the community is put to death by the sword,
O.   Therefore their property is lost.

The city as a whole is penalized, as was Sodom, when it conforms to the stated conditions. The importance for the larger argument is self-evident.[5]

As if to underline the proposition that what people do together dictates their fate, we end with the apostate town. That is as it should be, since we began with an account of those convictions and actions that constitute examples of apostasy. Here we conclude with the sanction inflicted upon an entire community by the nation at large. And that, too, is as it should be, since political sanctions preserve the public order that secures for the nation now and in time to come ("the world to come") ongoing life.

Not surprisingly, the penalty for the apostate group is to be gathered together and killed together, to be subjected to that one form of the death penalty that does not right the relationship with God. Only as individuals can we correct that relationship. This penalty, then, extinguishes for all time the political entity that has ultimately and finally denied God. There is a certain exact justice in such a sanction: one loses what one has denied. But it is a terrible justice indeed, imposing upon the system as a whole responsibility for matters, private as much as public, that the human being rightly or wrongly settles for himself or herself. Freedom to affirm is also liberty to perish.

As we review the catalogue of those who have lost life beyond the grave, we notice a curious disjuncture between the initial catalogue and the illustrative materials. Our account of who has no share in the world to come begins with those who commit crimes or sins against God. Such crimes or sins are individual, since they concern matters of conviction, on the one side, and misappropriation of divine power by the individual, on the other. But the account goes on to deal with kings and ordinary folk as public figures. Its kings are those who made Israel sin; its ordinary folk are false prophets, again, persons who have access to legitimate

---

[5]The remainder of the passage is given in *The Social Study of Judaism*, Chapter Eight.

power and who have misused it. And then, as if to underline the utterly public and shared political sanction at hand, the catalog provides a series of gentile, then Israelite, political entities that are denied eternal life. This means that a share in the world to come is something one gains, or loses, as part of an entire community, and that the condition of the public interest dictates the fate of the private person. Entire generations of gentiles, groups, and an entire generation of Israelites form such entities.

So the political entity, Israel, will endure forever: *eternity is relative to Israel.* That political entity, Israel, moreover is made up of persons who will never really die, in that, in the world to come, they will live forever. What is changeless is not time beyond time; there, as we know, there is promised a series of great events indeed, culminating after all in the last judgment. What is changeless, permanent, absolute, is Israel; the nations form the opposite, being ephemeral, transient, contingent. And as to time and eternity, these, as we have seen, take on importance in relationship to what is permanent and authentic and unchanging, which is Israel. To answer how "eternity" is conceived in the theology of the Judaism of the Dual Torah, I may then say very simply:

people individually did not want to die, and collectively wanted to stay right where they were and do pretty much what they then were doing. So, as we saw in those simple, but definitive words, "life in the world to come" means life in the Land, secured by God, living and not dying.[6]

The theological system of this Judaism, viewed as a whole, is meant to secure that here-and-now of life in the Land, the life of the people sustained by the Land, the life beyond death for individuals and for nation alike. And that teleological and eschatological vision forms not only the goal of politics but also the explanation and justification for the most violent media available to the political entity, which is denial of life. None then can miss the appropriate quality of the passion and its complement, the pathos, of the political theology that defines eternity: eternity is for Israel to live forever, or if merited, to lose life forever. Forever – eternity – is a strange thing, therefore, taking on meaning and consequence, for the theology of Judaism, solely within the social order.

---

[6]In his *Jewish Symbols in the Greco-Roman Period*, Erwin R. Goodenough underlined the passion for eternal life contained within the symbols used by Jewish artists for synagogues and cemeteries. Here in the depths of the Mishnah, in its politics for Israel, I find the same source of passion, in a context never considered by Goodenough, since these literary evidences fell (quite properly) outside of his range of analysis. That the results converge is suggestive. In my *Symbol and Theology in Judaism* (Minneapolis, 1991: Fortress Press) I have dealt at greater length with the same problem of convergence and divergence of the symbolic vocabulary of Judaic canonical writings and of synagogues and burial places.

Can John of Patmos, with his vision of "a new heaven and a new earth" have concurred? In detail, of course, no. But in mode of thought and argument, in uniting this "new heaven and new earth" with a radical change in the social order, I think he will have found much to affirm, and modes of thought entirely congruent with his own. Whether or not the great philosophical and Christian theological statements of eternity found in John of Patmos a suitable model, either for language of discourse or for categories of thought, is not for me to say. But when the Judaic counterparts in medieval theology spoke of eternal Israel, they paraphrased the Mishnah language before us – and went on to other things.

So to conclude, when we address to alien cultures and their languages categories that we deem self-evidently valid in *every* context and circumstance, we turn out to ask for a word in some other language to serve for what we mean in ours, only to discover that that other language has no word that fits. And since the limits of my language form the limits of my world, we discover at each further stage in asking how that alien culture defines and interprets a category deemed normal by our own the full intransigeance of categories, those of the other culture and also those of our own. The labor of comparison and contrast begins when we realize that categories so natural to our own conception scarcely retain their self-evidence in cultures other than our own. How is "eternity" to be understood in the theology of Judaism? It is by realizing that so far as we understand "eternity" in the context of Western thought, both philosophical and theological, "eternity" simply is not conceived at all within the theology of Judaism. As with so many other things, so with "eternity," we now see, the theology of Judaism means simply to speak of different things to different people altogether. That is, the category "eternity" in Judaism simply does not correspond to the category "eternity" in Western philosophical and Christian theological thought at all, but functions in a different way, refers to other things, and bears its own meaning and significance. So, as I said at the outset, when we understand how "eternity" is conceived within the theology of Judaism, what we learn concerns not "eternity" but the theology of Judaism.

Part Two

ANALYSIS OF LITERATURE

11

What Is the Tosefta?

The Tosefta forms the centerpiece of the Oral Torah.[1] The reason is that the Tosefta forms the bridge between the Mishnah and the two Talmuds. In terms of its own time, the Tosefta was compiled sometime after the conclusion of the Mishnah in ca. 200 but before the formation of the Talmud of the Land of Israel, ca 400, and my guess is that it is a work of the third century, 200-300. A small fraction of its contents can have reached final formulation prior to the closure of the Mishnah, but most of the document either cites the Mishnah verbatim and comments upon it, or can be understood only in light of the Mishnah even though the Mishnah is not cited verbatim, and that is sound reason for assigning the whole to the time after the Mishnah was concluded. So temporally we deal with the midpassage. But in substance the document's claim proves still stronger. For the Tosefta's materials, incoherent and cogent not among themselves but only in relationship to the Mishnah, serve as the Mishnah's first commentary, first amplification, and first extension – that is, the initial Talmud, prior to the one done in the Land of Israel by ca. 400 and the one completed in Babylonia by ca. 600. No important commentary to the Mishnah after the two Talmuds (and there were not very many in any event) read the Mishnah out of phase with the two Talmuds (particularly the Babylonian one), and the really perspicacious commentators appealed first of all to the Tosefta. So in these pages we really find out where it all began.

---

[1]This essay is drawn from the preface of *Tosefta. VI. Tohorot.* Second printing. With a new preface. Atlanta, 1990: Scholars Press for *South Florida Studies in the History of Judaism.* I call attention, also, to my *The Tosefta. An Introduction* (Northvale, 1991: Jason Aronson, Inc.), in which I provide a large selection of Mishnah and Tosefta passages in translation for more extended discussion than can be presented in a mere translation.

But that does not mean the Tosefta is a very accessible document. The opposite is the case. And the reason derives from the Tosefta's very character as a document of mediation, expansion, and extension of another piece of writing. If Judaism can be defined and described only in relationship to the Mishnah and two Talmuds, joined as they are by the Tosefta, the Tosefta, for its part, makes sense only in relationship to the Mishnah. That is so not only for its program and order, which are defined by the Mishnah, but also for its individual compositions. Each completed unit of thought of the Tosefta is to be understood, to begin with, in relationship with the Mishnah: is it a citation of and commentary to the Mishnah passage that forms its counterpart? Is the passage fully to be comprehended on its own or only in relationship to a counterpart passage of the Mishnah? Or is the passage free-standing? The answers to these three questions define the first step in making any sense at all of a passage of the Tosefta.

That explains why the Tosefta is a problem in the unfolding of the writings of Judaism, since its importance lies in its relationship to three other documents, the Mishnah, which came earlier, and the Talmud of the Land of Israel and the Talmud of Babylonia, which were completed later on. The Tosefta does not present a system of its own, as does the Mishnah, nor does it present both an inherited system and one of its own, as do both Talmuds. Rather, like a vine on a trellis, the Tosefta rests upon the Mishnah, having no structure of its own; but it also bears fruit nourished by its own roots.

Unlike the Mishnah, the Tosefta is not a free-standing document, one that presents its own viewpoint, propositions, and even system, but rather is secondary, derivative, dependent. That is not because it is a commentary upon the Mishnah, the Mishnah's first Talmud. For the criterion for knowing a free-standing from a contingent document is not the form; a commentary may, in fact, present in the form of a tradition and augmentation what is in fact a quite fresh and original system of its own; a fair part of the Yerushalmi, and an even larger component of the Bavli, fit the description of a systemic statement in commentary form. The dependent status of the Tosefta derives from the simple fact that, for most of the document – my estimate is in excess of 80 percent of the whole – we cannot understand a line without first consulting the Mishnah's counterpart statement. Once a text derives its first level of meaning from some other document, we no longer can maintain that we have a free-standing statement, let alone a systemic one.

The reader will soon perceive – in this part of the translation of the whole as in the other five volumes – that the Tosefta not only depends for structure, order, and sense, upon the Mishnah, but, in general, the materials assembled in the Tosefta set forth no viewpoint other than that of the Mishnah's counterpart materials, clarified, refined, and improved. Standing apart from the Mishnah, the greater part of the Tosefta's materials is incomprehensible gibberish, bearing no autonomous meaning to be discovered wholly within the limits of a discrete passage. the Tosefta's units relate to corresponding ones in the Mishnah in one of three ways:

1. The Tosefta cites the Mishnah verbatim and then supplies glosses or further discussions of the Mishnah's rules;
2. the Tosefta complements the Mishnah without directly citing the corresponding passage;
3. the Tosefta supplements the Mishnah with information relevant to, but in theme and meaning autonomous of, the principal document.

The first sort of relationship characterizes about half of the pericopae of the document, the second about another third, and the last, about a sixth. the Tosefta's aggregations of materials normally are grouped in accord with their respective relationships to the Mishnah. A sequence serving a given chapter of the Mishnah, for example, may begin with pericopae in which the Mishnah is cited, then proceed to another set in which the Mishnah is complemented, and finally, present materials in which the Mishnah is given supplementary but essentially separate materials. The formulary traits of the Tosefta run parallel to those of the Mishnah in the first, and, to a lesser extent, the second sort of materials. But in the main the Tosefta in language is a far less formalized document than the Mishnah. The Mishnah's redaction tends to produce aggregates of materials characterized by a common formulary pattern and a common theme. So far as the Tosefta may be divided into sizable groups of materials, by contrast, it is redacted primarily in accord with a single relationship to the Mishnah exhibited by a sequence of otherwise formally and thematically discrete units. In size, the Tosefta is approximately four times larger than the Mishnah.

The Tosefta is important within rabbinical literature for two reasons. First, pericopae of the Tosefta (or versions of pericopae, attributed to authorities of the first and second century, strongly resembling those now found in the Tosefta) commonly form the foundation of the treatment, by both Palestinian and Babylonian Talmuds, of the corresponding pericopae in the Mishnah. Indeed, the Tosefta supplement to the Mishnah often stands at the outset, and generates the two Talmuds' analyses of that same Mishnah. Second, the entire exegetical tradition of the Mishnah in later times depends upon the Tosefta's original exegesis of that document at all points at which the Tosefta is available and cited. If, therefore, one wants to understand how the Mishnah has been interpreted for nearly eighteen centuries, the place to begin is in the Tosefta. It hardly needs saying that the Tosefta, separate from its importance within the other principal documents of rabbinic Judaism, contains innumerable sayings which bear considerable value of their own. For the period after the redaction of the Mishnah and before the conclusion of the Talmuds, from ca. 200 to ca. 600, the Tosefta, including, especially, formulations of sayings which ultimately found their way into the Tosefta, constitutes a document of paramount importance.

The Tosefta depends upon the Mishnah in that its whole redactional framework, tractates and subdivisions alike, depends upon the Mishnah's. The Tosefta's redactors or arrangers tend to organize materials, within a given tractate, in line with two intersecting principles of arrangement. First, they follow the general outline of the Mishnah's treatment of a topic. Accordingly, if we set up a block of materials in the Tosefta side-by-side with a corresponding block of those of the Mishnah, we should discern roughly the same order of discourse. But, second, the Tosefta's arrangers also lay out their materials in accord with their own types. That is to say, they will tend (1) to keep as a group passages that cite and then comment upon the actual words of the Mishnah's base passage, then (2) to present passages that amplify in the Tosefta's own words opinions fully spelled out only in response to the Mishnah's statements, and, finally, (3) to give at the end, and as a group, wholly independent and autonomous sayings and constructions of such sayings. I stress that that redactional pattern may be shown only to be a tendency, a set of common policies and preferences, not a fixed rule. But when we ask how the Tosefta's editors arranged their materials, it is not wholly accurate to answer that they follow the plan of the Mishnah's counterparts. There will be some attention, also, to the taxonomic traits of the units of discourse of which the Tosefta itself is constructed. That is why two distinct editorial principles come into play in explaining the arrangement of the whole.

When we turn from the definition of the Tosefta and of its editorial and redactional character to the contents of the document as a whole, the Mishnah once more governs the framework of description. For the Tosefta, as is already clear, stands nearly entirely within the circle of the Mishnah's interests, rarely asking questions about topics omitted altogether by the Mishnah's authors, always following the topical decisions on what to discuss as laid down by the founders of the whole. For our part, therefore, we cannot write about the Tosefta's theology or law, as though these constituted a system susceptible of description and interpretation independent of the Mishnah's system. At the same time, we must recognize that the exegetes of the Mishnah, in the Tosefta, and in the two Talmuds, stand apart from, and later than, the authors of the

Mishnah itself. Accordingly, the exegetes systematically say whatever they wish to say by attaching their ideas to a document earlier than their own, and by making the principal document say what they wish to contribute. The system of expressing ideas through reframing those of predecessors preserves the continuity of tradition and establishes a deep stability and order upon the culture framed by that tradition. But it makes the labor of teasing out the ideas of the later generations parlous.

To see how the Tosefta fits into the sweep of the rabbinic literature extending from the Mishnah, ca. 200, through the Tosefta, ca. 200-300, to the Talmud of the Land of Israel or Yerushalmi, ca. 400, and on to the Talmud of Babylonia or Bavli, ca. 600, we follow a single passage. This allows us to place the Tosefta into its larger context. What is important, we shall observe, is how the Tosefta receives the Mishnah and transmits it forward; in the passage before us, the two Talmuds address not so much the Mishnah as the Mishnah as transmitted by the Tosefta. Even though this is not necessarily the pattern throughout, still, Saul Lieberman was more right than wrong when he observed that the Tosefta is the hinge on which the door of the Yerushalmi swings. When we see in great detail precisely how the Tosefta adds its amplification and explanation to the Mishnah, and then how the Yerushalmi and the Bavli in sequence take up the Tosefta's reading of the Mishnah, we shall grasp how profoundly the whole of rabbinic literature in its formative age focuses upon not the Mishnah as the Tosefta, the kind of hub of the whole.

The following pages present a chapter of the Mishnah, Mishnah-tractate Berakhot Chapter Eight. I then give the Tosefta to that chapter, following the text of Saul Lieberman, and compare the Mishnah and Tosefta. There follows the Yerushalmi's treatment of the same chapter, and, finally, the Bavli's as well. In giving the whole of both Talmuds' chapters, I mean to show how the Tosefta precipitates discourse, which then proceeds in quite unanticipated directions. In this way we get a good sense of proportion and balance: where the Tosefta matters, where it is left behind as the later authorities develop new interests altogether. I have already presented and carefully explained in detail every line of this passage in my *Invitation to the Talmud. A Teaching Book* (San Francisco, 1987: Harper & Row, second edition, completely revised). Readers who wish an explanation of the details of what follows will find it there. The main point I wish to register here is the position of the Tosefta in relationship to the Mishnah before and the two Talmuds afterward. Still more important, I want the reader to assess the matter of composition and proportion, with special reference to how the two Talmuds utilize passages of the Tosefta in forming their own discourse. To see the importance, but not the predominance, of the Tosefta in shaping the composition of the two Talmuds, the reader is given a picture of the entire chapter in those Talmuds, even though from a certain point in each case, the exposition of the Mishnah, as the Tosefta reads the Mishnah, falls away and others interests come to the fore.

I realize that this overview of the structure, order, proportions, and composition of the two Talmuds, neglecting as it does the exposition of the sense of phrases and sentences, represents a different approach to the representation of the rabbinic documents from the more familiar one of word-for-word exposition. But the very predominance of that atomistic reading of words, phrases, and, at the most, sentences makes it important to show a quite other angle of vision: the whole, seen whole, rather than the parts, seen in parts. Neither is ideal, but what follows – and the experience of the reader in surveying the whole as a whole – serves to remedy what is at present a considerable flaw in our approach to rabbinic writings. The best is the enemy of the good: here is one useful, and I think for its particular purpose defensible – way of approaching rabbinic writings, that is, in the largest possible context. The other, more familiar way of reading the same writings, as noted, is in my *Invitation to the Talmud*, which clarifies what, in the pages that follow, will of necessity be left in obscurity. For the main point here is to see the main point: structure, order, composition, proportion. These, after all, tell us what we need to know, which is, how to understand the Tosefta in context.

I. Mishnah-tractate Berakhot Chapter Eight

I

8:1. A   These are the things which are between the House of Shammai and the House of Hillel in [regard to] the meal:

B   The House of Shammai say, "One blesses over the day, and afterward one blesses over the wine."
And the House of Hillel say, "One blesses over the wine, and afterward one blesses over the day."

8.2. A   The House of Shammai say, "They wash the hands and afterward mix the cup."
And the House of Hillel say, "They mix the cup and afterward wash the hands."

8:3. A   The House of Shammai say, "He dries his hands on the cloth and lays it on the table."
And the House of Hillel say, "On the pillow."

8:4. A   The House of Shammai say, "They clean the house, and afterward they wash the hands."
And the House of Hillel say, "They wash the hands, and afterward they clean the house."

8:5. A   The House of Shammai say, "Light, and food, and spices, and *Havdalah*."

And the House of Hillel say, "Light, and spices, and food, and *Havdalah."*

B.   The House of Shammai say, "'Who created the light of the fire.'"
     And the House of Hillel say, "'Who creates the lights of the fire.'"

II

8:6.   A   They do not bless over the light or the spices of gentiles, nor the light or the spices of the dead, nor the light or the spices which are before an idol.

     B.   And they do not bless over the light until they make use of its illumination.

III

8:7.   A.   He who ate and forgot and did not bless [say Grace] –

     B.   The House of Shammai say, "He should go back to his place and bless."
     And the House of Hillel say, "He should bless in the place in which he remembered."

     C.   Until when does he bless? Until the food has been digested in his bowels.

8:8.   A.   Wine came to them after the meal, and there is there only that cup –

     B.   The House of Shammai say, "He blesses the wine, and afterward he blesses the food."
     And the House of Hillel say, "He blesses the food, and afterward he blesses the wine."

     C.   They respond *Amen* after an Israelite who blesses, and they do not respond *Amen* after a Samaritan who blesses, until hearing the entire blessing.

The Mishnah chapter goes over rules on the conduct of meals, first for Sabbaths and festivals, then in general, with special concern for preserving the cultic purity of the meal. That means the people at the meal keep the laws of cultic cleanness set forth in the book of Leviticus, as these are interpreted by the sages of the Torah. The details are explained in the Tosefta, Yerushalmi, and Bavli, and we do well to allow the course of rabbinic thought and writing to carry us into the matter. Here is how the Tosefta confronts the same themes and also cites some of the passages verbatim.

II. Tosefta to Mishnah Berakhot Chapter Eight

5:21 (Lieberman, p. 28, lines 41-2).

They answer *Amen* after a gentile who says a blessing with the Divine Name. They do not answer *Amen* after a Samaritan who says a blessing with the Divine Name until they have heard the entire blessing.

5.25 (Lieberman, p. 29, lines 53-57).

A. [The] things which are between the House of Shammai and the House of Hillel in [regard to] the meal:

B. The House of Shammai say, "One blesses over the day, and afterward he blesses over the wine, for the day causes the wine to come, and the day is already sanctified, but the wine has not yet come."

C. And the House of Hillel say, "One blesses over the wine, and afterward he blesses over the day, for the wine causes the Sanctification of the day to be said.

"Another explanation: The blessing over the wine is regular [= always required when wine is used], and the blessing over the day is not continual [but is said only on certain days]."

D. And the law is according to the words of the House of Hillel.

5:26 (Lieberman, pp. 29-30, lines 57-61).

A. The House of Shammai say, "They wash the hands and afterward mix the cup, lest the liquids which are on the outer surface of the cup be made unclean on account of the hands, and in turn make the cup unclean."

B. The House of Hillel say, "The outer surfaces of the cup are always deemed unclean.

"Another explanation: The washing of the hands must always take place immediately before the meal.

C. "They mix the cup and afterward wash the hands."

5:27 (Lieberman, p. 30, lines 61-65).

A. The House of House of Shammai say, "He dries his hand on the napkin and leaves it on the table, lest the liquids which are in the napkin be made unclean on account of the cushion, and then go and make the hands unclean."

B. And the House of Hillel say, "A doubt in regard to the condition of liquids so far as the hands are concerned is resolved as clean."

C. "Another explanation: Washing the hands does not pertain to unconsecrated food.

D. "But he dries his hands on the napkin and leaves it on the cushion, lest the liquids which are in the napkin be made unclean on account of the table, and they go and render the food unclean."

5:28 (Lieberman, p. 30, lines 65-68).

A. The House of Shammai say, "They clean the house, on account of the waste of food, and afterward they wash the hands."

B. The House of Hillel say, "If the waiter was a disciple of a sage, he gathers the scraps which contain as much as an olive's bulk.

C. "And they wash the hands and afterward clean the house."

5:29 (Lieberman, p. 30, lines 68-72).

A. The House of Shammai say, "He holds the cup of wine in his right hand and spiced oil in his left hand."

He blesses over the wine and afterward blesses over the oil.
B. And the House of Hillel say, "He holds the sweet oil in his right hand and the cup of wine in his left hand."
C. He blesses over the oil and smears it on the head of the waiter. If the waiter was a disciple of a sage, he [the diner] smears it on the wall, because it is not praiseworthy for a disciple of a sage to go forth perfumed.

5:30 (Lieberman, pp. 30-31, lines 72-75).

A. R. Judah said, "The House of Shammai and the House of Hillel did not dispute concerning the blessing of the food, that it is first, or concerning the *Havdalah,* that it is at the end.
"Concerning what did they dispute?
"Concerning the light and the spices, for –
"'The House of Shammai say, 'Light and afterward spices.'
"And the House of Hillel say, 'Spices and afterward light.'"

5:30 (Lieberman, p. 31, lines 75-77).

B. He who enters his home at the end of the Sabbath blesses the wine, the light, the spices, and then says *Havdalah.*
C. And if he has only one cup [of wine] he leaves it for after the meal and then says all [the liturgies] in order after [reciting the blessing for] it.

5:31 (Lieberman, p. 31, lines 81-85).

A. If a person has a light covered in the folds of his garment or in a lamp, and sees the flame but does not use its light, or uses its light but does not see its flame, he does not bless [that light]. [He says a blessing over the light only] when he both sees the flame and uses its light.
As to a lantern – even though he had not extinguished it (that is, it has been burning throughout the Sabbath), he recites a blessing over it.
B. They do not bless over the light of gentiles. One may bless over [the flame of] an Israelite kindled from a gentile, or a gentile who kindled from an Israelite.

5:32 (Lieberman, p. 31, lines 80-81).

In the house of study –
The House of Shammai say, "One [person] blesses for all of them."
And the House of Hillel say, "Each one blesses for himself."

Clearly, the Tosefta has a variety of materials Some of the materials are free-standing, but some simply cite and gloss the Mishnah. We see in the following comparison just how these things come to the surface. I add in italics the amplificatory language of the Tosefta.

III.   The Tosefta and the Mishnah Compared

Mishnah	Tosefta
M. 8:1. A. These are the things which are between the House of Shammai and the House of Hillel in [regard to] the meal:	Tos. 5:25. [The] things which are between the House of Shammai and the House of Hillel [as regards] the meal:
B. The House of Shammai say, "One blesses the day, and afterward one blesses over the wine."	The House of Shammai say, "One blesses the day, and afterward one blesses over the wine, *for the day causes the wine to come, and the day is already sanctified, but the wine has not yet come.*"
And the House of Hillel say, "One blesses the wine, and afterward one blesses over the day."	And the House of Hillel say, "One blesses over the wine, and afterward one blesses the day, *for the wine causes the Sanctification of the day to be said.*"
	"*Another matter: The blessing of the wine is continual, and the blessing of the day is not continual.*"
	And the law is according to the words of the House of Hillel.
M. 8:2.A. The House of Shammai say, "They wash the hands and afterward mix the cup."	Tos. 5:26. The House of Shammai say, "They wash the hands and afterward mix the cup, *lest the liquids which are on the outer surfaces of the cup may be made unclean on account of the hands, and they may go back and make the cup unclean.*"

And the House of Hillel say, "They mix the cup and afterward wash the hands."

The House of Hillel say, "*The outer surfaces of the cup are perpetually unclean.*

"*Another matter: The washing of the hands is only [done] near [at the outset of] the meal.*"

They mix the cup and afterward wash the hands."

8:3.A. The House of Shammai say, "He dries his hands on the napkin and lays it on the table."

And the House of Hillel say, "On the cushion."

5:27. The House of Shammai say, "He dries his hand on the napkin and lays it on the table, *lest the liquids which are in the napkin may be made unclean on account of the pillow, and they may go and make the hands unclean.*

The House of Hillel say, *A doubt in regard to the condition of liquids so far as the hands are concerned is clean.*

"*Another matter: Washing the hands does not pertain to unconsecrated food. But he dries his hands on the napkin and leaves it on the cushion lest the liquids which are in the pillow may be made unclean on account of the table, and they may go and render the food unclean.*"

M. 8:4.A. The House of Shammai say, "They clean the house and afterward wash the hands."

And the House of Hillel say, "They wash the hands and afterward clean the house."

Tos. 5:28. The House of Shammai say, "They clean the house *on account of the waste of food* and afterward wash the hands."

The House of Hillel say, "*If the waiter was a disciple of a sage, he gathers the scraps which contain as much as on olive's bulk.*"

They wash the hands and afterward clean the house."

8:5.A. The House of Shammai say, "Light, and food and spices, and *Havdalah.*"

And the House of Hillel say, "Light, and spices, and food, and *Havdalah.*"

5:30. R. Judah said, "*The House of Shammai and the House of Hillel did not dispute concerning the blessing of the food, that it is first, and concerning the* Havdalah *that it is the end. Concerning what did they dispute? Concerning the light and the spices, for* the House of Shammai say, 'Light and *afterward* spices,' and the House of Hillel say, 'Spices and *afterward* light.'"

B. The House of Shammai say, "'Who created the light of the fire.'"

And the House of Hillel say, "'Who creates the lights of the fire.'"

[No equivalent.]

M. 8:8.A. Wine came to them after the meal, and there is there only that cup –

B. The House of Shammai say, "He blesses over the wine and afterward he blesses over the food."

Tos. 5:30 (Lieberman, p. 31, lines 75-77). A. *He who enters his home at the end of the Sabbath blesses over the wine, the light, the spices, and then says* Havdalah.

And the House of Hillel say, "He blesses over the food and afterward he blesses over the wine."

[If wine came to them after the meal and] there is there only that cup House of Shammai say, "He blesses the wine and then the food."

(House of Hillel say, "He blesses the food and then the wine.")

B. *And if he has only one cup* [of wine], *he leaves it for after the meal and then says them all in order after* [blessing] *it.*

If he has only one cup [of wine] [he leaves if for after the meal and then says them all in order, thus:] Wine, then food.

M. 8:6.A. They do not bless the light or the spices of gentiles, nor the light or the spices of the dead, nor the light or the spices which are before an idol.

B. And they do not bless the light until they make use of its illumination.

Tos. 5:31.B. They do not bless the light of gentiles. *An Israelite who kindled* [a flame] *from a gentile, or a gentile who kindled from an Israelite – one may bless* [such a flame].

Tos. 5:31 (Lieberman, p. 31, lines 81-85). A. *If a person has a light covered in the folds of his garment or in a lamp, and he sees the flame but does not use its light, or uses its light but does not see its flame, he does not bless.* [He blesses only] *when he both sees the flame and uses its light.*

M. 8:8.C. They respond *Amen* after an Israelite who blesses, and they do not respond *Amen* after a Samaritan who blesses, until one hears the entire blessing.

Tos. 5:21 (Lieberman, p. 28, lines 41-2). *They answer "Amen" after a blessing with the divine name recited by a gentile.*

They do not answer *Amen* after a Samaritan who blesses *with the divine name* until they hear the entire blessing.

The pattern is now clear. We simply cannot understand a line of the Tosefta without turning to the Mishnah. That means that the Tosefta passage before us must have been composed after the Mishnah was in hand, that is, after 200, and that the authorship of the Tosefta had in mind the clarification of the received document, the Mishnah. So in a very simple sense, the Tosefta is the first Talmud, that is to say, it is the first sustained and systematic commentary to the Mishnah. Not only so, but as a Talmud, the Tosefta succeeds in ways in which the later Talmuds do not, simply because the Tosefta covers nearly the whole of the Mishnah, nearly all lines of all tractates, while the two Talmuds take up only a selection of the Mishnah tractates, thirty-nine in the Yerushalmi of the Mishnah's sixty-two tractates (excluding tractate Abot, the fathers, which is post-Mishnaic by about a generation, or fifty years), and the Bavli, thirty-seven of the Mishnah's tractates.

We come now to the Yerushalmi. To understand what follows we must know that the Yerushalmi will address a chapter of the Mishnah by citing the Mishnah in small blocks, not reading it whole but only in phrases and clauses. Our special interest is in the place of the Tosefta in the Yerushalmi's structure. What we shall see is that the Yerushalmi is consecutive upon not the Mishnah but the Tosefta's reading of the Mishnah.

How do the Yerushalmi's exegetes read the Mishnah and the Tosefta? A few general remarks will prepare us for what is to follow. They brought to the documents no distinctive program of their own. I perceive no hidden agenda. To state matters negatively, the exegetes did not know in advance of their approach to a law of the Mishnah facts about the passage not contained (at least implicitly) within the boundaries of the language of the Mishnah passage itself (except only for facts contained within other units of the same document). Rejecting propositions that were essentially a priori, they proposed to explain and expand precisely the wording and the conceptions supplied by the document under study. I cannot point to a single instance in which the Yerushalmi's exegetes in retrospect appear to twist and turn the language and message of a passage, attempting to make the words mean something other than what they appear to say. Whether the exegetical results remain close to the wording of a passage of the Mishnah, or whether they leap beyond the bounds of the passage, the upshot is the same. There is no exegetical program revealed in the Yerushalmi's reading of the Mishnah other than that defined, to begin with, by the language and conceptions of one Mishnah passage or another.

What, then, are the sorts of approaches we are apt to find? These are four, of which two are nearly indistinguishable, the third highly distinctive, and the fourth barely consequential.

1.   Citation and gloss of the language of the Mishnah (meaning of a phrase or concrete illustration of a rule). A unit of discourse of this kind will contain a direct citation of a sentence of the Mishnah. The word choices or phrasing of the Mishnah will be paraphrased or otherwise explained through what is essentially a gloss. Or the rule of the Mishnah will be explained through an example or a restatement of some kind.

2.   Specification of the meaning of the law of the Mishnah or the reason for it. Items of this kind stand very close to those of the former. What differentiates the one from the other is the absence, in the present set of units of discourse, of direct citation of the Mishnah or close and explicit reading of its language. The discussion then tends to allude to the Mishnah or to generalize, while remaining wholly within its framework. In some units of discourse scriptural prooftexts are adduced in evidence of a Mishnah passage. These frequently spill over into discussion of the reason for a rule.

3. Secondary implication or application of the law of the Mishnah. Units of discourse of this catalog generalize beyond the specific rule of the Mishnah. The discussion will commonly restate the principle of the rule at hand or raise a question invited by it. Hence if the Mishnah's law settles one question, participants in this sort of discourse will use that as the foundation for raising a second and consequent question. Two or more rules of the Mishnah (or of the Mishnah and Tosefta) will be contrasted with one another and then harmonized, or two or more rulings of a specific authority will be alleged to conflict and then shown not to stand at variance with one another.

4. The matter of authorities and their views: case law. In a handful of items, concrete decisions are attached to specific laws of the Mishnah, or the harmonization or identification of the opinions of Mishnah's authorities forms the center of interest. From this taxonomy it follows that there was a severely circumscribed repertoire of intellectual initiatives available to the authorities of the Yerushalmi.

Approaching a given rule of the Mishnah, a sage would do one of two things: (1) explain the meaning of the passage, or (2) extend and expand the meaning of the passage. In the former category fall all the items in the first and second approaches, as well as those units of discourse in which either a scriptural prooftext is adduced in support of a law or an alleged variant reading of a text is supplied. In the latter category fit all items in the third and fourth approaches, as well as those in which the work is to harmonize laws or principles, on the one side, or to cite and amplify Tosefta's complement to the Mishnah passage, on the other. Within these two categories, which produce, in all, four subdivisions, we may find a place for all units of discourse in which the focus of discussion is a passage of the Mishnah. Of the two sorts, the work of straightforward explanation of the plain meaning of a law of the Mishnah by far predominates. If we may state the outcome very simply: what the framers of the Yerushalmi want to say – whatever else their purpose or aspiration – is what they think the Mishnah means in any given passage.

Then when does the Yerushalmi speak for itself, not for the Mishnah and its close companion, the Tosefta? If we collect all units of discourse, or larger parts of such units, in which exegesis of the Mishnah or expansion upon the law of the Mishnah is absent – about 10 percent of all the Yerushalmi's units of discourse in my probe – we find at most four kinds, which in fact are only two:

1. Theoretical questions of law not associated with a particular passage of the Mishnah. Some tendency exists to move beyond the legal boundaries set by the Mishnah's rules themselves. More general inquiries are taken up. These, of course, remain within the framework of the topic of one tractate or another, although some larger modes of thought are characteristic of more than a single tractate. To explain, I point to the mode of thought in which the scriptural basis of the law of the Mishnah will be investigated, without regard to a given tractate. Along these same lines, I may point to a general inquiry into the count under which one may be liable for a given act, comments on the law governing teaching and judging cases, and the like. But these items tend not to leave the Mishnah far behind.
2. Exegesis of Scripture separate from the Mishnah. It is under this rubric that we find the most important instances in which the Yerushalmi presents materials essentially independent of the Mishnah. They pursue problems or themes through what is said about a biblical figure, expressing ideas and values simply unknown to the Mishnah.
3. Historical statements. The Yerushalmi contains a fair number of statements that something happened or narratives about how something happened. While many of these are replete with biblical quotations, in general they do not provide exegesis of Scripture, which serves merely as illustration or reference point.
4. Stories about, and rules for, sages and disciples, separate from discussion of a passage of the Mishnah. The Mishnah contains a tiny number of tales about rabbis. These serve principally as precedents for, or illustrations of, rules.

The Yerushalmi, by contrast, contains a sizable number of stories about sages and their relationships to other people. Like the items in the two afore-mentioned lists, these, too, may be adduced as evidence of the values of the people who stand behind the Yerushalmi, the things they thought important. These tales rarely serve to illustrate a rule or concept of the Mishnah. The main, though not the only, characteristic theme is the power of the rabbi, the honor due to the rabbi, and the tension between the rabbi and others, whether the patriarch, on the one side, the heretic on the second, or the gentile on the third. Units of discourse (or large segments of such units) independent of the interests of the Mishnah are not numerous. Varying in bulk from one tractate to the next, as I said, in my probe of five tractates of the Yerushalmi they added up to not much more than 10 percent of the whole. Furthermore, among the four sorts of units of discourse before us, the items on the first do not move far from the principles and concerns of the Mishnah. And this brings us to our task, which is to examine the Yerushalmi's treatment of the Mishnah and therefore also of the Tosefta to Mishnah-tractate Berakhot Chapter Eight. The reader will readily recognize how the Tosefta's materials make their appearance.

IV.   Yerushalmi to Mishnah Berakhot Chapter Eight

8:1.   **The House of Shammai say, "One blesses the day and afterward one blesses over the wine."**
                And the House of Hillel say, "One blesses over the wine and afterward one blesses the day."

I.   A.   *What is the reason of the House of Shammai?*
                The Sanctification of the day causes the wine to be brought, and the man is already liable for the Sanctification of the day before the wine comes.
                What is the reason of the House of Hillel?
                The wine causes the Sanctification of the day to be said.
                Another matter: Wine is perpetual, and the Sanctification is not perpetual. [What is always required takes precedence over what is required only occasionally.]

        B.   R. Yosé said, "[It follows] from the opinions of them both that with respect to wine and *Havdalah*, wine comes first."
                "*It is not the reason of the House of Shammai* that the Sanctification of the day causes the wine to be brought, and here, since *Havdalah* does not cause wine to be brought, the wine takes precedence?"
                "*Is it not the reason of the House of Hillel that* the wine is perpetual and the Sanctification is not perpetual, and since the wine is perpetual, and the *Havdalah* is not perpetual, the wine comes first?"

        C.   R. Mana said, "From the opinions of both of them [it follows] that with respect to wine and *Havdalah*, *Havdalah* comes first."
                "*Is it not the reason of the House of Shammai that* one is already obligated [to say] the Sanctification of the day before the wine comes, and here, since he is already obligated for *Havdalah* before the wine comes, *Havdalah* comes first?"
                Is it not the reason of the House of Hillel that the wine causes the Sanctification of the day to be said, and here, since the wine does not cause the *Havdalah* to be said, *Havdalah* comes first?"

        D.   R. Zeira said, "From the opinions of both of them [it follows] that they say *Havdalah* without wine, but they say the Sanctification only with wine."

        E.   *This is the opinion of R. Zeira, for R. Zeira said, They may say Havdalah over beer, but they go from place to place* [in search of wine] *for the Sanctification."*

II.   A.   R. Yosé b. Rabbi said, "They are accustomed there [in Babylonia], where there is no wine, for the prayer leader to go before the ark and say one blessing which is a summary of the seven, and complete it with, 'Who sanctifies Israel and the Sabbath Day.'"

        B.   *And thus the following poses a difficulty for the opinion of the House of Shammai: How should one act on the evenings of the Sabbath?*

He *who was sitting and eating on the evening of the Sabbath,* and it grew
dark and became Sabbath evening, and there was there only that
one cup – [The House of Shammai say, "Wine, then food," and the
House of Hillel say, "Food, then wine," so Mishnah 8:8].
Do you say he should leave it for the end of the meal and say all of
them [the blessings] on it?
What do you prefer?
Should he [first] bless the day? The food takes precedence.
Should he bless the food? The wine takes precedence.
Should he bless the wine? The day takes precedence.

C.   *We may infer* [the answer] *from this:*
If wine came to them after the meal, and there is there only that
cup –
R. Ba said, "Because it [the wine's] is a brief blessing, [he says it
first, for] perhaps he may forget and drink [the wine]. But here,
since he says them all over the cup, he will not forget [to say a
blessing over the wine in the cup]."

D.   What, then, should he do according to the opinion of the House of
Shammai?
Let him bless the food first, then bless the day, and then bless the
wine.

E.   *And this poses difficulty for the opinion of the House of Hillel: How
should one act at the end of the Sabbath?*
If he was sitting and eating on the Sabbath and it grew dark and the
Sabbath came to an end, and there is there only that cup –
Do you say he should leave it [the wine] for after the meal and say
them all on it?
What do you prefer?
Should he bless the wine? The food comes first.
Should he bless the food? The light comes first.
Should be bless the light? The *Havdalah* comes first.

F.   *We may infer* [the solution to the impasse] *from this:* R. Judah said,
"The House of Shammai and the House of Hillel did not differ
concerning the blessing of the food, that it comes first, nor
concerning *Havdalah,* that it comes at the end.
"Concerning what did they differ?
"Concerning the light and the spices, for:
"The House of Shammai say, 'The spices and afterward the light.'
"And the House of Hillel say, 'The light and afterward the spices.'"

G.   R. Ba and R. Judah in the name of Rav (said), "The law is according
to him who says, 'Spices and afterward light.'"]

H.   What should he do according to the opinion of the House of Hillel?
Let him bless the food, afterward bless the wine, and afterward
bless the light.

III. A.   As to [the beginning of the] festival day which coincides with the
end of the Sabbath –
R. Yohanan said, "[The order of prayer is] wine, Sanctification,
light, *Havdalah.*"
Hanina bar Ba said in the name of Rav, "Wine, Sanctification, light,
Havdalah, Sukkah, and season."
And did not Samuel rule according to this teaching of R. Hanina.

B.   R. Aha said in the name of R. Joshua b. Levi, "When a king goes out and the governor comes in, they accompany the king and afterward bring in the governor."

C.   Levi said, "Wine, *Havdalah*, light, Sanctification."

IV.   A.   R. Zeira asked before R. Yosé, "How shall we do it in practice?" He said to him, "According to Rav, and according to R. Yohanan." And so, too, did the rule come out in practice – according to Rav and according to R. Yohanan.

B.   *And when R. Abbahu went south, he would act in accord with R. Hanina, but when he went down to Tiberias, he would act in accord with R. Yohanan, for one does not differ from a man['s ruling] in his own place* [out of courtesy].

C.   *According to the opinion of R. Hanina this poses no problem.*

D.   *But it poses a problem to the opinion of R. Yohanan:* In the rest of the days of the year does he not bless the light, lest it go out [because of a draft, and he lose the opportunity to say the blessing]? And here, too, he should bless the light before it goes out!

E.   *What did R. Yohanan do in this connection?* [How did he explain this difficulty?]

F.   Since he has wine [in hand], his light will not go out [for it is protected].

G.   Then let him bless the light at the end?

H.   So as not to upset the order [of prayer; lit.: time of the coming Sabbaths, [he does not do so].

8:2.   The House of Shammai say, "They wash the hands and afterward mix the cup." And the House of Hillel say, "They mix the cup first and afterward wash the hands."

I.   A.   *What is the reason of the House of Shammai?* So that the liquids which are on the outer side of the cup may not be made unclean by his hands and go and make the cup unclean. *What is the reason of the House of Hillel?* The outer side of the cup is always unclean [so there is no reason to protect it from the hands' uncleanness]. Another matter: One should wash the hands immediately before saying the blessing.

B.   *R. Biban in the name of R. Yohanan* [said], *"The opinion of the House of Shammai is in accord with R. Yosé and that of the House of Hillel with R. Meir, as we have learned there* [M. Kel. 25:7-8]: "[In all vessels an outer part and an inner part are distinguished, and also a part by which they are held.]" "R. Meir says, 'For hands which are unclean and clean.'" "R. Yosé said, 'This applies only to clean hands alone.'"

C.   R. Yosé in the name of R. Shabbetai, and R. Hiyya in the name of R. Simeon b. Laqish [said], "For *Hallah* [dough-offering] and for washing the hands, a man goes four miles [to find water]." R. Abbahu in the name of R. Yosé b. R. Hanina said, "This is what he said, '[If the water is] before him [that is, on his way, in his vicinity, or near at hand, he must proceed to it and wash]. But if it is behind him [that is, not on his way], they do not trouble him [to obtain it and wash].'"

D.   Regarding those who guard gardens and orchards [and who cannot leave their posts], what do you do for them as to the insides and the outer sides [of a cup]? [How do we rule in their case? Do we judge them to be in the status of those for whom the water is] on their way, or in the status of those who would have to backtrack?

Let us infer the answer from this [M. Hal. 2:3]:

The woman sits and cuts off her dough-offering [Hallah] while she is naked, because she can cover herself up, but a man cannot.

Now does not a woman sit in the house, yet you say they do not bother her? So, too, here they do not bother him.

II.   A.   *It has been taught:*

Washing before the meal is a matter of choice, but afterward it is a matter of obligation.

But in respect to the first washing, he washes and interrupts, and in the case of the second washing, he washes and does not interrupt.

B.   What is the meaning of "he washes and interrupts?"

R. Jacob b. Aha said, "He washes and then repeats the washing."

R. Samuel bar Isaac said, "*If he is required* to repeat the washing, *how do you claim it is a matter of choice?*

["Or if you want, I may point out you require one to go four miles (in search of water], *so how do you claim* it is a matter of choice!"

C.   R. Jacob bar Idi said, "On account of the first [washing of hands], a pig's flesh was eaten; on account of the second [washing of hands], a woman left her house.

"And some say, three souls were killed on her account. [It is not a matter of choice at all.]"

III.   A   *Samuel went up to visit Rav. He saw him eating with* [his hands covered by] *a napkin. He said to him, "How so?* [Did you not wash your hands?]"

He said to him, "I am sensitive."

B.   *When R. Zeira came up here* [to Palestine], *he saw the priests eating with a napkin. He said to them, "Lo, this is in accord with the story of Rav and Samuel."*

C.   R. Yosé bar Kahana came [and said] *in the name of Samuel,* "One washes the hands for heave-offering, not for unconsecrated food."

D.   R. Yosé says, "For heave-offering and for unconsecrated food."

E.   R. Yosah in the name of R. Hiyya bar Ashi, and R. Jonah and R. Hiyya bar Ashi in the name of Rav [said], "They wash the hands for heave-offering up to the wrist, and for unconsecrated food up to he knuckles."

F.   *Measha the son of the son of R. Joshua b. Levi said, "If one was eating with my grandfather and did not wash his hands up to the wrist, grandfather would not eat with him."*

G.   R. Huna said, "Washing the hands applies only for bread."

H   R. Hoshia taught, "Whatever is unclean on account of liquid [is protected by washing the hands]."

I.   R. Zeira said, "*Even for cutting beets, he would wash his hands.*"

IV.   A   Rav said, "He who washed his hands in the morning is not required to do so in the afternoon."

B   *R. Abina ordered his wine steward, "Whenever you find sufficient water, wash your hands and rely on this washing all day long."*

C.   *R. Zeira went up to R. Abbahu in Caesarea. He found him saying, "I shall go to eat."*

D.   *He gave him a chunk of bread to cut. He* [Abbahu] *said to him* [Zeira], *"Begin, bless."*

E.   *He* [Zeira] *said to him* [Abbahu], *"The host knows the value of his loaf."* [You should bless.]

F.   *When they had eaten, he* [Abbahu] *said to him* [Zeira], *"Let the elder bless."*

G.   *He said to him, "Rabbi, does the rabbi* [you] *know R. Huna, a great man, who would say, 'He who opens* [blesses first] *must close* [and say Grace after Meals]'?"*

H.   *A Tannaitic teaching differs from R. Huna, as it has been taught:*

I.   The order of washing the hands is this: With up to five people present, they begin with the greatest. [If] more than this [are present], they begin with the least. In the middle of the meal, they begin with the eldest. After the meal they begin with the one who blesses.

J.   Is it not [done] so that he may prepare himself for the blessing? [So he did *not* bless at the beginning!

K.   *If you say* the one who opens is the one who closes, he is already prepared [having opened the meal].

L.   *R. Isaac said, "Explain it in regard to those who come in one by one and did not know which one had blessed* [at the outset]."

8:3.   **The House of Shammai say, "He dries his hands on the napkin and puts it on the table."**
And the House of Hillel say, "On the cushion."

I.   A.   The Mishnah deals with either a table of marble [which is not susceptible to uncleanness] or a table that can be taken apart and is not susceptible to becoming unclean.

      B.   *What is the reason of the House of Shammai?*
So that the liquids which are on the napkin may not become unclean from the cushion and go and render his hands unclean.
And what is the reason of the House of Hillel?
The condition of doubt[ful uncleanness] with respect to the hands is always regarded as clean.
Another reason: The [question of the cleanness of] hands does not apply to unconsecrated food [which in any case is not made unclean by unclean hands which are unclean in the second remove].

      C.   *And according to the House of Shammai, does* [the question of the cleanness of] hands [indeed] apply to unconsecrated food?

      D.   *You may interpret* [the tradition] either in accord with R. Simeon b. Eleazar or in accord with R. Eleazar b. R. Saddoq.
According to R. Simeon b. Eleazar, as it has been taught:
R. Simeon b. Eleazar says in the name of R. Meir, "Hands unclean in the first remove of uncleanness can affect [even] unconsecrated food, and in the second remove of uncleanness can affect [only] heave-offering."

      E.   Or according to R. Eleazar b. R. Saddoq, *as we have learned there:*

F.   Unconsecrated food which has been prepared along with consecrated [food] is like unconsecrated food [and subject to the same, less strict cleanness rules].

G.   R. Eleazar b. R. Saddoq says, "Lo, it is like heave-offering, capable of becoming unclean from [something unclean in the] second remove of uncleanness and being rendered unfit from [something unclean in] still a further remove of uncleanness."

H.   *There we have learned:*

I.   He who anoints himself with a clean oil and is made unclean and goes down and bathes [in ritual pool] –

J.   The House of Shammai say, "Even though he drips [with oil], [the oil] is clean."

K.   And the House of Hillel say, "It is unclean [so long as there remains enough to anoint a small member]."

L.   And if the oil was unclean in the first place –

M.   The House of Shammai say, "[It remains unclean, even after he has immersed himself, so long as there remains] sufficient for anointing a small limb."

N.   And the House of Hillel say, "[So long as it remains] a dripping liquid."

O.   R. Judah says in the name of the House of Hillel, "So long as it is dripping so as to moisten something else."

P.   *The principle of the House of Hillel has been turned around.*

Q.   *There* [in the just-cited law] *they say it is* unclean. *And here* [in our Mishnah] *they say it is* clean.

R.   *There* it is present. *But here* it is absorbed in the napkin.

8:4.   **The House of Shammai say, "They clean the house and afterward wash the hands." And the House of Hillel say, "They wash the hands and afterward clean the house."**

I.   A.   *What is the reason of the House of Shammai?*
      B.   Because of the waste of food.
      C.   *And what is the reason of the House of Hillel?*
      D.   If the servant is clever, he removes the crumbs which are less than an olive's bulk, and they wash their hands and afterward they clean the house.

8:5.   **The House of Shammai say, "Light, and food, and spices, and *Havdalah*." And the House of Hillel say, "Light, and spices, and food, and *Havdalah*." The House of Shammai say, "'Who created the light of the fire.'" And the House of Hillel say, "'Who creates the lights of the fire.'"**

I.   A.   It was taught:
      B.   R. Judah said, "The House of Shammai and the House of Hillel did not differ concerning the [blessing for] the mean, that it comes at the beginning, or concerning *Havdalah*, that it comes at the end. And concerning what did they differ? Concerning the light and spices, for the House of Shammai say, 'Spices and light.' And the House of Hillel say, 'Light and spices.'"

C.   R. Ba and R. Judah in the name of Rav [said], "The law is in accord with him who says, 'Spices and afterward light.' [That is, Judah's House of Shammai.]"

D.   The House of Shammai say, "The cup [should be] in his right hand, and the sweet oil in his left hand. He says [the blessing for] the cup and afterward says the blessing for the sweet oil."

E.   The House of Hillel say, "The sweet oil [should be] in his right hand and the cup in his left hand, and he says [the blessing for] the sweet oil and rubs it on the head of the servant. If the servant is a disciple of a sage, he rubs it on the wall, for it is not fitting for a disciple of a sage to go forth scented in public."

F.   *Abba bar bar Hanna and R. Huna were sitting and eating, and R. Zeira was standing and serving them. He went and bore both of them* [oil and cup] *in one hand.*

G.   *Abba bar bar Hanna said to him, "Is one of your hands cut off?" And his* [Abba's] *father was angry at him.*

H.   *He* [the father] *said to him* [Abba], *"Is it not enough for you that you are sitting and he is standing and serving? And furthermore, he is a priest, and Samuel said, 'He who makes* [secular] *use of the priesthood has committed sacrilege.' You make light of him.*

I.   *"I decree for him to sit and you to stand and serve in his place."*

J.   How do we know that he who makes use of the priesthood has committed sacrilege?

K.   R. Aha in the name of Samuel said, "'And I said to them, You are holy to the Lord and the vessels are holy' [Ezra 8:28]. Just as one who makes use of the vessels commits sacrilege, so he who makes use of the priests commits sacrilege."

L.   **[The House of Shammai say, "'Who created ...'"]**

M.   According to the opinion of the House of Shammai, [one should say as the blessing for wine], "Who created the fruit of the vine" [instead of "who creates ...," as actually is said].

N.   According to the opinion of the House of Hillel, [one should say,] "Who creates the fruit of the vine" [as is indeed the case].

O.   [The Shammaite reply:]

P.   The wine is newly created every year, but the fire is not newly created every hour.

Q.   The fire and the mule, even though they were not created in the six days of creation, were thought of [entered the Creator's mind] in the six days of creation.

R.   Proof of the mule: "These are the sons of Zibeon: Aiah and Anah; he is the Anah who found the hot springs (HYYMYM) in the wilderness [as he pastured the asses of Zibeon his father (Genesis 36:24]."

S.   *What is the meaning of* hot springs (HYYMYM)?

T.   R. Judah b. Simeon says, "Mule." [Greek: *hemiovos.*]

U.   *And the rabbis say,* "Half-a-horse [Greek: *hemi-hippos*], half was a horse, half an ass."

V.   And what are the marks [to know whether the father was a horse, the mother an ass, or vice versa]?

W. R. Judah said, "If the ears are small, the mother was a horse and the father an ass. If they are big, the mother was an ass and the father a horse."

X. *R. Mana instructed the members of the Patriarchate, "If you want to buy a mule, buy those whose ears are small,* for the mother was a horse and the father an ass."

Y. What did Zibeon and Anah do? They brought a female ass and mated her with a male horse, and they produced a mule.

Z. The Holy One, blessed be He, said to them, "You have brought into the world something which is destructive. So I, too, shall bring upon that man [you] something which is destructive."

AA. What did the Holy One, blessed be He, do?

BB. He brought a snake and mated it with a lizard and it produced a *havarbar*-lizard.

CC. A man should never say to you that a *havarbar*-lizard bit him and he lived, or a mad dog nipped him and he lived, or a she-mule butted him and he lived. We speak only of a white she-mule.

DD. As to the fire:

EE. R. Levi in the name of R. Nezira [said], "Thirty-six hours that light which was created on the first day served [the world]. Twelve on the eve of the Sabbath [Friday], twelve on the night of the Sabbath, and twelve on the Sabbath.

FF. "And the First Man [Adam] looked at it from one end of the world to the other. When the light did not cease [from shining], the whole world began to sing, as it is said, 'Under the whole heaven, he lets [his voice] go, and his light to the corners of the earth' [Job 37:3].

GG. "When the Sabbath ended, it began to get dark. Man became frightened, saying, 'This is the one concerning whom it is written,"He will bruise your head, and you shall bruise his heel" [Genesis 3:15].

HH. "'Perhaps this one has come to bite me.' And he said, 'Let only darkness cover me'" [Psalm 139:11].

II. R. Levi said, "At that moment the Holy One, blessed be He, prepared two flints and struck them against each other, and the light came forth from them. This is the meaning of that which Scripture says, 'And the night around me be light' [Psalm 139:11].

JJ. "And he [man] blessed it, 'Who creates the lights of the fire.'"

KK. Samuel said, "Therefore they bless the fire at the end of the Sabbath, for that is when it was first created."

LL. R. Huna in the name of R. Abbahu in the name of R. Yohanan [said], "Also at the end of the Day of Atonement one blesses it, for the light has rested that entire day."

8:6. **They do not bless the light or spices of gentiles, nor the light or spices of the dead, nor the light or spices which are before an idol. They do not bless the light until they make use of its illumination.**

I. A R. Jacob taught before R. Jeremiah, "They do bless the spices of gentiles."

B. *What is the difference* [between this view and the Mishnah's]?

C. *We explain that the latter refers to the* gentile's deeds before his òwn store [while the Mishnah refers to a banquet].
D. Even though it has not gone out [but burned the entire Sabbath], they may bless [the light of] a lantern [because no prohibited work has been done by its light].
E. As regards a flame in the folds of one's garment, in a lamp, or in a mirror, if one sees the flame but does not make use of its light, or makes use of its light but not see the flame, one may not bless it. [One may bless] only when one may see the flame and makes use of the light.
F. Five things were said in regard to the burning coal, and five with regard to the flame.
    1. A coal of the sanctuary is subject to the law of sacrilege, but a flame is neither used for pleasure nor subject to the law of sacrilege.
    2. A burning coal used for idolatry is prohibited, but a flame is permitted.
    3. He who vows not to have enjoyment from his fellow may not use his burning coal, but may use his flame.
    4. He who brings a coal out to the public way [on the Sabbath] is liable, but if he brings a flame, he is not liable.
    5. They bless the flame, but not the burning coal.
G. R. Hiyya bar Ashi in the name of Rav said, "If the coals were glowing, they may bless them."
H. R. Yohanan of Kerasion in the name of R. Nahum bar Simai [said], "On condition that it was cut off." [That is, the flame was shooting up from the coal.]
I. *It was taught:*
J. Now the [light of] a gentile who kindled [a light from the flame of] an Israelite, and an Israelite who kindled [a light from the flame of a gentile] – *this poses no problems.*
K. But [the light of] a gentile who kindled [a light from the flame of] an Israelite [may be blessed]. If so, even [the flame of] a gentile who kindled from a gentile [should be allowed].
L. *It is indeed taught:* They do *not* bless [a light kindled by] a gentile from a gentile.
M. R. Abbahu in the name of R. Yohanan [said,] "As to an alleyway which is populated entirely by gentiles with a single Israelite living in its midst – if the light comes from there, they may bless it on account of that one Israelite who lives there."
N. R. Abbahu in the name of R. Yohanan [said], "They do not bless either the spices on Sabbath evenings in Tiberias or the spices on Saturday nights in Sepphoris, or the light or the spices on Friday mornings in Sepphoris, for these all are prepared only for another purpose [cleaning clothes]."
O. Nor over the light or spices of the dead.
P. R. Hezekiah and R. Jacob b. Aha in the name of R. Yosé b. R. Hanina [said], "This refers to the following case: 'When they are placed over the bed of the dead. But if they are placed before the bed of the dead, they may be blessed [that is, a blessing may be recited over them].'"

Q.   "[For] I say, they are prepared for the purposes of the living."

R.   **Nor the light nor the spices of idolatry.**

S.   But is not that of gentiles the same as that of idolatry? [Why repeat the same rule?]

T.   Interpret it as applying to an Israelite idol.

They do not bless the light until they make use of its illumination.

I.   A.   R. Zeira, son of R. Abbahu expounded, "'And God saw the light, that it was good' [Gen. 1:4]. And afterward, 'And God divided the light from the darkness'" [Gen. 1:5]. [That is, first it was seen and used, then comes the *Havdalah.*]

B.   R. Berekiah said, "Thus the two great men of the world [age], R. Yohanan and R. Simeon b. Laqish, expounded: 'And God divided – a certain division.'" [That is, he did so literally.]

C.   R. Judah b. R. Simon said, "They divided for Him."

D.   And the rabbis say, "They divided for the righteous who were destined to come into the world.

E.   "They drew a parable: To what is the matter to be likened? To a king who has two generals. This one says, 'I shall serve by day,' and this one says, 'I shall serve by night.'

F.   "He calls the first and says to him, 'So-and-so, the day will be your division.'

G.   "He calls the second and says to him, 'So-and-so, the night will be your division.'

H.   "That is the meaning of what is written, 'And God called the light day, and the darkness he called night.'

I.   "To the light he said, 'The day will be your province.' And to the darkness he said, 'The night will be your province.'"

J.   R. Yohanan said, "This is what the Holy One, blessed be He, said to Job [Job 38:12], 'Have you commanded the morning since your days began, and caused the dawn to know its place?'

K.   "What is the place of the light of the six days of creation – where was it hidden?"

L.   *R. Tanhuma said,* "I give the reason: 'Who creates light and makes darkness, and makes peace' [Isa. 45:7]. When he went forth, he made peace between them."

M.   **They do not bless the light until they make use of its illumination.**

N.   Rav said, "They *use* [spelled with an *'alef*]."

O.   And Samuel said, "They *enjoy* [spelled with an *'ayin*]."

P.   He who said "they *use*" [may draw support from the following]:

Q.   "Only on this condition will we *consent* to you" [Gen. 34:15].

R.   He who said "*enjoy*" [may draw support from the following]:

S.   "How to sustain with a word him that is weary" [Isa. 50:4].

T.   There we have learned: "How do they extend (M'BR) the Sabbath limits of cities?"

U.   Rav said, "*Add*" ['*alef*].

V.   And Samuel said, "*Increase*" ['*ayin*].

W.   He who said it is with an *'alef* means they add a limb to it.

X. He who said it with an *'ayin* means it is [increased] like a pregnant woman.

Y. There we learned, "Before the festivals ('YD) of gentiles."

Z. Rav said, *"Testimonies" ['ayin].*

AA. And Samuel said, *"Festivals" ['alef].*

BB. He who said it is with an *'alef* [may cite this verse], "For near is the day of their calamity ['YD]" [Deut. 32:35].

CC. He who said it is with an *'ayin* [may cite], "Their testimonies neither see nor know, they may be put to shame" [Isa. 44:9].

DD. How does Samuel deal with the reason of Rav? [He may say,] "And their *testimonies* are destined to *shame* those who keep them on the day of judgment."

EE. **They do not bless the light until they have made use of its illumination.** [How much illumination must there be?]

FF. R. Judah in the name of Samuel said, "So that women may spin by its light."

GG. R. Yohanan said, "So that one's eye can see what is in the cup and what is in the saucer."

HH. R. Hanina said, "So that one may know how to distinguish one coin from another."

II. R. Oshaia taught, "Even [if the flame is in] a hall ten-by-ten, they may say the blessing."

JJ. *R. Zeira drew near the lamp. His disciples said to him, "Rabbi, why do you rule so stringently for us? Lo, R. Oshaia taught, "One may bless even in a hall ten-by-ten."*

8:7 **He who ate and forgot and did not bless –**
The House of Shammai say, "He should go back to his place and bless."
And the House of Hillel say, "He may bless in the place in which he remembered."
"Until when may he say the blessing? Until the food has been digested in his bowels."

I. A R. Yusta b. Shunam said, "[There are] *two authorities. One gives the reason of the House of Shammai and the other the reason of the House of Hillel."*

B *"The one who gives the reason of the House of Shammai* [says], 'If he had forgotten a purse of precious stones and pearls there, would he not go back and take his purse? *So, too,* let him go back to his place and bless.'

C *"The one who gave the reason of the House of Hillel* [states], 'If he were a worker on the top of the palm or down in a pit, would you trouble him to go back to his place and bless? But he should bless in the place where he remembers [to do so]. *Here, too,* let him bless in the place where he remembers.'"

D. **Until when does he recite the blessing?**

E. R. Hiyya in the name of Samuel says, "Until the food has been digested in his bowels."

F. And the sages say, "So long as he is thirsty on account of that meal."

G. R. Yohanan says, "Until he becomes hungry again."

8:8.　　　　　If wine came to them after the food, and there is there only one cup –
The House of Shammai say, "He blesses the wine and afterward blesses the food."
And the House of Hillel say, "He blesses the food and afterward blesses the wine."
They answer *Amen* after an Israelite who blesses, and they do not answer *Amen* after a Samaritan who blesses until the entire blessing has been heard.

I.　　A　　R. Ba said, "Because it is a brief blessing, he may forget and drink the wine. But because it is joined to the [blessings for] cup, he will not forget."

　　　B.　　After an Israelite they answer *Amen*, even though he has not heard [the Grace]. Has it not been taught, "If he heard [the Grace] and did not answer, he has carried out his obligation [to say Grace]. If he answered *[Amen]* and did not hear [the Grace], he has not carried out his obligation."

　　　C.　　Hiyya the son of Rav said, "The Mishnah speaks of him who] did not eat with them as much as an olive's bulk."

　　　D.　　*So, too, it has been taught:* If he heard and did not answer, he has carried out his obligation. If he answered and did not hear, he has not carried out his obligation.

　　　E.　　Rav in the name of Abba bar Hanna [said], *and some say Abba bar Hanna in the name of Rav* [said], "And this applies to a case in which he answered at the chapter [paragraph] headings."

　　　F.　　*R. Zeira asked, "What are these chapter headings?"*

　　　G.　　"Praise the Lord, praise the servants of the Lord, praise the name of the Lord" [Ps. 113:1].

　　　H.　　*They asked before R. Hiyya b. Abba, "How do we know that, if one heard and did not answer [Amen], he has carried out his obligation?"*

　　　I.　　*He said, "From what we have seen the great rabbis doing, so they do in public, for they say this:* 'Blessed is he that comes.' *And the others say,* 'In the name of the Lord.' *And both groups thus* complete their obligation."

　　　J.　　R. Oshaia taught, "A man responds *Amen*, even though he has not eaten, and he does not say, 'Let us bless him of whose bounty we have eaten,' unless he actually ate."

　　　K.　　*It has been taught,* They do not respond with an orphaned *Amen*, a cut-off *Amen*, or a hasty *Amen*.

　　　L.　　Ben Azzai says, "If one answers an orphaned *Amen*, his sons will be orphans. A cut-off one – his years will be cut off. A hasty one – his soul will be cut down. A long one – his days and years will be lengthened with goodness."

　　　M.　　What is an orphaned *Amen*?

　　　N.　　R. Huna said, *"This refers to a person who sat down to bless,* and he answered, but did not know to what [prayer] he answered *[Amen]."*

　　　O.　　It was taught: If a gentile blessed the Divine Name, they answer *Amen* after him.

　　　P.　　R. Tanhum said, "If a gentile blesses you, answer after him *Amen, as it is written,* 'Blessed will you be by all the peoples'" [Deut. 7:14].

Q A gentile met R. Ishmael and blessed him. He said to him, *"You have already been answered."*

R *Another met him* and cursed him. He said to him, *"You have already been answered."*

S His disciple said to him, *"Rabbi, how could you say the same to both?"* He said to them, *"Thus it is written in Scripture: 'Those that curse you will be cursed, and those that bless you will be blessed'"* [Gen. 27:29].

We come now to the Bavli and how it receives and reworks the entire antecedent heritage. We see immediately the simple fact that the Bavli's authorship appeals directly to the Tosefta, without addressing the program of the Yerushalmi. While, therefore, both Talmuds are organized as commentaries to the Mishnah, they are entirely autonomous of one another. The Babylonian Talmud does not expand upon the earlier one but forms its own discussions in accord with its own program. While the Bavli treats the Mishnah in the same way as does the Yerushalmi, in addition, the authorship of the second Talmud moved in a direction all its own, systematically commenting in large and cogent compositions upon not only the Mishnah but also Scripture, that is, on both the Oral and the Written Torahs. This difference between the two Talmuds may account for the greater acceptance of the later one. In the Land of Israel, Mishnah commentary went into the Talmud of the Land of Israel, Scripture commentary went into the Midrash compilations. But in Babylonia both were encompassed within the Talmud of that country, and the one substantial literary redactional difference between the Bavli and the Yerushalmi is the Bavli framers' inclusion of sizable sequences and proportionately substantial compositions – 30 to 40 percent – of Scripture units of discourse. These they inserted whole and complete, not at all in response to the Mishnah's program. The Yerushalmi presents large composites of scriptural commentary in only limited volume and in significantly modest proportion. Both Talmuds are laid out as a commentary to the Mishnah. These commentaries to the Mishnah are called *gemara*, and the Talmuds are often called simply Gemara.

By extensive resort to units of discourse providing an exegesis of Scripture, the Bavli's framers read their values into the texts of Scripture. In omitting such units of discourse, the Yerushalmi's authors lost the opportunity to spell out in a whole and complete way the larger system of Judaism that both Talmuds portray. The key to the success of the Bavli lies in the very foundations of its literary structure, in the redactional literary decision to lay the basis of the main beams of the Bavli's composition upon not only the Mishnah but also upon passages of Scripture. The compositors of the Bavli were encyclopaedists. Their creation turned out to be the encyclopaedia of Judaism, its summa, its point of final reference, its court of last appeal, its definition, its conclusion, its closure. Now let us turn to their final presentation of matters.

V. Bavli

I.1 A. [51B] *Gemara: Our rabbis have taught:*

B. The things which are between the House of Shammai and the House of Hillel in [regard to] a meal:

C. The House of Shammai say, "One blesses over the day and afterward blesses over the wine, for the day causes the wine to come, and the day has already been sactified, while the wine has not yet come."

D. And the House of Hillel say, "He blesses over the wine and afterward blesses over the day, for the wine causes the Sanctification to be said.

E. "Another matter: The blessing over the wine is perpetual, and the blessing over the day is not perpetual. Between that which is perpetual and that which is not perpetual, that which is perpetual takes precedence" [T. Ber. 5:25].

F. And the law is in accordance with the words of the House of Hillel.

G. *What is the purpose of* "another matter"?

H. *If you should say that there* [in regard to the opinion of the House of Shammai] *two* [reasons are given] *and here* [in regard to the opinion of the House of Hillel] *one, here, too,* [in respect to the House of Hillel], *there are two* [reasons, the second being]: "The blessing of the wine is perpetual and the blessing of the day is not perpetual. That which is perpetual takes precedence over that which is not perpetual."

I. And the law is in accord with the opinion of the House of Hillel.

J. *This is obvious* [that the law is in accord with the House of Hillel], *for the echo has gone forth* [and pronounced from heaven the decision that the law follows the opinion of the House of Hillel].

K. *If you like, I can argue that* [this was stated] before the echo.

L. *And if you like, I can argue that* it was after the echo, and [the passage was formulated in accord with the] opinion of [52A] R. Joshua, who stated, "They do not pay attention to an echo [from heaven]."

I.2 A. *And is it the reasoning of the House of Shammai that the blessing of the day is more important?*

B. *But has a Tanna not taught:* "He who enters his house at the close of the Sabbath blesses over the wine and the light and the spices and afterward he says *Havdalah*. And if he has only one cup, he leaves it for after the food and then says the other blessings in order after it." [*Havdalah* is the blessing of the day, yet comes last!]

C. *But lo, on what account* [do you say] *this is the view of the House of Shammai? Perhaps it is the House of Hillel['s opinion]?*

D. *Let* [such a thought] *not enter your mind, for the Tanna teaches:* "Light and afterward spices." *And of whom have you heard who holds this opinion? The House of Shammai, as a Tanna has taught:*

E. R. Judah said, "The House of Shammai and the House of Hillel did not differ concerning the [blessing of the] food, that it is first, and the *Havdalah*, that it is at the end.

F. "Concerning what did they dispute? Concerning the light and the spices.

G. **"For the House of Shammai say, 'Light and afterward spices.'**

H **"And the House of Hillel say, 'Spices and afterward the light'"** [T. Ber. 5:30].

I *And on what account* [do you suppose that] *it is the House of Shammai as* [interpreted by] *R. Judah? Perhaps it is* [a teaching in accord with] *the House of Hillel* [as interpreted by] *R. Meir?*

J. *Do not let such a thing enter your mind, for lo, a Tanna teaches here in our Mishnah:* The House of Shammai say, "Light and food and spices and *Havdalah*."

K. And the House of Hillel say, "Light and spices, food and *Havdalah*."

L. But there, in the "baraita,", *lo he has taught:* "If he has only one cup, he leaves it for after the food and then says the other blessings in order after it."

M *From this it is to be inferred that it is the House of Shammai's teaching, according to the* [interpretation] *of R. Judah.*

N *In any event there is a problem* [for the House of Shammai now give precedence to reciting a blessing for the wine over blessing the day].

O. *The House of Shammai suppose that the coming of the holy day is to be distinguished from its leaving. As to the coming of the [holy] day, the earlier one may bring it in, the better. As to the leaving of the festival day, the later one may take leave of it, the better, so that it should not seem to us as a burden.*

P. *And do the House of Shammai hold the opinion that* Grace requires a cup [of wine]? *And lo, we have learned:* [If] wine came to them after the food, and there is there only that cup, the House of Shammai say, "He blesses over the wine and afterward blesses over the food" [M. Ber. 8:8]. [So Grace is said *without* the cup.]

Q. *Does this not mean that he blesses it and drinks* [it]?

R. *No. He blesses it and leaves it.*

S. But has not a master said, "He that blesses must [also] taste [it]."

T. *He does taste it.*

U. And has not a master said, "Tasting it is spoiling it."

V. *He tastes it with his hand* [finger].

W. And has not a master said, "The cup of blessing requires a [fixed] measure." *And lo, he diminishes it from its fixed measure.*

X. [We speak of a situation in which] *he has more than the fixed measure.*

Y. *But lo, has it not been taught:* If there is there *only* that cup... [so he has no more].

Z. *There is not enough for two, but more than enough for one.*

AA. *And has not R. Hiyya taught:* The House of Shammai say, "He blesses over the wine and drinks it, and afterward he says Grace."

BB. Then we have two Tannas' [traditions] in respect to the opinion of the House of Shammai.

I.3 A. **The House of Shammai say** [They wash the hands and afterward mix the cup]... [M. 8:2A].

B. *Our rabbis have taught:*

C. The House of Shammai say, "They wash the hands and afterward mix the cup, for if you say they mix the cup first, [against this view is] a [precautionary] decree to prevent the liquids on the outer sides of the cup, which are unclean by reason of his hands' [touching them], from going back and making the cup unclean" [T. Ber. 5:26].

D. *But will not the hands make the cup itself unclean* [without reference to the liquids]?

E. The hands are in the second remove of uncleanness, and the [object unclean in] the second remove of uncleanness cannot [then] render [another object unclean] in the third [remove] in respect to profane foods, [but only to heave-offering]. But [this happens] only by means of liquids [unclean in the first remove].

F. And the House of Hillel say, "They mix the cup and afterward wash the hands, for if you say they wash the hands first, [against this view is] a [precautionary] decree lest the liquids which are [already] on the hands become unclean on account of the cup and go and render the hands unclean."

G. *But will not the cup* [itself] *make the hands unclean?*

H. A vessel cannot render a man unclean.

I. *But will they* [the hands] *not render the liquids which are in it* [the cup] *unclean?*

J. *Here we are dealing* with a vessel the outer part of which has been made unclean by liquid. The inner part is clean but the outer part is unclean. *Thus we have learned:*

K. [If] a vessel is made unclean on the outside by liquid, the outside is unclean, [52B] but its inside and its rim, handle, and haft are clean. If, however, the inside is unclean, the whole [cup] is unclean.

L. *What, then, do they* [the Houses] *dispute?*

M. *The House of Shammai hold that* it is prohibited to make use of a vessel whose outer parts are unclean by liquids, as a decree on account of the drippings. [There is] *no* [reason] *to decree* lest the liquids on the hands be made unclean by the cup.

N. *And the House of Hillel reckon* that it is permitted to make use of a vessel whose outer part is made unclean by liquids, *for drippings are unusual. But there is reason to take care* lest the liquids which are on the hands may be made unclean by the cup.

I.4 A. Another matter: [So that] immediately upon the washing of the hands [may come] the meal [itself].

B. *What is the reason for this additional explanation?*

C. *This is what the House of Hillel said to the House of Shammai:* "*According to your reasoning, in saying that* it is prohibited to make use of a cup whose outer parts are unclean, *we decree on account of the drippings. But even so,* [our opinion] *is better,* for immediately upon the washing of the hands [should come] the meal."

I.5 A. The House of Shammai say, "He dries his hand on the napkin..." [M. 8:3A].

B. *Our rabbis have taught:*

C. The House of Shammai say, "He wipes his hands with the napkin and lays it on the table, for if you say, 'on the cushion,' [that view is wrong, for it is a precautionary] decree lest the liquids which are

> on the napkin become unclean on account of the cushion and go
> back and render the hands unclean" [T. Ber. 5:27].

D. *And will not the cushion* [itself] *render the napkin unclean?*

E. A vessel cannot make a vessel unclean.

F. And will not the cushion [itself] make the man unclean?

G. A vessel cannot make a man unclean.

H And the House of Hillel say, "'On the cushion,' for if you say, 'on
the table,' [that opinion is wrong, for it is a] **decree lest the liquids
become unclean on account of the table and go and render the
food unclean"** [T. Ber. 5:27].

I. *But will not the table render the food which is on it unclean?*

J. *We here deal with a table which is unclean in the second remove,* and
something unclean in the second remove does not render
something unclean in the third remove in respect to unconsecrated
food, except by means of liquids [which are always unclean in the
first remove].

K. *What* [principle] *do they dispute?*

L. *The House of Shammai reckon that* it is prohibited to make use of a
table unclean on the second remove, as a decree on account of those
who eat Heave-offering [which is rendered unfit by an object
unclean in the second remove].

M *And the House of Hillel reckon that* it is permitted to make use of a
table unclean in the second remove, for those who eat Heave-
offering [the priests] are careful.

N Another matter: There is no scriptural requirement to wash the
hands before eating unconsecrated food.

O. *What is the purpose of* "another explanation"?

P. *This is what the House of Hillel said to the House of Shammai: If you ask
what is the difference in respect to food, concerning which we take care,
and in respect to the hands, concerning which we do not take care – even
in this regard* [our opinion] *is preferable, for there is no scriptural
requirement concerning the washing of the hands before eating
unconsecrated food.*

Q It is better that the hands should be made unclean, *for there is no
scriptural basis for* [washing] *them,* and let not the food be made
unclean, *concerning which there is a scriptural basis* [for concern about
its uncleanness].

I.6 A The House of Shammai say, "They clean house and afterward
wash the hands..." [M. 8:4A].

B. *Our rabbis have taught:*

C. The House of Shammai say, "They clean the house and afterward
wash the hands, for if you say, 'They wash the hands first,' it
turns out that you spoil the food" [T. Ber. 5:28].

D. *But the House of Shammai do not reckon that one washes the hands first.*

E. *What is the reason?*

F. *On account of the crumbs.*

G. And the House of Hillel say, "If the servant is a disciple of a sage,
he takes the crumbs which are as large as an olive [in bulk] and
leaves the crumbs which are not so much as an olive [in bulk]."

H   (*This view supports the opinion of R. Yohanan, for* R. Yohanan said, "Crumbs which are not an olive in bulk may be deliberately destroyed.")

I.   *In what do they differ?*

J.   *The House of Hillel reckon that it* is prohibited to employ a servant who is an ignorant man, *and the House of Shammai reckon that* it is permitted to employ a servant who is an ignorant man.

K   *R. Yosé bar Hanina said in the name of R. Huna, "In our entire chapter the law is in accord with the House of Hillel, excepting this matter, in which the law is in accord with the House of Shammai."*

L   *And R. Oshaia taught the matter contrariwise. And in this matter, too, the law is in accord with the House of Hillel.*

I.7   A.   **The House of Shammai say, "Light and food..."** [M. 8:5A].

B.   *R. Huna bar Judah happened by the house of Rava. He saw that Rava blessed the spices first.*

C   *He said to him, "Now the House of Shammai and the House of Hillel did not dispute concerning the light,* [it should come first].

D.   *"For it was taught:* The House of Shammai say, 'Light, and food, spices, and *Havdalah,*' and the House of Hillel say, 'Light, and spices, and food, and *Havdalah.*'

E   *Rava answered him, "This is the opinion* [= version] *of R. Meir, but R. Judah says, 'The House of Shammai and the House of Hillel did not differ concerning the food, that it comes first, and concerning the Havdalah, that it is at the end.*

F.   "'Concerning what did they differ?'

G.   "'Concerning the light and the spices.'

H   "For the House of Shammai say, 'The light and afterward the spices.'

I.   "And the House of Hillel say, 'The spices and afterward the light.'

J.   And R. Yohanan said, "The people were accustomed to act in accord with the House of Hillel *as presented by* R. Judah."

I.8   A.   **The House of Shammai say, "Who created..."** [M. 8:5C].

B.   Rava said, "*Concerning the word 'bara'* [created] *everyone agrees that 'bara' implies* [the past tense]. *They differ concerning 'boré'* [creates]. *The House of Shammai reckon that 'boré' means, 'Who will create in the future.' And the House of Hillel reckon that 'boré' also means what was created* [in the past]."

C   *R. Joseph objected,* "'Who forms light and creates darkness' [Isa. 45:7], 'Creates mountains and forms the wind' [Amos 4:13], 'Who creates the heavens and spreads them out'" [Isa. 42:5].

D.   "But," R. Joseph said, "*Concerning 'bara' and 'boré' everyone agrees that* [the words] *refer to the past. They differ as to whether one should say 'light' or 'lights.'*

E.   "*The House of Shammai reckon there is one light in the fire.*

F.   "*And the House of Hillel reckon that there are many lights in the fire."*

G.   *We have a Tannaite teaching along the same lines:*

H   The House of Hillel said to the House of Shammai, "There are many illuminations in the light."

II.1   A.   **A blessing is not said...** [M. 8:6A].

B. *Certainly,* [in the case of] *the light* [of idolators, one should not say a blessing] *because it did not rest on the Sabbath. But what is the reason that for spices* [one may not say the blessing]?

C. R. Judah said in the name of Rav, "*We here deal with a banquet held by idolators, because* the run-of-the-mill banquet held by idolators is for the sake of idolatry."

D. *But since it has been taught at the end of the clause,* "Or over the light or spices of idolatry," *we must infer that the beginning of the clause does not deal with idolatry.*

E. R. Hanina from Sura said, "What is the reason is what it explains, namely, what is the reason that they do not bless the light or spices of idolators? Because the run-of-the-mill banquet held by idolators is for the sake of idolatry."

II.2 A. *Our rabbis have taught:*

B. One may bless a light which has rested on the Sabbath, but one may not bless a light which has not rested on the Sabbath.

C. *And what is the meaning of* "which has not rested on the Sabbath"?

D. [53A] *Shall we say* it has not rested on the Sabbath on account of the work [which has been done with it, including] even work which is permitted?

E. *And has it not been taught:* They do bless the light [kindled on the Sabbath for] a woman in confinement or a sick person.

F. R. Nahman bar Isaac said, "*What is the meaning of* 'which enjoyed Sabbath-rest'? Which enjoyed Sabbath-rest on account of work, the doing of which is a trangression [on the Sabbath]."

G. We have learned likewise in a *baraita:*

H. They may bless a lamp which has been burning throughout the day to the conclusion of the Sabbath.

II.3 A. *Our rabbis have taught:*

B. They bless [a light] kindled by a gentile from an Israelite, or by an Israelite from a gentile, but they do not bless [a light] kindled by a gentile from a gentile.

C. *What is the reason one does not do so* [from a light kindled by] a gentile from a gentile?

D. *Because it did not enjoy Sabbath rest.*

E. *If so, lo,* [a light kindled by] *an Israelite from a gentile also has not enjoyed Sabbath rest.*

F. *And if you say this prohibited* [light] *has vanished, and the one* [in hand] *is another and was born in the hand of the Israelite,* [how will you deal] *with this teaching?*

G. He who brings out a flame to the public way [on the Sabbath] is liable [for violating the Sabbath rule against carrying from private to public property].

H. *Now why should he be liable?* What he raised up he did not put down, and what he put down he did not raise up.

I. *But* [we must conclude] *that the prohibited* [flame] *is present, but when he blesses, it is over the additional* [flame], *which is permitted, that he blesses.*

J. *If so, a gentile*['s flame kindled] *from a gentile*['s flame] *also* [should be permitted].

K.   *That is true, but* [it is prohibited by] *decree, on account of the original gentile and the original flame* [of light kindled on the Sabbath by the gentile].

II.4   A.   *Our rabbis have taught:*

B.   [If] one was walking outside the village and saw a light, if the majority [of the inhabitants of the village] are gentiles, he does not bless it. If the majority are Israelites, he blesses it.

C.   *Lo, the statement is self-contradictory. You have said,* "If the majority are gentiles, he does not bless it." *Then if they were evenly divided, he may bless it.*

D.   *But then it teaches,* "If the majority are Israelites, he may bless." *Then if they are evenly divided, he may not bless it.*

E.   *Strictly speaking, even if they are evenly divided, he may bless. But since in the opening clause* [the language is], "The majority are gentiles," *in the concluding clause,* [the same language is used:] "A majority are Israelites."

II.5   A.   *Our rabbis have taught:*

B.   [If] a man was walking outside of a village and saw a child with a torch in his hand, he makes inquiries about him. If he is an Israelite, he may bless [the light]. If he is a gentile, he may not bless.

C.   *Why do we speak of a child? Even an adult also* [would be subject to the same rule].

D.   *Rav Judah said in the name of Rav,* "In this case we are dealing with [a time] *near sunset. As to a gentile, it will be perfectly clear that he certainly is a gentile* [for an Israelite would not use the light immediately after sunset]. *If it is a child, I might say it is an Israelite child who happened to take up* [the torch]."

II.6   A.   *Our rabbis have taught:*

B.   [If] one was walking outside of a village and saw a light, if it was as thick as the opening of a furnace, he may bless it, and if not, he may not bless it.

C.   *One Tanna* [authority] [says], "They may bless the light of a furnace," *and another Tanna* [says], "They may not bless it."

D.   *There is no difficulty. The first speaks at the beginning* [of the fire], *the other at the end.*

E.   *One authority says,* "They may bless the light of an oven or a stove," *and another authority says,* "They may not bless it."

F.   *There is no problem. The former speaks of the beginning, the latter of the end.*

G.   *One authority says,* "They may bless the light of the synagogue and the schoolhouse," *and another authority says,* "They may not bless it."

H.   *There is no problem. The former speaks* [of a case in which] an important man *is present, the latter* [of a case in which] an important man *is not present.*

I.   *And if you want, I shall explain both teachings as applying to a case in which* an important man *is present. There still is no difficulty. The former* [teaching speaks of a case in which] *there is a beadle* [who eats in the synagogue], *the latter in which there is none.*

J.   *And if you want, I shall explain both teachings as applying to a case in which a beadle is present. There still is no difficulty. The former teaching* [speaks of a case in which] *there is moonlight, the latter in which there is no moonlight.*

II.7 A. *Our rabbis have taught:*

B. [If] they were sitting in the schoolhouse, and light was brought before them –

C. The House of Shammai say, "Each one blesses for himself."

D. And the House of Hillel say, "One blesses for all of them, as it is said, 'In the multitude of people is the King's glory'" [Prov. 14:28].

E. *Certainly* [we can understand the position of the House of Hillel because] *the House of Hillel explain their reason.*

F. *But what is the reason of the House of Shammai?*

G. *They reckon* [it as they do] *on account of* [avoiding] *interruption in* [Torah study] *in the schoolhouse.*

H. *We have a further Tannaitic tradition to the same effect:*

I. The members of the house of Rabban Gamaliel did not say [the blessing] "Good health" [after a sneeze] in the schoolhouse on account of the interruption [of study] in the schoolhouse.

II.8 A. **They say a blessing neither on the light nor on the spices of the dead...** [M. 8:6A].

B. *What is the reason?*

C. *The light is made for the honor* [of the deceased], *the spices to remove the bad smell.*

D. Rav Judah in the name of Rav said, ["Light made for] whoever [is of such importance that] they take out [a light] before him both by day and by night is not blessed. [And light made for] whoever [is not important, so that] they take out [a light] before him only by night, is blessed."

E. R. Huna said, "They do not bless spices of the privy and oil made to remove the grease."

F. *Does this saying imply that wherever* [spice] *is not used for smell, they do not bless over it? It may be objected:*

G. He who enters the stall of a spice dealer and smells the odor, even though he sat there all day long, blesses only one time. He who enters and goes out repeatedly blesses each time.

H. *And lo, here is a case in which it is not used for the scent, and still he blesses.*

I. *Yes, but it also is used for the odor – so that people will smell and come and purchase it.*

II.9 A. *Our rabbis have taught:*

B. If one was walking outside of a village and smelled a scent, if most of the inhabitants are idolators, he does not bless it. If most are Israelites, he blesses it.

C. R. Yosé says, "Even if most are Israelites, he *still* may not bless, because Israelite women use incense for witchcraft."

D. *But do they "all" burn incense for witchcraft!*

E. *A small part is for witchcraft and a small part is also for scenting garments, which yields a larger part not used for scent, and wherever the majority* [of the incense] *is not used for scent, one does not bless it.*

F. R. Hiyya bar Abba said in the name of R. Yohanan, "He who walks on the eve of the Sabbath in Tiberias and at the end of the Sabbath in Sepphoris and smells an odor does not bless it, because it is presumed to have been made only to perfume garments."

G.   *Our rabbis taught:* If one was walking in the gentiles' market and was pleased to scent the spices, he is a sinner.

III.1 A.   [53B] **They do not recite a blessing over the light until it has been used.. [M. 8:6B]:**

B.   Rav Judah said in the name of Rav, "Not that he has actually used it, but if anyone stood near enough so that he might use the light, even at some distance, [he may say the blessing]."

C.   So, too, R. Ashi said, "We have learned this teaching even [concerning] those at some distance."

D.   *It was objected* [on the basis of the following teaching]: If one had a light hidden in the folds of his cloak or in a lamp, or saw the flame but did not make use of its light, or made use of the light but did not [actually] see the flame, he may not say the blessing. [He may say the blessing only when] he [both] sees the flame and uses its light.

E.   *Certainly one finds cases in which* one may use the light and not see the flame. *This may be when the light is in a corner.*

F.   *But where do you find a case in which* one may see the flame and not make use of its light? *Is it not when he is at a distance?*

G.   *No, it is when the flame keeps on flickering.*

III.2 A.   *Our rabbis have taught:*

B.   They may say a blessing over glowing coals, but not over dying coals (*'omemot*).

C.   *What is meant by* glowing coals?

D.   R. Hisda said, "If one puts a chip into them and it kindles on its own, [these are] all [glowing coals]."

E.   *It was asked: Is the word* 'omemot ['alef] *or* 'omemot ['ayin]?

F.   *Come and hear, for R. Hisda b. Abdimi said,* "'The cedars in the garden of God could not darken [*'amamuhu*] it'" [Ezek. 31:8].

G.   And Rava said, "He must make actual use of it."

H.   *And how* [near must one be]?

I.   Ulla said, "So that he may make out the difference between an *issar* and a *pundion* [two small coins]."

J.   Hezekiah said, "So that he may make out the difference between a *meluzma* [a weight] of Tiberias and one of Sepphoris."

K.   *Rav Judah would say the blessing* [for the light of the] *house of Adda the waiter* [which was nearby].

L.   *Rava would say the blessing* [for the light of the] *house of Guria bar Hama.*

M.   *Abayye would say the blessing* [for the light of the] *house of Bar Abbuha.*

N.   R. Judah said in the name of Rav, "They do not go looking for the light in the way they go looking for [means to carry out other] commandments."

O.   *R. Zera said,* "At the outset, I used to go looking [for light]. *Now that I have heard this teaching of R. Judah in the name of Rav, I, too, will not go searching, but if one comes my way, I shall say the blessing over it.*"

IV.1 A.   **He who ate [and did not say Grace]... [M. 8:7A]:**

B.   R. Zevid, and some say, R. Dimi bar Abba, said, "The dispute [between the Houses] applies to a case of forgetfulness, but in a case in which a person deliberately [omitted Grace], all agree that he should return to his place and say the blessing."

C. *This is perfectly obvious. It is* [explicitly] *taught, "And he forgot."*

D. *What might you have said? That is the rule even where it was intentional, but the reason that the Tanna taught,* "And he forgot," *is to tell you* how far the House of Shammai were willing to go [in requiring the man to go back to where he ate. They did so even if a man accidentally forgot]. *Thus we are taught* [the contrary. Even if one forgot, unintentionally, he must go back].

IV.2 A. *It was taught:*

B. The House of Hillel said to the House of Shammai, "According to your opinion, someone who ate on the top of the Temple Mount and forgot and went down without saying Grace should go back to the top of the Mount and say the blessing."

C. The House of Shammai said to the House of Hillel, "According to your opinion, someone who forgot a purse on the top of the Temple Mount would not go back and retrieve it.

D. "For his own sake, he [assuredly] will go back. For the sake of Heaven [should he] not all the more so [go back]?"

E. *There were these two disciples. One did it* [forgot Grace] *accidentally, and, following the rule of the House of Shammai,* [went back to bless], *and found a purse of gold. And one did it deliberately* [omitted Grace], *and following the rule of the House of Hillel* [did not go back to say it], *and a lion ate him.*

F. *Rabbah bar bar Hanna was traveling in a caravan. He ate and was sated but* [forgot and] *did not say Grace.*

G. *He said, "What shall I do? If I tell the men* [of the caravan with me] *that I forgot to bless, they will say to me, 'Bless here. Wherever you say the blessing, you are saying the blessing to the Merciful* [God].' *It is better that I tell them I have forgotten a golden dove."*

H. *So he said to them, "Wait for me, for I have forgotten a golden dove."*

I. *He went back and blessed and found a golden dove.*

J. *And why was a dove so important?*

K. *Because the community of Israel is compared to a dove, as it is written,* "The wings of the dove are covered with silver, and her pinions with the shimmer of gold" [Psalm 68:14]. *Just as the dove is saved only by her wings, so Israel is saved only by the commandments.*

IV.3 A. **Until when can he say the Grace? Until the food is digested in his bowels...** [M. 8:7D]:

B. How long does it take to digest the food?

C. R. Yohanan said, "As long as one is no longer hungry."

D. Resh Laqish said, "As long as one [still] is thirsty on account of his meal."

E. *R. Yemar bar Shelamia said to Mar Zutra – and some say, Rav Yemar bar Shizbi said to Mar Zutra – "Did Resh Laqish really say this? And did not R. Ammi say in the name of Resh Laqish, 'How long does it take to digest a meal? The time it takes to go four miles.'"*

F. *There is no problem:* Here [we speak of] a big meal, there [we speak of] a small meal.

IV.4 A. **If wine came to them...** [M. 8:8A]:

B.   *This implies that in the case of an Israelite[*'s saying Grace], even though one has not heard the entire blessing, he responds *[Amen].*

C.   *But if he has not heard* [the whole Grace], *how can he have performed his duty by doing so* [assuming he has eaten also]?

D.   Hiyya bar Rav said, "[We speak of a case] in which he did not eat with them."

E.   So, too, did R. Nahman say in the name of Rabbah bar Abbuha, "[We speak of a case] in which he did not eat with them."

F.   *Rav said to Hiyya his son, "My son, seize* [the cup] *and bless."*

G.   *So did R. Huna say to Rabbah his son, "Seize and bless."*

H.   *This implies that he who says the blessing is better than he who answers Amen. But has it not been taught:*

I.   R. Yosé says, "The one who answers *Amen* is greater than the one who says the blessing."

J.   R. Nehorai said to him, "By heaven! It is so. You should know it, for behold, common soldiers go ahead and open the battle, but the heroes go in and win it."

K.   *It is a matter of dispute between Tannaites, as it has been taught:*

L.   Both the one who says the blessing and the one who answers Amen are implied [in the Scripture (Neh. 9:5)]. But the one who says the blessing is more quickly [answered] than he who answers Amen.

IV.5 A.   *Samuel asked Rav, "Should one answer [Amen] after [the blessings of] children in the schoolhouse?"*

B.   *He said to him, "They answer Amen after everyone except children in the schoolhouse, since they are [saying blessings solely] for the sake of learning."*

C.   *And this applies when it is not the time for them to say the* "Haftarah," *but in the time to say* "Haftarah," *they do respond [Amen].*

IV.6 A.   *Our rabbis have taught:*

B.   "The absence of oil holds up the blessing [Grace]," the words of Rabbi Zilai.

C.   R. Zivai says, "It does not hold it up."

D.   R. Aha says, "[The absence of] good oil holds it up."

E.   R. Zuhamai says, "Just as a dirty person *[mezuham]* is unfit for the Temple service, so dirty hands are unfit for the blessing."

F.   *R. Nahman Bar Isaac said, "I know neither Zilai nor Zivai nor Zuhamai. But I know a teaching which R. Judah said in the name of Rav, and some say it was taught as a 'baraita':*

G.   "'And be you holy' [Lev. 20:7] – this refers to washing the hands before the meal.

H.   "'And you shall be holy' – this refers to the washing after the meal."

I.   "'For holy' – this refers to the oil."

J.   "'Am I the Lord your God' – this refers to the blessing [Grace]."

The place of the Tosefta in the formation of the two Talmuds is now clear. In both instances, principal exegetical studies of the Mishnah commence with not the Mishnah but the Tosefta's re-presentation of the Mishnah. When at the outset I said that the Tosefta forms the bridge between the Mishnah and the two Talmuds, it is to this critical role in the exegetical process that I referred.

12

Turning to the Bavli

Clearly, the next stage in my research requires me to turn back to the Bavli, the starting point of my research thirty years ago.[1] To understand

---

[1]After my dissertation, a *Life of Yohanan ben Zakkai* (Leiden, 1962: E. J. Brill), I turned to my *A History of the Jews in Babylonia*. Leiden: Brill, 1965-1970. I-V. I. *A History of the Jews in Babylonia. The Parthian Period*. 1965. Second printing, revised, 1969. Third printing: Chico, 1984: Scholars Press for Brown Judaic Studies; II. *A History of the Jews in Babylonia. The Early Sasanian Period*. 1966; III. *A History of the Jews in Babylonia. From Shapur I to Shapur II*. 1968; IV. *A History of the Jews in Babylonia. The Age of Shapur II*. 1969; V. *A History of the Jews in Babylonia. Later Sasanian Times*. 1970. This was followed by an appendix, covering the one important source on the Jews and Judaism in Iranian Babylonia that my *History* had neglected: *Aphrahat and Judaism. The Christian-Jewish Argument in Fourth Century Iran*. Leiden, 1971: Brill. By that point I had fully realized the uncritical character of the method that was then paramount in the study of Judaism and the Jews in ancient times: total and complete gullibility in regard to literary sources. People collected and arranged and paraphrased and free-associated about stories and sayings they found in the rabbinic writings, and this they called history. I founded the critical enterprise with three experimental works: *Development of a Legend. Studies on the Traditions Concerning Yohanan ben Zakkai*. Leiden, 1970: Brill; *The Rabbinic Traditions about the Pharisees before 70*. Leiden, 1971: Brill. I-III. I. *The Rabbinic Traditions about the Pharisees before 70. The Masters*; II. *The Rabbinic Traditions about the Pharisees before 70. The Houses*. III. *The Rabbinic Traditions about the Pharisees before 70. Conclusions*; and, finally, *Eliezer ben Hyrcanus. The Tradition and the Man*. Leiden, 1973: Brill. I. *Eliezer ben Hyrcanus. The Tradition and the Man. The Tradition*. II. *Eliezer ben Hyrcanus. The Tradition and the Man. The Man*. At that point I realized that the entire canon had to be reconsidered, beginning to end, and in 1973 I began my *History of the Mishnaic Law*, which was completed in forty-three volumes. The heroic support of the late Mr. F. C. Wieder, Jr., E. J. Brill, in disseminating my research should be remembered. Until 1980, I was unable to publish a scholarly book in the USA. From 1960 to 1980, when his directorship of Brill ended, he accepted and published without subsidy every manuscript I submitted to him. Without him it would have been exceedingly difficult to publish my monographs and books. Since he left Brill, I have not been able to

what I now seek to find out, let me start back with my formulation of the problem.

The Talmud of Babylonia (a.k.a. the Bavli), which reached closure in ca. 600 A.D., defined the world order of Judaism from the end of late antiquity at the rise of Islam to nearly the present day. Anonymous and the statement of a consensus, addressing whom it may concern, anywhere and at any time, the document lays down its judgment on everywhere and every age. It sets forth the theory of a holy society. And, in point of fact, its writers achieved their goal. For the intellectual foundations of social action, the beliefs and values of culture, the national consensus that defined ways of forming a family and the conduct of the everyday life – the ethos and ethics of the diverse people of Israel, wherever they lived, to begin with responded to, and aimed to realize in concrete ways, the religious system set forth in that vast document. If, therefore, we wish to understand the relationship between the ideas that people hold and the world that they make for themselves, we find in that Talmud an example rich in promise. For writing, as people now appreciate not only sets forth messages through the statement of propositions. Writing also bears signification through how things are set, perhaps in a more effective and profound way than through what is said. If, therefore, we wish to move from writing to the world that that writing is meant to formulate, we can do well to pay close attention to a document that made the world that its authors intended to make, to begin with within the intellectual life of the readers that the authors proposed to influence and shape. Few documents in the entire history of the West – the Christian Bible is one, the writings of Aristotle another – have so informed and shaped society in the way in which, within the community of Israel, the Jewish people, the Bavli did. So in the study of the relationship of ideas and society, writing and the message that is communicated and realized through writing, this document bears special interest.

But to read a document in its social context, we have to form a theory of the context to which the writing speaks, and in the case of a document that at no point identifies its authorship or context, time of writing or circumstance of composition, that requirement is not easily met. How are we to move from a document that sets down the law applicable anywhere to the setting to which, to begin with, the anonymous writers meant to speak? And if, as seems reasonable, we suppose that those

---

publish with the firm again, though, happily, I have not had to. But that fact underlines how entirely personal was his support, which extended even to appointing me editor of two scholarly series, *Studies in Judaism in Late Antiquity*, and *Studies in Judaism in Modern Times*.

writers made choices out of a vast received heritage of thought, writings on the social order and justifications, by appeal to the Torah, of that order, then what concerns precipitated and shaped their work? In the theory that a well-crafted and cogent theory of society responds with a self-evidently valid and ineluctable answer to an urgent and inescapable problem – for urgent response to an acute challenge best accounts for the cogency and coherence of a theory of the social order – then how shall we identify the urgent and critical question to which in its dreary and repetitive, small and careful way, the law of the document grandly and massively presents its solution? That set of problems has occupied my attention for thirty years.

The Talmud of Babylonia covers thirty-seven of the Mishnah's sixty-three tractates, and, in discussing these thirty-seven Mishnah tractates, the authorship of the Talmud speaks in a single way. A fixed rhetorical pattern and a limited program of logical inquiry governs throughout. Whatever authors wish to say, they say within a severely restricted repertoire of rhetorical choices, and the intellectual initiatives they are free to explore everywhere dictate one set of questions and problems and not any other. The document's "voice," then, comprises that monotonous and repetitious language, which conveys a recurrent and single melody. In the ancient and great centers of learning in which the Talmud of Babylonia is studied today, masters and their disciples – studying out loud and in dialogue with one another and with the text – commonly and correctly say, "the Talmud says...," (Yiddish: *zogt die gemara*; Hebrew: *hattalmud omeret*), meaning, the anonymous, uniform, ubiquitous voice of the document, speaking in the name of no one in particular and within an indeterminate context of space and time, makes a given statement or point. Through years of encounter with the document, within the conventions of centuries of study in continuing circles of learning, by reference to "the Talmud says," the masters express the result of innumerable observations of coherence, uniformity, and cogency. I represent their usage when I speak of "the Talmud's one voice."

The Bavli's one voice governs throughout, about a considerable repertoire of topics speaking within a single restricted rhetorical vocabulary. "The Bavli's one voice" refers to a remarkably limited set of intellectual initiatives, only this and that, initiatives that moreover always adhere to a single sequence or order: this first, then that – but never the other thing. I can identify the Bavli's authorships' rules of composition. These are not many. Not only so, but the order of types of compositions (written in accord with a determinate set of rules) itself follows a fixed pattern, so that a composition written in obedience to a given rule as to form will always appear in the same point in a sequence of compositions that are written in obedience to two or more rules: type A first, type B next, in fixed sequence. The Talmud's one voice then represents the outcome of the work of the following:

1. an author preparing a composition for inclusion in the Bavli would conform to one of a very few rules of thought and expression; and, more to the point,
2. a framer of a cogent composite, often encompassing a set of compositions, for presentation as the Bavli would follow a fixed order in selecting and arranging the types of consequential forms that authors had made available for his use.

With a clear and specific account of the facts yielding that anticipated result, I shall be well justified in asking about the message of the rhetorical and logical method of the Bavli.

The Talmud of Babylonia is made up of large-scale composites – completed units of discourse, with a beginning, middle, and end, which supply all of the data a reader (or listener) requires to understand the point that the framer of that composite wishes to make. A composite commonly draws upon available information, made available in part by prior and completed composites, for example, Scripture, the Mishnah, the Tosefta, and in part by compositions worked out entirely within their own limits, which we might compare with a paragraph of a chapter; or a free-standing composition of a few lines. By "rules of composition" I mean the laws that dictated to the framers of a cogent and coherent composites – such as I allege comprise the whole of the Talmud of Babylonia – precisely how to put together whatever they wished to say, together with the supporting evidence as well as argument, in the composition that they proposed to write. Here, then, "rules of composition" govern how people formed composites that comprise the Bavli: how they are classified, how they are ordered.

The Talmud is made up of compositions, which set forth, beginning to end, proposition, argument, and evidence, together with what we should now call footnotes and appendices: all the information necessary to follow a complete, and sustained, thought. I know the rules for making up such compositions, and in *The Rules of Composition of the Talmud of Babylonia* (Atlanta, 1991: Scholars Press for South Florida Studies in the History of Judaism), I show what they were. This I do specifically by a classification of the types of compositions and the rhetorical and logical forms that dictate how they are to be made up. It is clear that the Bavli's authorships followed not only rules of language but also laws of composition. Now I claim to set forth the laws of composition, then, which dictate how to form composites or conglomerates that comprise coherent statements; and how to write sustained and coherent essays, the smallest complete units of proposition, evidence, and argument, of which the Talmud is made up. These laws told them what issues must come first, which ones may be treated later. Furthermore, if we classify the rhetorical laws that governed the translation of thought into formal prose, we readily identify certain patterns ("forms" in a very broad and loose sense), and we can show a close kinship between a rhetorical form and the logic that infuses statements made within the model of that form with coherence and cogency. The match of rhetoric and logic of coherent discourse produces those rules of composition: can I identify the "forms" (in the sense just now defined)? Can I show that all authors employ the same limited repertoire of forms, and, further, that they make use of these forms in the same, fixed order – form A always prior to form B, type of composition C always prior to type of composition D – throughout the document? Then, if I can, I shall know the rules of composition, just as, in the present work, I set forth the rules of linguistic taxonomy.

What is at stake in identifying the rules of composition? It is the demonstration of the well-crafted and orderly character of the sustained discourse that the writing sets forth: learning how to listen to the Talmud's one voice. Specifically, I show that all authors found guidance in the same limited repertoire of rules of composition. Not only so, but a fixed order of discourse – a composition of one sort, A, always comes prior to a composite of another type, B. A simple logic instructed framers of composites, who sometimes also were authors of compositions, and who sometimes drew upon available compositions in the making of their cogent composites. When we understand that logic, which accounts for what for a very long time has impressed students of the Talmud as the document's run-on, formless, and meandering character, we shall see the writing as cogent and well crafted, always addressing a point that, within the hegemony of this logic, and not some other, was deemed closely linked to what had gone before and what was to follow.

And on that basis we see as entirely of a piece, cogent and coherent, large-scale constructions, not brief compositions of a few lines, which therefore become subject to classification whole and complete. So the work of uncovering the laws of composition involve our identifying the entirety of a piece of coherent writing and classifying that writing – not pulling out of context and classifying only the compositions that, in some measure, form constituents of a larger whole. Were we to classify only the compositions, we should gain some knowledge of types of writing accomplished by authors, but none concerning types of writing that comprise our Talmud.

The word "composition" bears the double meaning of [1] composing a piece of writing, and also [2] forming a composite of completed pieces of writing. A composite may indeed be classified with all its parts held together in a coherent formation, meant to serve a single purpose, to make a single type of point. Here we classify the pieces of writing – the composites, made up of compositions – and find out the order in which these types of writing are presented. A limited repertoire of syntactic rules instructed an author of a composition in the Talmud of Babylonia on how to formulate his thought in words so as to convey within the intellectual conventions of the document – not merely grammatical or syntactical conventions of the language of the document – whatever issue or idea he wished to address. A counterpart repertoire also determined the range of analysis and inquiry: this, not that. And the premises of the rules for intelligible thought and intelligible formulation of thought defined the document's frame of reference: how to think, what to think, about what to pursue thought.

In this way all thought to be included in that writing would be immediately intelligible to whoever read what was written or heard what was formulated and transmitted orally. When we can identify the rules of composition and specify how they work, we therefore understand not how people correctly framed their sentences, the grammar of their language, but how they properly generated, organized, and, of course, conveyed their thought, the grammar of their thought. And that is what I seek to describe. I show that the hypotheses formed out of the analysis of the rules of composition of a single tractate in fact describe the rules that govern in a huge sample of the Talmud of Babylonia, and in this way I set forth precisely how the authors of compositions and framers of composites of that document conducted their intellectual enterprise.

A composition may – and in the Bavli generally does – constitute a composite, in that available materials are quoted; relevant data cited in its own context; pertinent, secondary facts and evidence included in a properly signified setting. That is to say, we state our point, in footnotes present sources and points of clarification, and in appendices include also pertinent data that, in the text itself, would impede the argument. The framers of the Talmud of Babylonia did not have access to the technical means of clarifying a sustained thought, without inserting right in their text itself their footnotes and appendices, necessary to what is said but disruptive of the flow of argument. When I speak of a "composite," then it is in the context of a text that bears the burden of footnotes and appendices right within the text itself, and what imparts the character of a composite, sometimes a tediously augmented composite, to what we see is a perfectly clear and simple composition, is the technical limitations of that age. What I classify here are whole and complete statements, consisting of a problem or proposition, a full exposition of the matter, the entire repertoire of footnotes and appendices, inserted into the writing itself rather than subordinated as they would be in our mode of setting forth ideas.

Accordingly, when we wish to discover the rules of composition, that is, the making of composites, of the Bavli, we have to undertake a vast labor of classification. We must know what types of composites people were instructed to make, and the answer will lie in a classification of all the types of composites that we find. But what about the compositions, with their clear and cogent statements, that commonly find a place within a larger composite? Are these to be classified within the large composite, or as free-standing and autonomous items on their own? In my judgment, what is subordinate to a large-scale composite is to be classified entirely within the rubric in which that composite finds its place. The reason is that the subordinated composition serves a purpose beyond itself, therefore has been selected by the framer of the composite to accomplish a goal not in the mind of the (original) author of said composition. I can show the ways in which ready-made compositions are utilized by framers of composites, and in my graphic re-presentation of two large composites, showing in a manner visual to the untutored eye just how subordinated compositions serve in a complex composite, I do just that.

When we know the rules of composition of thought, the issues that would arise in response to any topic that would be treated, the analytical questions that would be addressed without regard to subject matter, the premises of all inquiry – the fixed limns of all intellect – we know how thought was framed, formulated, and conveyed. And when we understand the rules of composition defined in this way, we also can move from detail to main point, holding together within a single descriptive framework the myriad of details that served the Bavli's authors and framers in making the few fundamental points that they wished to make. For identifying and cataloguing the rules of composition make possible the precise definition of the repertoire of thought – recurrent types of questions, repeated methods of answering those question, yielding the premises of all inquiry, reflection, thought, and discourse – of the Talmud of Babylonia, and that is why discovering those rules of composition is important.

These I call rules of composition, meaning not only correct usage of language, the grammar of (socially, contextually) proper and educated expression, but something of more profound weight. I refer to the rules that told someone the conventions of thought by defining the accepted conventions of expression: "the limits of my language are the limits of my world" in this context means, how I express myself properly tells me that about which I may properly think. In a writing of an analytical character, rules of composition dictate the repertoire of appropriate questions, indicating what issues demand sustained attention and (implicitly) which ones may be ignored.

These rules of composition in the Talmud of Babylonia, a remarkably uniform and conceptually simple writing, were few, readily learned, and easily discerned. One who knows the rules of expression – and anyone who has studied a sufficient volume of the document knows the rules implicitly, even though he or she may not grasp every detail of their application to an articulated case – always is able to define the analytical context, say what is at stake, define an appropriate solution to a properly framed problem, answer a question to the point and grasp both the point and what is at stake in the question.

Rules of composition therefore were not merely formal rules of correct arrangement of various classifications of words, for example, nouns, verbs; they encompassed more than correct usage of language in such a way that how things were said would be socially acceptable and intellectually comprehensible. Rules of composition always involved recurrent forms, but – and this must be fully appreciated – while formal and routine, they were never mere formalities, and they never were to be distinguished from the substance of things. For the rules of composition in the Bavli governed not only how a writer (or formulator of a thought for oral transmission) would make his statement, but also what he would say. Rules of composition place limitations upon thought for the purpose of communication within a given society, for the medium ubiquitously dictates the message in any determinate context, and the document before us, deriving as it did from a textual community of a clearly defined and limited order, sets forth its messages not only through what was said about some specific subject, but through how anything might be said about any subject that came under consideration. Anyone who has studied a large sample of the Talmud of Babylonia will readily list a variety of fixed syntactic forms, on the one side, and a substantial catalogue of examples of how a great many subjects are formulated within that limited variety of syntactic forms, on the other. But a generalized impression of how things are is not the same thing as a specific and comprehensive account, based on a systematic sampling of evidence, providing clear and concrete definitions of the rules of translating thought into words that can communicate thought within shared conventions of intellectual community, and that is what I provide here.

So, it is clear, I am engaged in addressing the problem, who speaks through the Bavli? Is it the voice of the penultimate and ultimate authorship, or does the document resonate with the voices of a variety of authors and authorships? The full weight of the problem to be solved here and the meaning of the results take on consequence only in the broader context of three decades of research of mine, which therefore require a brief summary, beginning with the immediately preceding studies.

I began with a general theory of how we are to differentiate the types of writing in any canonical writing of the Judaism of the Dual Torah, which seemed to me the required starting point for any further analysis: how do I know one thing from something else?

1. *Making the Classics in Judaism: The Three Stages of Literary Formation* (Atlanta, 1989: Scholars Press for Brown Judaic Studies): Two questions in the framing of a theory of the history of the anonymous literature of formative Judaism form the program of my studies of the Bavli, beginning here. The first is, What is the correct starting point of analysis of a document and its formative history? The second is, What are the principal results of starting from that designated point of entry? I test the hypothesis that the discrete sayings (lemmas) form the correct point of entry and show, through the formation and testing of a null hypothesis, that that hypothesis is false. We cannot begin work in the assumption that the building block of documents is the smallest whole unit of thought, the lemma, nor can we proceed in the premise that a lemma traverses the boundaries of various documents and is unaffected by the journey. The opposite premise is that we start our work with the traits of documents as a whole, rather than with the traits of the lemmas of which documents are (supposedly) composed. Since, in a variety of books[2] I have set forth the documentary hypothesis for the analysis of the rabbinic literature of late antiquity, I proceeded immediately to the exploration of the second of the two possibilities.

If we take as our point of entry the character and conditions of the document, seen whole, what is the point of entry into the data? And what are the results of doing so? I show the first steps dictated by the entry into documents as a whole. Once I have demonstrated beyond any doubt that a rabbinic text is a document, a well-crafted text and not merely a compilation of this and that, and further specified in acute detail precisely the aesthetic, formal, and logical program followed by each of those texts, I am able to move to the logical next step. That is to show that in the background of the documents that we have is [1] writing

---

[2]These are as follows: *From Tradition to Imitation. The Plan and Program of Pesiqta deRab Kahana and Pesiqta Rabbati, Canon and Connection: Intertextuality in Judaism, Midrash as Literature: The Primacy of Documentary Discourse,* and *The Bavli and its Sources: The Question of Tradition in the Case of Tractate Sukkah,* as well as *The Talmud of the Land of Israel. 35. Introduction. Taxonomy,* and *Judaism. The Classic Statement. The Evidence of the Bavli.*

that is not shaped by documentary requirements, [2] writing that is not shaped by the documentary requirements of the compilations we now have, and also [3] writing that is entirely formed within the rules of the documents that now present that writing. These, then, are the three kinds of writing that form, also, the three stages in the formation of the classics of Judaism.

Identifying stages in the formation of materials that finally surface in a given document raised the question: Do framers of documents take an active role in the formation of their writing, or do they merely receive and repeat what they have from prior authors and even authorships? My answer to that question derives from a comparison of how two distinct authorships dealt with the same document. Showing that each set of compilers or writers realized its own, distinctive theory of how that one document should be analyzed, I demonstrated that in both cases the recipients of the document each worked out its respective program of thought. The shared document is the Mishnah, the two distinct authorships were the writers of the Tosefta, on the one side, and the Bavli, on the other.

2. *The Bavli that Might Have Been: The Tosefta's Theory of Mishnah Commentary Compared with the Bavli's.* I here compare the program of a tractate of the Tosefta for the amplification of a Mishnah tractate, and the corresponding program, for the same tractate, of the Talmud of Babylonia. This study demonstrates the distinct approaches to the same task that characterize the Tosefta's and the Bavli's authorships. Both sets of authors have made decisions and followed each its own program of exegesis. The distinctive traits of documents therefore express and recapitulate in form the intellectual program of writers of documents. What proves that fact is not that there are differences between Tosefta's and Bavli's theory of Mishnah commentary, but that the differences are fixed and systematic, which means that just as the one document's authorship followed rules throughout, so did the other's.

That result drew me directly to the Bavli, which had been the goal of my research. I wanted to know whether I could read the Bavli as a single, cogent document, in which a fixed set of rules governed how things were said. Or did I have to read the Bavli as a miscellany of writings, in which diverse rules dictated how various components of the miscellany were to be written? I took as my question the matter of utilizing the two languages of the writing, Hebrew and Aramaic, and I asked whether I could state as a general rule the considerations that dictated when Hebrew would be used, and where and why Aramaic would serve as the document's medium.

3. *Language as Discourse. The Rules for Using Hebrew and Aramaic in the Babylonian Talmud.* Here – following upon the results of the prior *Beistudie*, I ask how writers in the Talmud of Babylonia knew when to use Hebrew and where and how to use Aramaic. The answer to that question tells us the signals they proposed to give their readers by the use of the one or the other. This book is based on the mode of translation of Bekhorot which systematically marks the use of the two languages. The upshot is to prove that the document carefully delineates the boundaries between its own statements and those of prior documents that are cited and expounded. This work provides that the classification of the canonical writings of Judaism within the framework of a literature of "intertextuality" is a gross error and a profound misrepresentation of this uniformly intratextual literature.

Once I could demonstrate that a single rule dictated language choice, and that rule everywhere operated in the Bavli, I was ready to move from language to the forms of discourse. For now I knew that the Bavli was to be read as not only distinctive – the Tosefta comparison had shown me that fact – but also as single and cogent, a document of integrity, governed everywhere by a single set of rules of language choice.[3] So it was time to move from a simple demonstration that one fundamental rule governed everywhere within the writing, but nowhere (except in the counterpart and parallel Talmud) outside of it, to the document itself. I took as my problem the simple question, how is the Talmud of Babylonia put together? Having shown that the framers of the document drew upon prior writings but also contributed writing of their own, I wanted to know how the three kinds of writing held together in a single cogent composition. My first problem was to devise an analytical system. By that I mean, a way of identifying what I think are the whole units of thought, text and footnotes alike, with which the document's authors, authorships, or compilers did their work. Only by a sustained and detailed account of my theory of the identification and arrangement of the parts could I proceed to a picture of how I maintain these parts are put together. That yielded the fourth *Vorstudie.*

4. *The Rules of Composition of the Talmud of Babylonia.* "Composition" here refers to the rules that instructed framers on how to put together composites of completed materials so as to make a single,

---

[3]While Aramaic occurs in other writings, it does not serve as the base language of any other canonical document of the Judaism of the Dual Torah except for the two Talmuds. A comparison of the Bavli's use of Aramaic with the use of the same language in any Midrash compilation will show that simple fact, which need not detain us.

coherent statement; and it also refers to the rules that instructed authors (or formulators of passages for oral transmission) on how to put together sentences to set forth a single, cogent, statement. Thus "composition" refers to both a complex conglomerate, that is, a composite of completed essays and also to a single, simple essay. How are these composites composed into compositions? The answer to that question depends upon how we identify the various components of a composite. In this book I set forth the theory of analysis, the method, that guides the present work on the Bavli's one voice.

The main problem in analyzing a sample of the Talmud of Babylonia is presented by the run-on character of the writing. Visually, what we see are long columns of undifferentiated words, the sole division between between a set of sentences drawn from the Mishnah and (ordinarily) much longer and more elaborate discussion of those sentences. Substantively, what we quickly perceive is that a passage of the Bavli moves far beyond the limits of Mishnah commentary, and that movement twists and turns, so that a vast amount of information will be introduced that is only tangentially relevant to the starting point in the Mishnah. Before any picture of the rules of composition of the document can emerge, we have to devise a method of identifying a whole unit of thought – beginning to end – and differentiating among its parts. This is not merely a formal problem, readily solved, as I had solved it two decades ago, by marking off chapters, paragraphs, and sentences (to draw on the metaphor of contemporary division).[4] It is a problem of a very substantial order. The reason is that the Bavli on the surface appears to be run-on, and many people have found the writing to be not only confusing but confused, the result of a stream of consciousness, not propositional, not crafted and purposive at all.

The run-on and meandering quality of a Talmudic discussion is difficult to analyze as a single, cogent composition, and therefore impossible to classify as the work of showing how the Bavli's one voice speaks, until we realize a simple fact. The Talmud of Babylonia in

---

[4]I published my results, in the context of the analysis of the Mishnah's division of purities, in *A History of the Mishnaic Law of Purities*. Leiden, 1977: Brill. XXI. *The Redaction and Formulation of the Order of Purities in the Mishnah and Tosefta*. There I showed how "chapter, subdivision of a chapter, a paragraph, and a sentence" (marked in my reference system by a capital Roman numeral, a Roman numeral in small letters, an Arabic numeral, and a capital letter) serve as metaphors for "completed unit of systematic exposition, subunit of exposition, formation of the smallest whole units of thought into a cogent statement, and the smallest whole units of thought," respectively, would do its work. I do not believe that that volume ever received a review, and I cannot say that, after nearly fifteen years, its proposals have been grasped in any way whatsoever.

contemporary terms would be presented heavy with footnotes and appendices. That is, in our mode of setting forth our ideas and the documentation for them, we include in our text the main points of proposition, evidence, and argument; we relegate to footnotes the sources upon which we draw; we place in appendices substantial bodies of secondary material, relevant to the main body of our text only tangentially, yet required for a full presentation of what we wish to say. The authorship of the Talmud of Babylonia accomplishes, within the technical limitations that governed its formulation of its proposition, evidence, and argument, what we work out through footnotes and appendices. Much of the materials subordinated to the proposition, evidence, and argument, derive from finished pieces of writing, worked out for use in a document we do not now have (and cannot even imagine!), now providing useful, if not essential, documentation for the document that we do have.

In *The Rules of Composition* I demonstrated that in classifying a piece of writing, a composition within a composite that constitutes a complete and fully articulated discourse, I must and should include within my scheme the entire mass of not only proposition, evidence, and argument, but also footnotes and appendices. The whole, then, is treated as what has been classified, even though only parts form that active and determinative discussion. Accordingly, I include within a given act of classification not only what is relevant to the flow and thrust of discourse, *but also the associated documentation*, meaning, everything upon which the framers drew. Then the whole of the Talmud under discussion will be seen fully to fall into place in accord with the proposed rules of composition. A protracted passage, which seems run-on, when properly set forth, forms a cogent and coherent statement: proposition, evidence, arguments, fully exposed, but, alas, glossed and amplified and extended through footnotes and appendices as only intellectuals who also are scholars can gloss, amplify, and extend their remarks.

So much for the present work, seen in its context. What is to follow? I next propose to ask what we learn from the *method* of the Bavli concerning the *message* of its authorship. This will be in two parts. The first, following upon the translation of Bavli-tractate Zebahim, will systematically ask what premises of thought routinely define the substrate of discourses in the Bavli, which is to say, what is at stake in general, when discussion about a detail is undertaken: if so, then what? I continue in this study, based on an appropriate portion of Zebahim, to try to generalize out of detail, finding the recurrent tensions and the critical propositions that everywhere animate discourse. This will be a two-part study, a matched set, as before, one of a case (Zebahim, parallel to Abodah Zarah), the other of all cases (rules of composition, message of the method of composition):

5. *The Message of the Method of the Talmud of Babylonia. The Case of Bavli-Tractate Zebahim.* What message can we derive from the methods of logical and cogent discourse that are paramount in the Bavli? This volume, to begin with, focuses upon Bavli-tractate Zebahim. A theory begun there is tested against the other tractates I shall have translated to that time.

6. *The Bavli's One Statement.* In this study I generalize on the results of the foregoing and test the generalizations against the tractates translated in the analytical manner and hence prepared for analysis. The principal question is, So what? If so, over and over again, then what, everywhere and all the time? Can I state the recurrent concerns that define what is at stake in a vast range of detailed inquiries? The results of these latter two studies – six in all – will produce generalizations about the character of the Bavli.

From that point, the goal of the entire project comes into sight. The Bavli adumbrates a system and forms its principal canonical expression. But in the same period – the fifth, sixth, and early seventh centuries – and among the same authorities, other writings, compilations of exegesis of Scripture known as Midrash compilations, reached closure. Accordingly, I have then to bring the Bavli into relationship with its associated Midrash compilations, Ruth Rabbah, Song of Songs Rabbah, Lamentations Rabbati, and Esther Rabbah I, just as in earlier work I aligned the Talmud of the Land of Israel with its associated Midrash compilations, Genesis Rabbah, Leviticus Rabbah, Pesiqta deRab Kahana, in *The Transformation of Judaism: From Philosophy to Religion.* So, too, in a variety of studies, I have brought into juxtaposition and alignment the Mishnah and Tosefta with their associated Midrash compilations, Sifra, Sifré to Numbers, and Sifré to Deuteronomy, for example, in *The Canonical History of Ideas. The Place of the So-called Tannaite Midrashim; Mekhilta Attributed to R. Ishmael; Sifra; Sifré to Numbers; and Sifré to Deuteronomy.*

These works on the Bavli and its related Midrash compilations prepare the way for the religious-historical study of the third stage in the formation of the Judaism of the Dual Torah, which, I anticipate, will prove to be a highly systematic, theological stage. After I have completed the translation of all of the Bavli tractates that at that time have not appeared, I shall turn to the systematic work:

7. *The Transformation of Judaism. From Religion to Theology in the Talmud of Babylonia and the Late Midrash Compilations.* Once I have

established the method and message of the Bavli, I return to the question addressed in *The Transformation of Judaism. From Philosophy to Religion.* This project requires me to reread the Bavli alongside the roughly contemporary Midrash compilations, just as in the work on the movement from philosophy to religion, I reread the Yerushalmi alongside the roughly contemporary Midrash compilations, Genesis Rabbah, Leviticus Rabbah, and Pesiqta deRab Kahana. As I compared the category formations of the Yerushalmi and its related Midrash compilations with those of the Mishnah, with the Tosefta, and related Midrash compilations, such as Sifra and the two Sifrés, so here my plan is to compare the category formations of the Yerushalmi and related writings with those of the Bavli and related writings and specify the category structure of the final system of late antiquity. Do I find paramount the same categories or other categories? The principal question finally answered here is, Since I identify the statements of norms, and I demonstrate that these norms are cogent with one another, what do these norms set forth as a system, and why do I maintain that it is a theological system, within my definition of theology?

And this will lead me to a further analytical stage, which is the comparison of religions in an appropriate context. The goal of history of religion has always been to encompass the comparison of religions, which lends perspective to work on a single religion or (in my language) set of religious systems, in the case of Judaism, sequential set of Judaic systems within the unfolding of the canon of the Dual Torah. The Bavli took shape in the same time and age – the end of late antiquity, the early emergence of Islam – as the Good Religion of the Worshipers of Mazda. This religious system, which we know as Zoroastrianism, forms in the age and circumstance of its ultimate statement the mythic counterpart to "the one whole Torah of Moses, our rabbi," which we know as Judaism or normative, or classical, or Talmudic, or rabbinic Judaism). The Bavli was reaching its final literary statement not a long time before the ninth century Pahlavi books, which form the counterpart to the Bavli, were coming to conclusion and closure.

More to the point, at the same time that the Judaic theological apologists for the writing down of the Bavli – lest the great tradition perish – gave the same reason for the writing, the Zoroastrian theological apologists accounted in the same way for the writing down of the Denkart and related documents. So the parallel that precipitates comparison and contrast is not merely adventitious and circumstantial but substantive and structural. Therefore I choose for my comparison the Bavli and the Denkart.

8. *The Bavli and the Denkart: The Judaic and Zoroastrians Response to the Challenge of Nascent Islam.* Are the Zoroastrian sages writing on the same range of issues, or is this simply the collection and arrangement of inherited information, as the prior accounts of the ninth century Pahlavi books have maintained and as counterpart accounts of Judaism, deriving from the same age, the early Islamic, allege?

Clearly, these projects of literary analysis in the service of the history of Judaism within the context of the history of religion (as I shall explain) are aimed at an issue that seems to me critical in the study of the formative history of Judaism. For now that I have translated twelve of the thirty-seven tractates of the Talmud of Babylonia (Abodah Zarah, Berakhot, Sukkah, Sotah, Bava Mesia, Sanhedrin, Bekhorot, Arakhin, Temurah, Keritot, Niddah, and Zebahim), I am moving toward the conclusion of a thirty-year project of rereading the entire canon of Judaism in its formative age.

More to the point, I am opening what I hope will be another protracted project, beyond the rereading of the entire canon, which is, to move from the history of (an important) Judaism to the history of religion. I mean to redefine the study of the history of Judaism by integrating the history of Judaism, in its formative age, to the history of religion, in that same age and circumstance. That is, I propose to transform the history of Judaism into an important component of the sector of the humanities comprised by the history of religion. I have defined the work of the history of (a) religion as a systematic effort is made to analyze the canonical evidence for the formation of systemic statements, treating the canon as recapitulative, but also historical and sequential, to try to identify within the social and historical circumstances of canonical writings the precipitating considerations, and, finally, proposing to define the generative, critical, urgent question to which, in one detail after another, a systematic statement through its canon proposes to respond. Now, admittedly, a systematic effort to study the formation of another canonical religion the way I am in process of studying that of Judaism has no counterpart known to me.

Certainly work on Christianity, Zoroastrianism, and earlier Islam in the Near and Middle East, in the same time and place, is episodic, isolated, and hardly aimed at generalizing about the character of religion in its formative age. From the greatest age in the history of religion known to humankind, the age that witnessed the formation as they would flourish of Christianity, Zoroastrianism, Islam, and Judaism, has come not a single generalization that can help us understand the formation of religion(s) in our own time and place. So the history of religion has yet to keep the promise it made in its formative time and among its formative intellects, which was to teach us lessons about not religions but religion, to transform humanistic learning about this and that into a chapter in *Geisteswissenschaft, sciences humaines, limmudé haruah, scienze politiche*, the study of humanity in a systematic and orderly way. So up to now, history of religion, in its socially acceptable definition, histories of religions, proves little more than the learned statement of argument through episode and anecdote – about nothing in particular beyond mere impressions.

But the study of the histories of religions within the setting of the history of religion is just now completing its first century or so, and if my work on the study of Judaism gains the exemplary status that I intend for it, then I shall have shown historians of other religions how to move from work on the history of a religion (or a given formation, or system, within a religion) to the history of religion. Without taking that step, our work lacks perspective and our results, meaning beyond themselves. The one thing I have not done, which I think all former historians of Judaism have done (and that does not encompass a great many competing works at all, in any language) is not merely recapitulate and paraphrase what I find in the writings; and not merely sift and sort out evidence in isolation from any articulated generalization or proposed proposition: If so, so what? That leads me to the way in which, through a process of generalization beginning now I shall move from anecdote to argument, and from episode to proposition, about religion, now not only exemplified by Judaism but demonstrated through the case of Judaism in its broader *religionsgeschichtlich* context of comparison and contrast. The work of preparation is nearly over.

Where, in the context of my unfolding *oeuvre*, shall I situate my interest in re-presenting the Bavli? Having placed this work into its largest humanistic context, I turn back to locate it within my own *oeuvre*. For three decades I have followed a single, straight path of scholarly inquiry. The program just now outlined will require yet another decade or so of sustained and continuous inquiry, so I plan to continue on that same undeviating course to its conclusion. To explain why have I organized this project and taken so considerable a part in re-translating the Talmud of Babylonia is possible only in the setting of my lifelong study of the formation of Judaism, of which the Bavli marks the third and final stage. Because I have now reached the preliminary levels of that third stage, I assign to the work of re-presenting the Bavli, in a form that makes possible detailed analysis of literary structure and order, the central importance at a turning in my long-term program. It gains priority now that my work on the description, analysis, and interpretation of the first two of the three stages in which, in my view, the Judaism of the Dual Torah took shape in late antiquity, unfolded.

As already hinted, the work on the second stage reached its conclusion in *Transformation of Judaism*. Corresponding to my *Judaism: The Evidence of the Mishnah* (Chicago, 1982: University of Chicago Press; Atlanta, 1989: Scholars Press for Brown Judaic Studies. Second edition, augmented), my *Transformation of Judaism. From Philosophy to Religion* (Champaign, 1991: University of Illinois Press), sets forth, whole and complete, the results of nearly a decade of research, from 1980, on the Judaic system (the "Judaism") portrayed by the documents that reached closure from the conclusion of the Mishnah at the end of the second century to the completion of the Talmud of the Land of Israel, Genesis Rabbah, Leviticus Rabbah, and Pesiqta deRab Kahana, in ca. the fourth and fifth centuries.

The now-completed research has systematically described the documents of that span of approximately two hundred years and, further, equally systematically analyzed those same documents through comparison and contrast, thus exposing important traits of the system and history of the Judaism portrayed by those documents.   In *Transformation* I take the two sets of documents as evidence of systems to which they refer or attest, and it is the systems that I claim exhibit traits I can describe and connections – comparisons and contrasts – I can analyze and interpret. So that work formed an exercise in the study of category formation, following upon a rather protracted labor of description of texts, analysis of the systems adumbrated or attested by them, and then interpretation of the systems within a single context of comparison and contrast. So much for the literature that conveys to us the first and the second stages in the formation of Judaism, the philosophical and the religion.   I have in mind now to find out whether or not we may characterize the third and last stage as the theological.

Specifically, in the next decade or so, upon the foundations of my present studies of the Bavli and the related Midrash compilations, particularly Lamentations Rabbah, Song of Songs Rabbah, Esther Rabbah I, and Ruth Rabbah, I shall accomplish the same work for the third and final stage in the formation of Judaism, from ca. 450 to ca. 600 Some of the descriptive and analytical work is now complete,[5] but a fair amount

---

[5]This work is in the following eight parts (nine volumes): *Lamentations Rabbah. An Analytical Translation*. Atlanta, 1989: Scholars Press for Brown Judaic Studies; *Esther Rabbah I. An Analytical Translation*. Atlanta, 1989: Scholars Press for Brown Judaic Studies; *Ruth Rabbah. An Analytical Translation*. Atlanta, 1989: Scholars Press for Brown Judaic Studies; *Song of Songs Rabbah. An Analytical Translation*. Volume One. *Song of Songs Rabbah to Song Chapters One through Three*. Atlanta, 1990: Scholars Press for Brown Judaic Studies; *Song of Songs Rabbah. An Analytical Translation*. Volume Two. *Song of Songs Rabbah to Song Chapters Four through Eight*. Atlanta, 1990: Scholars Press for Brown Judaic Studies; *The*

of descriptive study of texts and a still larger labor of analytical study of contexts stands between this work and the third and final interpretive enterprise I have in mind at this time, which is the passage from religion to theology. The ten tractates of the Bavli that I shall have translated will form the sample for the analysis of some of the problems associated with the coming inquiry. I hardly need say that – as is my way – the theoretical labor in my mind is now well under way for the final stage. I generally compose in my mind my major theoretical work, only afterward putting the whole down on paper – and catching up, in research, with the results of my abstraction, imagination, and sheer daydreaming. The translation work has stimulated much of that kind of thought: by small detail much is provoked.

Catching up means another go-around in the literary evidence. So to undertake systemic analysis on the strength of written evidence, I have systemically to complete the rereading of the classic documents of the Judaism that took shape in the first to the seventh centuries A.D. and that has predominated since then, the Judaism of the Dual Torah. These documents – the Mishnah, Midrash compilations, the two Talmuds – represent the collective statement and consensus of authorships (none is credibly assigned to a single author and all are preserved because they are deemed canonical and authoritative) and show us how those authorships proposed to make a statement to their situation and – so I argue – upon the human condition. For, when we study religions in quest of the definition and understanding of religion, that is what we study: God's perspective on humanity.

Midrash Compilations of the Sixth and Seventh Centuries. An Introduction to the Rhetorical, Logical, and Topical Program. I. Lamentations Rabbah. Atlanta, 1990: Scholars Press for Brown Judaic Studies; *The Midrash Compilations of the Sixth and Seventh Centuries: An Introduction to the Rhetorical, Logical, and Topical Program. II. Esther Rabbah I.* Atlanta, 1990: Scholars Press for Brown Judaic Studies; *The Midrash Compilations of the Sixth and Seventh Centuries: An Introduction to the Rhetorical, Logical, and Topical Program. III. Ruth Rabbah.* Atlanta, 1990: Scholars Press for Brown Judaic Studies; and *The Midrash Compilations of the Sixth and Seventh Centuries: An Introduction to the Rhetorical, Logical, and Topical Program. IV. Song of Songs Rabbah.* Atlanta, 1990: Scholars Press for Brown Judaic Studies.

13

The Bavli's One Voice and the Bavli's One Statement:
The Literary-Rhetorical Foundations of an Inquiry into the Bavli's Metapropositional Repertoire

The Talmud of Babylonia, a.k.a. the Bavli, throughout speaks in a single and singular voice.[1] That is what justifies asking what statement that that single voice chooses to make.[2] Different from, much more than, a haphazard compilation of traditions, the Bavli shows itself upon examination to be a cogent and purposive writing, in which through a single determinate set of rhetoric devices, a single program of inquiry is brought to bear on many and diverse passages of two inherited documents, the Mishnah and Scripture. The voice is one and single because it is a voice that expresses the same limited set of notes

---

[1] I have demonstrated that fact through analysis of the evidence of rhetoric and the logic of cogent discourse – and demonstrated at great length in *The Rules of Composition of the Talmud of Babylonia. The Cogency of the Bavli's Composite.* Atlanta, 1991: Scholars Press for South Florida Studies in the History of Judaism and in *The Bavli's One Voice: Types and Forms of Analytical Discourse and their Fixed Order of Appearance.* Atlanta, 1991: Scholars Press for South Florida Studies in the History of Judaism. Principal findings of the latter monograph are summarized here.

[2] I take up that question in the following monograph, which is now under way: *The Bavli's One Statement. The Metapropositional Program of Babylonian Talmud Tractate Zebahim Chapters One, Two, and Five, and of Babylonian Talmud Tractate Niddah Chapter One.* This work will yield a hypothesis and will be followed, after the completion of my analytical translations of eight more tractates of the Bavli, by *The Message of the Method of the Talmud of Babylonia. The Metapropositional Program of Babylonian Talmud Tractates Erubin, Yebamot, Qiddushin, Gittin, Baba Qamma, Baba Batra, Zebahim, and Menahot.*

everywhere. It is singular because these notes are arranged in one and the same way throughout. The Bavli's one voice, sounding through all tractates, is the voice of exegetes of the Mishnah. The document is organized around the Mishnah, and that order is not merely formal, but substantive. At *every* point,[3] if the framers have chosen a passage of Mishnah exegesis, that passage will stand at the head of all further discussion. *Every* turning point in a sustained composition and even in a large composite of compositions brings the editors back to the Mishnah, *always* read in its own order and sequence. So the Bavli's speaks in a single way about some few things, and that is the upshot of this sustained inquiry. It follows that well-crafted and orderly rules governed the character of the sustained discourse that the writing in the Bavli sets forth. All framers of composites and editors of sequences of composites found guidance in the same limited repertoire of rules of analytical rhetoric: some few questions or procedures, directed always toward one and the same prior writing. Not only so, but a fixed order of discourse dictated that a composition of one sort, A, always comes prior to a composite of another type, B. A simple logic instructed framers of composites, who sometimes also were authors of compositions, and who sometimes drew upon available compositions in the making of their cogent composites. So we have now to see the Bavli as entirely of a piece, cogent and coherent, made up of well-composed large-scale constructions.

The Bavli's one voice utilizes only a few, well-modulated tones: a scale of not many notes at all, yielding only a few, rather monotonous, melodies. When we classify more than three thousand composites, spread over eleven tractates, we find that nearly 90 percent of the whole comprises Mishnah commentary of various kinds; not only so, but the variety of the types of Mishnah commentary is limited, as a review of the representation of Temurah in detail, and of the ten tractates of our sample in brief characterization, has shown. Cogent composites are further devoted to Scripture or to topics of a moral or theological character not closely tied to the exegesis of verses of Scripture; these form in the aggregate approximately 10% of the whole number of composites, but, of tractates to begin with not concerned with scriptural or theological topics (in our sample these are Sanhedrin and Berakhot), they make up scarcely 3 percent of the whole. So the Bavli has one voice, and

---

[3]The "every" and "always" refers to the more than three thousand composites that I examined and classified in the eleven tractates treated by *The Bavli's One Voice: Types and Forms of Analytical Discourse and their Fixed Order of Appearance.* Some tractates present anomalies, so the consistent quality of the evidence is underlined.

it is the voice of a person or persons who propose to speak about one document and to do so in some few ways. Let me spell out precisely what I mean. The results of the survey of eleven tractates and classification of all of the composites of each one of them yields firm and one-sided results.

First, we are able to classify *all* composites (among the more than three thousand that I examined) in three principal categories: [1] exegesis and amplification of the law of the Mishnah; [2] exegesis and exposition of verses of, or topics in, Scripture; [3] free-standing composites devoted to topics other than those defined by the Mishnah or Scripture. That means that my initial proposal of a taxonomic system left no lacunae. These classifications were not forced or subtle; the grounds for making them were consistent; appeal throughout was to gross and merely formal characteristics, not to subjective judgments of what unstipulated consideration might underlie, or define the intention of the framer of, a passage.

Second, with the classification in place, it is a matter of simple fact that much more than four-fifths of all composites of the Bavli address the Mishnah and systematically expound that document. These composites are subject to subclassification in two ways: Mishnah exegesis and speculation and abstract theorizing about the implications of the Mishnah's statements. The former type of composite, further, is to be classified in a few and simple taxa, for example, composites organized around [1] clarification of the statements of the Mishnah, [2] identification of the authority behind an anonymous statement in the Mishnah, [3] scriptural foundation for the Mishnah's rules; [4] citation and not seldom systematic exposition of the Tosefta's amplification of the Mishnah. That means that most of the Bavli is a systematic exposition of the Mishnah.

Third, the other fifth (or less) of a given tractate will comprise composites that take shape around [1] Scripture or [2] themes or topics of a generally theological or moral character. Distinguishing the latter from the former, of course, is merely formal; very often a scriptural topic will be set forth in a theological or moral framework, and very seldom does a composite on a topic omit all reference to the amplification of a verse or topic of Scripture. The proportion of a given tractate devoted to other-than-Mishnah exegesis and amplification is generally not more than 10 percent. My figure, as we shall note presently, is distorted by the special problems of tractates Sanhedrin and Berakhot, and, in the former, Chapter Eleven in particular.

These two tractates prove anomalous for the categories I have invented because both of them contain important components that are devoted, to begin with, to scriptural or theological topics. Tractate-

Sanhedrin Chapter Eleven, for example, lists various scriptural figures in catalogues of those who do, or do not, inherit the world to come; it further specifies certain doctrines that define the norms of the community of Israel that inherits the world to come. It will therefore prove quite natural that numerous composites will attend to scriptural or theological topics. Tractate Berakhot addresses matters of prayer and other forms of virtue, with the same consequence. In the analysis that follows, therefore, I calculate the averages of proportions of various types of composites both with and without these anomalous tractates. The upshot is that a rather inconsequential proportion of most tractates, and a small proportion of the whole, of the Bavli, is devoted to the systematic exposition of either verses of Scripture or topics of a theological or moral character. Let us now consider in detail the eleven tractates' proportions of types of composites, to see the foundation for these generalizations.[4]

1. Temurah

		Number	Percent
1.	Exegesis of the Mishnah	58	75%
2.	Exegesis of Mishnah law	8	10%
3.	Speculation and Abstract Thought on Law	8	10%
4.	Scripture	3	4%
5.	Free-standing Composites	Not calculated	
6.	Miscellanies	0	-
		77	

2. Sukkah

1.	Exegesis of the Mishnah	141	89%
2.	Exegesis of the Mishnah's Law	8	5%
3.	Speculation and Abstract Thought on Law	4	2%
4.	Scripture	1	-
5.	Miscellanies	5	3%
		159	

[4]The figures derive from *The Bavli's One Voice*, where I analyze and classify all composites of the named, eleven tractates, and explain the reasons for the classification; I further am able to show a fixed order of types of composites, signaled by the order in which my classifications are given here. Where a composite includes an exegesis of the Mishnah, it will always commence with that exegesis; where it includes an exegesis of the Mishnah's law, that is the point at which it will invariably start; and so, too, throughout. Very commonly, to be sure, exegesis of the Mishnah's law will address the question of the scriptural foundations for the Mishnah's rule. But this is classified only as Mishnah exegesis and not Scripture exegesis, for obvious reasons.

3. Keritot

1.	Exegesis of the Mishnah	80	94%
2.	Exegesis of the Mishnah's Law	4	4%
3.	Speculation and Abstract Thought on Law	0	-
4.	Scripture	1	1%
5.	Free-standing Composites	0	-
6.	Miscellanies	0	-
		85	

4. Arakhin

1.	Exegesis of the Mishnah	127	91%
2.	Exegesis of the Mishnah's Law	8	6%
3.	Speculation and Abstract Thought on Law	2	1.5%
4.	Scripture	0	-
5.	Free-standing Composites	2	1.5%
6.	Miscellanies	0	-
		139	

The importance of the free-standing composites is not reflected by the count, since both items are enormous and the first of the two serves as the prologue to the tractate as a whole.

5. Niddah

1.	Exegesis of the Mishnah	290	97%
2.	Exegesis of the Mishnah's Law	6	2%
3.	Speculation and Abstract Thought on Law	0	-
4.	Scripture	0	-
5.	Free-standing Composites	3	1%
6.	Miscellanies	0	-
		299	

6. Abodah Zarah

1.	Exegesis of the Mishnah	244	85%
2.	Exegesis of the Mishnah's Law	3	1%
3.	Speculation and Abstract Thought on Law	0	
4.	Scripture	28	10%
5.	Free-standing Composites	12	4%
6.	Miscellanies	0	
		287	

7. Sotah

1.	Exegesis of the Mishnah	193	91%
2.	Exegesis of the Mishnah's Law	0	-
3.	Speculation and Abstract Thought on Law	0	-
4.	Scripture	10	5%
5.	Free-standing Composites	8	4%
6.	Miscellanies	1	0.5%
		212	

8. Baba Mesia

1.	Exegesis of the Mishnah	334	86%
2.	Exegesis of the Mishnah's Law	42	11%
3.	Speculation and Abstract Thought on Law	0	-
4.	Scripture	2	0.5%
5.	Free-standing Composites	10	3%
6.	Miscellanies	0	
		388	

9. Bekhorot

1.	Exegesis of the Mishnah	281	98%
2.	Exegesis of the Mishnah's Law	2	1%
3.	Speculation and Abstract Thought on Law	-	
4.	Scripture	-	
5.	Free-standing Composites	2	1%
6.	Miscellanies	-	
		285	

10. Berakhot

1.	Exegesis of the Mishnah	330	59%
2.	Exegesis of the Mishnah's Law	3	0.5%
3.	Speculation and Abstract Thought on Law	0	-
4.	Scripture	34	6%
5.	Free-standing Composites	187	34%
6.	Miscellanies	2	0.4%
		556	

11. Sanhedrin

1. Exegesis of the Mishnah	313	45%
2. Exegesis of the Mishnah's Law	6	0.8%
3. Speculation and Abstract Thought on Law	6	0.8%
4. Scripture	163	23%
5. Free-standing Composites	214	30%
6. Miscellanies	0	-
	702	

Seen in the aggregate, 83 percent of the eleven tractates is devoted solely to Mishnah exegesis. If we omit reference to the two clearly anomalous tractates, Berakhot and Sanhedrin, the proportion of Mishnah exegesis rises to 89.5 percent. If, then, we combine exegesis of the Mishnah and exegesis of the broader implications of the Mishnah's law – and in the process of classification, it was not always easy to keep these items apart in a consistent way – we see a still more striking result. More than 86 percent of the whole of our tractates is devoted to the exegesis of the Mishnah and the amplification of the implications of its law; without the anomalous tractates, the proportion is close to 94 to 95 percent.[5]

Composites devoted to Scripture, not the Mishnah, are calculated in two ways. In the first nine tractates, I counted each composite as one entry, just as, overall, I counted each composite devoted to the Mishnah as one entry. On the surface such a mode of counting understated the proportions of the anomalous tractates that are devoted to Scripture exegesis, or to topics drawn from Scripture. Overall, we should expect to find something on the order of 4 percent of a given tractate made up of Scripture composites. If we eliminate the two anomalous tractates, the anticipated proportion would be 2 percent. Free-standing composites, formed in general around themes, rather than passages of the Mishnah or sequences of verses of Scripture or topics provided by Scripture, average 10 percent for eight tractates (omitted: Temurah, Sukkah, Keritot, where I found none), and, without the anomalous ones, 1.5 to 3 percent. The latter figure seems to me more probable than the former. So it is simply the fact that the Talmud speaks through one voice, that voice of logic that

---

[5]I early on dismissed as a taxon that did not serve any useful purpose the one that was supposed to identify "speculation and abstract thought on law." As a matter of fact, nearly all speculative or abstract thought on law, measured by the number of composites devoted to that purpose, treats the Mishnah's concrete laws; nearly all speculation is precipitated by an inquiry into the premises of those laws. There is virtually no abstract thought on law that does not aim at the clarification of the Mishnah's laws in particular. That simply unanticipated result is as stunning as the foregoing.

with vast assurance reaches into our own minds and by asking the logical and urgent next question tells us what we should be thinking. Fixing our attention upon the Mishnah, the Talmud's rhetoric seduces us into joining its analytical inquiry, always raising precisely the question that should trouble us (and that would trouble us if we knew all of the pertinent details as well as the Talmud does).

The upshot is simple and demands heavy emphasis: *the Bavli speaks about the Mishnah in essentially a single voice, about fundamentally few things.* Its mode of speech as much as of thought is uniform throughout. Diverse topics produce slight differentiation in modes of analysis. The same sorts of questions phrased in the same rhetoric – a moving, or dialectical, argument, composed of questions and answers – turn out to pertain equally well to every subject and problem. The Talmud's discourse forms a closed system, in which people say the same thing about everything. The fact that the Talmud speaks in a single voice supplies striking evidence [1] that the Talmud does speak in particular for the age in which its units of discourse took shape, and [2] that that work was done toward the end of that long period of Mishnah reception that began at the end of the second century and came to an end at the conclusion of the sixth century.

When I speak of the Bavli's one voice, as now is clear, I mean to say it everywhere speaks uniformly, consistently, and predictably. The voice is the voice of a book. The message is one deriving from a community, the collectivity of sages for whom and to whom the book speaks. The document seems, in the main, to intend to provide notes, an abbreviated script which anyone may use to reconstruct and reenact formal discussions of problems: about this, one says that. Curt and often arcane, these notes can be translated only with immense bodies of inserted explanation. All of this script of information is public and undifferentiated, not individual and idiosyncratic. We must assume people took for granted that, out of the signs of speech, it would be possible for anyone to reconstruct speech, doing so in accurate and fully conventional ways. So the literary traits of the document presuppose a uniform code of communication: a single voice.

The ubiquitous character of this single and continuous voice of the Talmud argues for one of two points of origin. First, powerful and prevailing conventions may have been formed in the earliest stages of the reception and study of the Mishnah, then carried on thereafter without variation or revision. Or, second, the framing of sayings into uniform and large-scale constructions of discourse – composites – may have been accomplished only toward the end of the period marked by the formation of the Talmud's units of discourse and their conglomeration into the Talmud as we know it. In the former case, we posit that the mode of reasoned analysis of the Mishnah and the repertoire of issues to be addressed to any passage of the Mishnah were defined early on, then persisted for four or five hundred years – the span of time that separates us from Columbus. The consequent, conventional mode of speech yielded that nearly total uniformity of discourse characteristic of numerous units of discourse of the Talmud at which the interpretation of a law of the Mishnah is subject to discussion. In the latter case we surmise that a vast corpus of sayings, some by themselves, some parts of larger conglomerates, was inherited at some point toward the end of the two hundred years under discussion. This corpus of miscellanies was then subjected to intense consideration as a whole, shaped and reworded into the single, cogent and rhetorically consistent Talmudic discourse before us.

As between these two possibilities, the sustained and relentless inquiry I have shown to characterize the Bavli's rules of discourse set forth in the works listed above makes the latter by far the more likely. The reason is simple. I cannot find among the units of discourse in the Talmud evidence of differentiation among the generations of names or schools. There is no interest, for instance, in the chronological sequence in which sayings took shape and in which discussions may be supposed to have been carried on. That is to say, the Talmudic unit of discourse approaches the explanation of a passage of the Mishnah without systematic attention to the layers in which ideas were set forth, the schools among which discussion must have been divided, the sequence in which statements about a Mishnah law were made. That fact points to formation at the end, not agglutination in successive layers of intellectual sediment. In a given unit of discourse, the focus, the organizing principle, the generative interest – these are defined solely by the issue at hand. The argument moves from point to point, directed by the inner logic of argument itself. A single plane of discourse is established. All things are leveled out, so that the line of logic runs straight and true. Accordingly, a single conception of the framing and formation of the unit of discourse stands prior to the spelling out of issues. More fundamental still, what people in general wanted was not to create topical anthologies – to put together instances of what this one said about that issue – but to exhibit the logic of that issue, viewed under the aspect of eternity. Under sustained inquiry we always find a theoretical issue, freed of all temporal considerations and the contingencies of politics and circumstance.

Once these elemental literary facts make their full impression, everything else falls into place as well. Arguments did not unfold over a long period of time, as one generation made its points, to be followed by the additions and revisions of another generation, in a process of gradual increment and agglutination running on for two hundred years. That theory of the formation of literature cannot account for the unity, stunning force and dynamism, of the Talmud's dialectical arguments. To the contrary, someone (or small group) at the end determined to reconstruct, so as to expose, the naked logic of a problem. For this purpose, oftentimes, it was found useful to cite sayings or positions in hand from earlier times. But these inherited materials underwent a process of reshaping, and, more aptly, refocusing. Whatever the original words – and we need not doubt that at times we have them – the point of everything in hand was defined and determined by the people who made it all up at the end. The whole shows a plan and program. Theirs are the minds behind the whole. In the nature of things, they did their work at the end, not at the outset. There are two possibilities. The first is that our document emerges out of a gradual increment of a sedimentary process. Or it emerges as the creation of single-minded geniuses of applied logic and sustained analytical inquiry. But there is no intermediate possibility.[6]

It follows that the whole is the work of the one who decided to make up the discussion on the atemporal logic of the point at issue. Otherwise the discussion would be not continuous but disjointed, full of seams and margins, marks of the existence of prior conglomerations of materials that have now been sewn together. What we have are not patchwork quilts, but woven fabric. Along these same lines, we may find discussions in which opinions of Palestinians, such as Yohanan and Simeon b. Laqish, will be joined together side by side with opinions of Babylonians, such as Rab and Samuel. The whole, once again, will unfold in a smooth way, so that the issues at hand define the sole focus of discourse. The logic of those issues will be fully exposed. Considerations of the origin of a saying in one country or the other will play no role whatsoever in the rhetoric or literary forms of argument. There will be no possibility of differentiation among opinions on the basis of where, when, by whom, or how they are formulated, only on the

---

[6]One qualification is required. I do not mean to say that the principles of chronology were wholly ignored. The opposite is the case – when it is relevant to the proposition or discourse at hand. Rather, the considerations of sequence of authorities cited in a composite simply were not determinative of the structure of argument. So I do not suggest that the framers of the Talmud would likely have an early authority argue with a later one about what is assigned only to the later one. That I cannot and do not expect to instantiate. I do not think we shall find such slovenly work in the Talmud. These sages were painstaking and sensible. But no attention ever is devoted in particular to the temporal sequence in which various things are said. Everything is worked together into a single, temporally seamless discourse. Discussion will always focus upon the logical point at hand. The sequence of authorities is not temporal but logical: which problem has to be addressed first, and which is logically next in sequence.

basis of what, in fact, is said. The upshot is that we may fairly ask about the message of the method of those who followed this one and single, prevailing method: a fixed set of rules on choice of language, a fixed repertoire of problems, a fixed received text governing the whole – the Bavli as we have it.

On the page of the Bavli, the role of individuals is both ubiquitous – numerous statements are joined to specific names – and also unimportant.[7] The paramount voice is that of "the Talmud." The rhetoric of the Talmud may be described very simply: a preference for questions and answers, a willingness, then, to test the answers and to expand through secondary and tertiary amplification, achieved through further questions and answers. The whole gives the appearance of the script for a conversation to be reconstructed, or an argument of logical possibilities to be reenacted, in one's own mind. In this setting we of course shall be struck by the uniformity of the rhetoric, even though we need not make much of the close patterning of language. The voice of "the Talmud," moreover, authoritatively defines the mode of analysis. The inquiry is consistent and predictable; one argument differs from another not in supposition but only in detail. When individuals' positions occur, it is because what they have to say serves the purposes of "the Talmud" and its uniform inquiry. The inquiry is into the logic and the rational potentialities of a passage. To these dimensions of thought, the details of place, time, and even of an individual's philosophy, are secondary. All details are turned toward a common core of discourse. This, I maintain, is possible only because the document as a whole takes shape in accord with an overriding program of inquiry and

---

[7]One has to be sure to ask about the role of individuals. Many still want to maintain that sayings assigned to particular names circulated for a long time and only at the very end of a process of transmission were they given their place in a conglomerate or composite. This is a principal fact that leads them to see the document as a compilation and not a composition. While named authorities and sayings assigned to them do occur, the dialectic of argument is conducted outside the contributions of the specified sages. Sages' statements serve the purposes of the anonymous voice, rather than defining and governing the flow of argument. So the anonymous voice, "the Talmud," predominates even when individuals' sayings are utilized. Selecting and arranging whatever was in hand is the work of one hand, one voice. The materials are organized so as to facilitate explanations of the law's inner structure and potentiality, not to present a mere repertoire of ideas and opinions of interest for their own sake. The upshot is a sustained argument, not an anthology of relevant sayings. Such a cogent and ongoing argument is more likely the work of a single mind than of a committee, let alone of writers who lived over a period of ten or fifteen decades. So even though "he really said it," that fact hardly mattered when it came to working out a composition or even putting together a composite; it was trivial and in no way indicative.

comes to expression in conformity with a single plan of rhetorical expression. To state the proposition simply: it did not just *grow*, but rather, someone *made* it up.

The Talmudic argument is not indifferent to the chronology of authorities. But the sequence in which things may be supposed to have been said – an early third century figure's saying before a later fourth century figure's saying – in no way explains the construction of protracted dialectical arguments. The argument as a whole, its direction and purpose, always govern the selection, formation, and ordering of the parts of the argument and their relationships to one another. The dialectic is determinative. Chronology, if never violated, is always subordinated. Once that fact is clear, it will become further apparent that "arguments" – analytical units of discourse – took shape at the end, with the whole in mind, as part of a plan and a program. That is to say, the components of the argument, even when associated with the names of specific authorities who lived at different times, were not added piece by piece, in order of historical appearance. They were put together whole and complete, all at one time, when the dialectical discourse was made up. By examining a few units of discourse, we clearly see the unimportance of the sequence in which people lived, hence of the order in which sayings (presumably) became available. The upshot is that chronological sequence, while not likely to be ignored, never determines the layout of a unit of discourse. We can never definitively settle the issue of whether a unit of discourse came into being through a long process of accumulation and agglutination, or was shaped at one point – then, at the end of the time in which named authorities flourished – with everything in hand and a particular purpose in mind. But the more likely of the two possibilities is clearly the latter. It seems to me likely that the purposes of dialectical argument determined not only which available sayings were selected for inclusion, but also the order and purpose in accordance with which sayings were laid out.

It follows that the whole – the composites of discourse as we know them, the sequence of composites as we have them – was put together at the end. At that point everything was in hand, so available for arrangement in accordance with a principle other than chronology, and in a rhetoric common to all sayings. That other principle will then have determined the arrangement, drawing in its wake resort to a single monotonous voice: "the Talmud." The principle is logical exposition, that is to say, the analysis and dissection of a problem into its conceptual components. The dialectic of argument is framed not by considerations of the chronological sequence in which sayings were said but by attention to the requirements of reasonable exposition of the problem. That is what governs.

So it is time to ask the purpose of that composition: what the authors, authorships, or framers of the document wished to say through the writing that they have given us. If there is a single governing method, then what can we expect to learn about the single, repeated message? The evidence before us indicates that the purpose of the Talmud is to clarify and amplify selected passages of the Mishnah. We may say very simply that the Mishnah is about life, and the Talmud is about the Mishnah. That is to say, while the Mishnah records rules governing the conduct of the holy life of Israel, the holy people, the Talmud concerns itself with the details of the Mishnah. The one is descriptive and free-standing, the other analytical and contingent. Were there no Mishnah, there would be no Talmud. But what is the message of the method, which is to insist upon the Mishnah's near monopoly over serious discourse? To begin with, the very character of the Talmud tells us the sages' view of the Mishnah. The Mishnah presented itself to them as constitutive, the text of ultimate concern. So, in our instance, the Mishnah speaks of a quarrel over a coat, the Talmud, of the Mishnah's provision of an oath as a means of settling the quarrel in a fair way: substance transformed into process. What the framers of the Bavli wished to say about the Mishnah will guide us toward the definition of the message of their method, but it will not tell us what that message was, or why it was important. A long process of close study of texts is required to guide us toward the center of matters.

The upshot is that now we have solid grounds in literary evidence on the basis of which really to speak about "the Talmud," *its* voice, *its* purposes, *its* mode of constructing a view of the Israelite world. The reason is that, when we claim "the Talmud" speaks, we replicate both the main lines of chronology and the literary character of the document. These point toward the formation of the bulk of materials – its units of discourse – in a process lasting (to take a guess) about half a century, prior to the ultimate arrangement of these units of discourse around passages of the Mishnah and the closure and redaction of the whole into the document we now know. What comes next? Well, now that we know that the Bavli is a document of remarkable integrity, repeatedly insisting upon the harmony of the parts within a whole and unitary structure of belief and behavior, we want to know what the Bavli says: the one thing that is repeated in regard to many things. Dismantling ("deconstructing") its components and identifying them, perhaps even describing the kinds of compilations that the authors of those components can have had in mind in writing their compositions – these activities of literary criticism yield no insight into the religious system that guided the document's framers. But the Talmud of Babylonia recapitulates, in grand and acute detail, a religious system, and the generative problematic of that writing directs our attention not to the aesthetics of writing as literature, but to the religion of writing as a document of faith in the formation of the social order. So we have now to turn to the message of the method of the Bavli: what the Bavli's one voice always wishes to convey. The formidable task of finally providing reliable charts for "the sea of the Talmud" is now well under way. We stand where Prince Henry did when he rounded the coast of Africa. But Good Hope is, as yet, far beyond our most distant horizon.

Part Three
THE ONGOING DEBATE

14

Mr. Sanders's Pharisees –
and Mine

Despite the risible misnomer of his book of miscellaneous essays, claiming to speak of "Jewish law to the Mishnah" while discussing mere anecdotes and episodes in Jewish law in the first century with special reference to the Gospels, Professor Edward P. Sanders's current account of his views should not be dismissed as the merely random thoughts of one who wanders aimlessly beyond the fence of his field of first-hand knowledge. Holding Sanders to his claim that he knows something about what he calls "Jewish law," let us take seriously his conception of the Pharisees of the first century. Since, intending to persuade colleagues that his picture of, and apologia for, the Pharisees, not mine, accurately portray how things really were in the first century, Sanders devotes two of his five chapters to that subject,[1] we turn forthwith to the contrasting results contained in his current book.

I. What I Maintain We Know about the Pharisees and How in My View We Know It

Since the announced purpose of the pertinent chapters is to criticize my position and set forth a different one, to begin with let me rapidly summarize my views.[2] Viewed as a historical problem, identifying the

---

[1] I ignore Sanders's uninformed discussion of my *Judaism: The Evidence of the Mishnah*. This "critique" hardly commands attention, either among New Testament scholars, who have no pressing reason to want to know about that document and its place in Judaism, or among Mishnah scholars, to whose field Sanders has yet to make a serious and original contribution.

[2] My principal results are in two major works, first, *The Rabbinic Traditions about the Pharisees before 70*. Leiden, 1971: Brill. I-III. I. *The Rabbinic Traditions about the Pharisees before 70. The Masters*. II. *The Rabbinic Traditions about the Pharisees before 70. The Houses*. III. *The Rabbinic Traditions about the Pharisees before 70. Conclusions*.

Pharisees begins with attention to the sources that refer to them. No historical knowledge reaches us out of an a priori corpus of principles, and what we cannot show, we simply do not know. A principal problem in arguing with Sanders is his rich capacity to make up distinctions and definitions as he goes along,[3] then to impose these distinctions and definitions upon sources that, on the face of it, scarcely sustain them. Sanders proceeds to form out of a priori distinctions and definitions a deductive argument, which makes it exceedingly difficult to compose an argument with him. For how are those of us who appeal to evidence and the results of the analysis of evidence to compose an argument against fabricated definitions and distinctions, which to begin with derive not from evidence and analysis thereof? The fundamental difficulty in dealing with Sanders, therefore, begins with the basic problem of reading scholarship that is accessible only within its own framework of premises and even language.[4] Looking at the evidence in its own terms, by

---

And second, *Eliezer ben Hyrcanus. The Tradition and the Man.* Leiden, 1973: Brill: I. *Eliezer ben Hyrcanus. The Tradition and the Man. The Tradition.* II. *Eliezer ben Hyrcanus. The Tradition and the Man. The Man.* I am not sure that Sanders has fully grasped the methodological issues that I have worked out in doing my analysis in this way, rather than in some other. I have given reprises of some of these results in the following: *Oral Tradition in Judaism: The Case of the Mishnah.* New York, 1987: Garland Publishing Co. *Albert Bates Lord Monograph Series* of the journal, *Oral Tradition; Das pharisäische und talmudische Judentum.* Tuebingen, 1984: J.C.B. Mohr (Paul Siebeck). Edited by Hermann Lichtenberger. Foreword by Martin Hengel, and *The Pharisees. Rabbinic Perspectives.* New York, 1985: Ktav Publishing House. On problems of method – how we claim to know what we know, on the basis of sources that exhibit the traits of those on which we work – my summary of matters is in *Reading and Believing: Ancient Judaism and Contemporary Gullibility.* Atlanta, 1986: Scholars Press for Brown Judaic Studies.

[3]One example: "Shall we call these 'oral law'? That is just the question. To get at it, I wish to make further distinctions: [1] between conscious and unconscious interpretation of the written law; [2] between interpretation and consciously formulated supplements, alterations or additions, which are known not to be in the law at all. These distinctions are easier to state than to demonstrate, since exegesis can be fanciful and produce results which are now thought to be remote from the text, and since we have no direct access to what was 'conscious' and 'unconscious.' Nevertheless, if we bear these distinctions in mind and consider some examples, we shall improve our understanding of the problem" (*Jewish Law*, pp. 102-103). The most powerful arguments against Sanders's distinctions are stated in his presentation of them: there is no evidence; we also do not know what was "conscious" and what was "unconscious." But these powerful considerations do not impede Sanders's progress. He simply dismisses them and moves ahead. That seems to me a fine instance of how he just make things up as he goes along.

[4]As a matter of fact, Sanders's prose is so turgid and obscure, not to say deliberately obfuscatory, that reading him produces few of the ordinary

contrast, requires us to classify our documents and analyze them, only afterward turning to the issues of special concern to us.

The Pharisees formed a social entity, of indeterminate classification (sect? church? political party? philosophical order? cult?), in the Jewish nation in the Land of Israel in the century or so before A.D. 70. They are of special interest for two reasons. First, they are mentioned in the synoptic Gospels as contemporaries of Jesus, represented sometimes as hostile, sometimes as neutral, and sometimes as friendly to the early Christians represented by Jesus. Second, they are commonly supposed to stand behind the authorities who, in the second century, made up the materials that come to us in the Mishnah, the first important document, after Scripture, of Judaism in its classical or normative form. Hence the Mishnah and some related writings are alleged to rest upon traditions going back to the Pharisees before A.D. 70. These views impute to the Pharisees greater importance than, in their own day, they are likely to have enjoyed. My description of the Pharisees, in order of closure: (1) the Gospels, (2) the writings of Josephus, and (3) the later rabbinic compositions, beginning with the Mishnah, hence, in time of closure, ca. A.D. 70-90, ca. A.D. 90-100, and ca. A.D. 200-600, respectively. No writings survive that were produced by them; all we do know is what later writers said about them.

The three separate bodies of information – the historical narratives of Josephus, a Jewish historian who, between 75 and ca. 100 A.D., wrote the history of the Jews from the beginnings to the destruction of Jerusalem; biographical traditions about, and sayings attributed to, Jesus; and the laws and sayings attributed to pre-70 Pharisees by their successors and heirs, the rabbis of late first and second century Palestine – are quite different in character. The first is a systematic, coherent historical narrative. The second is a well-edited collection of stories and sayings. The third consists chiefly of laws, arranged by legal categories in codes and commentaries on those codes. Moreover, the purposes of the authors or compilers of the respective collections differ from one another. Josephus was engaged in explaining to the Jewish world of his day that Rome was not at fault for the destruction of the Temple, and in telling the Roman world that the Jewish people had been misled, and therefore not to be held responsible for the terrible war. The interest of the Gospels is not in the history of the Jewish people, but in the life and teachings of

---

pleasures of scholarship. Not only so, but his years in Oxford have left him isolated from the mainstream of learning, with the result that a certain self-indulgence, even solipsism, has taken over in his prose. Following Sanders's arguments requires us to examine evidence, the relevance of which to begin with is never entirely clear. A stream of consciousness seems to provide the momentum for much of his learning.

Jesus, to which that history applies. The rabbinical legislators show no keen interest in narrative, biographical, or historical problems, but take as their task the promulgation of laws for the government and administration of the Jewish community.

The several sources concerning pre-70 Pharisaic Judaism were generally shaped in the aftermath of the crisis of 70 A.D. With the Temple in ruins it was important to preserve and, especially, to interpret, the record of what had gone before. Josephus tells the story of the people and the great war. The Gospels record the climactic moment in Israel's supernatural life. The rabbis describe the party to which they traced their origin, and through which they claimed to reach back to the authority of Moses at Sinai. The issue in all three cases was: What is the meaning of the decisive history just passed? To Josephus the answer is that Israel's welfare depends upon obedience to the laws of the Torah as expounded by the Pharisees and upon peaceful relationships with Rome. The Gospels claim that, with the coming of the Messiah, the Temple had ceased to enjoy its former importance, and those who had had charge of Israel's life – chief among them the priests, scribes, and Pharisees – were shown through their disbelief to have ignored the hour of their salvation. Their unbelief is explained in part by the Pharisees' hypocrisy and self-seeking. The rabbis contend that the continuity of the Mosaic Torah is unbroken. Destruction of the Temple, while lamentable, does not mean Israel has lost all means of service to the Creator. The way of the Pharisees leads, without break, back to Sinai and forward to the rabbinical circle reforming at Yavneh. The Oral Torah revealed by Moses and handed on from prophet to scribe, sage, and rabbi remains in the hands of Israel. The legal record of pre-70 Pharisaism requires careful preservation because it remains wholly in effect.

The theological side to Pharisaic Judaism before A.D. 70, however, is not easily accessible, for the pre-70 beliefs, ideas, and values have been taken over and revised by the rabbinical masters after that time. We therefore cannot reliably claim that an idea first known to us in a later rabbinical document, from the third century and afterward, was originally both known and understood in the same way. For pre-70 Pharisaic Judaism, our sources of information tell little of theological interest. A number of books in the Apocrypha and Pseudepigrapha of the Old Testament are attributed to Pharisaic writers, but none of these documents positively identifies its author as a Pharisee. Secure attribution of a work can only be made when an absolutely peculiar characteristic of the possible author can be shown to be an essential element in the structure of the whole work. No reliance can be placed on elements which appear in only one or another episode, or which appear in several episodes but are secondary and detachable details. These may be accretions. Above all, motifs which are not certainly peculiar to one sect cannot prove that sect was the source. No available assignment of an apocryphal or pseudepigraphical book to a Pharisaic author can pass these tests. Most such attributions were made by scholars who thought that all pre-70 Palestinian Jews were either Sadducees, Pharisees, Essenes, members of the "Fourth Philosophy," or Zealots, and therefore felt obliged to attribute all supposedly pre-70 Palestinian Jewish works to one of these groups. That supposition is untenable. That is why, in my account of the Pharisees, I omit all reference to apocryphal and pseudepigraphical

The rabbinic traditions about the Pharisees before 70 are those pericopae in the Mishnah (ca. A.D. 200) and Tosefta (ca. A.D. 300), often subject to exegesis in later rabbinic writings, in which we find names of either pre-70 masters or the Houses of Shammai and Hillel. Pre-70 masters are the men named in the chains of authorities down to and including Simeon b. Gamaliel and masters referred to in pericopae of those same authorities. The reason these pericopae are held to refer to Pharisees and their authorities is that Gamaliel and Simeon b. Gamaliel are identified by Acts and Josephus, respectively, as Pharisees. They occur, in Mishnah-tractate Abot and other lists of authorities, and it is therefore generally assumed that all others on these same lists or chains of authorities also were Pharisees. Traditions of others who were evidently presumed by the tannaitic tradents both to have lived before 70 and to have been Pharisees do not add up to much; the traditions are mostly concerned with the masters named in the Pharisaic chains. Few others are known. Authorities who began teaching before 70 but whose traditions derive chiefly from Yavneh, rather than pre-70 Jerusalem, are excluded. These figures in any event do not occur on the lists or chains of authorities, beginning at Sinai and ending with Gamaliel I and his son Simeon.

The rabbinic traditions about the Pharisees before 70 A.D. consist of approximately 371 separate items in the Mishnah – stories or sayings or allusions – which are spread over approximately 655 different pericopae. Of these traditions, 75 percent – 280, in 456 pericopae – pertain to Menahem, Shammai, Hillel, and the Houses of Hillel and Shammai. A roughly even division of the materials would give twenty-three traditions in forty pericopae to each name or category, so the disparity is enormous. Exact figures cannot be given, for much depends upon how one counts the components of composite pericopae or reckons with other imponderables. As to subject matter covered by the rabbinic traditions that allude to persons or groups we assume to have been Pharisees, approximately 67 percent of all legal pericopae deal with dietary laws. These laws concern [1] ritual purity for meals and [2] agricultural rules governing the fitness of food for Pharisaic consumption. Observance of Sabbaths and festivals is a distant third. The named masters normally have legal traditions of the same sort; only Gamaliel greatly diverges from the pattern, Simeon b. Shetah somewhat less so. Of the latter we can say nothing. The wider range of legal topics covered by Gamaliel's legal lemmas and stories goes to confirm the tradition that he had an important position in the civil government.

The rabbinic traditions about the Pharisees as a whole may be characterized as self-centered, the internal records of a party concerning its own life, its own laws, and its own partisan conflicts. The omission of records of what happened outside of the party is not only puzzling, but nearly inexplicable. Almost nothing in Josephus's picture of the Pharisees seems closely related to much, if anything, in the rabbis' portrait of the Pharisees, except the rather general allegation that the Pharisees had "traditions from the fathers," a point made also by the synoptic storytellers. The rabbis' Pharisaic conflict stories, moreover, do not tell of Pharisees' opposing Essenes, Christians, or Sadducees, but of Hillelites' opposing Shammaites. Pharisaic laws deal not with the governance of the country but with the party's rules for table fellowship. The political issues are not whether one should pay taxes to Rome or how one should know the Messiah, but whether in the Temple the rule of Shammai or that of Hillel should be followed in a minor festal sacrifice. From the rabbinic traditions about the Pharisees we cannot reconstruct a single significant public event of the period before 70 – not the rise, success, and fall of the Hasmoneans, nor the Roman conquest of Palestine, nor the rule of Herod, nor the reign of the procurators, nor the growth of opposition to Rome, nor the proliferation of social violence and unrest in the last decades before 66 A.D., nor the outbreak of the war with Rome. We do not gain a picture of the Pharisees' philosophy of history or theology or politics. We should not even know how Palestine was governed, for the Pharisees' traditions according to the rabbis do not refer to how the Pharisees governed the country. The rabbis never claim the Pharisees did run pre-70 Palestine, at least not in stories told either about named masters or about the Houses, nor do they tell us how the Romans ran it. Furthermore, sectarian issues are barely mentioned, and other sects not at all. The rabbis' Pharisees are mostly figures of the late Herodian and Roman periods. In the rabbinic traditions, they were a nonpolitical group, whose chief religious concerns were for the proper preservation of ritual purity in connection with eating secular (not Temple) food, and for the observance of the dietary laws of the day, especially those pertaining to the proper nurture and harvest of agricultural crops. Their secondary religious concern was with the proper governance of the party itself.

When we compare the rabbinic traditions about the Pharisees, upon which I have concentrated, with Josephus's and the Gospels' traditions, we find the sources not entirely symmetrical. Josephus's Pharisaic records pertain mostly to the years from the rise of the Hasmoneans to their fall. They were a political party which tried to get control of the government of Jewish Palestine, not a little sect drawn apart from the common society by observance of laws of table fellowship. Josephus's Pharisees are important in the reigns of John Hyrcanus and Alexander Jannaeus, but drop from the picture after Alexandra Salome. But the synoptics' Pharisees appropriately are much like those of the rabbis; they belong to the Roman period, and their legal agendae are virtually identical: tithing, purity laws, Sabbath observance, vows, and the like.

The rabbinic tradition thus begins where Josephus's narrative leaves off, and the difference between them leads us to suspect that the change in the character of Pharisaism from a political party to a sect comes with Hillel. If Hillel was responsible for directing the party out of its political concerns and into more passive, quietistic paths, then we should understand why his figure dominates the subsequent rabbinic tradition. If Hillel was a contemporary of Herod, then we may commend his wisdom, for had the Pharisees persisted as a political force, they would have come into conflict with Alexander Jannaeus. The extreme rarity of materials of masters before Simeon b. Shetah, except those of Yohanan the High Priest (John Hyrcanus), suggests that few survived Jannaeus's massacres, and that those few did not perpetuate the policies, nor, therefore, the decisions of their predecessors. Hillel and his follows chose to remember Simeon b. Shetah, who was on good terms with Salome, but not his followers, who were almost certainly on bad terms with Aristobulus and his descendants, the leaders of the national resistance to Rome and to Antipater's family (see Josephus's story of Aristobulus's protection of the Pharisees' victims). As Herod's characteristics became clear, therefore, the Pharisees must have found themselves out of sympathy alike with the government and the opposition. And at this moment Hillel arose to change what had been a political party into a table fellowship sect, not unlike other, publicly harmless and politically neutral groups, whatever their private eschatological aspirations. All this is more than mere conjecture, but less than established fact. What is fact is that the vast majority of rabbinic traditions about the Pharisees relate to the circle of Hillel and certainly the best attested and most reliable corpus, the opinions of the Houses, reaches us from that circle's later adherents. The pre-Hillel Pharisees are not known to us primarily from the rabbinic traditions, and, when we begin to have a substantial rabbinic record, it is the record of a group very different from Josephus's pre-Hillelite, pre-Herodian party.

Clear-cut and well-defined forms were used for the transmission of some of the rabbinic traditions about the Pharisees. This does not prove that these materials originally were orally formulated and orally transmitted. Part of the corpus seems to me to have been ritually shaped according to the myth of how Moses orally dictated, and Aaron memorized, lemmas, namely, those in the Aqiban Mishnah. But the allegation that the present rabbinic material about the pre-70 Pharisees consists of the written texts of traditions, originally orally formulated and orally transmitted, is groundless. The only allegation we find about pre-70 Pharisees is that they had traditions. Nothing is said about whether these traditions come from Moses, nor about whether they were in oral form. They generally are ascribed to the 'fathers,' and their form is not specified. No mention of an Oral Torah or a Dual Torah occurs in pre-70 pericopae, except for the Hillel-and-the-convert story, certainly not weighty evidence. Moreover the Pharisaic laws contain no instructions on how materials are to be handed on, nor references to how this actually was done. Allegations that Moses dictated an Oral Torah to Aaron in much the same way as rabbis taught Mishnah first occur with Aqiba, who in fact undertook exactly that process in the formulation of his Mishnah. The myth of oral formulation and oral transmission is first attested by Judah b. Ilai, although a dispute between Eliezer and Aqiba presupposes oral formulation and transmission in Yavnean circles. The myth of the Oral Torah is first attested much later in the formation of the rabbinic literature and is never in a document prior to ca. A.D. 200 assigned to a Pharisaic authority (the attribution to Hillel of such a belief appears for the first time in the Talmud of Babylonia, ca. A.D. 600).

If, therefore, we ask, precisely what is known from the Mishnah about pre-70 Pharisaism, the answer is clear. The traditions pertain chiefly to the last half-century or so before the destruction of the Temple – at most, seventy or eighty years. Then the Pharisees were (whatever else they were) primarily a society for table fellowship, the high point of their life as a group. The laws of table fellowship predominate in the Houses disputes, as they ought to – three-fourths of all pericopae – and correspond to the legal agenda of the Pharisees according to the synoptic stories. As we saw, some rather thin and inadequate traditions about masters before Shammai-Hillel persisted, but these do not amount to much and in several cases consist merely of the name of a master, plus whatever opinion is given to him in the chain in which he appears. The interest of the nonlegal materials concentrates on the relationships of Shammai and Hillel, on the career of Hillel, and related matters. Materials on their successors at best are perfunctory, until we come to men who themselves survived to work at Yavneh, such as Hananiah Prefect of the Priests and, of course, Yohanan b. Zakkai. The chief interest of Hillel tradents, apart from the preservation of favorable stories of Hillel and the attribution of wise sayings to him, was Hillel's predominance in Pharisaism.

After the Houses disputes ceased to matter much, by the Bar Kokhba War, the growth of Hillel materials was undiminished. The rise-to-power stories then begin, very likely at Usha, and are rapidly glossed by patriarchal and anti-patriarchal hands, so that by Judah the Patriarch's time everyone knows Hillel is the ancestor of the patriarchate in general, and of Judah in particular. The attribution of a Davidic ancestor to Hillel naturally means that the patriarch Judah also derives from the Messianic seed. The work of Yavneh consisted, therefore, in establishing viable forms for the organization and transmission primarily of the Houses materials. The Ushans continued to make use of these forms, and further produced a coherent account of the history of the Oral Torah from Moses onward. The Yavneans probably showed greater interest in the development of stories about the relationships between the Houses than did later masters, for whom the disputes were less interesting. The Ushans may have augmented the traditions of other early masters, besides Shammai-Hillel, and otherwise broadened the range of interests.

So, in all, we have from the rabbis a very sketchy account of the life of Pharisaism during less than the last century of its existence before 70, with at most random and episodic materials pertaining to the period before Hillel. We have this account, so far as it is early, primarily through the medium of forms and mnemonic patterns used at Yavneh and later on at Usha. What we know is what the rabbis of Yavneh and Usha regarded as the important and desirable account of the Pharisaic traditions: almost entirely the internal record of the life of the party and its laws, the party being no more than the two factions that predominated after 70, the laws being mainly rules of how and what people might eat with one another. The focus of interest of the rabbinic traditions about the Pharisees is the internal affairs of the Pharisaic party itself. The primary partisan issues center upon Shammai's and his House's relationship to Hillel and his House. The competing sects, by contrast, are ignored. Essenes and Christians make no appearance at all. The Sadducees are first mentioned by Yohanan b. Zakkai. The Romans never occur. The Hasmonean monarchy is reduced to a single name, Yannai the King, for Yohanan the High Priest, so far as the rabbinic traditions about the Pharisees are concerned, was a good Pharisee. In all, the traditions give the impression of intense concentration on the inner life of the party, or sect, whose intimate affairs take precedence, in the larger scheme of history, over the affairs of state, cult, and country. The state is a shadowy presence at best. The cult is of secondary importance. The country's life and the struggle with Rome as a whole are bypassed in silence. What we have, therefore, are the records of the party chiefly in regard to the life of the party itself.

There is a striking discontinuity among the three principal sources which speak of the Pharisees before 70, the Gospels, and the rabbinic writings of a later period, on the one side, and Josephus, on the other. What Josephus thinks characteristic of the Pharisees are matters which play little or no role in what Mark and Matthew regard as significant, and what the later rabbis think the Pharisees said scarcely intersects with the topics and themes important to Josephus. In this regard, the picture drawn by Matthew and Mark and that drawn by the later rabbis are essentially congruent, and together differ from the portrait left to us by Josephus. The traits of Pharisaism emphasized by Josephus, their principal beliefs and practices, nowhere occur in the rabbinic traditions of the Pharisees. When we compare what Josephus says about the Pharisees to what the later rabbinic traditions have to say, there is scarcely a point of contact, let alone intersection. Josephus says next to nothing about the predominant issues in the rabbinic traditions about the Pharisees. Shammai and Hillel are not explicitly mentioned, let alone their Houses. Above all, we find not the slightest allusion to laws of ritual purity, agricultural taboos, Sabbath and festivals, and the like, which predominate in the traditions of the Houses. In the detailed account of the reign of Alexander Jannaeus, Simeon b. Shetah does not occur. Apart from the banquet of John Hyrcanus, we could not, relying upon Josephus, recover a single significant detail of the rabbinic traditions about the Pharisees, let alone the main outlines of the whole.

As to the topical program of the Pharisees, Josephus's agenda of Pharisaic doctrine hardly coincides with those of the rabbis. For example, while Josephus seems to paraphrase Aqiba's saying, that all is in the hands of heaven yet man has free choice, that saying is nowhere attributed to pre-70 Pharisees, certainly not to the Pharisees who would have flourished in the period in which Josephus places such beliefs. We find no references to the soul's imperishability, all the more so to the transmigration of souls. The Houses' debate on the intermediate group comes closest to Josephus's report. As to Josephus's allegation that the Pharisees are affectionate to one another, we may observe that is not how the Hillelites report matters. Josephus knows nothing of the Shammaites' slaughter of Hillelites, their mob action against Hillel in the Temple, and other stories that suggest a less than affectionate relationship within the Pharisaic group. So, for Josephus, the three chief issues of sectarian consequence are belief in fate, belief in traditions outside of the Laws of Moses, and influence over political life. The Pharisees believe in fate, have traditions from the fathers, and exercise significant influence in public affairs. The Sadducees do not believe in fate, do not accept other than Mosaic laws, and have no consequence in public life. For the rabbinic traditions about the Pharisees, the three chief issues of sectarian consequence are ritual purity, agricultural taboos, and Sabbath and festival behavior.

The relationship between the rabbinic traditions about the Pharisees and the Gospels' accounts of the Pharisees by contrast strikes me as entirely symmetrical. There is one topic on which these sources are apt to be essentially sound, namely, the themes of the laws they impute to the figures before 70 who we believe were Pharisees. The congruity in the themes of the laws attributed to the Pharisees by both the Gospels and the later rabbinic sources is striking. What it means is that, from speaking of traditions about the Pharisees, we are apt to address the historical Pharisees themselves in the decades before the destruction of the Temple in A.D. 70. The historical Pharisees in the decades before the destruction of Jerusalem are portrayed by legal traditions that seem to me fundamentally sound in topic, perhaps also in detailed substance, and attested by references of masters who may reasonably supposed to have known what they were talking about. Which laws pertained primarily to Pharisaism, and which were part of the law common to all of Palestinian Jewry? Most of the laws before us, verified early or late, affect primarily the sectarian life of the party. The laws that made a sect sectarian were those which either were interpreted and obeyed by the group in a way different from other groups or from common society at large, on the one hand, or were to begin with observed only by the group, on the other. In the latter category are the purity laws, which take so large a place in the Pharisaic corpus. One primary mark of Pharisaic commitment was the observance of the laws of ritual purity outside of the Temple, where everyone kept them. Eating one's secular, that is, unconsecrated, food in a state of ritual purity as if one were a Temple priest in the cult was one of the two significations of party membership. The manifold circumstances of everyday life required the multiplication of concrete rules. Representative of the other category may be the laws of tithing and other agricultural taboos. Here we are less certain. Pharisees clearly regarded keeping the agricultural rules as a primary religious duty. But whether, to what degree, and how other Jews did so is not clear. And the agricultural laws, just like the purity rules, in the end affected table fellowship, namely, what one might eat.

The early Christian traditions on both points represent the Pharisees as reproaching Jesus because his followers did not keep these two kinds of laws at all. That is, why were they not Pharisees? The answer was that the primary concern was for ethics. Both the question and the answer are disingenuous. The questioners are represented as rebuking the Christians for not being Pharisees, which begs the question, for everyone presumably knew Christians were not Pharisees. The answer takes advantage of the polemical opening: Pharisees are not concerned with ethics, a point repeatedly made in the anti-Pharisaic pericopae, depending upon a supposed conflict between rules of table fellowship, on the one side, and ethical behavior on the other. The obvious underlying claim is that Christian table fellowship does not depend upon the sorts of rules important in the table fellowship of other groups. As to the Sabbath laws, the issue was narrower. All Jews kept the Sabbath. It was part of the culture of their country. The same applies to the festivals. Here the Pharisaic materials are not so broad in interest as with regard to agricultural rules and ritual purity. They pertain primarily to gentiles' working on the Sabbath for Jews, on the one hand, and to the preparation of the 'erub, on the other. Like the levirate rule, the 'erub laws must be regarded as solely of sectarian interest. The references to the unobservant Sadducee make this virtually certain. Since the tithes and offerings either went to the Levites and priests or had to be consumed in Jerusalem, and since the purity rules were to begin with Temple matters, we note that the Pharisees claimed laymen are better informed as to purity and Temple laws than the Temple priesthood.

The fact is, therefore, that the laws we have are the laws we should have: the rules of a sect concerning its own sectarian affairs, matters of importance primarily to its own members. That seems to me further evidence of the essential accuracy of the representation of the Houses in the rabbinic traditions. To be sure, not all laws before us portray with equal authenticity the life of pre-70 Pharisaism. But the themes of the laws, perhaps also their substance in detail, are precisely what they ought to have been according to our theory of sectarianism. When we review the substance of the laws, we find they pertain either immediately or ultimately to table fellowship, involve preparation of food, ritual purity, either purity rules directly relating to food, or purity rules indirectly important on account of the need to keep food ritually clean, and agricultural rules pertaining to the proper growing, tithing, and preparation of agricultural produce for table use. All agricultural laws concern producing or preparing food for consumption, assuring either that tithes and offerings have been set aside as the Law requires or that the conditions for the nurture of the crops have conformed to the biblical taboos. Ritual slaughter, appropriately, occurs in only one minor matter, likewise the taboo against milk with meat is applied to chicken and cheese. The laws of ritual cleanness apply in the main to the preservation of the ritual cleanness of food, of people involved in preparing it, and of objects used in its preparation. Secondary considerations include the ritual pool. These matters became practically important in the lives of Pharisees in regard to the daily preparation of food, in the lives of all

Jews only in connection with visiting the Temple, and of the priests in the cult itself. Laws regarding Sabbath and festivals furthermore pertain in large measure to the preparation and preservation of food on festivals and the Sabbath. The ritual of table fellowship also included blessings and rules of conduct at meals.

If the Pharisees were, as has often been taken for granted, primarily a group for Torah study (as the Qumranian writers describe themselves) then we should have looked for more rules about the school, perhaps also scribal matters, than we actually find. Indeed, we have only one, and that, while attested at early Yavneh, merely involves sneezing in the schoolhouse. Surely other, more fundamental problems presented themselves. Nor do we find much interest in defining the master-disciple relationship, the duties of the master and the responsibilities and rights of the disciple, the way in which the disciple should learn his lessons, and similar matters of importance in later times. That is not to suggest that the historical Pharisees were only or principally a table fellowship commune. It is only to say that, whatever else they were, they surely identified themselves as Pharisees by the dietary rules, involving cultic cleanness, and certain other sectarian practices as to marital relationships, that they observed. More than this we do not know on the basis of the rabbinic evidence, as correlated with the Gospels' accounts. Josephus's picture of the group is asymmetrical to this picture, and a simple hypothesis is to assign his account to the period of which he speaks when he mentions the Pharisees as a political party, which is the second and first centuries B.C., and the rabbis' and Gospels' account to the period of which they speak, which is the first century A.D. But the matter remains open for continued inquiry, and no picture of the Pharisees has gained complete acceptance in twentieth-century scholarship. That is my picture of the matter.[5]

Now to Sanders's critique and his concomitant reconstruction of the matter. He deals with two consequential matters, first, "Did the Pharisees have oral law?" and second, "Did the Pharisees eat ordinary food in purity?" To these questions I state my answer up front. So far as Sanders claims to argue with me in particular, I have not called into question the proposition that, in addition to Scriptures, Pharisees, like pretty much every other group, had some further law or tradition, and that that additional material can have been formulated and transmitted orally, in memory. But, as a matter of fact, no evidence pertaining in

---

[5]Most recently I have summarized my views as set forth in my *Theologische Real Encyclopädie* (forthcoming). In that restatement, I have taken account of important criticism of some of my earlier ideas and removed from the picture elements that no longer seem to me to be viable.

particular to the Pharisees permits us to impute to them the fully exposed myth of the Dual Torah, part in writing, part oral, that comes to complete expression only in the later documents of the Judaism of the Dual Torah, in particular, in the Talmud of Babylonia. As to whether Pharisees ate ordinary food in a state of cultic cleanness, I of course do not know what they actually did. I claim to know only how the earlier strata of the Mishnah's law represents matters in sayings attributed to authorities before 70. And the answer is, the earlier strata of the law take for granted that the laws of cultic cleanness, applicable to priests' eating their Temple food, are assumed to apply outside of the Temple, and also to persons who were not members of the priestly caste.

II. Did the Pharisees Have Oral Law?

While announcing that he agrees with me, Sanders claims to find confusing my treatments of this matter. But the source of his confusion is that he imputes to me that same confusion between history and theology that characterizes his work. I am consistently explicit on that distinction, for example, *"viewed from the perspective of Judaic faith,* the teachings of the named sages of late antiquity...preserve principles...handed on by tradition from Sinai."[6] I am equally clear that, *described historically,* the conception that "Moses received the Torah at Sinai in two media" emerges at a given point, fairly late in the formative history of the Judaism of the Dual Torah. Obviously, a critical historical account presents information of one kind, a theological statement, information of another.[7] Sanders states: "He continues to publish things whose [sic!] fundamentalism would embarrass the most conservative talmudists."[8]

What Sanders means by "fundamentalism" is not clear to me, since, in Judaism, we have no "fundamentalism" in the Protestant sense. I have never misrepresented myself. I am a believing and practicing Jew,

---

[6]Sanders, p. 111.

[7]Sanders's representation of the matter becomes not merely contemptible but libellous when he says, "It is possible that one of these completely contradictory stances is Neusner's real position, and that the other is adopted simply for tactical purposes, perhaps to sell books to a different audience." I would not have thought that a scholarly debate would sink to such a level, but, as I said above, perhaps the ambience at Oxford has made its impact, so that Sanders has lost such capacity as he once might have had to conduct civil discourse. I am amazed that a publisher of the repute of Trinity Press International and SCM Press would include such libelous statements in a book under their imprint. But suing for libel would be no fun; and anyhow, my books sell too well for me to require subterfuge; perhaps Sanders means to impute to me motives that in his mind would lead him to do what he says I have done?

[8]*Jewish Law*, p. 244.

without apology. I affirm with all my heart that God revealed the one whole Torah, oral and written, to Moses, our rabbi, on Mount Sinai. I have produced historical results that impart to that statement of faith and theology a set of meanings that are not historical at all. This I have shown in many passages (which as a Christian Sanders evidently finds offensive) of my writing, but especially in *Uniting the Dual Torah: Sifra and the Problem of the Mishnah.*[9] The closing lines of that book form a statement of what we can mean by "Moses received Torah at Sinai," when that is taken to refer to not historical but other matters altogether, matters of eternity, sanctification, and salvation, for example. I have not confused history with theology, nor have I followed the model of those biblical theologians whose historical work leads them to modify theological truth in light of facts of a different order altogether. In my view history contains no truth for theological consideration. A deeper understanding of Judaism as a living religion would have helped Sanders avoid the dreadful confusion that characterizes these remarks, which impede his appreciation of Judaism then as much as now.

In point of fact, however, Sanders concurs with everything that I have maintained on this topic. Explicitly concurring with my results, Sanders proceeds to give a survey of matters on Oral Torah that he finds in various rabbinic documents. Some of these passages attribute views to pre-70 authorities we assume were Pharisees; most do not, and therefore his account draws upon evidence not pertinent to the Pharisees in particular. Since Sanders himself admits that "we have come to a view proposed by Neusner on the basis of a partially different body of evidence," it hardly seems interesting to spell out all of the mistakes Sanders makes in selecting and interpreting the evidence he deems pertinent, nor is time devoted to pointing out the confusion of distinct bodies of evidence well spent.[10] In this chapter Sanders affirms precisely the results that I have set forth, and I congratulate him.

III. Did the Pharisees Eat Ordinary Food in Purity?

Here again, Sanders's conclusion is "Neusner's standards for collective evidence mark a distinct advance." He concurs with much that I say, tinkering with nuance and emphasis, rather than with fact and substance.[11] But there can be an argument, since he also maintains, "He

---

[9]Cambridge and New York, 1990: Cambridge University Press.

[10]Sanders discusses so many groups that quite how evidence drawn from any one of them pertains to the principal group under discussion is not at all clear.

[11]Perhaps this fundamental agreement with my methods and results accounts for the captious and often deliberately insulting character of his treatment of not only my work but also my person. I cannot, for example, find in any of his writings a

misinterpreted his own material. Use of his analytical work leads to other conclusions about the Pharisees than the ones which he drew."[12] On method Sanders and I differ in one fundamental way. He takes as generally reliable attributions of sayings to named authorities. Since in

single point, beginning to end, at which he refers to me as a professor or by any other honorific title, only "Neusner." This is not merely a matter of form. Sanders takes up two conflicting positions – [1] respect for my methods and replication, with his own emphases, of most of my results, and [2] deep disrespect for me as a person and a scholar. These lead him to characterize in a thoroughly dishonest manner the reception of my books, for example, in published book reviews. He says, "He has also produced a vast number of translations, to which there are only a few critical responses." Here he footnotes *one* book review alone, Saul Lieberman's in *Journal of the American Oriental Society* 1984, 104:315-319. There were other negative reviews, and also a great many more positive reviews, to which a footnote meant to be fair also would have alluded. Not that I have found much to learn, other than corrections of minor details, in even the most offensive reviews; my impression is that Sanders approves the intention of Lieberman and Zeitlin, among others, which always was merely to discredit, rather than to argue; but for his part, to his credit, he does argue. I take pride in the literature of discrediting that has been devoted to me; it has shown me the worst criticism a critic can fabricate, and that has proven lightweight and unpersuasive. Sanders, to his credit, has not gone along with the campaign of sustained *Todschweigen* – murder by silence, meaning, not reviewing, not citing, not arguing with my work, – that Israeli and Yeshiva scholarship (including university-based yeshivas) has practiced against me for thirty years. Indeed, lest anyone imagine that I would suppress the writings of these critics, I have included an entire volume of negative reviews of books of mine, by not only Lieberman, but also Zeitlin, S. J. D. Cohen, H. Maccoby, and others, in my edition of reprinted articles, *The Origins of Judaism. Religion, History, and Literature in Late Antiquity*. With William Scott Green. New York, 1991: Garland Press. Twenty volumes of reprinted scholarly essays, with introductions. He further states, "There are comments to be made at each point of his publishing enterprise." Here his footnote is as follows: "On Neusner's undergraduate textbooks, see my review of *Judaism in the Beginning of Christianity*, *Theology* 88, 1985, pp. 392ff." (He said the same thing about the same book in the same review in *Journal of Religion*.) A fair representation of positive reviews of my textbooks would have required pages of citations. The point is that he seems to find himself forced over and over again to affirm my methods and my results, revising only details, mainly of emphasis or evaluation, but that fact does not persuade him to treat with even minimal courtesy and respect someone from whom, by his own word, he has learned so much. I regret that it is necessary to call attention to this disagreeable fact about Sanders, but any reader of the book to which I am called upon to respond will have made the same observation, and it should be made explicit – and regretted. He could have disagreed with courtesy and even amiability – and above all, with honesty and objectivity. I do not believe that he has. And I do not think he has gained anything or made his position more plausible by expressing his disagreement, which turns out to be trivial and niggling, in such offensive language.

[12]*Jewish Law*, p. 131.

historical study what we cannot show, we do not know, I am inclined to a more reserved position, asking for evidence that permits us to assign to a period in which a named authority is assumed to have lived a saying attributed to that authority. Beyond that point, the evidence in hand does not permit us to go, since we do not have books written by specific, named authorities, or even collections of sayings formed prior to, and demonstrably utilized by, the compilers and editors of the late, anonymous documents that we do have. Sanders concedes that materials attributed to the Houses in fact were formulated after 70. But that does not prevent him from using those materials he chooses for evidence on the *topics* under discussion.[13] If, however, the attributions are not reliable, then how can we know for sure that people at that time talked about the topics?

Sanders accuses me of not noting "the importance of the distinctions which the Houses made between the priests' food and their own with regard to harvesting, handling, and processing it." The *locus classicus* for those distinctions between food prepared in conditions of cultic cleanness for use in the Temple by the priests, and food prepared in conditions of cultic cleanness for use other than in the Temple by the priests, must be Mishnah-tractate Hagigah 2:5-3:3. Because it is fundamental, let me place it into the hands of the reader, and only then specify why I think it is important.[14]

2:5 A. They wash the hands for eating unconsecrated food, tithe, and heave-offering;

B. and for eating food in the status of Holy Things they immerse;

C. and as to [the preparation of] purification water through the burning of the red cow, if one's hands are made unclean, his entire body is deemed to be unclean as well.

2:6 A. He who immerses for the eating of unconsecrated food and is thereby confirmed as suitable for eating unconsecrated food is prohibited from eating tithe.

B. [If] he immersed for eating tithe and is thereby confirmed as suitable for eating tithe, he is prohibited from eating heave-offering.

C. [If] he immersed for eating heave-offering and is thereby confirmed as suitable for eating heave-offering, he is prohibited from eating food in the status of Holy Things.

---

[13]*Jewish Law*, p. 171.

[14]But there are equally probative examples to be adduced, for instance, from Mishnah-tractate Tohorot Chapter Two, which, like the passage at hand, place within a single continuum, so far as cultic cleanness of food in the Temple and not in the Temple is concerned, priests and nonpriests. That passage does not make explicit reference to the Pharisees, which is why I have given the present one as my single example, among countless candidates.

D.   [If] he immersed for eating food in the status of Holy Things and is thereby confirmed as suitable for eating food in the status of Holy Things, he is prohibited from engaging in the preparation of purification water.

E.   [If, however], one immersed for the matter requiring the more stringent rule, he is permitted to engage in the matter requiring the less stringent rule.

F.   [If he immersed but was not confirmed, it is as though he did not immerse.

2:7 A.   The clothing of ordinary folk is in the status of midras uncleanness for abstainers [=Perushim, Pharisees].

B.   The clothing of abstainers is in the status of midras uncleanness for those who eat heave-offering [priests].

C.   The clothing of those who eat heave-offering is in the status of midras uncleanness for those who eat Holy Things [officiating priests].

D.   The clothing of those who eat Holy Things is in the status of midras uncleanness for those engaged in the preparation of purification water.

E.   Yosef b. Yoezer was the most pious man in the priesthood, but his handkerchief was in the status of midras uncleanness so far as eating Holy Things was concerned.

F.   For his whole life Yohanan b. Gudegedah ate his food in accord with the requirements of cleanness applying to Holy Things, but his handkerchief was in the status of midras uncleanness so far as those engaged in the preparation of purification water were concerned.

3:1 A.   A more stringent rule applies to Holy Things than applies to heave-offering,

I.   B.   for: They immerse utensils inside of other utensils for purification for use with [food in the status of] heave-offering,

C.   but not for purification for use with [food in the status of] Holy Things.

II. D.   [They make a distinction among] outer parts, inside, and holding place in the case of use for heave-offering,

E.   but not in the case of use for Holy Things.

III. F.   He who carries something affected by midras uncleanness [may also] carry heave-offering,

G.   but [he may] not [also carry food in the status of] Holy Things.

IV. H.   The clothing of those who are so clean as to be able to eat heave-offering

I.   is deemed unclean in the status of midras uncleanness for the purposes of Holy Things.

J.   The rule for Holy Things is not like the rule for heave-offering.

V.   K.   For in the case of [immersion for use of] Holy Things one unties a knot and dries it off, immerses and afterwards ties it up again.

L.   And in the case of heave-offering one ties it and then one immerses.

3:2
VI. A   Utensils which are completely processed in a state of insusceptibility to uncleanness [and so when completed are clean] require immersion for use in connection with Holy Things,

B.   but not for use in connection with heave-offering.

VII. C   A utensil unites everything contained therein for the purposes of Holy Things,

D.   but not for the purposes of heave-offering.

VIII.   E   [That which is made unclean in] the fourth remove from the original source of uncleanness in the case of Holy Things is invalid,

F.   but only [that which is made unclean in] the third remove in the case of heave-offering.

IX. G   And in the case of heave-offering, if one of one's hands is made unclean, the other is clean.

H.   But in the case of Holy Things one has to immerse both of them.

X. I   For one hand imparts uncleanness to the other for the purposes of Holy Things,

J.   but not for the purposes of heave-offering.

3:3
XI. A   With unclean hands they eat food which has not been wet down in the case of heave-offering,

B.   but not in the case of Holy Things.

XII. C   He who [prior to interment of the deceased] mourns his next of kin [without having contracted corpse uncleanness] and one whose atonement rite is not complete [because an offering is yet required] require immersion for the purposes of Holy Things,

D.   but not for the purposes of heave-offering.

The passage distinguishes between the cleanness required for eating unconsecrated food, food that has been designated as tithe or priestly rations ("heave-offering"), and food that is in the status of Holy Things. "Holy Things" are the share of the officiating (or other) priests in what has been offered on the altar, for example, the priests' share of the sin-offering. Priestly rations comprise the share of a crop that the farmer designates for transfer to the priesthood. Scripture certainly takes for granted that Holy Things will be eaten in the Temple, therefore in a state of cultic cleanness, and priestly rations are supposed likewise to be eaten in a condition of cultic cleanness; since the family of the priest likewise eats priestly rations, it is assumed that women and children not located in the Temple at the time of their meal likewise will be concerned about cultic cleanness when it comes to eating this food as well. The nub of the matter is the classification of food called "unconsecrated." Unconsecrated food is food that has no relationship to the cult or the Temple. If one eats it with considerations of cultic cleanness in mind at all, then, there can be only one reason, and that is, that someone proposes to eat unconsecrated food in a state of cultic cleanness. That seems to me the simple fact of the matter, and Sanders's ingenious distinctions and definitions notwithstanding, that remains the plain sense of the numerous passages that distinguish among unconsecrated food, priestly rations, and Holy Things.

We see that there are diverse standards of cultic cleanness that pertain to food that is unconsecrated, priestly ration, and Holy Things, and these standards are of course hierarchical,[15] with the most stringent rules (the details of which we may bypass) required for Holy Things, less stringent ones for priestly rations, and least stringent for unconsecrated food. Now to my way of thinking, when at M. Hagigah 2:7A-C we are told that the clothing of ordinary folk is in the status of midras uncleanness for Pharisees, and that of Pharisees in the same state for those who eat heave-offering, in the present context it seems to me that a single conclusion must be drawn. Pharisees, 2:7A, are concerned with cultic cleanness; they are not the same as priests, who are dealt with at 2:7B, but are of a lesser standing in the hierarchy of cultic cleanness. Then priests eating priestly rations or heave-offering are hierarchically situated as well, now at a lesser status than priests who are going to eat Holy Things deriving from the altar. The context throughout is preparation for eating food, as the language that is used demonstrates. The explicit reference to Pharisees certainly yields the thesis that Pharisees are not classified as priests, that is, as persons who eat priestly rations or heave-offering. But they are persons who are placed within the hierarchy of cultic cleanness in eating food. The food that they eat is not food that is reserved for priests, so it can only be food that is not reserved for priests, which is to say, secular or unconsecrated food. That passage on the face of it therefore sustains the view that Pharisees are persons who eat unconsecrated food in a state of cultic cleanness, or, more accurately, within the hierarchy of states of cultic cleanness that the Mishnah's paragraph's framer proposes to spell out.

Now let us turn directly to Sanders's own thesis.[16] It is best to turn directly to the passage I have cited, since where and how Sanders's

---

[15]The hierarchical classification of all things defines the Mishnah's authorships' principal concern, as I have shown in my *Judaism as Philosophy. The Method and Message of the Mishnah*. Columbia, 1991: University of South Carolina Press.

[16]I cannot imagine that anyone is interested in my point-by-point refutation of either Sanders's critique of my work or Sanders's interpretation – or rather, systematic misinterpretation – of a vast number of passages. He constantly alludes to passages that he does not present and analyze, and he imputes to said passages positions and opinions that are not obvious to others who have read the same passages; we are left only with his claims. His catalogue of "rather a lot of things wrong with Neusner's work" (p. 183) serves to state merely that he disagrees with me about this and that, which I may stipulate as fact.

Pharisees differ from mine is best discerned on the common ground of shared evidence. He states the following:

> Hagigah 2.7 fits Pharisees into a hierarchy...it indicates that Pharisees were more scrupulous with regard to one (minor) form of impurity than were other laypeople.[17]

> How important were these rules to the Pharisees? Purity was certainly important to them, and protecting the priesthood and the temple from impurity was a very substantial concern. The purity of their own food seems to have been of less importance....[18]

> ...since Pharisees did not observe the purity laws of the priesthood with regard to their own food, why did they have so many rules about corpse impurity and midras impurity? I propose, To make minor gestures towards extra purity. I call them minor gestures in comparison with what they are thought to have done: expelled their wives, done all the domestic work one week in four, and so on. The word 'minor,' however, probably misleads us with regard to their own intention. It sounds as if they made the comparison which I have made, and found their own efforts trivial. This is most unlikely. We cannot assign precise motives, but I think we can safely assign a general one: to be pure, because purity is good.[19]

Apart from the rather subjective judgment at the end, which begs the question, I could not have said it better myself. That is precisely what my reading of this, and various other, passages tells me. When Sanders proceeds to announce that the Pharisees also did other things, for instance, "they worked from dawn to dusk...and they had to study," he cannot imagine anyone is going to be surprised. But he proceeds,

> The legal discussions attributed to Pharisees never take study as their topic, and thus mechanical counting failed to reveal to Neusner that it is a main theme. It is the basis of the entirety of the material, and every discussion rests on it.

Here, alas, Sanders confuses an activity with the mythology attached to the activity. No one doubts people acquired information, that is, studied. What I have called into question is whether Torah study as the principal mode for the imitation of God, which the later rabbinic Torah myth set forth as a critical and central proposition, is attested in the rabbinic traditions about the Pharisees. I did not find it there, and Sanders's reminder that people learned things is, like much else that he says, monumentally irrelevant to the issue. In the successor system, first attested by writings that reached closure long after the first century,

---

[17]*Jewish Law*, pp. 206-207.
[18]Ibid, p. 234.
[19]Ibid, p. 235.

knowledge more than merely informs, it saves. What happens to me in Torah study in the theory of the religious successor system that does not happen to me in Torah study in the theory of the Mishnah – itself no Pharisaic writing – is that I am changed in my very being. This transformation of the one who knows is not alone as to knowledge and understanding (let alone mere information), nor even as to virtue and taxic status, but as to what the knower *is*. The one who knows Torah is changed and saved by Torah knowledge, becomes something different from, better, and more holy than, what he was before he knew, and whether the complement is "the mysteries" or "the Torah [as taught by sages]" makes no material difference.[20] When Sanders tells me that people learned things and so alleges that Torah study was a "main theme" of Pharisaism, he shows that he does not grasp the point of the myth of Torah study within the Judaism of the Dual Torah. Scarcely a single passage that is supposed to pertain to the pre-70 Pharisees imagines such a gnostic Torah. But of this Sanders grasps absolutely nothing.

IV. Sectarianism, Exclusivism, and Sanders's Protestant Theological Apologetic for a Judaism in the Protestant Model

What is at stake? My reading of the evidence leads me to treat the Pharisees as ordinary people eating meals at home in conditions that are analogous to the conditions required of priests in the Temple or in their homes. Sanders treats Pharisees as people who were "more scrupulous with regard to one (minor) form of impurity than were other laypeople." I see here a distinction that yields no difference at all. Anyone who can tell me how this difference – scarcely in degree, but not at all in kind, – has persuaded Sanders to spend so much time on details of the law of the Mishnah and Tosefta, which he time and again either reads out of context or simply does not understand at all, will win my thanks. Sanders minimizes purity laws, it would seem, because he wants to argue against the notion of Pharisaic "exclusivism."[21] Sanders wishes to deny that the category, "sect," applies to the Pharisees:

> ...we should reserve the word "sect" for a group which was to an appreciable degree *cut off* from mainline society. It should *reject* some important part of the rest of society, or it should *create* an alternative structure. Neusner frequently compared the Pharisees to the Dead Sea Sect, finding basic agreements and minor differences. But the

---

[20]I spell out this matter in my *The Transformation of Judaism. From Philosophy to Religion*. Champaign, 1991: University of Illinois Press.

[21]*Jewish Law*, pp. 236-242.

differences are large and clear, and they show that one was a sect and the other not.[22]

Of course a group that did not set up a commune off all by itself is different from a group that by all evidence remained within the common society, and if the former is a sect, then the latter is something else. We need not quibble; I think my definition functions well: a group of people who interpreted and obeyed law "in a way different from other groups or from society at large."[23] But if he means that the Essene community was exclusivist but the Pharisees were not, then we really do differ in a fundamental way. In my judgment every Judaism, including the Pharisees' Judaic system, by definition is exclusivist, in that it identifies who is saved and who is not. That the authors of the Gospels saw the Pharisees as a distinct "group," whether the group be classified as a sect, a party, a club, or something else, seems to me to underline that the group was exclusivist, as indeed were the various Christianities and the other Judaisms of the same time and place – by nature, by definition. Why not?

Sanders responds to a long tradition of anti-Judaism and even anti-Semitism in New Testament scholarship. He denies that Judaism was what its academic and theological enemies maintain. His book in the context of contemporary Protestant theological debate makes a point important in its context:

The Pharisees had a positive concern for purity; it was better to be pure than not. They were not alone. The same was true of a lot of Jews and of a lot of pagans...." Ritual purity "...now has to many people an unfavorable connotation, and it is thought that what is wrong with the Pharisees is that they favored it. But this would only mean that what is wrong with them is that they lived in the ancient world – where most people favored it. Most Christian scholars...think that it was precisely "ritual" which Jesus and Paul attacked. Since the major point of the Jewish law which is treated negatively in both the synoptic gospels and Paul is the sabbath, the assumption that they attacked "ritual" implies that rest on the sabbath should be considered "ritual." It was instead commemorative (of God's rest) and ethical (not only men, but also women, servants, animals, and the land itself were allowed to rest. The Pharisees concern to be pure went beyond the requirements of the law – as did that of others....People thought that purity was a good thing, and they tried to avoid impurity, even though it had no practical consequence. There were many who wanted to be able to "distinguish between the holy and the common...." The Pharisees fully participated

---

[22]Ibid., pp. 240-241.

[23]Ibid., p. 240; Sanders tends to attribute more language to me than I ordinarily use; he routinely uses ten words when one suffices. In the passage at hand, he adds words I do not require to say what I mean.

in this spirit. They differed from others in many particulars, they defined certain impurities very carefully, they probably extended corpse impurity more than did most, and they may have tried harder than did most to avoid the new sources of this impurity. The desire to be pure, however, they shared with the populace in general.[24]

I cite the passage at length because it seems to me to point toward the benevolent intent of Sanders's scholarship. But the result is historically puzzling and theologically condescending.

It is puzzling because, first, there is no evidence that, in general, people wanted to be pure; the Mishnah and related sources take for granted ordinary folk wanted to be, and were, cultically clean when they observed the pilgrim festivals in Temple and in Jerusalem. I find in Sanders's book no evidence that *in other contexts* Jews of the first century other than Pharisees and Essenes may be described as desiring to be cultically pure (which is what is at stake in the debate). That absence of evidence probably accounts for the number of times he repeats his never-substantiated assertion.[25] It is condescending because Sanders affirms that, if the Pharisees practiced "ritual," then they, and the Judaism that claims descent from them, would be subject to condemnation by Jesus and Paul. Throughout its history, Orthodox and Roman Catholic Christianities have not concurred, of course, and the conception of a religion without ritual of some kind – perhaps not this kind, but some other kind – scarcely matches the reality of Protestant Christianity as well.

As a believing Jew, I practice Judaism, and I do not appreciate – or require – a defense that dismisses as unimportant or inauthentic what in my faith is very important indeed: the observance of rituals of various kinds. They are mine because they are the Torah's. I do not propose to apologize for them, I do not wish to explain them away. I do not reduce them to their ethical significance. "Commemorative" and "ethical" indeed! The Sabbath is holy, and that is why I keep it, not because it may also be "commemorative" or "ethical." Judaism is not a culture that merely commemorates, nor is it a sociology that advances social policy. It is a religion that believe we serve God by what we say and do, and doing involves not only life with neighbor but also life with God: nourishing life in accord with God's revealed rules of sanctification.

Nor do I value a defense of my religion that implicitly throughout and explicitly at many points accepts at face value what another religion

[24]Ibid., pp. 245-246.

[25]Like the turgidity of his prose, the rambling and disorganized and run-on character of his exposition, so, too, the utter vulgarity of Sanders's mind and intellectual processes has impressed more than a few reads of his books.

values and rejects what my religion deems authentic service to the living God. In the end Sanders wants to defend Judaism by his re-presentation of Pharisaism in a form that, in his view, Christianity can have affirmed then and should appreciate today – and now ceases to denigrate. That approved Judaism turns out to be a Judaism in the model of Christianity (in Sanders's pattern). So if Sanders's Pharisees result from a mere tinkering with some details of mine, his "Judaism" is only a caricature and an offense. With friends like Sanders, Judaism hardly needs any enemies.[26]

---

[26]It is only in this context that I can make sense of an apologia for Judaism that treats with such disdain theological formulations of Judaism such as I have made. Sanders's word choice in announcing his confusing of historical and theological discourse, "He continues to publish things whose [sic!] fundamentalism would embarrass the most conservative talmudists." This is repulsive and ignorant.

15

Mr. Maccoby's Red Cow – and Mine: A Reply to Critics

Mr. H. Maccoby, Richmond, Surrey,[1] has just now advanced discussion of some proposals of mine on the description, analysis, and interpretation of the Judaism of the Dual Torah in its formative age. What is at issue between Mr. Maccoby and me is a fundamental methodological problem: the relationship of a religious system to its own canon.[2] Mr. Maccoby takes the view that if in a received holy book, we may locate support ("prooftexts" or pretexts, depending on one's taste) for a position taken by heirs of that holy book, then we may interpret said position as a "mere" continuation and amplification of the received position. My view is that the canon recapitulates the system, not the system, the canon. Maccoby represents a single, continuous Judaism, the rabbinic one, as though in antiquity there were such a singular, harmonious, unitary, and normative system. But at the time of which he

---

[1] H. Maccoby, "Neusner and the Red Cow," *Journal for the Study of Judaism* 21 (1990):60ff. This essay goes over issues treated in more general terms in Chapter Twelve. Readers may benefit from seeing how the main point made there is worked out in debate on very particular problems. No one can then suppose that I have invented a shadow opponent, altogether too easy to refute. Maccoby is quite explicit in supposing that resort to prooftexts accounts for why an authority says what he does; he has not understood the simplest problems inherent in the processes of selectivity and does not grasp the indicative character of choice. Issues of method take on immediacy when confronted in debates of precisely how a given rite is to be described and interpreted.

[2] To be sure, Maccoby personalizes, and so trivializes, debates with other scholars. But there is a methodological issue worth addressing, despite his difficulty in formulating an academic debate in an appropriate, academic way. I am not inclined to anticipate that further exchanges with him will prove intellectually productive, the issues as he formulates them in the end not pertaining to the analysis of ideas. He is a mere apologist.

speaks, there was no such thing, but only Judaisms. Not only so, but he imagines that, from Scripture forward, there was a linear and singular progression, his normative Judaism unfolding, generation by generation, out of that same scripture. That is the nub of argument.

In point of fact, just as there cannot be one history of a single Judaism, so also there cannot be a continuous story that tells how first came this, then came that, there can be an exercise of description, analysis, interpretation: examination of system after system. There never has been a single, unitary and linear Judaism, any more than as a matter of mere fact there has been a single, linear and incremental *History of the Jewish People*, let alone a single People, "One People."[3] These statements of theological or ideological program do not describe how things have been or are today. But there have been Judaisms, and, as historical entities, there have been groups of Jews. There can be histories of Judaisms and histories of Jewish groups. And these Judaic systems, these Judaisms, we can describe, analyze through comparison and contrast, interpret by locating the ineluctable questions, the self-evidently true answers, and the circumstances and context that imparted urgency to both questions and answers. Accordingly, appeal to Scripture to explain how a given group made the choices that it did – which verses of Scripture to identify, how to read them, with what hermeneutical purpose in mind – is proven post facto by the variety of choices that various Judaisms made for themselves.

Each Judaism invented for itself such past as it found necessary. Part of that invention involved selecting verses of Scripture that would contribute authority to the fully formed system. In the case of the Red Cow, for example, the Judaism represented by the Mishnah devoted attention to that subject and so read with care – as both Maccoby and I have demonstrated – the pertinent verses of Numbers 19. Other Judaisms found nothing in those same verses. The act of selection then is prior to the act of hermeneutics, just as the variety of verses chosen as critical by various Judaisms (Matthew's school's choices, Philo's choices, the Essenes' choices, for example) attests. The fact that many Judaisms, and Christianities as well, appealed to the same Scriptures renders null any claim that all we have in any rabbinic document is a recapitulation and a paraphrase of the plain meaning of Scripture. Accordingly, the invented past of any Judaism has ordinarily consisted of a set of

---

[3] I have expanded on this matter in J. Neusner, ed., *Essays in Jewish Historiography* [=*History and Theory* Beiheft 27, edited by Ada Rapoport-Albert]. With a new Introduction and an Appendix. Atlanta, 1991: Scholars Press for South Florida Studies in the History of Judaism. I go over this matter in Chapter Six of these essays.

selections not so much of particular events – set into a linear and incremental story of how things came to be what they are – but singular documents, passages in holy books purported to tell the story and therefore also to justify and validate the Judaism at hand.

To be sure, in other work,[4] I account for the shape and character of all Judaisms that have ever flourished and predict the structure of any Judaism that will ever come into existence. Specifically, because the Mosaic Torah's interpretation of the diverse experiences of the Israelites after the destruction of the Temple in 586 invoked – whether pertinent or not – the categories of exile and return, so constructing as paradigmatic the experience of only a minority of the families of the Jews (most in Babylonia stayed there, many in the Land of Israel never left), through the formation of the Pentateuch, the Five Books of Moses, the events from 586 to 450 B.C., became for all time to come the generative and definitive pattern of meaning. Consequently, whether or not the paradigm precipitated dissonance with their actual circumstances, Jews in diverse settings have constructed their worlds, that is, shaped their identification, in accord with that one, generative model. They therefore have perpetually rehearsed that human experience imagined by the original authorship of the Torah in the time of Ezra. That pattern accordingly was not merely preserved and perpetuated. It itself precipitated and provoked its own replication in age succeeding age.

A Judaism – that is, a Judaic system, way of life, worldview, worked out by a distinct social group (an "Israel") – therefore would for time to come represent a reworking of the theme of exile and return, alienation and reconciliation, by an Israel, a group troubled by the resentment of that uncertain past and of that future subject to stipulation. Each Judaism therefore recapitulates the original experience. To state matters in more general terms, religions recapitulate resentment. All Judaisms that have come into being have conformed to that paradigm, and, so long as framers of Judaic systems – ways of life, worldviews, addressed to an Israel subject to particular definition – refer to that same holy scripture, the Five Books of Moses in particular, all Judaisms that will emerge will focus, in one way or another, upon that same generative resentment.

My general theory of the history of Judaism[5] is that a particular experience, transformed by a religious system into a paradigm of the life

---

[4] *Self-Fulfilling Prophecy: Exile and Return in the History of Judaism*. Boston, 1987: Beacon Press. Second printing: Atlanta, 1990: Scholars Press for South Florida Studies in the History of Judaism. With a new introduction. This is worked out in the present context in Chapter Twelve. There is some overlap between that essay and the present one.

[5] My field theory of the history of Judaism beginning to the present rests on a number of completed works, the following in particular: *Foundations of Judaism:*

of the social group, became normative – and therefore generative. Under other circumstances, in other times and places, that experience preserved in authoritative Scripture consequently imparted its form and substance upon Jewish polities that, in point of fact, faced the task of explaining a social world quite different from the one that, to begin with, had generated that original and paradigmatic experience. That is why I maintain that the social world recapitulates religion, not that religion recapitulates that social and political datum, the given of society, economy, politics, let alone of an imaginative or emotional reality. It must follow, of course, that the canon ("verses of Scripture, prooftexts," in context of the debate with Maccoby) recapitulates the system, not the system, the canon.

One may well ask, however, what of the role of the Pentateuch, which by definition is critical to every Judaism. It is a simple fact that the original reading of the Jews' existence as exile and return derives from the Pentateuch, the Five Books of Moses, which were composed as we now have them (out of earlier materials, to be sure) in the aftermath of the destruction of the Temple in 586 B.C. and in response to the exile to Babylonia, the experience selected and addressed by the authorship of the document is that of exile and restoration. So the document itself serves the system that comes to expression in the document; the Pentateuch itself attests to a process of selection and revision. Its framing of events into the pattern at hand represents an act of powerful imagination and interpretation.

The pentateuchal account is fabricated in not only a historical sense, as everyone knows, but also in an existential sense as well. It is an experience that is invented, because no one person or group both went into "exile" and also "returned home." Diverse experiences have been sorted out, various persons have been chosen, and the whole has been worked into a system by those who selected history out of happenings, and models out of masses of persons. I say "selected," because no Jews after 586 actually experienced what in the aggregate Scripture says happened. None both went into exile and then came back to Jerusalem. So, to begin with, Scripture does not record a particular person's experience. More to the point, if it is not autobiographical, writing for society at large the personal insight of a singular figure, it also is not an account of a whole nation's story. The reason is that the original exile

---

Method, Teleology, Symbol (Philadelphia, 1983-1985: Fortress Press) I-III, *Judaism in the Matrix of Christianity* (Philadelphia, 1986: Fortress Press), *Judaism and Christianity in the Age of Constantine* (Chicago, 1987: University of Chicago Press), and *The Death and Birth of Judaism: From Self-Evidence to Self-Consciousness in Modern Times* (New York, 1987: Basic Books).

encompassed mainly the political classes of Jerusalem and some useful populations alongside. Many Jews in the Judea of 586 never left. And, as is well known, a great many of those who ended up in Babylonia stayed there. Only a minority went back to Jerusalem. Consequently, the story of exile and return to Zion encompasses what happened to only a few families, who identified themselves as the family of Abraham, Isaac, and Jacob, and their genealogy as the history of Israel. Those families that stayed and those that never came back had they written the Torah would have told as normative and paradigmatic a different tale altogether.

That experience of the few that formed the paradigm for Israel beyond the restoration taught as normative lessons of alienation. Let me state with emphasis the lessons people claimed to learn out of the events they had chosen for their history: the life of the group is uncertain, subject to conditions and stipulations. Nothing is set and given, all things a gift: land and life itself. But what actually did happen in that uncertain world – exile but then restoration – marked the group as special, different, select.

There were other ways of seeing things, and the pentateuchal picture was no more compelling than any other. Those Jews who did not go into exile, and those who did not "come home" had no reason to take the view of matters that characterized the authorship of Scripture. The life of the group need not have appeared more uncertain, more subject to contingency and stipulation, than the life of any other group. The land did not require the vision that imparted to it the enchantment, the personality, that, in Scripture, it received: "The land will vomit you out as it did those who were here before you." And the adventitious circumstance of Iranian imperial policy – a political happenstance – did not have to be recast into return. So nothing in the system of Scripture – exile for reason, return as redemption – followed necessarily and logically. Everything was invented: interpreted.

That experience of the uncertainty of the life of the group in the century or so from the destruction of the First Temple of Jerusalem by the Babylonians in 586 to the building of the Second Temple of Jerusalem by the Jews, with Persian permission and sponsorship returned from exile, formed the paradigm. With the promulgation of the "Torah of Moses" under the sponsorship of Ezra, the Persians' viceroy, at ca. 450 B.C., all future Israels would then refer to that formative experience as it had been set down and preserved as the norm for Israel in the mythic terms of that "original" Israel, the Israel not of Genesis and Sinai and the end at the moment of entry into the promised land, but the "Israel" of the families that recorded as the rule and the norm the story of both the exile and the return. In that minority genealogy, that story of exile and return, alienation and remission, imposed on the received stories of pre-exilic

Israel and adumbrated time and again in the Five Books of Moses and addressed by the framers of that document in their work over all, we find that paradigmatic statement in which every Judaism, from then to now, found its structure and deep syntax of social existence, the grammar of its intelligible message. I therefore offer these principles by way of generalization:

1. No Judaism recapitulates any other, and none stands in a linear and incremental relationship with any prior one.
2. No Judaism merely recapitulates the canon of Scripture; all make choices therein: which verses, which issues, define the generative problematic of a system.
3. But all Judaisms recapitulate that single paradigmatic experience of the Torah of "Moses," the authorship that reflected on the meaning of the events of 586-450 selected for the composition of history and therefore interpretation.

Accordingly, a Judaic religious system recapitulates a particular resentment, the one to which the Pentateuch in its general shape and structure precipitates. In this one way each Judaism relates to other Judaisms, religious systems. Each one in its own way, on its own, will address and go over that same pattern, all addressing the same original experience. That is why a sequence of happenings, identified as important history and therefore paradigmatic event, then, is recapitulated in age succeeding age, whether by one Judaism in competition with another or by one Judaism after another. But, as a matter of systemic fact, no Judaism recapitulates any other, though each goes over the same paradigmatic experience.[6] Maccoby errs because he treats the canonical writing as primary to the formation of a Judaic system. But a book is not a Judaism and a Judaism is not a book – except after the fact.[7]

---

[6]That is the argument of my *Death and Birth of Judaism* (New York, 1987: Basic). There I argue at some length that no Judaism stands in a linear relationship with any other, none forms an increment on a predecessor, and all constitute systems that, once in being, select for themselves an appropriate and useful past – that is, a canon of useful and authoritative texts. And that is the order: the system creates its canon.

[7]The importance of this principle of selection cannot be missed. Let me explain by way of example. I do not see the writings of Philo as a Judaism, though they may represent a Judaism. We have distinctive books that represent social groups, for instance the apocalyptic writings of the Second Temple period, but our knowledge of those social groups – their way of life, their worldview, their identification of themselves as Israel – is imperfect. Consequently we cannot relate the contents of a system to its context or account for the substance of a system by appeal to its circumstance. We therefore know the answers provided by a system – that is, the contents of the book – but have not got a clear picture of

Maccoby thinks that, because he can find some prooftexts for a rabbinic document, he has explained the system to which that document testifies. But his premise, that the framers of the document set about merely to paraphrase the canonical writing they have chosen, answers no question but begs all questions. Recapitulating the story a religious system tells about itself does not help us understand the religious system – let alone account for it. The story – the chosen prooftext – tells not why people made their choices, let alone what happened on the occasion to which the story refers (the creation of the world, for instance) but how (long afterward and for their own reasons) people determined to portray themselves. The tale therefore recapitulates that resentment, that obsessive and troubling point of origin, that the group wishes to to explain, transcend, transform – and to that formative process in the making of a religious system, the prooftext is post-facto.[8]

If, therefore, in Maccoby's conception a mere narrative of history – discovering prooftexts or pretexts for positions of a later document – is supposed to serve the purpose of explanation, it is because of an evasion, on the one side, and a deep misunderstanding of the character of Judaisms on the other. The evasion represents the easier side to perceive: people find it easier to recite and paraphrase than to analyze and explain. That is why – as in the rather clumsy article of Maccoby in this journal – they play out the conventions of show-and-tell and let the answers come from they know not where: self-evidence, mostly. The incomprehension of Judaisms derives from accepting as fact the claim of a Judaism to constitute Judaism: as it was in the beginning, as it is, and on through time. The linear and incremental story of Judaism that today serves – beginning from Abraham, ending with this morning's events in Jerusalem or Jewish Providence – constitutes a profound theological judgment. It does not record how things really were. For no Judaism – Judaic system made up of a worldview, a way of life, and a particular group of Jews, an Israel, whose collective life is explained by the one and patterned by the other – stands in a linear and incremental relationship with any other. Indeed, none relates to any other at all, except in making selections from a common treasury of historical detritus. But the selections from the rubbish heap of history – the holy books, the customs

---

the questions that the answers take up, or, still more important, the political or social forces that made those questions urgent and inescapable, in just that place, in just that time.

[8]Since all Christianities share the same books, the Torah, that for Judaisms portray the paradigmatic experience of exile and return, Maccoby's certainty about the determinative power of the received canon is not only puzzling, it is incomprehensible.

and ceremonies (so to speak) always follow the inner logic of a system, which, after the fact, makes its choices, pronounces its canon.

Now this brings us back to Mr. Maccoby's point. The principal objection advanced by Mr. H. Maccoby to my account of the red cow in Mishnah-tractate Parah is this:

> His general thesis...is that the Mishnah expresses, through the details of ritual, a philosophy of holiness that is, in significant respects, different from that of the Bible, being a response to the historical circumstances of Jewish political helplessness after the destruction of the Temple. It may be objected, however, that this schema is flawed by considerable special pleading and inaccuracy [sic!] on Neusner's part. Details of rabbinic law which Neusner wishes to attribute to innovative rabbinic philosophy turn out, time after time, to be mere responses to the biblical text. The 'myth' which Neusner wishes to extract from alleged rabbinic ritual innovations is constructed out of non-existent materials; while the myth to which the rabbis really subscribed is that of the Bible itself, with its major themes of Exodus, Revelation, Desert, and Promised Land – a myth powerful enough to induce submission to the text of scripture and faith in its ability to provide answers to all possible difficulties. Neusner's offered paradigm case of the Mishnah's treatment of the Red Cow rite may serve to illustrate the above criticisms.

For a critique who claims to contrast his "accuracy" as against his allegation of errors I am suppose to have made, this vague, inaccurate and misleading, précis of my ideas hardly supplies much validation. Maccoby has not proved himself a careful and accurate reader of other people's work.

A brief account of positions of mine, clearly stated and broadly known, suffices to show how slovenly is his précis. In my work, I maintain that the Mishnah took shape after the Bar Kokhba War, not "after the destruction of the Temple." It is represented by me as a response not to "Jewish political helplessness," which vastly understates Judah the Patriarch's power, but to the religious crisis represented by the failure of the scriptural paradigm, destruction, three generations, return and renewal. It is not the destruction of the Temple in 70 that precipitated a crisis, but the debacle of Bar Kokhba's effort to replicate the rebuilding in the time of the second Isaiah, that I think accounts for the distinctive emphases of the Mishnah upon the enduring sanctification of the Land and of the people, Israel.

On the face of it, Maccoby puts forward the claim that the rabbinic system "merely" restated what the Written Torah said to begin with: "the plain sense."[9] That hoary apologetic[10] hardly serves the authentic

---

[9]Maccoby's "Bible," but of course he cannot mean that the rabbis drew also upon the New Testament, which is one-half of the Bible. Here is a fine case in which methodological naiveté extends even to the simplest terminology. No Christian

Judaism of the dual Torah, which alleges that the oral part of the Torah complements and completes the written part, but also is free standing. Since numerous Mishnah tractates take up subjects of which the written Torah knows nothing, Maccoby's basic allegation is simply ignorant and inaccurate. But – despite his obvious program of theological apologetics for his particular Judaism to accord him a fair hearing – if I understand Maccoby, what he wishes to claim is that "details...turn out...to be mere responses to the biblical text." I gather that his argument is that since the framers of tractate Parah found support for some of their propositions in verses of Scripture, therefore any claim that they did more than state the plain meaning of Scripture must be rejected.

If that is what he wishes to say, then his criticism is simply charming for its naiveté. As my opening remarks have emphasized, every writer from Ezra's closure of the Pentateuch in 450 found in Scripture whatever he wanted, whether Bar Kokhba, Philo, Jesus, or the Teacher of Righteousness, the School of Matthew, or the authorship of a tractate of the Mishnah. Mentioning those six who can well have claimed merely to say what the Written Torah had said ("not to destroy but to fulfill") underlines that people could find not only what they wanted, but also the opposite of what they wanted. So at stake in explaining a piece of writing is not whether verses of Scripture can have been adduced in support of what an authorship wished to say, for they always can and were found, ready at hand, when wanted. At issue, rather, is why someone went looking for proof, chose a given subject to begin with.

---

can be assumed to "know" that when Maccoby refers to "Bible," he does not mean the New Testament as well as the Old, and hence his focus of discourse is private and highly restricted. Word choices do matter, though Maccoby has shown himself obtuse and uncomprehending in such an extreme way that he has difficulty finding precise words for what he wishes to say.

[10]The same apologetic surfaces in the dreadful work of Daniel Boyarin, *Intertextuality and the Reading of Midrash* (Bloomington & Indianapolis: Indiana University Press, 1990). The difficult in following Boyarin is that he writes in a strange, turgid jargon. Furthermore, without telling us why this is important, he identifies himself early on as an Orthodox Jew (p. ix); He calls himself a participant observer, so as to win credibility, I suppose; this confuses religious authenticity with intellectual accuracy. But as a matter of fact, the apologetic point of the work is clear: "What in the Bible's text might have motivated this gloss on this verse?" He states at the end (p. 128), "Midrash is best understood as a continuation of the literary activity which engendered the Scriptures themselves." This sounds suspiciously like the familiar claim that Midrash says what Scripture really means, and that *is* the theology of some Orthodox Judaisms. In this book the literary critical frosting covers a stale but kosher cake. Boyarin thus represents in connection with rabbinic exegesis of Scripture that proposition that Maccoby puts forth in the context of the origins and growth of law within the system of the Judaism of the Dual Torah.

Maccoby begs the question, of course, unless he can explain why a particular verse of Scripture to begin with attracted attention. Maccoby does not seem to take seriously that the school of Matthew as much as the authorship of Mishnah-tractate Parah found ample support in Scripture for whatever they wished to say.

Precisely what he says about the authorship of Mishnah-tractate Parah can and should be said about Mark, Luke, Matthew (for Isaiah, for instance), and John (among many!). Then are we to dismiss the School of Matthew or the authorship of Mishnah-tractate Parah therefore can be dismissed as mere epigones of Scripture? Not very likely. To the contrary, when we wish to understand a document, the first question (in this context) must be, why this particular topic, as against a vast range of other scriptural topics that are neglected? If the Red Cow, then why not the flight to Egypt. I should be interested in Maccoby's evidence for his allegation that "the rabbis" (I assume in this context he means the authors of the tractate under discussion) have found in "Exodus, Revelation, Desert, and Promised Land" anything pertinent to their Red Cow. I should be curious to know just where, in the tractate under discussion, Maccoby finds his grand themes of "Exodus...," etc. Maccoby persistently exhibits the deplorable tendency to make things up as he goes along. The wide-spread realization that his writings on Jesus and Paul are simply bigoted joins with the broad recognition that he is scarcely a master of the sources.

Whenever I have had occasion to test an allegation on which Maccoby displays his marvelous certainty, I have found no evidence in support of that allegation, but rather, evidence of Maccoby's incomprehension of the sources and also of the considerations that have led scholars to the conclusions that they have reached. There seems to me no reason to pay more attention to Maccoby; I have the impression that colleagues in New Testament scholarship have reached that conclusion as well. In any event the most decisive refutation of Maccoby is given in Jewish Law from Jesus to the Mishnah by E. P. Sanders: "The idea of human intention, greatly and correctly emphasized by Neusner, is original to the Pharisees so far as we know. Thus even when they are only defining or clarifying biblical law, they are operating with some post-biblical categories."[11] What is said in this small context applies throughout, and with that we may dismiss Maccoby as not merely uninformed but, alas, simply uncomprehending.

---

[11]*Jewish Law*, p. 187.

16

Mr. Kraemer's Intellectual History of the Bavli – and Mine

The Mind of the Talmud: An Intellectual History of the Bavli. By David Kraemer. New York: Oxford University Press, 1990. 217 pp.

Claiming to "trace the development of the literary forms and conventions of the Babylonian Talmud and analyze those forms as expressions of emergent rabbinic ideology," which expresses the conviction of "the inaccessibility of perfect truth," and concluding that [not the determination, but the mere] "pursuit of truth...becomes the ultimate act of rabbinic piety," Kraemer spells out his program in these terms:

> [The book is]...a literary history. It traces the development of the literary forms and conventions by which rabbinic sages...recorded their opinions and rulings. What motivates this examination is the assumption...that literary conventions are reflections of ideological choices and that by tracing the history of literary developments we can say something of the history of ideas. This is also, therefore, intended as an intellectual history of the Jews who produced the Bavli.

While Kraemer claims not to rely for his history upon the attributions of sayings to given authorities, he alleges, "We can...know, at the very least, that certain forms of expression were typical in certain generations, and, given additional data, we can even say that it is likely that the essence of a certain opinion was held in the circle of disciples of a particular sage. Since this work is a history of literary forms as ideological expressions, we do have access to the sort of information needed to write such a history." Upon that formulation, the historical half of this book rests. But the formulation evokes the notion that, even though I cannot prove A, the accumulation of evidence of the same kind as A – "typical in certain generations," "circle of disciples of a particular sage" – provides proof that A on its own cannot. I doubt that many will find persuasive this rather facile and blatantly circular solution to the problem of the historicity of attributions; to his credit Kraemer himself calls it circular (p. 24). But then for several chapters he walks around in circles, supposedly proving we can rely on attributions as a whole, if not one by one. The whole of his elaborate proof, resting not on individual names but on groups of names ("generations of sages, but not individuals...are so distinguished") alleging that "verification...will extend only to the level of the generation, not to particular individuals," is therefore hardly compelling. Since Kraemer's "history of Amoraic literary expression" does not command assent, the claim that he has described "an intellectual history of the Bavli" rests on infirm foundations.

But we cannot dismiss the book as another exercise in pseudorthodoxy and pietistic gullibility. For in the succeeding chapters Kraemer also claims accurately to characterize the document as a whole, as it existed at the end of its formation. His descriptive proposition therefore is to be addressed entirely distinct from the claim to account for the history of the formation of the document. He alleges that the anonymous and commanding discourse of the document concerns not conclusion but argumentation. While received materials (Kraemer: "for the Amoraim") contain "both brief and discursive" writing, "conclusion and argumentation," for the unattributed and definitive discourse ("for the stam" not italicized, a foreign word meaning, "what is not attributed to a named authority") "*there is only argumentation.*" In the words he has italicized is Kraemer's principal descriptive allegation. All else rests upon that characterization.

Now it is certainly the fact that on occasion derivative cases are set forth, sometimes at great length, to put forward theoretical possibilities on sorting out conflicting principles, and these not uncommonly conclude, "the question stands." The argument, then, is the main thing: conflict of principles, left unresolved. So there is ample anecdotal material in the document – we know not the proportion or place in the composition of the whole – to validate Kraemer's claim in detail. But the passages that present conundrums invariably attend to interstitial issues, and none of them, so far as I have observed, present without resolution the conflict of fundamental principles (e.g., contradictions between the premises of two distinct Mishnah paragraphs are never left in conflict but always harmonized). So that phenomenon, which does conform to Kraemer's description, is not primary to the document, its modes of thought and argument.

Kraemer adduces in evidence of his claim that the document concerns itself with argument, not decision, by showing a variety of specific traits characteristic of what he calls the anonymous layer of the writing. He finds, for instance, that the redactor will "extend the range of the original argumentation" (p. 80). "The authors of the gemara also saw fit to create argumentation out of amoraic sources that were originally not argumentational" (p. 84). They created "fictional argumentation" (p. 87), "argumentation for its own sake" (p. 90). He then claims to have illustrated the point that "the Babylonian gemara is, at the level of its anonymous composition, an uncompromisingly deliberative/argumentational text." He properly compares this Talmud to the other one, the Talmud of the Land of Israel (a.k.a., the Yerushalmi) and finds that a principal difference is that the Yerushalmi reaches conclusions, the Bavli does not.

A considerable problem in assessing his evidence, argument, and, therefore, proposition, has to be specified here. All of these cases are treated as exemplary, but, unfortunately, Kraemer never tells us what proportion of the document as a whole, or of some sizable sample thereof, is comprised by them. So we have argument from anecdote and episode, without any sustained demonstration of the determinate characteristics of the writing as such. Nonetheless, from this point forward, Kraemer regards it as established fact that the Bavli has been given "an argumentational form." The remainder of the book is devoted to "the indeterminability of truth," an issue that the document under discussion on its own terms hardly portrays as urgent. Indeed, I am inclined to suspect the authors of the Bavli will have been amazed to be told that their document was more interested in argument than in "truth," meaning, determinate conclusions. To the contrary, since, as a matter of fact, the Bavli forms a highly systematic representation of a complete, proportionate, and authoritative system, Kraemer seems to wish to answer a question the document itself does not require that we ask.

What apparently has happened is that Kraemer has evidently found compelling a couple of philosophical books on the subject of the indeterminacy of truth and has identified his philosopher's stone. So he finds in the issue (his idiosyncratic reworking of the claims, along these same lines, of the literary critics of the deconstructionist school) a basis on which to explain the traits of the document in terms that are intellectually generally accessible, a worthwhile exercise, if carried out in a somewhat mechanical manner. If, then, the meaning is indeterminate, as deconstructionism wants us to believe, so, too, must be the message, Kraemer wishes us to conclude; all that is left is process. The entire history of the reception of the Bavli testifies that the document was meant to teach truth, not merely exemplify process. But the implausibility of Kraemer's result does not form an important reason to disbelieve his book.

Rather, let us ask ourselves whether, in his representation of the document, Kraemer has accurately described its paramount traits. It seems to me that, to do so, he will have wanted to answer a variety of fairly basic questions. The first must be, does the document seen in the aggregate repeatedly utilize a few fixed forms and time and again take up a few determinate intellectual initiatives? If it does, then we may speak, as Kraemer does, of "the Talmud," and if not, we may not. Second, if it can be shown that the document is cogent, saying the same thing of many things, then what is the principal focus of the document? I am inclined to wonder whether Kraemer's characterization will stand up to the scrutiny made possible by the answers to these questions. For from Kraemer's description of the Bavli, we should hardly know the simple fact that, while cogent and coherent as he claims, the rhetorical focus of coherence is upon a prior document, the Mishnah. My analysis of eleven tractates, presented in *The Bavli's One Voice: Types and Forms of Analytical Discourse and Their Fixed Order of Appearance* (Atlanta, 1991: Scholars Press for South Florida Studies in the History of Judaism), has shown that the Bavli is set forth in a systematic way as a commentary to the Mishnah, and, depending upon the tractate, from 85 percent to 97 percent (by my admittedly rough-and-ready reckoning) of the whole serves as Mishnah commentary. Kraemer does not deal with that fact, to which his characterization of the writing is monumentally irrelevant.

Further, from Kraemer's description, we should hardly have realized that the Bavli does set forth a highly propositional program, which it repeats time and again throughout. The allegation that the purpose of the document is to represent argument, not conclusion, contradicts that fact, spelled out in my *The Bavli's One Statement. The Metapropositional Program of Babylonian Talmud Tractate Zebahim Chapters One and Five* (Atlanta, 1991: Scholars Press for South Florida Studies in the History of Judaism). In other words, it is difficult for me to identify, in the terms of Kraemer's description, the paramount literary and propositional program of the Bavli, as sustained, and not merely episodic and exemplary, analysis has shown it to be. So not only is his proposition on the indeterminacy of truth on the face of it implausible, his characterization of the document as a matter of fact simply fails to encompass the document's fundamental and indicative traits, since he has not bothered to tell us what he thinks the Bavli is. I hasten to add, in Kraemer's defense, that the results to which I have alluded are very recent, so he is not to be blamed for not knowing what, when he was writing his book, no one knew. But my characterization of the Bavli, even before Kraemer produced his book, did not end with my *Judaism: The Classical Statement. The Evidence of the Bavli* (Chicago, 1986: University of Chicago Press), and *The Bavli and its Sources: The Question of Tradition in the Case of Tractate Sukkah* (Atlanta, 1987: Scholars Press for Brown Judaic Studies), two books of mine that Kraemer does know and utilize.

But, as a matter of fact, there were two other works, that take up precisely the same problem of description as the one treated in the second half of Kraemer's book, in print when he was at work. These are *The Making of the Mind of Judaism* (Atlanta, 1987: Scholars Press for Brown Judaic Studies), and *The Formation of the Jewish Intellect. Making Connections and Drawing Conclusions in the Traditional System of Judaism* (Atlanta, 1988: Scholars Press for Brown Judaic Studies). In these two works I formulated precisely the same question that Kraemer's book asks, but I framed it in terms and categories quite different from his. The results were what led me precisely to the results, as to the overall characteristics of the writing, set forth just now: we deal with a sustained and systematic commentary to the Mishnah, and the problem of the intellectual history of the document is to be defined in the framework of a writing in exegetical form, but with a well-framed propositional program. Of all of this Kraemer knows nothing. How might he have framed his research, had he chosen to see the document as a whole from the perspective of the writing at the end of its formation? For one thing, he will have dropped the words "history" and "historical" from the numerous sentences in which they occur, beginning with the title. But that hardly forms a weighty flaw in his work. In my view the intellectual interest of his inquiry will not have greatly suffered, given the rather formidable chasm that separates the first half of the book from the second (for instance, the authorities who take a principal place in the first four chapters play a negligible role in the final three, where philosophers, not Talmudists, predominate in the footnotes). Indeed, I am inclined to think he can have written Chapters Five through Eight without the results of Chapters One through Four.

But the accuracy of the description of the document that Kraemer puts forward will have gained. A brief account of how I have defined the task will explain why I think the flaws in his description are formidable. In the former work I describe the distinctive modes of thought that produced a kind of writing in Judaism quite different in the basic structure of its mentality and interior traits of logic and, especially, the formation of large-scale structures of knowledge, from the kind of writing carried out by contemporary Christian theologians – even on the same questions. I then described and analyzed, in the context of the concrete expression of mind provided by principal canonical writings, the four critical processes of thought, which I call logics, as I see them, three being propositional logics, the philosophical, teleological, and metapropositional, and one a nonpropositional logic, the logic of fixed association. In this description of the modes of coherent thought and cogent argument, I was able to characterize precisely what Kraemer claims to describe, namely, the intellectual traits of the writing. I cannot point to a single passage in his book in which he tells us about not "truth" (for instance, "truth in the classical philosophical tradition" p. 175) but logic in the framework of intelligible thought. Telling about "truth" leads us to attend to mere propositions, for example this is so, that is not so. But a description of the intellectual processes of a piece of writing should tell us about modes of thought: what is plausible and why, what is found cogent, how are connections made, for instance.

In the latter work, turning to the larger tasks of comparison and contrast of documents, where reliable intellectual history *is* possible (as what I call "the documentary history of ideas"), I claimed to account for how Judaic system builders framed their systems by comparison to the modes of cogent discourse characteristic of prior ones, beginning with the pentateuchal system of Judaism. "The formation of the Jewish intellect" interprets the word "formation" in two senses. The first is "formation" as the ways in which that intellect formed a Judaic system, and the second is, "formation" as an account also concerning the structure of that intellect, that is, of what modes of thought that intellect was formed. First I set forth the order, proportion, structure, and composition of a Judaic system, that is, a worldview and way of life addressed to a defined social entity called (an) "Israel." Second, I explained how framers of such a system made connections and drew conclusions in the setting up of their system. The order was deliberate. *For the order of the formation of the intellect is from the whole to the parts.* The reason is that it is the systemic statement that, to begin with, defines the logic needed to make that statement. The manner of making connections and drawing conclusions – the true life of intellect – does not percolate upward into the framing of the systemic statement.

What Kraemer has said about the traits of the Bavli therefore is not only dubious as a characterization of the writing as a whole. It is also monumentally beside the point, if the issue is the intellectual structure (if not history) of the Bavli. In this rather facile, shallow, and private work, therefore, Kraemer has presented an intellectual history which is neither historical, nor intellectual, since what he describes as the indicative intellectual traits of the document prove in fact to be subordinate and contingent, not systemic, not typical, and not determinative. Would that we could argue only from example, from select evidence, and ignore whether it is representative, characterizing what may not be characteristic at all! But plausible propositions rest upon a thorough and accurate knowledge of the document as a whole and in its parts. Kraemer simply has not done the slow, hard work of adducing literary evidence in behalf of the work of the description, analysis, and interpretation of "the mind of the Talmud." Whether the Bavli really favors argument over conclusion because its authors believe that truth is indeterminate simply is not settled in these pages. True, it can be shown that Kraemer is wrong as to the facts on every point he wishes to make about both the method and the propositional program of the document. But at issue here is not whether he is right or wrong, but only whether he has composed at least what we may judge to be a plausible, if arguable, case for his proposition, and I do not think he has done his homework adequately or set for himself a rigorous challenge, involving thorough research. The book misses the mark because the first half has evaded the problem of historicity, and the second has substituted argument by example, always aimed at propositional characterization, for analysis of the whole aimed at an encompassing and accurate description of the document's program of logic and its metapropositional consequence.

17

Mr. Young's *Parables* – and Mine

Brad H. Young: *Jesus and His Jewish Parables. Rediscovering the Roots of Jesus' Teaching.* New York & Mahway, 1989: Paulist Press. 366 pp.

Young presents an account of parables in general, and then turns to the Gospels' parables in detail. He covers these topics: parabolic teachings and the problem of hermeneutics; modern parable research; the parables and Talmudic literature: parable, agadah, and tradition; the parables and the Gospels: the synoptic problem; the parables and their context: reapplication and interpretation in the parables; the parables of the Kingdom of Heaven; Jesus, the Jewish sages and their parables; prophetic tension and the Temple: the parable of the wicked husbandmen; Jesus, the Jewish people, and the interpretation of the parables. The book proposes no thesis, pursues no line of inquiry, argues no sustained proposition. The author prefers, as he says, "an inductive approach," which "allows research into the wider range of meanings of the terms which are so important for a proper understanding of the development and emergence of the parable as a well-defined pedagogic technique" (p. 10).

The book appears to have been completed some time ago, perhaps as a dissertation at the Hebrew University, where the author studied for ten years. Omission of all reference to the important article by David Stern on the parable, published in *Prooftexts* a half decade ago, and of Stern's name in the index, points toward both conclusions, since, in general, Jerusalem scholarship reads Jerusalem scholarship and not much else. Further evidence of the overseas provenance of the work is that the language of the book is somewhat strange, and at many points it looks as though we have a translation from Israeli Hebrew.

Clearly, the purpose of Young's research derives from an interest in the parables attributed to Jesus. Young asks the right questions: "We see that the rabbinic parables are preserved in a literature that was compiled some time after the gospels." He further distinguishes the parables that occur in some rabbinic compilations – many hundreds of years after the time of Jesus – from those that occur in the Gospels. The latter draw heavily on verses of Scripture, the former rarely do. These observations, then, suggest that Young will systematically work out a thesis. But his presentation of his ideas is so prolix and disorganized that no thesis emerges. He just rambles onward and onward.

Let me give an example of his discourse, which captures the flavor of the book as a whole:

> The fable is an important forerunner of the parable. No fables appear in the gospels. It must be distinguished from the latter in that it employs animals and sometimes plants, attributing human characteristics to them. The antiquity of the fable is not disputed. Perry noted, "In the early period of Greek literature, and in the Alexandrian age, fables might be the subject matter of separate poems, but much more commonly they were used subordinately as illustrations in a larger context...." Hence Greek literature preserves fables in both prose and poetry. Also Schwarzbaum has stressed the antiquity of the fable: "It should also be pointed out that some of the antecedents of the so-called Aesopic fables are to be found...." Jacobs observed that many of the fables of rabbinic literature are paralleled in both Greek and Indian sources. Thus the fable was a widely circulated didactic mode. The well-known fable of the Oak and the Reeds appears in the Indian Mahabharata xii.4198, Avian and Babrius 64 as well as in Talmudic literature. The oak is not pliable and breaks as it stands against the powerful wind. The flimsy reed however bends with the wind and thus survives the storm. Flusser noted that the fable is probably behind the words of Jesus in regard to John the Baptist, 'What did you go out in the wilderness to behold? A reed shaken by the wind?' (Matthew 11:7; Luke 7:24). John's uncompromising nature put him on a collision course with Herod Antipas.
>
> In Exodus Rabbah a fable is used by the Amora R. Judah bar Shalom, (ca. 350 A.D.) to elucidate the predicament of Israel who in spite of their deliverer Moses still had to worry about Pharaoh.....

And so it goes. What is wrong with all this is that, through the introduction of a vast corpus of vaguely relevant information, Young simply makes no point. To be sure, readers familiar with the academic style of Jerusalem will find themselves right at home: this, that, the other thing, with no clear connection, no argument, no movement from fact to argument to proposition – just a stream of consciousness.

But that is misleading. In fact there is something at stake here. The author wishes to appeal to rabbinic compilations to bring us *"ipsissima verba"* of Jesus, and he says so in so many words:

> After examining the editorial aspects of the parable [of the two builders] in Matthew and Luke, one can propose a Hebrew reconstruction which more closely reflects the *ipsissima verba* of Jesus or at least the hypothetical Hebrew Urevangelium which underlies the texts of the synoptic gospels. More philological study is needed to determine to what extent one should look for a Hebrew closer to biblical or Mishnaic. Was the *vav* consecutive employed? It seems that in a popular story parable that the *vav* consecutive would have been considered too literary. Here the passage, "Saying Lord, Lord" has been attached to the parable because it appears in both Matthew and Luke and could be an original part of the text. Though this is true, it is possible that it was derived from a different context. Perhaps one of the more remarkable aspects of the parable is the phrase, "who hears my words and does them." The text stresses the teachings of Jesus. The phrase which refers to hearing and doing may allude to the passages from the Pentateuch which speak about the giving of the Lord...[p. 255].

The passage runs on, a single paragraph covering a variety of subjects, but the main point is clear at the outset. It suffices to note that the story in the rabbinic version occurs for the first time in the Fathers According to Rabbi Nathan, a document of indeterminate date but probably within the ambiance of the Talmud of Babylonia, so, let us say, something on the order of five centuries after Jesus is supposed to have made use of the parable. It is attributed to Elisha b. Avuyah. Even if we take the attribution as fact, Elisha can hardly attest to the state of affairs of Jesus, since he is a figure of the second century. But of course we cannot take the attribution as fact, and, consequently, the rabbinic version of the parable can hardly be adduced as evidence of what circulated in the time of Jesus.

In this day and age, we can hardly expect Young to ignore such considerations, and, formally, he pays attention to these issues. This is his language: "Elisha b. Avuyah's examples and Jesus Parable of the Two Builders have a number of common elements. I. Abrahams noted, 'All authorities are agreed that there can have been no direct, literary borrowing by the later Rabbis from the books of the New Testament.' Indeed, it seems unlikely that the parables of Jesus or of Elisha b. Avuyah could have directly influenced one another." So far, so good. But then we move back to *ipsissima verba*, by a circuitous route:

> It seems overly simplistic to consider only the question of dates between Elisha b. Avuyah and Jesus or the time of the final compilation of the gospels and that of Abot derabbi Nathan. Nor should the importance of the time difference be minimized. Nonetheless the parables are too close to one another to be completely independent. However, were Elisha b.

Avuyah's parable a secondary development from Jesus' illustration one would certainly expect that the parables would be more similar to one another and for the rabbinic version to betray signs of embellishment. The rabbinic version is shorter and conforms to the other parables in this chapter....Perhaps it is wise to recognize the fact that there is a third intermediate stage in the transmission of these parallel parables that connects the world in which Jesus operated with the sphere of the parable of Elisha b. Avuyah. Insufficient evidence has survived to speak with absolute certainty about this intermediate stage but it represents a common stream of Jewish thought that links Jesus with the world of rabbinic learning, the love of man and the love of his Creator [pp. 257-258].

If this is more then mere gibberish (and a case can be made that all we have is dust in the eyes of the scholars), then what Young seems to wish to say is something like this. First, we cannot take account only of the difference of a hundred years between the time of Jesus and the time of Elisha. The inference is that, if we did, for narrowly historical and biographical purposes, then we could not invoke Elisha's use of the parable to tell us anything about Jesus's use of the same parable. We also do not have to take account only of the fact that the rabbinic parable appears in a document that reached closure many hundreds of years after the time of Jesus. The inference is that, if we did, we could not posit any relationship of a historical character to permit us to comment on the use of the parable by Jesus.

Now why do we not take account of these paralyzing problems? Because the two versions of the parable ("the parables") are like one another ("too close to one another to be completely independent"). So what? Well, it would be nice to conceive that Elisha's use of the parable reflected knowledge of Jesus' use of the parable ("secondary development"), but the data do not suggest so. For Young what is at stake is only history, only biography, only finding out more about the setting in which Jesus lived and taught. If his interest were in the study of parables, the issues of attribution and redaction would play no role. It is solely the insistence on recovering what Jesus really said and meant that requires Young to worry about the accuracy of the transmission of sayings, the reliability of attributions, the veracity of what is attributed, the inconsequentiality of when documents reached closure, and other such ominous considerations.

So there is this "third intermediate stage." Of what it consists we know nothing. But even without evidence, we know that "it represents a common stream of Jewish thought that links Jesus with the world of rabbinic learning, the love of man and the love of his Creator." How we know it I cannot say, and Young does not tell us. So we have (on the surface) affirmed the critical premises of contemporary scholarship but forthwith ignored them, a phenomenon that Morton Smith classified as "pseudorthodoxy," meaning, the profession of critical principles accompanied by the practice of unalloyed fundamentalism. Still, if all that is at stake is the modifying language, "the love of man and the love of his Creator," then that "common stream of Jewish thought" has flowed directly from the Old Testament. In that case why take the trouble to call upon rabbinic compilations, spread over so long a span of centuries and two distinct empires, the Roman and the Iranian, to tell us what was going on in an age of which their authors had no direct knowledge whatsoever.

And, more to the point, why in any event ask these same compilations to tell us anything about the thought of a protean figure, who put the stamp of his own unique personality upon everything he used? For what is striking to those knowledgeable concerning rabbinic writings is not the points in common with the deeds and statements of Jesus, but the stunning contradictions between the "known" (the rabbinic) and the new. There is scarcely a saying or a story in the Gospels that does not astonish and amaze, and that is precisely what Jesus is supposed to have said over and over again: "You have heard it said...but I say to you...."

So we are left with the well-established fact that a single simile or parable may be used in a variety of settings, both gentile and Jewish, both rabbinic-Jewish and other-than-rabbinic Jewish (classifying the New Testament books written by authors who professed to be Jews as Jewish but not rabbinic). Young contributes nothing new to the recognition of that commonplace. His interest is in placing Jesus into the "common stream" of rabbinic Judaism. But that requires him at once to profess and to ignore the critical problems for appeal to rabbinic compilations in pursuit of scholarship on Jesus. These are, [1] attributions of sayings to named rabbis are notoriously uncertain and can be shown to be pseudepigraphic where they are not merely contradictory (the same saying given to two or more authorities, sayings manifestly invented out of logical inferences and then assigned to named authorities, and other routine fabrications); [2] redaction of documents in the rabbinic corpus took place from two hundred to six hundred years after the time of Jesus, and any utilization of their contents to describe the state of opinion prior to the time of closure requires demonstration that the contents antedate the closure of the compilations. Appeals to the reliability of processes of transmission rarely find support in systematic and sustained demonstration, and those who invoke the principle that "our sages would not lie" ignore a considerable corpus of scholarship, beginning with Y. N. Epstein's *Mavo lenussah hammishnah* (1954), which shows that veracity in a historical sense is simply beside the point.

Young has given us a very poor piece of work. His research is superficial, since he does not appear to have read many current and important works on his subject and on the documents on which he is working. As my brief abstracts show, his writing is clumsy and obscure. The book is disorganized and rich in irrelevant information. As a matter of fact his knowledge of the rabbinic sources is parlous and unreliable; a long list of misunderstandings can have been compiled to show how little, in Jerusalem, people really know about these writings. So, in all, his ten years of study in Jerusalem turned him into a Jerusalem scholar.

But his book has the considerable merit of showing us precisely how one approach to the use of the rabbinic evidence for the analysis of the New Testament is carried forward. In his crude and clumsy way, Young succeeds in presenting a thesis and illustrating a method and presenting results for all to see. The claim upon critical standing set forth by pseudorthodoxy stands refuted in the pages of this book. If all we are to gain is Young's "third intermediate stage" (he obviously means, "a third, intermediate stage"), why bother? Here are no consequential results of an other-than-theological character, and, as to theology, history and biography make no difference.

18

Mr. Boyarin's *Intertextuality* – and Mine

Intertextuality and the Reading of Midrash. By Daniel Boyarin. Indiana Studies in Biblical Literature. Bloomington & Indianapolis: Indiana University Press, 1990. 161 pp.

This rather thin, first book by the new Taubman Professor at University of California, Berkeley, proposes through examining a tiny segment of the anomalous and probably medieval exegetical text, Mekhilta, to clarify the nature of Midrash. The use of contemporary literary theory to explain Midrash is hardly news; the trend is more than a decade old. The results have proven trivial and dubious, as in Susan Handelman, *The Slayers of Moses: The Emergence of Rabbinic Interpretation in Modern Literary Theory* (Albany: SUNY Press, 1982). So Boyarin's is not a work of pioneering intellect, but of mere application and paraphrase. Unhappily, the application is not very compelling.

To be sure, using a medieval compilation for that purpose is exceedingly odd, and therefore certainly original, if perhaps ill-advised. Boyarin knows but dismisses B. Z. Wacholder, "The Date of the Mekilta de-Rabbi Ishmael," *Hebrew Union College Annual* 39 (1968), pp. 117-144. He maintains that Wacholder's view has been "decisively and definitively disproved by Menahem Kahana, 'The Editions of the Mekilta deRabbi Ishmael on Exodus in the Light of Geniza Fragments' *Tarbiz* 45, 1986, pp. 515-520." Indeed Boyarin goes on to state (p. 130, n. 3), "The Mekilta may be in the main, in fact, the earliest of rabbinic midrashic texts, although its final recension seems to have been a little later than some other early midrashim." This murky claim of his – what he means by "final recension" and how he knows what he says – is not spelled out but just tossed off.

Boyarin's ignorance of Mekhilta scholarship, the very text to which he devotes his entire book, is genuinely alarming. First of all, Dr. Mireille Hadas-Lebel's major paper, on loan words from Greek and Latin in Mekhilta, has definitively demonstrated that these loan words are terms that did not come into existence before the third or fourth century C.E. Borrowing these terms into Hebrew necessarily belongs to a subsequent date. That paper was written without reference to Wacholder's thesis but substantiated his views, point by point. Wacholder for his part has furthermore dismissed Kahana's article (which was in Tarbiz 55, pp. 489-524, not the pages Boyarin cites!) as based on "insubstantial evidence." Boyarin also does not seem to know that Mekhilta Attributed to R. Ishmael is asymmetrical in rhetoric and logic to the entire corpus of other, demonstrably early Midrash compilations – Sifra, and the two Sifrés for example – as shown in my *Mekhilta Attributed to R. Ishmael. An Introduction to Judaism's First Scriptural Encyclopaedia* (Atlanta, 1988: Scholars Press for Brown Judaic Studies). How can a work that purports to describe Midrash on the basis of a few passages of a single, atypical text win our confidence when the author does not even know the scholarly literature on the document he claims to describe and interpret?

The book is written in a strange, turgid jargon, for example, "...all of them [interpretations in Midrash compilations] are more or less different from the commentary of the European traditions in that they do not seem to involve the privileged pairing of a signifier with a specific set of signifieds," and again, "I intend to articulate a theory of this text which will explain its hermeneutic moves as hermeneutic – i.e., without reducing them to some other species of discourse." At many points Boyarin seems to be talking mainly to himself. Without telling us why this is important, he identifies himself early on as an Orthodox Jew (p. ix); He calls himself a participant observer, so as to win credibility, I suppose; this confuses religious authenticity with intellectual accuracy. The apologetic point of the work is clear: "What in the Bible's text might have motivated this gloss on this verse?" He states at the end (p. 128), "Midrash is best understood as a continuation of the literary activity which engendered the Scriptures themselves." This sounds suspiciously like the familiar claim that Midrash says what Scripture really means, and that *is* Orthodox Judaism. In this book the literary critical frosting covers a stale but kosher cake.

Lest readers suppose that I exaggerate the oddity of his representation of Midrash, let me give a typical passage (p. 35) among the half dozen or so that comprise the entire book. This shows us how Boyarin uses the language of literary criticism to tell us what a straightforward reading of the text shows without literary criticism of this sort. First the reader must know that the passage we consider is not in the Mekhilta at all, but in the Talmud of Babylonia. So we are introduced to the Mekhilta by other-than-Midrash texts, a fine instance of the intellectually vulgar Orthodoxy of this book: everything Jewish is the same as everything else Jewish, Midrash, Talmud, Bible – whatever. The reason he gives is that the names that occur in one document occur in another – and that's that. For Boyarin that gullibility does not pose a problem: "The Talmud preserves a story about the very rabbis of the Mekhilta which contains a nearly explicit commentary on midrashic intertextuality...."

> For this commandment which I command you today is not too difficult for you or too remote. *It is not in heaven* that one should say, Who will arise to heaven, take it and make it heard that we might do it. And it is not over the sea, that one might say, Who will cross to the other side of the sea and take it for us and make us hear it, that we might do it. Rather, the word [thing] is very close to you in your mouth and heart, to do it. [Deut. 30:11-14].

On this passage, Boyarin states the following:

> R. Yehoshua [to whom the passage is attributed (JN)] transforms the verse through his citation into meaning that the Torah is beyond the reach, as it were, of its divine author. The nature of R. Yehoshua's hermeneutic speech act here is vital to understand the text. If we do not perceive what he is doing with the verse from Deuteronomy, we could misunderstand him to be making precisely the opposite claim, namely, that the text is autonomous and sufficient in itself, not requiring the author to guarantee its true interpretation – a version of the New Criticism. By performing an act of tesseration of the language, however, the rabbi disables any such reading of his statement. Without fanfare, R. Yehoshua creates radical new meaning in this verse, simply by reinscribing it in a new context. "It is not in heaven" means not only that the Torah is not beyond human reach, but that it is beyond divine reach, as it were.

The "as it were"s do not help us much in figuring out what Boyarin wants to say here. "Not only that the Torah is not beyond human reach" should mean that the Torah is within human reach. "...but that it is beyond divine reach" means either, [1] "not only that it is not beyond human reach, but that it is [supply: not] beyond divine reach," or, [2] "it is within human reach but it is beyond divine reach." If we do not supply the *not* in version 1, we end up saying that Boyarin thinks that the author of the passage is saying that human beings can master the Torah, but God cannot. That strikes me within the context of the text he purports to interpret as little short of lunatic.

Adherents to the theory he expounds here will maintain that you can say pretty much anything you like about any text, and in the next paragraph of the same passage, Boyarin defends himself:

> This brings us squarely up against the dilemma of any hermeneutic theory that does not allow appeal to author's intention as a curb on interpretation. Once that control is gone, it seems that any interpretation is the same as any other, that anything at all can be said to be the meaning of the text. Such hermeneutic anarchy is clearly *not* the way that midrash presents itself. Within our text both the dilemma and an answer to it are offered.

The sentence that follows, we have a right to expect, will specify the dilemma and the answer. But here is Boyarin:

> Present within the narrative is a commentary on itself, namely: "What is 'it is not in heaven'? Said R. Yermia, Since the Torah has already been given from Mt. Sinai, we do not pay attention to heavenly voices, for You have written already at Mt. Sinai, 'Incline after the majority.'"
>
> R. Yermia's rereading of R. Yehoshua solves the problem of what constrains interpretation. The answer is surprisingly modern: the majority of the community which holds cultural hegemony controls interpretation. To put it another way: correctness of interpretation is a function of the ideology of the interpretive community.

Boyarin is saying that the message of the passage is: the community controls the interpretation of the Torah. That is quite so – but then, why write a whole book to say what we have always known Midrash to mean? If this is what intertextuality has to contribute to the reading of Midrash, it is not even trivial, but merely paraphrastic – just the *peshat*.

Much of the book walks over these same well-trodden paths; when we read his analysis of passage after passage, we know pretty much what we knew before we read his analysis. The publisher's blurb holds: "the best, most cogent and intelligent attempt to date to apply insights from modern literary criticism to the interpretation of midrash." But Indiana University Press appears to have forgotten its own publication of a far more original and compelling work, José Faur, *Golden Doves with Silver Dots* (Bloomington: Indiana University Press, 1986). Those who wish to gain whatever benefit a now-fading theory of literature may offer for the study of Midrash will do far better to dismiss Boyarin's vacuity and turn to Faur.

Part Four
STUDYING ABOUT RELIGION THROUGH THE CASE OF JUDAISM

19

Defining A Religion. A Method Exemplified in Defining Judaism

I. The Problem of Defining a Religion: *E Pluribus Unum?*

A critical problem in the study of any religion is that of definition: precisely what do we mean by "Christianity," or "Islam," or "Buddhism," or "Hinduism," or "Judaism."[1] These convenient terms – intellectual labor-saving devices, really – mean to organize and correlate quite diverse religious systems, each comprising a worldview, way of life, and theory of the social entity that explains itself and organizes its affairs within that worldview and way of life. When we consider the hardly irenic relationships among Christian systems – Orthodox, Roman Catholic, Protestant in numerous communions – we realize that "Christianity" covers a considerable family of religious systems. And the same is so for Islam, as people who have had to understand the difference between Sunnis' and Shiites' Islams have come to grasp. "Buddhism" is an invention of the West, and such convenient terms as "Hinduism" or "Confucianism" – no less than the invention of "*the* Maori*"* to solve problems of comprehension in the earliest European encounter with the twenty-four warring nations of New Zealand – serve as mere labor-saving devices as well. Anyone who asks whether, among Christianities, we may speak of Christianity, or among Judaisms, we may speak of Judaism, will then find compelling the experiment presented in this book. For no reasonable person can treat as final the judgment that there is no Judaism, but only Judaisms, no Christianity, but only

---

[1]This essay served as the new introduction of *Self-Fulfilling Prophecy: Exile and Return in the History of Judaism*. Boston, 1987: Beacon Press. Second printing: Atlanta, 1990: Scholars Press for South Florida Studies in the History of Judaism.

Christianities. Religious systems do form species that may be shown to form a genus, and in this book I show how all Judaic religious systems form a single genus, Judaism. This I do by showing how to form the genus out of the species, and, further, by setting forth the definition of that genus through an exercise in polythetic classification.

Defining a religion, therefore, forms the critical problem in the study of religion. At issue, to begin with, are the diverse kinds of data – produced within the religious community, produced by outsider observers, preserved by the community, preserved outside of the community – that enter into a definition, and the various sorts of definitions that can be undertaken. A considerable critical literature, of both theory and practice, is available, and since the problem is an abstract and general one, defining is a challenge to specialists in more than a single religion. In addressing the character of religion, the language we use conflicts with our everyday observations. We recognize that a given religion (or religious tradition) presents enormous diversity, so that, in reality, we observe not one Judaism but many, not one Christianity but many. But then when we speak of religion, we speak of Buddhism, not Buddhisms, Islam, not Islams, Judaism, not Judaisms. When scholars who study religion ask the closely correlated questions, How can we speak of Judaism but see only Judaisms? and, second, How can we speak of Judaism despite the diversity of the Judaic systems we observe both in history and nowadays?, the field of the study of religion will change. It will draw together the data with the theory.

II. The Case of Judaisms and Judaism

A good case in point is Judaism in ancient times. Of keen contemporary interest because in the first seven centuries A.D. Christianity was born and Judaism as it has flourished in the West took shape, Judaism comes to us in diverse documents and archaeological data. What we find in the Dead Sea scrolls cannot be correlated with what Philo tells us, and what Philo tells us scarcely intersects with what the apocryphal and pseudepigraphic writings take for granted; the vast corpus of writings from rabbis, all joined because of the common trait of appeal to a single symbolic structure and myth, has now been thoroughly analyzed and differentiated, with the result that, even within that canon, it is easier to differentiate one document from another than to say what all the documents have in common. The archaeological data conflict at important points with much of the literary data as well, and efforts to use the rabbinic literature as a handbook for the interpretation of the symbolic expressions in iconographic form have proven somewhat awkward. This problem of defining Judaism amid the welter of data originally was sidestepped by appeal to a normative Judaism, which allowed picking and choosing among the data; or to an "official" as against an "unofficial," or a "sectarian" as against an "orthodox" Judaism, and so forth. But that approach has lost all authority, for now when we wonder whether and how all the data attest to a single Judaism, we are not prepared to make theological judgments at the outset.

The case of Judaism in late antiquity and beyond is a compelling one because a variety of testimonies on who, or what, is a Jew, and how is Judaism to be defined, derive from diverse participants to the discussion, both in antiquity and in modern times. A rich corpus of ancient sources, found in archaeology, on the one side, and in written sources, on the other, address that issue and make it complicated. Jews and Judaism were defined both by Jews and by gentiles; both by Jews whose descendants remained Jewish and by Jews whose descendants took a different route. Debates in ancient time between Jews or Jews and Christians who regarded themselves, also, as "Israel," took up the subject as well. Many books and articles, some of them quite current, have been published as well. At issue is, what kind of evidence, arguments, and modes of thought and rhetoric serve to address the question of "defining Israel." For if no one now entertains the theory that [1] there was a single Judaism (which was orthodox), and [2] the Jews' ethnic affairs and their religious life were more or less the same thing or at least need not be differentiated, what are we now to do?

Specifically, once we do recognize difference, can we speak of Judaism or only of Judaisms? Defining a religion, or a religious system, has already yielded recognition of different systems, all of them Judaic, but work has yet to develop methods for finding out in what way it is legitimate to differentiate all Judaisms from any other religions, on the one side, and to treat as cogent or coherent all Judaisms, however distinct we recognize their respective systems were, on the other. Work on the characterization of distinct Judaic systems within the rabbinic framework, addressing the canonical writings stage by stage and document by document, has shown, for instance, that a given system may be classified in one way, another in a different way: one as a philosophy, the other as a religion, for example. The analysis of the category structures and the processes of category formation at work within the documents of rabbinic canonical origin, for instance, have yielded a variety of quite interesting conceptual tools: category and counterpart category, for instance, and this has served well in the comparison of one systemic composition with another, later one. In these pages I address the problem of how a religious system manages to set forth a statement that is well composed and cogent – not merely attitudes but beliefs that hang together and are internally coherent, for example.

That is not a problem of heresy and orthodoxy (in the framework of the debate of Walter Bauer and H. E. W. Turner, for instance) nor is it an issue of (descriptive) sociology, but, rather, a problem of the analysis of structures of ideas – as documented.

In what follows I try to show that a single paradigmatic experience is reworked in every Judaism from antiquity to the present day. It is the pentateuchal paradigm of exile and return, and it is reworked in Judaic systems over time. These systems do not recapitulate one another and they also do not continue or develop from one another. But all of them do recapitulate a single generative experience and are held together by that experience. Whether we deal with Zionism or the Judaism of the Dual Torah or any of the continuator Judaisms of the nineteenth and twentieth centuries, typified by the Judaism of Holocaust and Redemption, what we discern is that single paradigm. In Chapter Three of this book I set forth that paradigm and then in the subsequent chapters I demonstrate its persistence.

III. The Premises of this Field Theory of the History of Judaism: Three Theses

My field theory of the history of Judaism takes for granted three theses, one on the history of Judaism, the other two on the nature of religion as exemplified by the history of Judaism, which are set forth in its companion, *Death and Birth of Judaism. The Impact of Christianity, Secularism, and the Holocaust on Jewish Faith* (New York, 1987: Basic Books).

The first thesis is as follows: Judaism as it flourished in the West was born in the encounter with Christianity in the definition in which it defined the civilization of the West, and that same Judaism lost its power to persuade Jews of its self-evident truth when Christianity did. That thesis concerning the history of Judaism occupies the first part of *Death and Birth*, but is fully exposed in *Judaism and Christianity in the Age of Constantine* (Chicago, 1988: University of Chicago Press) and in these works: *The Foundations of Judaism. Method, Teleology, Doctrine* (Philadelphia, 1983-1985: Fortress Press). I-III. I. *Midrash in Context. Exegesis in Formative Judaism* (Second printing: Atlanta, 1988: Scholars Press for Brown Judaic Studies); *The Foundations of Judaism. Method, Teleology, Doctrine* (Philadelphia, 1983-1985: Fortress Press). I-III. II. *Messiah in Context. Israel's History and Destiny in Formative Judaism* (Second printing: Lanham, 1988: University Press of America Studies in Judaism Series); *The Foundations of Judaism. Method, Teleology, Doctrine* (Philadelphia, 1983-1985: Fortress Press). I-III. III. *Torah: From Scroll to Symbol in Formative Judaism* (Second printing: Atlanta, 1988: Scholars

Press for Brown Judaic Studies); and *Judaism in the Matrix of Christianity* (Philadelphia, 1986: Fortress Press. British edition, Edinburgh, 1988, T. & T. Collins).

The second, on what we learn about religion from the history of Judaism, is this: No Judaism – hence, as a matter of hypothesis, no religious system – recapitulates any other of its species let alone of the genus, religion. Each begins on its own and then – only then – goes back to the received documents in search of texts and prooftexts. Every Judaism, therefore, commences in the definition (to believers: the *discovery*) of its canon. All Judaisms, therefore, testify to humanity's power of creative genius: making something out of nothing. That something, that system, serves to suit a purpose, to solve a problem, in our context, to answer in a self-evidently right doctrine a question that none can escape or ignore.

The study of Judaisms as they form one Judaism draws our attention, quite naturally, to the nature of religion in a time of change, such as the modern age of the death of Judaism and the birth of Judaisms has been. The thesis of my *Death and Birth of Judaism*, therefore, proposes to account for the ongoing formation of new religious systems, the new Judaisms which take up inescapable questions and produce ineluctable answers. The thesis – which is critical to my field theory of the history of Judaism – is as follows: *religion recapitulates resentment.* A generation that reaches the decision to change expresses resentment of its immediate setting and therefore its past, its parents, as much as it proposes to commit itself to something better, the future it proposes to manufacture. So when, in the second of the three theses, I say that the urgent question yields its self-evidently true answer, my meaning is this: resentment produces resolution. The two, when joined, form a religious system, in this book, a Judaism.

Now to the substance of the matter. My field theory of the history of Judaism, spelled out in these and other works, deriving from a detailed study of the literature of ancient Judaism and the history of Judaism in modern times, tells the story of four great ages in the history of Judaism. The question of how we can speak of Judaism, not only Judaisms, derives from the fact that all Judaisms recapitulate a single issue, one that is initially set forth in the pentateuchal Judaism and persists, thereafter. But persistence of a single paradigm should not obscure the progression of historical developments: Judaisms.

First comes the birth of the Judaism of the Dual Torah, formed in the age of Constantine, in the fourth century. What do I mean by "the Judaism of the Dual Torah"? It is a Judaic religious system that rests on one conviction. When God revealed the Torah to Israel at Mount Sinai, that Torah came in two media, one in writing, the other in memory, that is, formulated and transmitted through oral, not written means. So the Dual Torah is the Torah that is in part in writing – the Hebrew Scriptures everyone knows – and in part oral, through formulation and transmission by memory. Only long after Sinai did the documents of this other, Oral Torah, reach writing, beginning with the Mishnah, closed at about 200 C.E. and ending, for late antiquity, with the Talmud of Babylonia, ca. 600. That, then, is what we mean when we speak of the Judaism of the Dual Torah – one among many Judaisms that have come into existence through the years. But that was the single important Judaism, for the simple reason that, from the fourth century to the nineteenth, that Judaism defined matters without substantial competence. That Judaism flourished in Israel in Christendom without significant competition from the fourth to the nineteenth century. So the first stage in the history of Judaism we consider is the formative one: the birth of the successful Judaism of the Dual Torah.

IV. The Problem of Judaisms in the Modern Age

The second, third, and fourth ages come about in the aftermath of the death, for many Jews, of the self-evident power and truth of the Judaism of the Dual Torah. The ages now pass in rapid succession – so our present perspective suggests. These ages coincide with the nineteenth, twentieth, and nascent twenty-first centuries. These I treat in *Death and Birth of Judaism*. I take up, in the nineteenth century the birth of three Judaic continuator systems of religious reflection, that is, three Judaisms, Reform, Orthodox, Conservative, each an exercise in theological reflection of a highly self-conscious order. I then turn to the birth of three Judaic systems of mythic consciousness – I mean, systems we hold to be self-evident truths – which are the Jewish version of Socialism, nationalism (in Zionism), and Americanism (in the American-Judaic system of Holocaust and redemption), received by believers as a matter of what is obvious and beyond all need for argument. These movements convey the dominant motifs of the Judaisms of the mid-twentieth century, from the turn of the century, through World War I, to nearly the present day. Finally, turning toward the twenty-first century, I ask about movements of reversion to something that, calling itself tradition, bears traits of a remarkably fresh and innovative character – not tradition but roots. We make the journey, therefore, from the end of self-evidence, through the age of self-consciousness, to the beginning of a new age of self-evidence. That forms this exercise in interpretation of religion. But I propose not merely to amass information but to interpret the history of Judaism and to explain matters as they now confront us.

Let me state at the outset the thesis of *Death and Birth*. In modern times a long-established system of Judaism formed in ancient days – a worldview, way of life, addressed to a distinctive Israel, framed in response to urgent and perennial questions – lost its paramount position. That received Judaic system gave way to a number of new Judaisms – that is, Judaic systems, each with its own set of self-evidently true answers to ineluctable questions. Each of these systems in its way claimed to take the natural next step in "Jewish History," or in "the Tradition" or to constitute the increment of Judaism ("the Tradition") in its unfolding, linear history. All of them were wrong, and, because they err gloriously in perfect self-delusion, each one testifies to the powerful imagination of humanity, the courage of people to face urgent questions and to compose, in solving them, systems of belief and behavior capable of creating whole worlds of meaning: sensibility and sense alike. So in the gallant courage of Jewry to create and call new creation old, in its capacity to renew hope in the face of despair, I find what it means, as I shall explain in a moment, to be in God's image, after God's likeness.

So I begin with the claim that, in calling itself reform or historical or authentic, or Torah true and traditional, in amassing prooftexts for its propositions, the new always errs in linking itself to the old. In fact there is no such thing as "the Tradition" to which to reconnect in a fresh beginning. There are only Judaic systems, each a response in a new way to a new day. The proof? The demonstration that people, knowing in advance something that in the received Judaism they did not find out and could not have found out, invariably proceed to pick and choose – after they have completed their (unself-conscious) work of invention.

Much, therefore, is at stake, for our understanding of humanity, in the interpretation of the Judaic systems of the modern and contemporary age: Are they what they say they are, which is reversion or reform?, or Are they what in perspective of the ages they prove to be, which is, all of them not rebirths but new beginnings, each one on its own not a recapitulation nor replication but a reworking of the received in the formation of a new given? I maintain that the Judaic systems – the Judaisms – of the nineteenth and twentieth century constitute, each on its own, a new birth, not a reversion or a reform. The received Judaism of the Dual Torah did not undergo a midlife crisis, for those whose questions that system did not address, that Judaism died. And the Judaism that did answer urgent questions for its devotees was born, not reborn (though they ordinarily said that is all it was).

V. Incremental History or Systemic Recapitulation?

To frame matters in not so homely terms, we sort out the difference between an incremental theory of the history of Judaism, in which, in a single line from Sinai, a long line of yesterdays leads directly to whatever we are and believe today, and the theory that there is no single Judaism, therefore no history of Judaism at all, only a sequence of fresh initiatives, new Judaisms resting on a long sequence of matters of self-evidence. My view is that there is not now, and never has been, a single Judaism, but only Judaisms, each with its distinctive system and new beginning, all resorting to available antecedents and claiming they are precedents, but in fact none with a history prior to its birth. Each system begins on its own, in response to a circumstance that strikes people as urgent and a question they find ineluctable. But I argue that all Judaisms recapitulate a single paradigm.

VI. Judaism's Persistent Recapitulaton of Resentment

From the opening lines of the preface of this book, I have emphasized I see no such thing as Judaism but only Judaisms. Surely that allegation contradicts the common sense view that "Judaism" differs from "Christianity." The search for a useful metaphor draws us back to human life. The several Judaic (or Christian, or Buddhist, or Islamic) systems form a family, with certain traits in common. But the family is made up of individuals, each with her or his biography. And, when it comes to families, we live and die pretty much alone, one by one. So it has been, and so it is, with Judaisms (Christianities, Buddhisms, Islams). Each forms both part of a family, with clear filiation, but, as it is born, lives, and dies, also and essentially a singular system to itself. That singular system possesses its own identity, each one with its distinctive definition, its way of life, its worldview, its address to (in the case of a Judaism) an Israel of its own designation (even the whole of Israel, the Jewish people, though that is ordinarily a matter of disbelieved rhetoric). Each demands study not in categories defined by its own claims of continuity, but in those defined by its own distinctive and characteristic choices. For a system takes shape and then makes choices – in that order. The choices, the selections out of the received materials of Judaisms – these come after the fact. The fact is formed by the (prior, fully formed) system: its points of stress, its values, above all, the problems that system has chosen for itself and has determined to solve (and has very commonly solved).

And what forms the fact? It is what the earliest generations of the new Judaism find self-evident, the truths that demand no articulation, no defense, no argument. What is self-evident forms the system and defines its generative exegetical principles. And if I want to know what people find self-evident, I have to uncover the questions they confront and cannot evade. These questions will dictate the program of inquiry, the answers to which then follow after the fact. If I know what issues of social existence predominate, I can also uncover the point – the circumstance – of origin of a Judaism. To be sure, no one claims to know the source of urgent questions: whether political, whether cultural, whether formed within the received condition of the faith, whether framed by forces outside. Debates on such issues of beginnings rarely yield consensus. The reason is simple. In the end no one is present at the beginning, so we have no information to settle any important questions. We work our way back from the known to the unknown. But all we wish to know is whether what we trace is old and continuous, as its apologists invariably claim, or essentially new and creative, a testimony to human will and human power and human intellect, as I maintain it is: a new Judaism, for a new circumstance.

Having begun at the end, let us move back to the beginning, the birth of the Judaism under discussion here. Judaism was born in the year 312, the year of Constantine's vision at the Milvian Bridge of a cross and the words, "By this sign you will conquer," and that same Judaism died – ceased to impress nearly all Jews as self-evidently true in the year 1789, with the American Constitution and the French Revolution, which for the first time established in the West a politics distinct from Christianity. With Constantine, Christianity became the definitive power in the politics of the West, and with the American Constitution and the French Revolution Christianity began its journey out of the political arena. The Judaism that took shape in the fourth century, attested by documents brought to closure in the fifth, responded to that Christianity and flourished, in Israel, the Jewish people, so long as the West was Christian. That same Judaism died – meaning, ceased to impress Israel, the Jewish people, as self-evidently true – when the Christian definition of Western civilization entered into competition with other systems of thought. The Judaism of the Dual Torah responded to a political question, and the Judaisms of the nineteenth and twentieth centuries addressed political change, and, finally, crisis and catastrophe.

VII. The Paramount Judaism and its Distinctive System

Political change therefore takes the critical role in shaping theological discourse. Specifically, the Judaism that took shape in the fourth century, in response to the political triumph of Christianity in the Roman Empire, governed the mind and imagination of Israel in Christendom for the next fifteen hundred years. The reason, I hold, is that that Judaism, for Israel, dealt effectively with the urgent issues deriving from the world defined by regnant Christianity. Received for that long epoch as self-evidently true, that same Judaism began to strike some Jews as not at all self-evident at that point, and in those places, at which Christianity (in one version or another) lost control of the politics of the West. When Christianity no longer governed the political life and, therefore, also the symbolic transactions, of the West, the Judaism that had taken shape in response to triumphant Christianity and that had so long and so successfully sustained the life of Israel, the Jewish people confronted skeptical questioning among people now standing essentially outside of its system of truths beyond all argument. That is why I say Judaism was born in 312 and died in 1789. But of course there is more to it than that. New Judaisms took shape, dealing with other agendae of urgent questions and answering those questions in ways self-evidently right for those who believed. Each of these Judaisms claimed to continue in linear succession the Judaism that had flourished for so long, to develop in an incremental succession and so to connect, through the long past, to Sinai. So we deal not only with the death of one Judaism but with the birth of several others. Here we deal, in all with eight, one I call "the Judaism of the Dual Torah," that is, the one that took shape in the fourth century, and seven others, as we shall see.

Why does the fourth century mark so critical an era in the history of Judaism? Because that was when the Judaism that would flourish in the West came to full definition and expression – and so did the Christianity that would define the civilization of the West for nineteen hundred years. The fourth century, therefore, marked the beginning, in a terrible union of cobra and mongoose, of the two great religious traditions of the West, unequal in numbers but well-matched in intellectual resources, Christianity and Judaism. While Christianity took shape around its own issues, the Judaism of the Dual Torah responded in a profound way to the challenge of Christianity in its triumphant form. Had a Judaism not done so, no Judaism could have survived the amazing events of that era: conversion of the enemy to the persecuted faith. For Jews had to sort out the issues defined by the triumph of Christianity as well as their own disappointment of the same age. And, through the sages, they succeeded in doing so.

So the Judaism that would thrive, that is, the Judaic system of the Dual Torah, came to expression in the matrix of Christianity. Before that time, the Christian and Judaic thinkers had not accomplished the feat of framing a single program for debate. Judaic sages had earlier talked about their issues to their audience, Christian theologians had for three centuries pursued their arguments on their distinctive agenda. The former had long pretended the latter did not exist. Afterward the principal intellectual structures of a distinctive Judaism – the definition of the teleology, method, and doctrine of that Judaism – reached definition and ample articulation. Each of these components of the system met head-on, and in a fundamental way, the challenge of politically regnant Christianity. The Judaic answers to the Christian *défi*, for believing Israel remained valid as a matter of self-evidence so long as Christianity dictated the politics in which the confrontation of Judaism and Christianity would take place.

VIII. Toward the Comparison of Judaisms. With Special Attention to Modern and Contemporary Systems

Obviously, this field theory requires that we compare one Judaic system to another, so as to see how they may form a common genus, Judaism all together. To compare Judaisms with one another we return to our point of departure, the Judaism of the Dual Torah. The Judaism of the Dual Torah took up a long perspective, situating Israel in the entire cosmos of creation and in the majestic unfolding of human history, a vast and noble vision. The Judaisms born from the death of the self-evidence of the system of the Dual Torah onward ask smaller questions. The great tradition of old overshadows the smaller ones of the age. Contrast the humble agenda at hand in the Judaisms of the twentieth and (as it would now appear) the twenty-first centuries to the crisis of late antiquity. The one unfolds out of a crisis of conscience and of confidence, but scarcely of culture and of politics. The other proceeds out of a calamity of political economy. The one asked, Given what has happened, what should the Jews do? The other: Given what is happening, what should someone – Jew, gentile – do with the Jews?

The questions of the formative age of the Judaism of the Dual Torah addressed the meaning and end of history. The issue was how to make sense of what was happening, viewed as part of a divine plan. Through typology, which compared Israel of the day to the Israel described in the book of Genesis, the sages answered that question: the meaning of events now derives from the story of the patriarchs and matriarchs of long ago. The definition of Israel called into question the standing and status of the Jews, since Christians maintained that they were the new Israel. The answer, worked out through genealogy, posited that the Jews now were the family, in a perfectly physical sense, of Abraham, Isaac, and Jacob. The Christians' ineluctable claim that Jesus had been, and now is, Christ, was countered through the doctrine that the Messiah would come at the end of days, and that the Messiah would be a sage. Now these issues invoked deep and far-seeing questions of human history from creation to redemption. They were framed in response to the conflict between Scripture's promises to Israel and history's disappointments for Israel. So these questions responded not to the hour, though precipitated by a critical moment. They turn the evanescent occasion into a moment in eternity, taking a long view of things. That perspective, I think, forms part of the power to abide and endure that we discern in the Judaic system of the Dual Torah.

Modern Judaic systems ask smaller questions and yield commensurately modest answers. The comparison of the issues of the Judaism of the Dual Torah to the agenda of the day produces a somewhat jarring effect. The issues, though matters of life and death, seem less in dimension, so, too, the answers: political answers to political questions, economic and social responses to a crisis of European society in its political economy. The Judaism of the Dual Torah invoked heaven and earth to do battle for the soul of disappointed Israel. The systems of the twentieth century call into being a culture of organizations and create not theologies but bureaucracies instead.

If we ask the source for the remarkable depth of vision of the Judaic system of the Dual Torah, we do well to turn to Scripture, which shaped that vision. Constant reference to Scripture and tradition produced that reading that yielded Judaism in the system of the Dual Torah. The questions derived from the world of imagination and sensibility, and so did the answers. The pressing issues of the age of Constantine and the birth of Christianity concerned not the Jews' political standing within the Roman Empire, nor their economic and social position. The Jews remained essentially what they had been: subordinated, but so was everyone within the empire; on the whole, this was satisfactory, as, in the region, most people lived lives they found acceptable. The agenda took up issues of eternal dimensions, reaching back to creation and forward to the end of time. Those issues proved perennial, and, for a long time, so did the responses.

In the nineteenth century, close to the received system, the continuator Judaisms, thriving in an age we now perceive as benign, dealt with questions of the same sort and answered them in essentially the same canonical way, that is, by reference to the Dual Torah. But the twentieth century – so it appears at its end – was different. And the Judaisms of reversion, pointing us toward the twenty-first century, different yet again. So at the surface, we see a radical break not in 1789, with the American Constitution and the French Revolution, but in 1897, with the founding of the Zionist Organization and of the Jewish Workers union called the Bund. To extend the *jeu d'esprit*, we may say that Judaism in the received form took a century to die, and the newborn Judaisms came forth, in paradigm, in a single year.

Yet how pertinent, in all, the comparison of the continuator Judaisms of the nineteenth century – the ones so long in dying, the present thesis proposes – and the new ideologies, framed out of the materials of the contemporary idiom of thought and politics, of the twentieth and twenty-first? The Judaic systems of a theological order, in full knowledge and self-consciousness, by self-aware decision in the nineteenth century created fresh systems out of available materials. The utterly new ideologies of the twentieth century formed ways of life and worldviews out of nothing particular to the Judaic systems that had gone before, instead forming a Jewish expression within a cosmopolitan and international idiom of sociology (class struggle), culture (linguistic basis for group life), and politics (nationalism). So how compare the one with the other at all, when we may find in hand not two species of a single genus but two genera?

Now the obvious objection – the point of continuity from century to century – derives from the Judaisms of reversion. Yet the claim to continuity of belief (in Israeli reversionism) and behavior (in the American kind) cloaks remarkable selectivity. For the theology of rejection of all that is secular and Western contradicts the perceptions of the continuator Judaisms that the received system presents no conflict between the West and the Torah. More to the point, that system, in its long history, managed quite comfortably to accommodate diverse worlds and to address Jews living in them. But that theology does conform in every substantive detail to the ideology of the very distinct moment at which it came to expression. It stated a no more distinctively Judaic viewpoint than did Jewish Socialism or Zionism which spoke only out of Judaic canonical writings and experience (worldview, way of life).

So, to proceed with the argument, how appropriate the comparison? For we talk now, in the twentieth century systems, of politics, scarcely of a worldview, of sociology, migration, demography, and the movement of generations, hardly of a way of life. Rejection of everything in favor of a made-up "authentic tradition" turns out, too, to express a general malaise with modernity – a cliché of experience, a banality no more nuanced, no less shallow, than the unspeakable banalities of "kibbutz Judaism." We wonder, therefore, whether we are comparing things that sustain comparison and contrast, things of a single genus but different species. We ask ourselves whether the effect of a circumstance, a condition brought on from the outside and cleared off by external forces deserves analysis as a Judaic system in the way in which the received compositions of thought and programs of behavior addressed to an Israel do. In all, the wildly attractive ideologies of the twentieth century, with their power to move people through their statement of self-evident (if diverse and contradictory) truths, which, like Jonah's castor oil plant, by morning sprout up and by evening wither.

So the question is this: Were they ever Judaisms? And what do their successes and (up to now) abrupt demises teach us about a Judaism? The answer depends upon our purpose in asking the question. If we propose to form judgments upon questions of content, then we err to consider the ideologies at hand at all. For proving that they do not continue and build upon the received system of the Dual Torah requires only that we cite their own ideologists. They, after all, said so, over and over again, to audiences eager to hear exactly that message of liberation from an unwanted past. And that was because, I think that past stood as a symbol for an unsatisfactory present. The treatment of the past as symbol and symbolization in no way differentiates any of the Judaisms before us, continuator and theological or fresh and ideological, or reversionary alike. That mode of thought pervaded the world. Claiming that the ideologies of the twentieth century in no way grew out of an incremental process generated within the logic of "the tradition" itself, moreover, scarcely requires effort except in the case of reversionism – and then, not much effort. The move from (at least) prooftexts to (at most) pretexts finds nearly universal recognition. It is not something people debate any more, except, again, in regard to reversionism, and then the debate hardly generates much heat. So the essentially new and utterly unprecedented Judaic systems of the present century prove somewhat less than meets the eye, since the basic propositions – not a linear history, not an incremental process – find ample substantiation right on the surface.

But – to revert – were they ever Judaisms? And what do their success and abrupt demise teach us about a Judaism? We review: a Judaism is constituted by a worldview, telling people who they are and why they must do what they have to do, a way of life, defining everyday activities in the context of a pattern of meaning transcending the mundane, addressed to an Israel (or to "all Israel"). So, of course, the systems at hand all constituted Judaisms – why not? The aspect of perfect faith that characterizes the three Judaic systems of the twentieth century and the ones of the twenty-first that we have considered testifies to the systemic power of each one. The source of that power? The system sorted out the real questions and answered them. So much for success. It derives from the strength of a system to identify urgent problems, issues that have crossed the line separating the chronic from the acute considerations confronting Jews. Each of the twentieth century systems succeeded in doing just that: answering extraordinarily pressing questions in a persuasive way. We learn, therefore, that a system succeeds, that is, attains the status of self-evidence, when it asks the right questions and proposes answers perceived, scarcely through argument, to work.

And what do we learn from the astounding instability of the systems at hand? It is that, given the character of society in this century, focus upon today guarantees nearly instant obsolescence, whether in machines or in the social constructs of humanity I call systems. Problems change because the world changes, and a Judaism that selects as urgent a social or political problem gains for itself nearly immediate currency but certain, rapid devaluation, too – even defalcation of all value. Jewish Socialism and Yiddishism, after all, did not die because people disbelieved; they died because the Israel to whom they spoke was murdered. Zionism did not perish because it failed but because it succeeded; the Jewish problem changed, and the success of Zionism itself created new problems for Jews. American Judaism thrives, so we cannot say where and how it will lose its presently supreme power of self-evidence. We need not doubt that Israeli and American reversionism has yet a way to run in its course. We can only maintain, with perfect certainty, that a Judaic system is like Jonah's castor oil plant, that shade that saved Jonah from his discomfort. By dawn a worm will attack the plant, so that it will wither. And none will be angry for the plant, for which none labored, which none made to grow, which came into being in a night and perished in a night. And so it is with Judaisms: come up in a night, pass in a night, whence and why and whither, no one knows.

So we may refer, for a probative analogy, to the taxonomy of botany: Are plants that perish in a night plants, too? Sure, why not. In our terms, we wonder how long a system has to survive to serve as a system. Doubtless they also serve who last but a brief generation, even form a system for a half-life of an hour. So that question proves trivial. But the consequent one does not: which plants last and resist the worm and which do not, and what is the difference? In our terms, why does one system last and another perish quickly? Among the eight systems we have surveyed, counting the Judaic system of the Dual Torah as well as its continuators in Reform, Orthodox, and Conservative Judaisms, as well as in its successors in Jewish Socialism and Yiddishism, Zionism, and American Judaism, and, finally, the Judaic system(s) of reversion, what points of differentiation present themselves?

First, a system that meets the definition at hand – worldview, complemented by a way of life, addressed to a clearly denoted Israel – however long it lasts, constitutes a system. No criterion of age or of longevity pertains. The reason is that a religious system presents a fact not of history but of immediacy, of the social present. The issue of survival by itself proves impertinent to the analysis of a system. A system is like a language. A language forms an example of language if it produces communication through rules of syntax and verbal arrangement. That paradigm serves full well however many people speak the language, or however long the language serves. Two people who understand each other form a language community, even, or especially, if no one understands them.

So, too, by definition religions address the living, constitute societies, frame and compose cultures. For however long, at whatever moment in historical time, a religious system always grows up in the perpetual present, an artifact of its day, whether today or a long-ago time. The only appropriate tense for a religious system is the present. A religious system always *is*, whatever it was, whatever it will be. Why so? Because its traits address a condition of humanity in society, a circumstance of an hour – however brief or protracted the hour and the circumstance.

When we ask that a religious composition speak to a society with a message of the *is* and the *ought* and with a meaning for the everyday, we focus on the power of that system to hold the whole together: the society the system addresses, the individuals who compose the society, the ordinary lives they lead, in ascending order of consequence. And that system then forms a whole and well-composed structure. Yes, the structure stands somewhere, and the place where it stands will secure for the system either an extended or an ephemeral span of life. But the system, for however long it lasts, serves. And that focus on the eternal present justifies my interest in analyzing why a system works (the urgent agenda of issues it successfully solves for those for whom it solves those problems) when it does, and why it ceases to work (loses self-evidence, is bereft of its Israel, for example) when it no longer works. The hypotheses that present themselves to fulfill that interest in no way depend for verification on the accidents of mass murder or migration, systemic success unprepared for, as with Zionism, even systemic exhaustion of undernourished intellects and overstrained emotions, as (I suspect) may yet afflict American Judaism. So the phrase, the *history* of a *system*, presents us with an oxymoron. Systems endure in that eternal present that they create. They evoke precedent, they do not have a history. A system relates to context, but, as I have stressed, exists in an enduring moment (which, to be sure, changes all the time). We capture the system in a moment, the worm consumes it an hour later. That is the way of mortality, whether for us one by one, in all mortality, or for the works of humanity in society.

Then we wonder which system lasts and which does not and how we are to know the difference. The systems before us in modern times, surveyed in *Death and Birth of Judaism* – seven acutely contemporary, one remarkable for its endurance – differ in one important way. Seven of them ask today's questions and answer them by appeal to facts and a

claim of mere facticity. One of them asks questions framed out of a long
perspective, seeks the answers in the interstices of a vast and persistent
canon of writings, makes provision for the active intellect and its ongoing
labor of exegesis. The Judaism of the Dual Torah appeals to the authority
of sages and stimulates a permanent confrontation between them and the
changing world at hand. They for their part sustained the system by
mediating between the one and the other: the system and the world of
change. The outcome is an exercise in harmonization within the system
and of mediation between temporal change and eternal verity beyond
the system. Change did not destroy, time did not attenuate, so long as
the fundamental issues persisted. The issues, moreover, possessed an
enduring urgency, for pretty much everyone in the world whom Jews
knew asked the same questions and answered them by appeal to the
same set of facts, diversely construed, to be sure.

And in the West the issues of the Judaism of the Dual Torah
registered somewhere between chronic and acute for so long as
Christianity controlled the West's systems of social bonding, of world
creating. Then the issues of a long perspective – a past to creation, a
future to the end of time – impended every day, but, for Judaism, came
to resolution on the seventh day (so to speak).

The Israel of the Judaism of the Dual Torah lived in a timeless world
of the everyday, for the *now* of sanctification, and of the future
redemption, for the *then* of salvation. And the larger circumstance of that
system spoke of God's will in the *now* and plan for the *then*. So the
system corresponded to the circumstance and lasted for that long. But
when it collapsed, a century of continuators saved what they could (and
it was a great deal). Then, a hundred years beyond, a set of systems,
acutely exemplified by the three we have surveyed, composed new
Judaisms, each out of the wherewithal of the world at hand. None of
these systems in its day exhibited profound flaws of composition and
construction, because each amply disposed of the urgent questions it, to
begin with, had selected. To state matters in a less anthropomorphic
way, the framers of each system produced systems adequate to deal with
the questions each set of framers thought urgent. The precipitating
catalyst and the consequent solution served full well. But none of the
theologies of continuation or the ideologies of the new age appealed to
more than the facts at hand. And when the facts changed, so did Jews'
minds.

This brings us back to the matter of what might have been: why
some circumstances yielded the formation of new systems and others did
not. In the three-quarters of a century beyond the decade after World
War I, with the stated exceptions, we look in vain for important and
influential Judaic systems aborning. I can think of examples of what

might have been, for example, in Reconstructionism, a handsomely articulated worldview, but altogether derivative, as to way of life, of Conservative Judaism, and lacking any considerable influence. Focused, after all, on the thought of a single individual, however noteworthy, a set of ideas hardly serve the composition of a system, and a philosophy is not a Judaism. That example is trivial. To take a stunning and important fact: we discern no Judaic system, taking shape from the decade after World War I to the decade after the Viet Nam War (for the unfolding of Jewish Americans' Judaic existence) and after the Yom Kippur War (for Israelis). Not one. Considering the mass appeal and power of Zionism, we look in vain to Israeli life for evidence of the formation of Judaic systems of cogent composition and distinctive character. Only with the reversionary systems of the late twentieth century do we see what might have been. It seems a valid observation, therefore, that no systems came into being between the 1890s and the 1970s, thus approximately three quarters of a century. We ask, what might have been, and why what might have happened did not happen.

To answer the first question – what might have been? – we turn to Israeli nationalism, which can have constituted such a system but thus far has failed to do so. To be sure, perhaps it has done so, but it made no impression outside of the country. True, an Israeli nationalism has framed a distinctive worldview and way of life for a defined Israel. Its way of life? Doing whatever you want, within a prescribed set of national boundaries. Its worldview? Citizenship in the Jewish state and the viewpoints connected with the duties of that citizenship. Its Israel? The question answers itself. That nationalism belongs in the classification of a Judaic system, no less than did Jewish Socialism and Yiddishism, on the one side, and Zionism, on the other. The fact, therefore, that that nationalism also falls into a genus in no way particular to Israel's taxonomic system is immaterial. A Judaic system that addresses only one segment of the Jews certainly does not suffer disqualification on that account.

But the definition of Israeli nationalism as a Judaic system produces one important flaw. For, by legal definition, Israeli nationalism – encompassing, after all, citizenship – presents a Judaic system that encompasses non-Jews, such as, in the nature of things, Israeli nationalism must do. That is a different matter, lacking all self-evident resolution. We can say that while Israelism, that is, a generalized sentiment of concern for the welfare of the State of Israel, joined to important activity to realize that sentiment, flourishes among nearly all Jews, Israelism scarcely explains the meaning of life to any sizable sector of world Jewry. Israelism, moreover, attracts non-Jews as well as Jews, so does not have a clear address to an Israel. Moreover, in the nature of politics, Israelism scarcely absorbs a substantial part of the life of the devotee, as did, for example, Zionism or Orthodoxy or Jewish Socialism and Yiddishism. And neither does Israeli nationalism for that heterogeneous and diverse population. For a Judaic system must tell me what I, a Jew, am not but also what I am and must become, why I must do what I must do, where I am heading and what my life means within the larger framework of Israel. Zionism answered those questions, Israeli nationalism for Israelis scarcely asks them. The country is too divided and diverse, the population too absorbed within its ordinary and mundane life, and such civil religion as any society puts forth to hold things together as a matter of national and state policy cannot serve, also, as a systemic structure. So, in all, there is no Judaic system here. Whether or not Israeli nationalism presents a species of the genus, civil religion, does not concern us.

IX. Comparing Judaisms: The Modern and the Classical

Let me conclude these remarks on the comparison of systems with a systemic comparison. It is between the list of the systems at hand and the prior ones. The movements of reversion, in both the State of Israel and America as well as other parts of the Diaspora, bring Jews to affirm what they think is the received system of the Dual Torah. And that fact must present a surprise. Who, standing in 1897, could reasonably predict that Zionism would achieve its objectives, and that Jewish Socialism would not? And who, nearly a century ago, could have outlined the urgent problems of explaining the world that would preoccupy Jews in the final decade of the twentieth century? For the issue today that moves people to change and to do derives from the one question people a century ago thought they dismissed: how to get back to the Judaism of the Dual Torah. The Judaisms of continuation answered the opposite question: how far may one go away from that received system? The twentieth-century Judaisms of an essentially original order ignored the received system as if it scarcely existed. Accordingly, all the mythopoeic, or, more really, system-generating or *systemo-poeic* energies of the age derived from the question, how to get away from that Judaism.

Every system except for Orthodoxy took as its premise a general alienation from that received Judaism, and Orthodoxy, for its part, proposed to attain a balance between separation from, and replication of, that system: this, not that. The selective piety so brilliantly validated by Hirsch explained the answer. But the orbits of other systems derived energy from the reaction against the received system. The force that sent on their way the six systems we have analyzed was the negative energy generated by the Judaism of the Dual Torah. True, in each case the issues of continuity and change required sorting out; in all cases the matter of dealing with the precedent and authority of the received Judaism demanded much thought. But the simple fact is this: everyone who from the eighteenth century forward made a Judaic system did so because he wanted out. The self-evident question for two hundred years concerned integration. At the dawn of the twenty-first century Jews fully at home in the West opted for segregation.

That fact indicates how the centrifugal force a hundred years ago has become a centripetal power today, a change of remarkable character, wholly beyond the imagination of anyone to predict. That is not to suggest the Judaic systems of the two hundred years between the self-evidence of the Judaism of the Dual Torah and the self-evidence of American Judaism exercised no centripetal power of their own. Quite to the contrary, we have seen how each one answered the question: How to get in? Zionism, for instance, attracted to its program and viewpoint Jews who formerly had slight interest in Judaic life in any form, Herzl being an outstanding example. The Jewish Socialists and Yiddishists – as I show in *Death and Birth of Judaism* – came back to the Jewish people after a journey far away. They credited Jewish Socialism and Yiddishism with the power to draw them back. American Judaism gave access to vivid participation in a Judaic system to sizable numbers of people whose interest in the continuator Judaisms in the synagogue at best proved formal and conventional. And Reform Judaism opened a two-way road, on which many chose to travel backward into a Judaic system. Its power to address the situation of Jews entirely remote in experience and upbringing found no match elsewhere. In all, therefore, the Judaisms at hand drew inward as much as they led outward. But, in all instances, the road back led not to the Judaism of the Dual Torah. And today, we find, the single most interesting systemic development produces precisely a reversion not to a generalized "Jewish identity," that is, identification with Jewish things. It yields a reappraisal of, a reentry into, that Judaism of the Dual Torah that for so long had repelled so many. That fact, above all, none can have predicted.

20

Talking Peace, Making War: The Paradoxical Record of Religion

Two challenges face anyone who wishes to speak in the name of religion about peace.[1] The first is how to find something to say on the subject of peace without merely rehearsing familiar, banal platitudes. The second is whether we who believe in God and affirm our respective religious traditions can address the paradox that religions, all of which affirm peace, form in the world a principal source for enmity, social disruption, political conflict.   And these two challenges prove complementary. For it is only by ignoring religion in the concrete context of world affairs that we can repeat banalities and platitudes. But when we address the simple fact that, today as for long centuries past, religions talk of peace but, in the nature of things, make war, we face the dreadful paradox at hand: talking peace, making war. It goes without saying that enemies of religion make much of that fact. But we who affirm not only our respective, very particular religions, but also religion, as God's instrument, have also to face the same fact. If in these days we may make of the occasion of a meeting for peace an opportunity to look inward, asking ourselves tough questions about religion even as we affirm and honor our own, and one anothers', religions, then we may meet the challenge. We may do more than rehearse familiar platitudes on how great is peace, how much each of our religious traditions prizes and affirms peace. Then, beyond platitude, we can contemplate that paradox that captures the nature of our being religious and of our religions.

Why is it that Buddhism and Hinduism in South Asia, Islam in the Middle East, Islam and Judaism in the Near East, Christianity in Europe

---

[1]Address to the Fourth International Meeting for Peace, Bari, Italy, Sept. 27, 1990, under the auspices of *Uomini e Religioni/Comunità di S. Egidio*, Roma.

both east and west, to name only outstanding cases in which religions praise peace but make war – why is it that the great religions of the world, where they exercise power and influence, teach peace but make war or cause war? I see three principle traits of religion that form of faith a cause of war.

The first is that religion, in its social context, defines an "us," and that "us" takes shape in contrast with a "them." So religion by nature sustains the social order. It identifies, within its group, those who are alike, and so it sets apart the like from the unlike. In setting forth its case in behalf of the like, it quite naturally marks the other as unlike – with all the heavy burden of dislike that goes with that characterization. The power of religion, therefore, in holding together believers and forming of them a vivid community, also defines the pathos of religion, in its insistence on marking this one as like, that one as other.

Second, religion in its psychological context teaches us to differentiate the near at hand and to homogenize the rest. Where there is a caste system, it will establish a minutely detailed hierarchy within the social order, treating as utterly undeserving of hierarchization or even close examination everyone else. So religion focuses our attention upon the like, teaching us how, within the framework of the faith, there is better and worse, greater or lesser – but then by its silences tells us that the other or the outsider simply demands no scrutiny at all. The power of religion in instructing us on how to identify and classify other persons within our group and place ourselves into relationship with them defines the pathos of religion, in its dismissal of the other or the outsider. Consequently, in the hierarchy of value and of consequence, the other loses all that humanity that the intense scrutiny of traits imputes to the one scrutinized: the outside does not matter.

Third, religion in its political context proposes social policy for a homogeneous political order that does not exist. Quite reasonably, religions address not only private life but also public policy, and drawing upon their own rich resources of ethical and moral doctrine, religions formulate proposals for the political community. But the diversity of the social entity that sustains the political process proves disjunctive, and, consequently, instead of holding together and sustaining the social order, religions prove disruptive.

The power of religion is its capacity to form community, to define "us," but the pathos is that, in forming community, religion also defines otherness. The power of religion is to teach us to look for God's image and likeness in the face of others, but the pathos is that, beyond "the others," whom we know and differentiate, lies the outsider, "the other," who is left without distinctive traits. The power of religion is to define worthy goals for the social order, setting forth components of public policy that accord with our vision of humanity "in our image, after our likeness." The pathos of religion is that, whether now or a thousand years ago, religion has proved unable to cope with difference and change: the social order never exhibited so homogeneous a character as to sustain that vision. So our power is our pathos, and where we are strong, we prove fallible and weak.

Some enemies of religion dismiss religion as a relic, a vanishing remnant of a repudiated past. Religion's very capacity to cause and make war proves them wrong; it is an argument that – alas! – is easy to win, wherever we look for evidence of the power of religion in the world today. But the more insidious enemies of religion recognize but deplore religion's remarkable influence in the world order. Their indictment proves considerably more difficult to dismiss, and it reaches into the heart of the matter. For, I think, whatever religions think of one another, all religions affirm that religion, in a given formulation if not in all formulations, is God's gift to us, in the language of the Sayings of the Fathers of Judaism, for example, *Beloved is the human being, who was created in the image [of God]. It was an act of still greater love that it was made known to him that he was created in the image [of God], as it is said," For in the image of God he made man" (Gen. 9:6) [The Sayings of the Fathers/Pirqé Abot 3:14]*. To generalize, no religious person can imagine that religion is the enemy of the welfare of humanity, and all religious people (speaking, at least, of their own religions in particular) stoutly affirm that religion is God's greatest gift to humanity.

Where, then, are we to begin the work of demonstrating for all to see the truth of our conviction that religion not only exercises power but forms God's greatest good bestowed upon humanity? In my judgment it is by starting with ourselves, specifically, by trying to learn how to do something we do not now know how to do, which is to carry on the war that we must fight against one another by talking peacefully with one another. If we can succeed in learning how to do that, we shall produce another and a greater paradox: making war in peaceful discourse. For, we cannot doubt, in the nature of things, given the claims that religions set forth for themselves – God's will, God's word, for example – religions must conduct an ongoing struggle among themselves, and when they fail to do so, they deny their power and their very nature.

Religions define the social order – for their own adherents. That definition includes but therefore excludes. Then those who stand outside the social order that a religion sets forth by definition are outsiders – and have to be. Religion differentiates within but homogenizes beyond; and that, too, is the way of the world, since what is near at hand and subject to our concern will be differentiated, and what is at a distance and unimportant will not. And religions by their nature address society at large, insisting that, since their teachings are true, no compromise can be made with difference, no legitimate accommodation can be attempted with diversity. So when we observe how religions speak of peace (for insiders) but call for war (against outsiders), we discern what are, in the end, the innate traits of religions.

Now ours is hardly the first generation of religious women and men to reflect upon the paradox that what we see as God's gift to all humanity can be perceived as God's joke upon us all. On the contrary, every religious system that precipitates reflection upon the world at large – and most do – asks itself how the same God can deliver so many conflicting messages. For most of the history of humanity, that question has proved chronic, but in the West from the age of the Protestant Reformation and the Catholic Reformation as well, and in the Near and Middle East even today, the question has become acute. We can no longer dismiss as merely interesting, or try to ignore, what a world so close to utter destruction must address: the different and conflicting messages that religions hear from one and the same God. The urgency derives not from what secular, atheistic, and antireligious persons and forces threaten to do to us, to discredit us, but from what we, ourselves, may do to the world, to destroy the world order beyond repair.

Now how over the four hundred years from the Reformations have we in the Christian West learned to deal with religious difference, with the challenge of one God's saying so many contradictory things through many religions? The first response was to appeal to politics: who governed the country decided its religion, and enough said. That response of course proved disingenuous; no one believed that the decision of the prince settled questions of religious truth. It was not a compromise but an evasion. The second response was to appeal to religious indifference. Differences among religions discredit them all equally. But that solution to the problem of religious difference, contributed by the Enlightenment, bore no relevance at all to religions themselves, which thrive because no one is indifferent. The third response, that of nineteenth century Romanticism married to Nationalism, subordinated religion to the nation, identified religion with the nation, to the detriment of religion. Accordingly, a kind of relativism in disguise treated religion as integral to the life of the nation – with the (generally unstated) corollary that other nations will have whatever religions they want, too. When to be a Pole meant to be, by the way, a Roman Catholic, or to be a German meant to be Evangelical (Lutheran), the many people living in Poland who were Ukrainian Orthodox, or Judaic, or Russian Orthodox, or German Lutheran (to give four examples among many) were excluded from the nation that was coming to be born, and, worse still, the Roman Catholic religion for its part was made an instrument, instead of the ultimate and goal of all of life, such as the faith (like all faiths) saw itself.

The human tragedy of our own century, in which millions of human beings were "exterminated" like insects, in which the Communists in the Soviet Union starved ten million Ukrainians to death, the Germans built factories to manufacture nearly six million dead Jews in the Holocaust, Hindus massacred Muslims and Muslims, Hindus, and Muslims, other Muslims not to mention Christians – this most tragic of all centuries has shown us the virtue of toleration. But toleration, too, is an evasion, and that in two ways. First, when we tolerate the other, we evade the truth claims made by the other, and so we dismiss them. Second, when we tolerate the other, we pretend that the other is so revolting that we can abide him or her only by a superhuman act of (mere) toleration. So if we found we did not have to tolerate, we would indeed eliminate difference.

Toleration or tolerance prove to be political, not theological virtues. They serve the social order, to be sure, but solely in its secular aspect. These are scarcely virtues that religions can commend. For insistence upon toleration for the truths of others imposes pretense that truths of others are really true, but we do not honestly think so. And our theological convictions, which shape our intellects, attitudes, and judgments, tell us one thing is right and another thing wrong, this true, that false. So to survive our century, we have had to make a virtue out of what is, at best, a mere necessity.

The result is that we believers, all in one God, but all in different things about that one God, really have not yet begun to think about thinking about difference. Let me give a concrete example of the issues that await attention. In Britain today a debate on religious education in a pluralistic society's public schools underlines how little religions have to contribute to the social order, and how much destruction their failure to date has wrought to the social order. But the same debate underlines how great a flaw in religions themselves opens to public scrutiny in our failure to learn how to make judgments of the other, beyond mere rejection, vilification, or indifference. Can there be religious education in the public schools at all? Christian evangelicals in Britain held there cannot: religious education is to show the Way, the Truth, and the Life." Muslims opposed the multiculturalism of the proposed curriculum, for "the ultimate aim of Muslim education lies in the realization of complete submission to God." Secular and agnostic opinion rejected the "multiculturalist" use of religious education "as a vehicle for politicization in the classroom." In this context, Mervyn Hiskett, in *The Salisbury Review*, June 1990 (pp. 13-16), asks whether religious education really can "promote respect, understanding, and tolerance for those who adhere to different faiths."

Hiskett raises this question, which, I think, really demands our attention: "The requirement of 'respect, understanding and tolerance for those who adhere to different faiths' begs some questions and adumbrates multiculturalist attitudes. Few would argue against senior pupils understanding Islam, Hinduism, Sikhism, and so on....The same applies to respect, provided this is understood to mean simply civilized and courteous behavior, not the sycophantic 'celebratory approach' of the multiculturalists." But, Hiskett goes on, "tolerance is a different matter," and I quote his language without endorsing or rejecting his view:

> Are we expected to tolerate a religion and its adherents that seeks to enforce the death penalty on apostates, or a religion whose fundamentalists advocate the return of slavery on scriptural authority, or the ritual death of widows on their husbands' funeral pyres; or one that continues to permit child marriage and the stoning of women for adultery? Tolerance, as the multiculturalists, with their dogma that world religions are to be judged solely from the standpoint of those who practise, understand and teach them, all too often means a denial of the right to criticize and disapprove. It shuns theological argument. It fears polemic lest this should cause offence. It will sacrifice principle for the wholly spurious appearance of harmony. Such teaching must lead in the end to the suspension of all moral judgment and thus to a relativistic amorality among those taught along such lines.

My point in citing the problem of religious education in Britain (a problem I hope in the near future we in the U.S.A. will face as well) is to point to a simple fact. None of the religions that comprise the constituents of the British religious order today has fully thought through doctrines of the other. Each speaks only to its own. All repress, for the sake of peace, what they really think of the other. But every one of them knows with perfect faith that the other is less, diminished by reason of difference. And when all religions join together in a single society – the classroom in the present case – the only conversation that appears possible is the implausible one: a discourse that takes as its premise the reign of relativism. So the message is, what they think is right for them, and what we think is right for us. And we are going to suppress our judgments of what we really find repulsive in the other. Now that is not peace between and among religions, it is merely hypocrisy raised to a principle of public policy. And if that is the only way in which so enlightened a state as the British one can address religions, what can we expect of the many societies across the globe that have yet to come to grips with the vast confusion of language and culture and religion that characterizes every nation. In our minds and in our hearts, we religious men and women think about the world as though at least our sector of it were cogent, harmonious, simple, and coherent. But when we walk out into the streets, we meet up with unbelievers as well as believers, and, more to the point, believers in things that, in God's name, we deny.

Where to begin? Once we agree that we have no time for platitudes, we have to take seriously the differences that are among us. And that means we have to cross the border into the dangerous territory of addressing religious difference *religiously!* What I mean is simple. Until now, when religions have addressed the outsider, they have done so within one of two motives. First of all, they have taken the outsider seriously within the labor of working out the full logic of the true faith itself. And every religion has a theory of the outsider – formed, to be sure, entirely within the frame of that religion's logic, its system and structure and sense of order. So the theory of the other, whether tolerant or otherwise, is one that affirms the self. Second, religions have taken the problem of the outsider seriously when they have had to, that is, when forces beyond the faith could not be ignored. It is only rarely in the history of religions that people have explored the resources of their faith to think seriously about the other – in terms that outsider themselves can comprehend and even affirm.

One such example derives from the Roman Catholic Church at Vatican II, when doctrines of Judaism and other religions came forth in full recognition of the faith of other people in other things; and other Christian communions have made equivalently radical efforts to rethink relationships with Judaism. But the Judaeo-Christian relationship is a very special one, and its traits scarcely characterize the relationships (to speak solely *pro domo*) of Judaism with any religion, or of Christianity with any other religion, in the same way. So what we have been given is a model, on the one side, and an example of how the work might be done. But Vatican II in the nature of things is only that: an example of what one might do, not a prescription for what we are to do. And the Protestant and Orthodox and Roman Catholic communions all together, with their power to think about the entirety of humanity and the whole of human culture and their commitment to a theory of a global order that is Christian, over time have tended to love the other in a rather aggressive way. It has been love with stipulations and conditions. But at least theirs is a theory that proposes a religious way of thinking about the outsider that the outsider can comprehend. To criticize my own faith and not to boast, I have to say that Judaism has yet to formulate a theory of the other that [1] affirms the otherness of the other; [2] differentiates among outsiders, and that [3] in theory (and not only in practice) acknowledges the pluralistic character of the world order not only across the globe, but even within the social structure in which Judaism dominates. And having confessed the pathos of the Judaism that I affirm, I may be forgiven to say that I discern the same unaccomplished tasks in all other religions equally: the beam is in my eye, but the mote, in yours, too.

So at stake here is what we are to make of the other, and how, beyond the human bonds that link us and make possible our discourse to begin with, we may move toward religious dialogue. The dialogue of which I speak is not with the outsider, but within ourselves – above the outsider. But the dialogue will take place, if it can take place, only when the outsider, hearing what we say among ourselves, can yet recognize the outlines of the humanity in God's image, after God's likeness, that that "other", too, claims to realize. This is a difficult task because we have few models for our work together, and because we have many examples of the failures of earlier generations. What they thought represented progress – toleration, relativism, the now-current "multiculturalism – we see as evasion, disingenuousness, or hypocrisy in the name of social harmony. But for believers, such as all of us are, what choices are there beyond toleration, which we take for granted, relativism, which we can never take seriously at all, and multiculturalism, which we reject every time we affirm what we believe by an act of prayer, for example, or other religious devotion. If we do not believe in mere toleration, if we reject the spurious truce of relativism, and if in word and deed we deplore (mere) multiculturalism as merely useful, then where do we find ourselves? It is, as a matter of fact, where all of us affirm we are: before God, and what we are, God's children. But then what? Children squabble, but grow up, sometimes, each fully realized and whole and different, but still, to love one another. The paradox of religion can be that we, too, can attain that *shalom*, that wholeness, that peace, that is in submission to God, in God's image and after God's likeness.

Index

South Florida Studies in the History of Judaism

DATE DUE
